ROUND TOWER CHURCHES OF SOUTH EAST ENGLAND

W J Goode
3 August 2003

AUTHOR
W.J. GOODE

ILLUSTRATED BY
DIANA BOWIE

With 40 Photo Plates by W.J. Goode
and Coloured Frontispiece by J. Scales

ISBN 0 9523058 0 1 (pbk)
ISBN 0 9523058 1 X (cased)

Published by Round Tower Churches Society.
Registered Address: Crabbe Hall, Burnham Market, Norfolk.

President: W.J. Goode
Chairman : J. Scales

Front Cover : St. Margaret's, Old Catton.
Back Cover : Thorpe Parva

Printed by Crowes of Norwich.

ACKNOWLEDGEMENTS

I would like to register my thanks to the many people who have helped me in my study. The late John Todhunter and Barbara Green, Keeper of Archaeology at the Castle Museum, Norwich, were valuable sources of advice, as were Brian Harmer and Charles Farrow for their assistance with my original book. My thanks are due to all the incumbents who have allowed me to study, measure and photograph these towers and churches and also for the many details they have added to my own survey.

My thanks are due especially to Diana Bowie who has designed the cover for this book and who has supplied the line drawings and maps that accompany this edition. The miniature sketches at the head of each church are all her work, and it was her idea that inspired their inclusion.

Finally my thanks are due to John Scales and Arnold Butler who have made such an improvement to my original script. The improvements are all their work, any errors are mine.

The Society is very grateful to the many generous people who have assisted in the publication of this book. Donations toward the cost have been received from: Brisely and Elmham book A/C. The proceeds of 'The First 1300 years' by H.D. Holbeach and R. Butler-Stoney. Mr A.R. West, Bernard Matthews (Turkeys), Bardfield Saling P.C.C., Bedingham P.C.C., Lt. Col. Leader, Mr J. Owles, Ruth Hadman, Ann Proctor, Miss K. Bartholomew, Rev. P. Gray, Betty Hall, Mrs Jane de Quincey, Mrs L. Wilkinson, Mrs Sterne, J. Cornforth, Miss C. Gould, W.G. Hudson, Mrs R.Q. Bareham, Mrs I. Everett and Mr I. Mitchell.

Interest free loans have also been received from Michael Coates, Mr and Mrs Drewery, Mr and Mrs Stilgoe, Mr and Mrs Spelman, John Scales, Mr A. Bayford, Ruth Hadman, Elsie Marley, Miss A. Assheton, Mr B.R. Cook, Mr G. Asker, Mr T. Gower, Major A. Crofton, Mr B.A. Morton and Mr A. Alldred. To all the above, our very grateful thanks.

Forncett St Peter, Norfolk.

To my dear wife, who for thirty years has
selflessly encouraged me in my study of
round tower churches.

FOREWORD

I am pleased and proud to be writing a Foreword to this excellent book. Mr Goode has visited and thoroughly examined every round tower church in England - all 181 of them (only 6 are outside East Anglia). He is fond of round towers and campaigns for their proper recognition: there are mistaken ideas about their origin, notably that they were built as defence posts against the Vikings, which Mr Goode rejects on historical grounds. His research is exceptionally thorough and he explains it carefully. He does not always agree with the accepted conclusions of other writers; this makes the reader think hard, and it will make church crawling very exciting as Mr Goode's clues are followed up. The greater knowledge of church history and architecture gained from this book will also, it may be hoped, encourage the care and protection of all our churches, which are threatened from many sides in these days. Mr Goode has done a splendid job, for which all lovers of churches will be deeply grateful.

Lady Harrod
President, Norfolk Churches Trust

CONTENTS

LINE DRAWINGS

ILLUSTRATIONS

PREFACE

It is quite remarkable that this fascinating group of Round Tower churches has never before been thoroughly studied in spite of their undoubted interest and the exhortations of Charles Cox. In the early days of this century he said; "It would indeed, be passing strange, considering the abiding character of flint, and the undoubted knowledge and use of mortar possessed by both Angles and Danes, if Norfolk was destitute of any traces of the places of worship where our forefathers gathered in days prior to the Norman Conquest. It is strange that no one has yet arisen of sufficient leisure, means and intelligence to produce a thorough and trustworthy monograph on this subject."

Way back in 1829 John Gage F.R.S. visited over 50 of these towers in the course of one summer, with a friend who made a number of sketches. As stated, he had barely seen a quarter of the towers, but yet pronounced that none were pre-Conquest.

Rev. Messent was the first person to produce a book entirely devoted to the Round Towers. His was a worth-while effort, for it did what had never been done before, listed just about all the round tower churches in England. Its usefulness finished there, for although he made a sketch of each one there were no measurements, and his notes contained nothing new, and were merely repeating what other writers had already described.

Many of the larger parish churches of East Anglia had round towers at one time, as the foundations of the old towers have been found during restorations. It has been estimated that there were probably around 1,000 round tower churches standing in the medieval period, but today there are only 175 left in addition to a number of ruins.

A remarkable coincidence is the fact that George Barrow, was studying the Irish Round Towers in depth from 1971 to 1976, when I was doing the same work on our East Anglian Round Towers; although neither of us knew of the other's research. His book is the best study to date on the "Irish Round Towers."

This shows the great interest in these unique towers and churches, and the following pages will attempt to show the reader how to look at these ancient buildings and learn some of their secrets.

I have not included a glossary of the architecture, but these terms can be found in most church guides, such as Pevsner's *"The Buildings of England"* series. I have included a bibliography and most of the relevant quotes in the text are plainly documented. The reader will find that this book is almost exclusively devoted to the buildings themselves and appears to ignore the church furniture. This is deliberate as many have already written at length about these fittings, and they are more qualified that I am on this subject. This book would be far too unwieldy to include this material, so I have reluctantly had to reduce such details. While more illustrations would undoubtedly clarify some of the statements made and help to prove the value of my studies, the cost factor has curtailed these very useful additions. I have tried therefore to give a balanced coverage to the most interesting and valuable aspects of these towers and churches.

At the reorganisation of Local Boundaries in 1974, Belton, Bradwell, Burgh Castle and Fritton in Suffolk, (where the church of St. Edmund stands), were transferred to Norfolk. Norfolk however, already has a Fritton, with a round tower church of St. Catherine. As all the previous books on churches list these churches in Suffolk, I have left them in this county to avoid confusion.

Some years ago the Ordnance maps were revised and a new series of map numbers came into use. This was the 1:50,000 First Series: that replaced the old 1" series. In this volume I have omitted reference to the one inch maps. I have included maps of Norfolk and Suffolk at each end of this volume so that readers can find the area of any church without having to look at any other map.

My last book followed the time scale of Baldwin Brown and H. M. Taylor, but in this volume I have simplified the dating to Early Saxon, 800 to 900; Middle Saxon 900 to 1,000 and Late Saxon 1,000 to the Conquest. Saxo-Norman work is from the Conquest to about 1100 A.D.

The headings of each church will be listed in the following order:- County number as : N1. (Acle in Norfolk), village and dedication. Church position on book map, followed by Ordnance map and reference numbers as (Acle Norfolk), K6. Sheet 134. Map ref. T.G. 401 103; or (Mutford Suffolk) L3. Sheet. 156. Map ref. T.M. 486 886. Then dating all or parts of church and tower, as far as my study has shown, followed by the main measurements. The church position follows this with the main plan of its parts.

HOW IT ALL BEGAN

At school my best subject was arithmetic. I had little interest in history, but I liked to see two and two make four and perhaps that has some bearing on my subsequent analytical approach to the puzzle presented by round towers and their origins.

I left school at 14 and it was many years later that I came to round towers. My interest in them started from photography. I had played with a simple Ensign camera as a lad and then in 1965 at the age of 53 I got hold of an Argus single lens reflex camera. I was always more interested in photographing things than people and I liked to take pictures of objects. I still retained some vague memories of something I had read about round towers in my teens and since these towers were available locally and were also very photogenic I started taking pictures of them.

As I was living in Lowestoft, I started with nearby Suffolk towers - Mutford, which was my first, followed by Rushmere. Then I was off. From Lowestoft Library I borrowed Messent's book, *"Round Towers to English Parish Churches"* and this opened up for me the world of round towers. At that time it was the only book dealing specifically with the subject. Excellent though it was as a catalogue, however, it gave no historical background and very soon I wanted more. This led me to all the expert sources listed later in this book and my study of them was the catalyst. As a simple enquirer after truth, I was surprised, indeed rather shocked, to discover how these renowned historians disagreed among themselves, and I could not escape the feeling at the same time that each tended to repeat or elaborate upon what proved to be earlier misconceptions, instead of making a fresh examination of the facts. Not only did their dating vary considerably between them, but quite often a writer would contradict himself. This did not suit me at all.

I decided then and there that I would find out for myself and started off on an investigation which has gone on until now, but of which the groundwork was largely laid in the years between 1965 and 1976.

In the early part of that period I visited every round tower in England, a total of 181 and all but 6 in East Anglia. I was taking pictures of the towers and their churches, noting and recording their features, reading all I could on the subject and I soon began to have suspicions about three widely held views - that the towers were built as defence posts against the invading Vikings, secondly that they were mostly built by the Normans, and lastly that their churches were nearly all built on later. It could be said that it became my life's work to refute these three mistaken ideas.

In 1975, when I was 63, I had the opportunity to take early retirement from my firm and so began two years really intensive study of the round towers of East Anglia. Whereas earlier I had spent most Saturdays with the towers, I was now able to be on the job daily and I revisited all of them. I had already learned that Norman walls were thicker than Saxon - their mortar was not so good - and that Saxon naves tended to be narrower, and now I came to realise the vital importance of measurements. I measured everything in sight - the height of the towers, the thickness of the walls, the towers' internal diameter as well as the width of the naves, the length of chancels and so on - and these measurements, which had never been done before in any extent or precision, were largely responsible for the conclusions to be outlined later in this book, which in summary are that most East Anglian round towers were built by the Saxons, not for the purpose of defence but were added on to existing Saxon churches as bell towers. At the same time, I began to think I would one day like to publish my findings and I gave my first thoughts to writing a book.

I worked alone, travelling in my little Volkswagen Beetle, which must have covered 70,000 miles in pursuit of round towers in the 19 years of its life from 1973 to 1992. It never let me down though the windscreen wipers did once pack up in a thunderstorm. For equipment I carried on the car roof a ladder which extended to 19 feet, a torch, tape recorder, tape measures, two 35mm. reflex cameras with extra lenses and two clothes-lines. One of the cameras was for colour slides for use in lectures and the other was for black and white photographs which I developed and printed myself for records. The clothes lines were tied together, marked off at one-foot intervals by a strip of black insulating tape, and lowered from the tops of towers to measure the height. Fortunately I have no problem with heights so did not mind leaning over the edge of the parapet to lower the line, weighed down with a bright piece of hardboard to show when it touched ground. I managed to get to the top of most of the towers - the few whose rickety ladders or rotten floorboards forbade ascent are indicated in the book - and it took two journeys to carry all my equipment to the top before working steadily down. One of the trickiest parts of the enterprise was lifting the heavy trap door in the final assault on the summit, the top of the tower, balancing on a long ladder and sometimes having to push up a trap door made of lead without the benefit of one side being hinged. Occasionally I had to climb over a bell-frame to get to the next stage. Measurement of wall thicknesses was done at the windows, measuring first from the inside as far as the glass, and then from the outside, and adding the two measurements. Of course I could not have got up the towers at all without the co-operation of the local parson, but it was always understood that I was on my own in every sense. Once I thought I had been locked in when I had forgotten which doorway I had used to enter the church. On another occasion I met an owl, sitting on its eggs, but it did not seem to mind as I walked past. Perhaps, in its wise way, it already knew the tower was Saxon not Norman. I never came across any bats in those days.

I could usually examine and measure three towers and their churches in one day and I spent the evenings transcribing my notes from the tape recorder. Writing in 1993, at the age of 81, I still like to get up to the top of a tower when anything of interest arises.

My final challenge was to get my findings published. Every publisher I approached was very polite and said it was all most interesting but not a commercial proposition. So in 1982 I used most of my own savings to finance publication myself. All 500 copies were sold and I got my money back and made a profit to put into the Round Tower Churches Society which I had set up in 1973 in order to spread interest in round towers and to provide funds towards their maintenance. After a slow start the Society is thriving, with 342 members (July 1993) and I am delighted to have found a nucleus of fellow-enthusiasts to carry forward my work on round towers.

INTRODUCTION

Hundreds of books have been written about the wonderful churches of England. The East Anglian churches in particular have been praised for their beauty by many writers, but when it comes to dating the churches this is generally ignored. The dates of windows and doors, as well as screens, fonts etc. are often given, but I wondered why a little more study had not been given to discover the early history of these buildings. I believe there are three reasons for this. The first is that most writers take only a cursory look at the church walls. Next, for the early history if any, they followed the views of earlier writers who had done much serious work but lacked the modern knowledge that is available to scholars of the present day. Since the last war, a great many Roman and Saxon sites have been found, and more knowledge of Christianity in the early days has been gained. Thirdly, the idea that nearly all Saxon churches in East Anglia were of wood and so did not endure has been so widely accepted without any real proof, that one wonders how much writers will accept without scientific evidence.

If we now examine these reasons, we find it is too easy to look at the windows and to say we have a 14th. century church here because the windows are from the Decorated period. But we should know that new and larger windows were almost always inserted into village churches when a village was prosperous. We must all be aware of some churches that have 13th., 14th., and 15th. century windows, sometimes even in the same wall. Edingthorpe is one such example, where there are all three styles of windows side by side. Such a building may then be called a 13th. century church, whereas the true position is that it is at least 13th. century with the possibility that it could be considerably earlier.

When I first began my study of the round towers and their churches, I tried to regard them as one building. Tradition, however, and a great many writers would have us believe that the towers came first, and only later were stone churches built against them. I did not at once contest the established theories, but serious study with tape measure and ladder meant that I could check the measurements from a number of churches and towers against the assertions of other writers. This study I look upon as archaeology above ground or archaeology without a spade; for it is truly the same type of research, trying to date each part and fathom the reason for the features no longer used. The history of the village, its people and industry are tied up with the local church as the most ancient building in the parish. It reflects the wealth and importance of the leading personalities as well as the skills of its artisans from age to age.

Why is it that so little effort is put into dating the walls of our churches? We are generally given the dates when the windows, doorways and arcades were built, and sometimes even the towers, but rarely is any attempt made to date the actual building of the church, unless there are documents to prove this. As we are told that there are almost no documents of churches built before the Conquest, we can date these churches only by a detailed study of them and the methods of their construction.

The study in depth that I began on round tower churches in 1965 convinced me of the shortcomings of the views generally held concerning these towers; and if my reasoning is correct, the Normans did not build or rebuild nearly as many churches in East Anglia as we are led to believe. The conclusion I have been forced to accept is that most of our modern writers have accepted without question the opinions of the earlier writers without subjecting them to very much further study. Thus it is only now that our round tower churches are finally revealing their secrets and their true antiquity.

Chapter 1

HISTORICAL EVIDENCE FOR CHRISTIANITY BEFORE THE 7TH CENTURY

In this section of our research we must rely on historians and the way they interpret the various sources of information open to them on the spread of Christianity. Their opinions must certainly carry more weight than I or any other writer wishing to put over his own particular point of view. I intend only to put forward the views expressed by a few well recognised historians, and then make a general assessment of the effect Christianity had on this area in pre-Conquest days. The book from which I have drawn most of my information on the Christian Church before the Conquest is *"The Church in Anglo-Saxon England"* by C.J. Godfrey. The foreword tells us the book is concerned not only with the narrow ecclesiastical concept of the conversion, but with notable personalities and the cultural achievements of the Saxons. The scope of the work carries on beyond the end of Saxon England into the Saxo-Norman period.

Godfrey concludes that the late 2nd. century was almost certainly the time when individual Christians were known in Britain. By the 3rd century, or shortly afterwards, Tertullian includes the Britons in a list of peoples who had accepted Christ.

The Church in Britain probably made small but steady progress during the 3rd. century, but then came a setback. According to Bede, the persecution of Diocletian, the last great effort of the Empire to extirpate Christianity, reached Britain. By the 4th. century Britain shared in the world Councils, and in 314 sent three bishops to the Council of Arles. Britain was definitely represented at the Council of Ariminum which met in 360. It is certain that at least three bishops attended.

It appears that by the 4th. century the Church was not only well established, but Britain was accepted on the continent as an integral part of the Universal Church. Although the invasions of the Saxons increased throughout the 5th. century, bringing their pagan religion with them, it is probable that they did not wholly submerge the Christian Faith, but were eventually converted to it.

Pope Gregory the Great sent a party of missionaries with Augustine to the Kingdom of Kent in 596. It was so successful that many new churches were built and some old ones restored in the area.

East Anglia played its part in the spread of Christianity throughout the Anglo-Saxon period. As well as the area's 9th century king and martyr St. Edmund, Godfrey records, "A monastic saint named Botolph of the East Anglian Church of whom scarcely anything is known, though he was highly regarded by his contemporaries. He founded, in 654, a monastery at Icanhoh, a place which has not been identified satisfactorily. He gathered a community around him, to whom he gave a rule." In 670 he was visited by Ceolfrith, who was subsequently Abbot of Jarrow, who had heard of his fame.

In the 7th century, two notable missionaries, St. Felix and St. Fursey, were active in promoting the faith throughout East Anglia. Little enough is known of their work and achievements, but the Church in the area must have been put upon a sufficiently sound footing in this century for Godfrey to record that the line of Bishops centred on Dunwich endured well into the 9th.

century. By the 9th century, the Viking raids had begun, and East Anglia did not escape. But for how long and how deeply was life disorganised by the raids? The *"Saxon Chronicle"* records, and it is agreed by both Godfrey and Stenton, that the Vikings settled down and in 866 wintered in East Anglia and in 867 they struck northwards and occupied York. It seems to follow therefore that East Anglia might have been less disturbed than the Northern districts, although some historians would suggest that East Anglia was constantly ravaged for over a century. The baptism of Guthrum the Dane, in 886 was virtually the beginning of the third wave of Christian conversion. The *"Saxon Chronicle"* records this and the other events. It is plain that Christianity first came to Britain relatively early, and it spread to East Anglia and was established by the 7th century. As is now widely accepted, East Anglia was a prosperous and a relatively highly populated part of the country, and there is no reason to suppose that it was backward in accepting the Christian doctrine. The evidence of the missions to the area and the saints all point to the extent of Christian belief.

The central theme of the historical evidence for pre-Conquest churches is confirmed as early as the 6th. century by the records of St. Augustine when he was here. It matters little if the churches built then were of wood or stone, for this was 500 years before the Conquest. In 1962, Godfrey recorded about 200 churches in England, in use that contain some part of Anglo-Saxon work. This admits a reasonable amount of building in stone. But only three years later, the Taylors, setting a very high standard of acceptance, listed 400 churches and 59 doubtful cases. They had many more cases referred to them which they had not seen, and in East Anglia I have carefully examined by their methods all the round tower churches and in doing so have found a great many more that fulfil their very high demands.

Just one more comparison, using the Taylors' figures for the whole of England, we find that while Yorkshire, the largest county today, has 32, and Kent 26 pre-Conquest churches, Norfolk has the most at 54. All these with the one exception of Greensted are stone-built.

Chapter 2

WRITERS AND THEIR VIEWS

The earliest record I have of any study being done on the round tower churches is in 1829, when two eminent men wrote to the *"Society of Antiquaries"* concerning the round tower churches of East Anglia. Both said that these churches had aroused great interest. Samuel Woodward said he had studied these towers to find out why they had been built of flints and why they were round. He decided that they had been built of flints because these were the only building stones available in the area, and they owed their circular shape not to any local style but for ease of building as there was no freestone to provide good quoins (corners) required for square towers. In other words, the circular shape suited the materials available when the towers were first erected.

The same year John Gage F.R.S. visited over fifty of these towers including five outside East Anglia, to discover their age, as it was widely held that they were very ancient, dating from pre-Conquest days. Considering the transport in those days, this number was a very good effort, but surely little close study was possible. Few towers were named in his treatise, and only generalisations given for dating the towers as Norman and Early English. His conclusions were that none was built before the Conquest. Tasburgh, he said, was the oldest, but even that he dated between 1066 and 1100. Most of them he declared to be Norman, and many even of the pointed period, which means the 13th. century. This pronouncement we now tend to dismiss rather unfairly, I think, when we realise that these early students and writers did not have the wealth of information that is now at our disposal.

However, it was seventy years before Gage's statements were challenged by Charles Cox, who declared that 23 of the round towers were pre-Conquest. Cox also pointed out that no one had so far fully studied these buildings, and the work of subsequent writers including Baldwin Brown, Arthur Mee, Munro Cautley, Nicholas Pevsner and H.M. and Joan Taylor, served to show that such a study was still awaited.

Cox felt certain that builders of pre-Conquest days knew about and used mortar and flints for their churches, and we know from Roman remains that walls so made stand up to the weather and passing years even when left unmaintained. He also considered that the Norman builders were energetic not only in sustaining and improving the large number of churches that they found in the country, but in adding considerably to their number.

Not all writers, however, shared the views of Charles Cox. In 1912 Hugh Bryant in his *"County Churches Suffolk"* said, "Many existing churches are built on the sites of these Saxon ones, but very little of the original architecture remains. Probably several of these small wooden edifices were soon replaced by larger ones erected by the Normans, who were far in advance of the Saxons in mechanical and artistic skills." However, this last assertion has for some time been called into question by modern research claiming that it was the Saxons who were in the lead both artistically and in the skills of the artisan.

Baldwin Brown was a foremost Anglo-Saxon scholar at this time. He discovered many more Saxon churches than were known before, and wrote his first book on Anglo-Saxon Architecture in 1905. In 1925 he revised and enlarged his work to four volumes. *"The Arts of Early*

England" Vol. 2. "Anglo-Saxon Architecture" is what mainly concerns us, as it covers the whole range of Saxon architecture. He indicates many new features by which we can identify Saxon churches, and so enables us to recognise more Saxon churches in East Anglia.

Then in 1937 Munro Cautley published his magnus opus *"Suffolk Churches and Their Treasures"*. Cautley was Surveyor to the Diocese of St. Edmundsbury and Ipswich and a recognised authority on churches in general. He considered that the majority of the round tower churches dated from the Norman period but that some were from the earlier centuries and that these were built as detached defence towers, only later being converted to bell towers when churches were ingeniously built on to the east of the towers.

Munro Cautley says, "As the Saxon invasion completely obliterated the buildings of the British Church, so the raids of the Norsemen destroyed the memorials of the work of such later pioneers as Theodore of Tarsus, to whom we owe our parochial system and the foundation of eighteen dioceses. Probably the sole remains we have of even these later buildings is the ruined old Minster in South Elmham. It is not till we reach the later Saxon days that we can claim much evidence in stone of the earlier church in Suffolk."

Munro Cautley believed that each invasion levelled all the churches then standing but apparently only in East Anglia, for all writers agree that Jarrow, Monkwearmouth and Escomb, to mention only a few, did not suffer this fate, although they were also in an area plundered and occupied by the invader. Why should the larger number of churches in East Anglia, a populous area, all be destroyed? Cautley offers no explanation.

He admits that, "Probably, however, in the centuries immediately preceding the Conquest, the rudest structures had given place to a more permanent form:" and "In 1086, when Domesday was compiled, it would appear that at least 390 churches existed in Suffolk, with the possibility of 448." This lead him to the conclusion "Now even if the Normans had not been fully occupied with the settlement of the country it seems impossible that this great number of churches could have been erected in the twenty years that had elapsed since the Conquest. Hence one is driven to the conclusion that the great majority of them were pre-Conquest in origin."

However, he then contradicts himself by saying of our Saxon churches, "If a few were of masonry, possibly the larger number were simple wooden or wattle and daub buildings. All seem to have been rebuilt or extensively altered and improved in the hundred years succeeding the Conquest, when there was such an outburst of building." The reasoning here is rather obscure, as Cautley had clearly said that the rudest churches had been replaced before the Conquest by permanent structures, yet he is still looking for wood or wattle and daub churches at the Conquest to be improved. Later he says, "The fact that the Normans were great builders is testified by the large number of buildings they erected and the magnificent conceptions often displayed. Yet, technically they were far from great builders. The mortar they employed was of poor quality. The stones they used were far too small to ensure good work." Yet we are asked to believe that only a few Saxon churches remain while a great many built in Norman times are still here.

A few years earlier, in 1934, Sir Alfred Clapham wrote, "The new Norman hierarchy, which, with few exceptions, dispossessed the native ecclesiastics within a few years of the Conquest, brought with it an established order both of church and governance and architecture which, almost without effort, overthrew the loosely knit organisation and somewhat haphazard architecture of the Anglo-Saxon Church." This judgement clearly implies that post - Conquest buildings would have been built in the Norman style, with freestone used for all the main features.

Yet most other writers suggest that Saxon features in flints carried on almost to the end of the Norman period. Of course this means that the Saxons built churches in stone and not only in wood or wattle and daub. But we are also told that hardly any Saxon churches survive in East Anglia, although many are known in other parts of the country. According to this view not only were a tremendous number of Norman churches built in one hundred years, but in spite of poor mortar and small stones all or nearly all have survived.

Surely these three statements are not compatible. One or more must be inaccurate. If all the Saxon churches were of wood, how could Saxon features be perpetuated in stone? If we say that in four hundred and fifty years the Saxons could build only a few churches that would last, how could the Normans, who are recognised as much poorer builders, construct hundreds of churches in East Anglia in only one hundred years, most of which are still standing today? Surely there must be something wrong with some of these statements? We are told from various quarters that the use of mortar and flints was well known to the Saxons and that their mortar was far superior to the Normans. We should therefore expect to see many more Saxon churches still standing. If Sir Alfred Clapham is to be believed, the Saxo-Norman Overlap was almost non-existent, for the Saxon culture was quickly submerged beneath the weight of the Norman domination. Sir Alfred has stated from an historical standpoint what I, from the viewpoint of the physical evidence I have seen in the churches, have concluded.

Cox's challenge was finally accepted in 1958 when Revd. Claude Messent A.R.I.B.A. published his book, *"Round Towers to English Parish Churches."* It covered all the round church towers in the country, with a sketch of each one, and a short summary of each tower beside the sketch. As a catalogue it was commendable, but it contained nothing new to add to the knowledge already available.

Three years later, Nicholas Pevsner declared in *"Buildings of England Suffolk",* "Suffolk is thus poor in Anglo-Saxon remains, at least Anglo-Saxon remains in situ....and as for the most conspicuous architectural survival, the round towers, it is not even certain how many are Saxon. While none of them are datable with certainty, some are evidently Norman and others may well belong to the familiar and ubiquitous so-called Saxo-Norman overlap of the 11th. century. That they must be late Saxon, if they are Saxon at all, there can be no question; for it seems that the earliest round campanili of Italy are not earlier than the 9th. century. 835 is the date of the two round campanili for St. Gall."

This constant assertion that these round towers cannot be dated has been stated by so many writers that it came to be believed without question, although no one had studied them as Charles Cox had plainly seen was required back in 1910. Certainly a few are Norman, and one in Essex dates from as late as the 14th century. But I consider that by far the greater number are pre-Conquest. The argument that none can be before the round towers of St. Gall of 835 can be ignored, for there were the round bastions of the Roman Fort at Burgh Castle, on the banks of the river Waveney in Suffolk, which was built about 350 thus providing a first class model for the Saxon builders in the area.

In 1962, E.A. Fisher in *"Greater Anglo-Saxon Churches"* wrote, "At first no doubt these churches were of timber, for the whole area was well wooded, and probably many or most would belong to the group of field churches." Once again we hear the familiar words of timber churches for this area, and also the probability that they belonged to the group of field churches. Both statements were made by earlier writers but with no positive evidence; they were merely suppositions. This again proves that writers of acknowledged authority were passing on evidence from other writers without further research or solid supporting facts. Even if these two statements are correct in relation to the earlier period, the timber churches would surely have been replaced by flint and mortar buildings by the 8th century.

About this time, the Taylors, a husband and wife team, received a University Grant to study the Saxon churches of Great Britain, as they were experts in this field. They were recognised as the foremost scholars of Anglo-Saxon architecture. They evidently did not subscribe to the ideas of other writers that the churches of East Anglia were of wood until after the Conquest, for they found that Norfolk had more Saxon churches than any other county in Britain. However, as they had looked at only those churches they were aware had been called Saxon, their list of Saxon round tower churches is much shorter than mine, as I have visited all of our East Anglian round tower churches at least twice. Yet old habits die hard for when, in 1983, Eric Fernie published his book *"Architecture of the Anglo-Saxons",* despite praising the work of the Taylors and admitting that almost all his references to British Anglo-Saxon churches, details and measurements were from the Taylors' books, he nevertheless still maintained there were no pre-Conquest churches in East Anglia. In spite of his praise of the Taylors' work, he seems to have closed his mind to those parts of their study that did not support his views.

In the recently published *"An Historical Atlas of Norfolk"* Stephen Heywood tells us that Norfolk churches were built with round towers not for functional reasons but because of "The strong cultural links which existed during the early Middle Ages with countries bordering the Baltic and North Seas." According to this theory East Anglian traders were so impressed by the round western towers of Schleswig-Holstein and the round stair turret-cum-bell towers on major buildings in the Empire that on their return home they hastened to imitate them by building single round western towers on minor churches. If this is correct we would expect to find many round tower churches around King's Lynn, as that was the port trading with north Germany but there are scarcely any. Even more puzzling is the presence of three round tower churches in Sussex and two in Berkshire which would hardly have enjoyed strong cultural links with the Baltic region. Is the fact that these two counties, like East Anglia, have no better building stone than flint an irrelevance?

Chapter 3

DEFENCE TOWERS OR BELL TOWERS?

Why were towers built round? Two theories are quickly disposed of. First the idea of the well. This it seems was common at least 150 years ago. The story goes that the towers were originally wells, but then a great flood washed away the soil and left the well shafts standing proud! The East Anglians then found a use for the well-cases by building their churches on to them and using them as bell towers. How this wild story came to be believed can be more readily understood by knowing this area. Throughout the centuries, the sea has been eroding the East Anglian coast and after many a severe storm, large sections of the cliffs have been washed away. So much so that entire villages have disappeared. In a number of cases a well-case has been left standing on the beach while surrounding buildings lay in ruins. Local people must have witnessed this sight many times over the years and someone dreamed up the story to fit what they had seen.

Our second story is from an article in the *"East Anglian Miscellany"* of 1924. The writer relates the towers to the circles of ancient pagan cults. Stonehenge and other heathen temples, he says, were circular and the ceremonies were always in the open. Therefore, round towers formed the circles and the service or ceremony would be held outside. The writer does not allow for the depth of the Christian life in the area which would scarcely have allowed pagan traditions so to influence the Christian worship. He also does not explain why round towers did not spread to other parts of Britain.

A third more important reason given for the building of these towers is Munro Cautley's Defence theory. This states simply that the towers were built before the churches as defence or watch towers during the time of the Viking raids. This idea is supported on several grounds and it is worth-while to examine them in turn.

Munro Cautley gave his reasons for believing that many of the Saxon towers dating from the 9th. or 10th. century were built as defence towers. He said that they were originally detached, that defence towers were as essential here as in Ireland against "The fury of the Northmen", that there were no openings in the ground stage of the towers, but that higher up there were narrow slit windows and often on the eastern side were narrow upper doorways for access by a rope ladder. Finally he argued that when later the church was built on to the east of the tower, and a doorway cut through the eastern wall of the tower into the nave, the roughness of the western side of the arch compared with the stone dressings on the eastern side, proves that the arch was a later insertion by the Normans who used dressed stone only on the visible east side of the tower arch, when a fireproof tower against the Danish invaders was no longer needed. Interestingly, while he mentions the need to provide the defenders with food against a siege he also says that most of these early towers were originally of little height (about 30 - 35ft.) in order to make them as inconspicuous as possible.

Messent, who also favours the Defence theory, puts forward as one of the reasons that they all occupy a commanding or hilltop position. But this was true of all Saxon and even later settlements. The high point of the village was generally chosen as the site of the church even in later times.

When were they built? So far only 25 to 40 out of 185 round towers (complete or ruinous) are generally accepted as Saxon. Where dates are given for these, they are invariably in the 11th. century, which of course is too late to have been used for defence against the Vikings. The following dates of the Viking raids are taken from the *"Saxon Chronicle"*. In 793 the monastery on Lindisfarne was destroyed and by 838 the Vikings had raided Kent and East Anglia. In 850 they wintered in East Anglia and in 866 they launched from there their raids on the north, by which time they were settling in this area. 871 to 878 were the years of the Danish Wars in the north. By 874 we have reached an age of Viking conquest and more permanent settlement.

Alfred won a decisive victory at Edington in 878, but Guthrum the Dane marched his army back into East Anglia. In 886 there was a treaty between the English under Alfred and the people who dwelt in East Anglia under Guthrum. We hear little more of East Anglia in the wars that still continued for a number of years.

So we come to Athelstan's law of 937 stating that "A bell tower must be built on the land of every Thegn." Some writers suggest that this law was for the building of these defence towers, but by now the Danes were as much a part of East Anglia as the Saxons. Bells are mentioned, but no words of defence. The next half century may well have witnessed a great increase in the number of bell towers throughout the land.

From Athelstan's reign there was a comparative peace until the accession of Ethelred the Unready in 979. During the second wave of Danish wars at the end of the 10th. century the Danes in East Anglia were generally sympathetic towards their brethren from overseas and assisted them. By 1013, Sweyn had forced Ethelred to flee the country and so in 1016 Sweyn's son Canute became King of England, coincident with a mass conversion of the Danes to Christianity.

The height of towers and the time needed to build them must surely play an important part in any defence work. I am certain that all the early towers were quite low, being only 30 to 35ft. in height, or just above the present nave roof (while the Irish round towers were about 90ft.) As a lookout in East Anglia these towers would have been poor vantage points from which to view the winding rivers. A tree would have provided a much better view. The towers would have taken from three to four years to build, as the maximum height possible in one year was ten feet. (See chapter 6 for the reason). This is far too long a period of construction to be of any use once raids had started.

East Anglian round towers are often compared to the Irish defence towers which also had upper doorways and no ground floor entrances. However, the Irish towers were so much taller, at about 90ft., they could hold more people on several floors. They could also be built much more quickly as they consisted of the local stone, had no buildings attached to them and were roofed in fireproof slates or stone. The local Irish stone used for these towers is similar to the rough stone used for field walls in the north of England. It is in much larger blocks than the East Anglian flints, therefore much more than nine inches could be built before being left to set, probably two or three feet. It is the similarity in shape which impresses many writers; but a 30ft. tower, whether attached to a thatched church or not, would not be a very safe refuge. Compare three of the Irish round towers from over 90 examples. Ratoo in County Kerry belonged to a sixth century monastery and was over 90ft, tall. In County Louth, Monasterboice was over 100ft. tall and belonged to another 6th. century monastery, and another early monastery at Swords, not far from Dublin had a tower 85ft tall. While all the Irish round towers were detached, only one in East Anglia was built this way, at Bramfield, but that was only 45ft. tall and not built until Norman times.

This brings us to the view that the towers were built first and the churches added on later. In my opinion many Saxon towers, and in particular most of the early towers, show clearly that they were built on to existing churches and I shall deal more fully with my reasons for believing this in chapter 8. Munro Cautley lays stress on the point that there were no doorways in the ground floor stage of the tower until the churches were built on later. He explains away the flint facings on the western side of the tower arches, while the eastern side had only flints, by saying they only used the more expensive dressed stone for the eastern nave side, where it would be seen more often. However, apart from tower arches, there are many south and west doorways to these towers although most are now blocked. A few are still open, or the blocked alcoves show clearly that they were pre-Conquest. A few that are certainly Saxon are Aylmerton and Forncett St. Peter, and Aslacton, Howe and Intwood, where although blocked, the alcove distinctly shows its Saxon features.

The fortified appearance of these towers does not need a lot of explaining when it is remembered that in Saxon and Norman times glass was almost unheard of, and certainly not cheap enough to glaze village church windows. Many Saxon windows are of the double-splayed type, to give maximum light with minimum penetration of wind and rain. What appear to be arrow slits are in fact the original slit windows, sometimes even belfry windows as at Risby in Suffolk. The battlements which now crown many of these towers and give a distinctly fortified appearance were not in fact added until the 13th. century, or in most cases much later, and are purely a decoration.

Furthermore, many Norfolk churches still have thatched roofs. In Saxon times all the churches would have been thatched and the towers also. This would have made them very vulnerable to attack by fire.

I therefore feel confident that the round towers were built as bell towers and not as defence towers: that the sites of round tower churches were not intrinsically different from the sites of any other churches and that many of the tower arches are the original Saxon entrances to the base of the tower which obviously precluded their use as defence. The question of why so many churches also have upper doorways I will attempt to answer in the next chapter.

Chapter 4

UPPER DOORWAYS

Before I give my opinion of their use and purpose, I must offer some more evidence derived from my observations. Upper doorways are rarely mentioned in towers other than round and readers may have the impression that they do not exist elsewhere. It is only since 1984 that I have started to record upper doorways in towers other than round, so there must be far more than I have noted to date. However, since 1984 I have seen upper doorways in over a dozen square towered churches which suggests that they had a wide-spread use.

Of the 73 upper doorways I have found in round towers, only 13 can be seen from the nave. The remainder can be seen only when the tower is climbed internally. Therefore, if such a small proportion of upper doorways is visible from the ground without climbing the tower, it is likely that the number of upper doorways in square towers is similarly far larger than can be seen from the nave.

Where these upper doorways are found in square towered churches they are usually of 13th. or 14th. century origin, as towers of the 15th. century generally had a stair turret built with the tower. This means that all these upper doorways were built before seating became common in churches. This implies that the doorways were to allow access to the first floor of the tower from the nave below. It was how they gained access that caused a further problem. A normal doorway was needed as it must have been into a room that was well used, though exactly just what for is uncertain. As we have no written or other evidence to determine its use, it could have been a vestry, priest's room, a place for the priest to rest between saying mass for souls through the night or even the village armoury.

We are left finally with the problem of the means of access. Had these been defence towers a rope ladder would have been used, but as we have seen the Viking raids were over before many of these towers were built. As it is we are left with an upper room needing some form of staircase. Therefore, the only questions remaining are, what form of staircase was it, and why was it removed? To both these questions we are unlikely to get a complete answer, for having been built at a time when church floors were trodden earth, no evidence would remain once the wooden staircase was removed. It would seem only logical that this would have been made of wood, perhaps starting with open stairs similar to a ladder, but soon these would have been improved to boarded-in steps and a handrail. We are now only left with the problem of the position of these stairs. While some people have suggested that many Saxon churches had a balcony at the west end, which would make access to this upper room simple, we have no proof of this, and many low churches have their upper doorways at eaves height or even higher. This would make a balcony of very little use. There are two other alternatives; either the stairs would have run beside the nave west wall with a small platform outside the door, or the stairs could have run from the upper doorway down the centre of the nave. This is the position I favour, although there is no proof. This position would explain why they were removed, and also when. Up to the 14th century, there were seats, or rather ledges, only for the elderly and infirm, against the north and south walls. Seating did not become common in small parish churches until the late 14th. and 15th. centuries, and then a staircase down the centre of the nave would have become an obstacle that could not be tolerated; so it was removed when the seats were installed. None of these early towers, either round, or square, had stair turrets built with them, but many stair turrets were built on to these towers during the 15th. century. This is another pointer to nave stairs getting in the way of seating. Towers from the 15th. century onwards, in nearly every case, had a stair turret built with the tower. There is thus a very strong probability that the stair turrets built on to the earlier towers were to replace some other form of entry into the tower

Here is a list of the round towers with an upper doorway. Those visible from the nave are marked * . Acle, Aslacton, Aylmerton, Bedingham, Beachamwell*, Brooke, Burnham Deepdale *, Burnham Norton *, Forncett, Framingham Earl, Fritton St. Catherine *, Gayton Thorpe, Haddiscoe *, Hales, Hardley, Hardwick, Great Hautbois *, Howe*, Letheringsett, East Lexham, Matlaske *, Mautby, Needham, Norton Subcourse, Norwich St. Benedict, Quidenham, Rockland St Peter, Roughton, Rushall, Great Ryburgh, Sedgeford, Seething, Little Snoring *, Long Stratton, Tasburgh, Titchwell, Welborne *, Witton, Woodton, Yaxham *, and Burgh St. Mary ruins *, in Norfolk.

Ashby *, Barsham, Blundeston, Little Bradley,Bungay, South Elmham All Saints, Gisleham, Hasketon, Hengrave, Herringfleet, Holton, Mettingham, Mutford *, Onehouse, Rickinghall, Risby, Little Saxham *, Spexhall, Theberton, Thorington*, Wissett, Wortham in Suffolk. Pentlow in Essex; Bartlow in Cambridgeshire; and Great Shefford in Berkshire.

The upper doorways in square towers seen by me are all visible from the ground and are at:- Aylsham, West Barsham, Brinton, Bergh Apton, Flitcham, Kettlestone, Sharrington, Sporle, Shottesham All Saints, Thornham, Tilney All Saints, Watlington, West Winch, Great Melton ruins, Shottesham ruins, and Tunstall ruins. These are in Norfolk.

Suffolk square towers with upper doorways visible from the ground are at:- Acton, Brandeston, Butley and Worlingworth.

Chapter 5

WOODEN CHURCHES

Most writers assert that most British churches were built of wood before and up to the Conquest. As late as 1969 E.A. Fisher in *"Anglo Saxon Towers"* wrote. "There can be no doubt that by far the greater number of structural churches existing in England even in the 12th century were still of wood, and this explains the remarkable activity of the church architects of this and the next century. They were replacing in stone the earlier wooden churches and rebuilding on a larger scale some of the few mason-built churches already in existence."

What are the facts? In 1912 Charles Cox believed that stone churches and towers existed in East Anglia from the 9th and 10th centuries. It is later that writers have asserted that no stone churches were built until after the Conquest, but they do not advance any positive facts to support their views. The Taylors, our foremost Anglo-Saxon scholars, list more Saxon churches in Norfolk than in any other county, but the only answer against this is to place all Saxon features in the Saxo-Norman period without offering any proof. Only one church in wood still exists, at Greensted-juxta-Ongar in Essex; the building date is given as 1016, and no other wooden churches are known to be still standing. Yet in the same county is the stone chapel of St Peter-on-the-Wall at Bradwell with a building date of 654. This early date of building for a stone church refutes the idea that no masonry work was carried on in Eastern England before the late Saxon period.

It is understood that buildings, except those of great importance, not only in East Anglia but throughout the country were of wood, generally half timbered or timber-framed structures. Most houses were in this style right through the middle ages until the mass production of bricks. But this does not mean that churches, and in particular East Anglian churches, were built in this fashion. A church was the most important building in any parish. King Alfred is recorded as giving half of his income to the Church, and Norman and later Earls and Dukes gave entire estates to monasteries, so the wealthy Church could afford to build in the best materials available.

Godfrey records, "In England today there are about 200 churches still in use, mostly as parish churches, which wholly or in part consist of late Anglo-Saxon work. They are generally in villages or out-of-the-way places, where there has been little need or temptation through the centuries to replace the original structures with larger buildings. Though scattered they form a homogenous group, members of which can usually be distinguished by certain well-defined characteristics." Some of our East Anglian villages appear to fulfil the description of 'out-of-the way places' very well. This statement must mean that, even in small communities, Godfrey recognised that stone churches were built before the Conquest. The evidence of the Taylors gives Norfolk 54 and Suffolk 11 churches with parts at least dating back to before the Conquest.

From the beginning of this century, the main features by which stone buildings could be designated pre-Conquest have been known from the careful and diligent work of a number of scholars, including Rickman, Baldwin Brown, Clapham, and later H.M. and Joan Taylor. But many writers have consistently ignored these features when they did not fit in with their own idea. When one of these scholars lists the Saxon features in a number of churches, the explanation will be, "They are Saxo-Norman, because all Saxon churches were of wood before the Conquest." But if all Saxon churches were of wood, there would have been no Saxon features in flints at any period.

There is visual evidence of pre-Conquest building in stone in churches with square towers as well as round. The Normans would never have built features with flint in churches where we can see large amounts of their dressed stone used in the doorways. In East Anglia, the Saxons built mostly in flints as no dressed stone was readily available. Why then is this evidence not acknowledged as far too much attention is given to the later features in dressed stone, that have in many cases replaced features that were in existence many years earlier? Churches were built to last, and generation after generation repaired, enlarged and altered their church but still in most cases left the shell almost intact. The large numbers of Norman doorways in Norfolk and Suffolk is proof of this, and yet these churches have few Norman windows left, for the later styles that let in more light and allowed the glorious stained glass to beautify the interior swept aside the smaller windows of earlier ages. If this example can show that many churches are as old as the 12th. century, why is it so hard to believe that many of these churches had Norman doorways fitted into earlier church walls? The most disturbing result to my mind, is that without any evidence to corroborate it, the foundation of any early church, whether or not it has a round tower, is usually dated no earlier than the 11th. or 12th century, especially if it is in East Anglia.

From the early days of my research into the round tower churches, I wondered why many experts constantly referred to the early East Anglian churches as wooden. Yet, they readily point to stone churches in other parts of the country as early as the 7th. century. These include Brixworth, and Brigstock in Northants; Wing in Bucks; Deerhurst in Gloucestershire; Reculver in Kent; Hexham in Northumberland; and Escomb and Jarrow in Durham. Lincolnshire also has many Saxon churches, while the chapel of St. Peter-on-the-Wall at Bradwell in Essex is dated to 654.

Why then should it be supposed that in Norfolk and Suffolk alone were men incapable of making and working with flint and mortar for so long? If pressed, those favouring a totality of wooden churches up to the Conquest will argue that East Anglia was covered with forests, and the trees cut down to make a clearing would be used to build their churches and houses. But though Britain was well wooded, East Anglia was more open than other areas even in Roman times for it was the main arable area of the country. Yet as East Anglia was throughout this period one of the most densely populated and prosperous regions of England, presumably the churches would always have been built with the best materials available. These factors suggest that instead of designating all East Anglian churches as made of wood until Norman times we should be looking for pre-Conquest churches in stone.

Chapter 6

BUILDING MATERIALS AND METHODS

The stones used by the Saxons were many and varied and not beautiful to the eyes of the Normans, but why spend large sums on transport when you can use materials close at hand? The walls they built from local stones, the roof timbers and doors from the common woodland or manor estate and the thatch would have been wheat straw. Reed thatch came into use much later.

We can usually tell what part of Britain we are in by the materials used in our churches. East Anglia has no dressed stone which is preferable for building the corners of the walls and for surrounding doorways and windows. This had to be transported over long distances and because of its weight it was, and still is, a very expensive material. In fact due to poor roads and vehicles capable of transporting only small loads, it was too expensive to move far in spite of cheap labour.

Let us begin by looking at the local building materials and the means of transport. Within the last 30 to 40 years archaeologists have come to the conclusion that East Anglia, from Roman times at least, has been a partly open landscape and not covered by dense forests as was once thought. It was certainly marshy in parts and this no doubt hampered land transport after the Roman roads were neglected. The many rivers of the area were probably fully utilised for transporting what the Saxons considered essential cargoes but this does not seem to have included building materials or there would certainly be more dressed stone of pre-Conquest date left in the area to confirm this.

The study of Saxon villages and churches seems to show that they were almost self-supporting and stone would have been a luxury material they do not appear to have enjoyed. Each parish would have had its wooded area, usually on the parish boundaries, which would have supplied fuel for the fires and timber for the houses and furniture. Transported materials would have been mainly small and light, and certainly until the coming of the Normans, not much dressed stone for building would have been brought in. There were probably Roman villas, and at least three Roman military forts in the round tower area from which bricks and other materials could be taken.

FLINTS These stones, of many sizes and colours, are very hard and durable. Those used for the outer face of churches and towers in Saxon times are still looking just the same today as they did one thousand years earlier. This is in contrast to the dressed stone used in Norman or even later periods, much of which has already had to be renewed. The flints were obtained from the beaches, from gravel deposits laid down by glacial drifts during the Ice Ages and from chalk beds. Flints in large quantities were also found in the fields, and would be removed prior to ploughing to save the iron tipped wooden ploughs. Even as late as the last century, women and children were paid 1d. a basket for collecting stones from farmers' fields. Flints from gravel deposits are brown in colour, while those black or white flints with a whitish outside are from the chalk beds. In some cases, hard chalk (clunch) can be found in the flint beds and was used as the centre core of flint walls, with flints for the surface. This can be seen inside the towers of

Fritton St. Edmund in Suffolk and in Feltwell St. Nicholas, East Lexham St Andrew and West Lexham St. Nicholas in Norfolk.

CARSTONE Carstone is frequently confused with conglomerate although they are entirely different and come from differing geological periods. Carstone is a brown stone, usually much lighter in colour than conglomerate. The colour is caused by iron oxides; it contains quartz or glass like particles, but these are not likely to be noticed in weather-worn blocks in situ in walls. It can easily be carved and is a form of sandstone that outcrops at Hunstanton cliffs in Norfolk. It is still quarried at Snettisham in Norfolk, and there used to be a quarry at Bexwell. It was used for building in West Norfolk until late in the 19th. century. In spite of this its use in the building of round tower churches is very limited, although a number of other churches in West Norfolk have much of this stone in their structures. The priory church of Castle Acre has bands of carstone as a decoration, but even there none was used for the doorways, windows or corners, and only as decorative bands along the nave walls. It is a very soft stone not standing up to the weather and rarely encountered outside West Norfolk.

CONGLOMERATE This is also called Norfolk ironstone or puddingstone. It is roughly similar to carstone in colour, but is more likely to be a very dark brown, almost black in some cases. Also it is impregnated with pebbles throughout its structure whereas carstone has none. While much harder than carstone, it is also a very intractable stone to carve, due mainly to the pebbles it contains. While carstone was used only near the quarries, conglomerate is to be seen in a large number of towers and church walls, giving the impression that it was found locally in surface soil. I was told that in West Dereham it is still being turned up by farmers' ploughs. All the walls containing this conglomerate appear to be pre-Conquest, except where it has been re-used. Yaxham and Little Snoring have re-used the quoins of this stone and Great Hautbois and West Dereham have had buttresses built of this material at dates after the Norman era to blend with the walls constructed almost entirely of conglomerate in pre-Conquest days.

SANDSTONE The only example that I know of sandstone being used extensively in round-tower churches is at Bungay in Suffolk. There small blocks of this yellow sandstone are used with the flints in the tower, but I do not know where they originated. Odd pieces are sometimes seen elsewhere but not in any quantity.

SEPTARIA This stone, a form of compressed London Clay, is to be found in the Deben and Stour estuaries of Essex and south Suffolk. It is rarely seen in round tower churches, due no doubt to there being so few in these districts. Ramsholt tower and church are built principally of this material.

ERRATICS Erratics are large blocks of very hard stone that are found in gravel beds. They have been deposited by the glacial drifts. Odd blocks of these stones are often seen in Saxon towers and churches, usually at the base of the tower or church walls. The north west corner at Syleham in Suffolk has a few blocks laid in long-and-short fashion. Plate 34 shows this corner.

BRICKS Bricks were made and used throughout the country during the Roman period, no doubt more so in the flint areas. Both Brampton and Hales have a scattering of Roman bricks while Broomfield in Essex has a complete corner, (plate 35), and Rickinghall Inferior has the interior of the Saxon belfry windows completely framed with these bricks. We are now beginning to realise that East Anglia restarted brickmaking much earlier than other parts of the country. The area's reliance on outside sources for dressed stone, which must have been expensive, no doubt served to promote the resurgence of this industry. Several of the octagonal tops to round towers are built with bricks as early as the 13th. century. Two examples are Ashby in Suffolk, (plate 11), and Heckingham in Norfolk.

DRESSED STONE. This must always have come either from the stone belt of the Midlands or, after the Conquest, from Caen. The fact that so much Caen stone was imported for church building highlights the great difficulty in transporting the Midland stone overland to East Anglia. From Caen it could have come by water nearly all the way - down the river Orne, across the

Channel then up one of the numerous East Anglian rivers. It was not impossible to transport heavy stones across country for we know that the stones of Stonehenge were transported long distances in the Bronze Age. In Saxon times however, a new factor operated; the economy was becoming linked to money. To transport stone at this time required money rather than the time of many people. So in East Anglia before the Conquest only rich patrons could afford to use dressed stone in their churches, and I have found very little in round tower churches pre-Conquest except re-used slabs.

BUILDING METHODS

If we study some dressed stone that is called Saxon, like the long-and-short work at Little Bradley, (plate 33), which has been inserted into a pre-Conquest church, we can see that these stones are too small to be Saxon. They must be Saxo-Norman of about 1100. The size of the stones and the careful cutting is the key here, for Saxon workmen always used very large stones and they were not so careful of the shape, as their tool, the adze, was not so precise as the Norman bolster. Norman masons used quite small stones carefully prepared and readily lifted and fitted by one man.

The belfry of Herringfleet in Suffolk must be Saxo-Norman, for the double-triangular-headed windows have Norman billet moulding round the jambs and round-headed arch that frames the double windows of the Saxon style. The windows and surrounding mouldings are all in the same dressed stone. Not far from Herringfleet and just over the Norfolk border is the tower of Haddiscoe (plate 7). The whole tower here is Saxo-Norman of about the same date. The abundance of Caen stone from Normandy in the tower is proof of its date. The wall of considerable thickness also favours a Norman date. The stone string-courses at each stage were built into the tower when it was constructed. The windows of Haddiscoe tower (plate 24). have remained the same throughout its life, something very rare in these towers. All the windows are carefully finished in dressed stone both within and without. There is no other medieval round tower save Bardfield Saling that has its tower windows treated in this way.

The use of dressed stone in East Anglian churches can tell us a lot if we first study how, why and when it was used. Most writers point to Norman or Early English windows and doorways in dressed stone, and categorically pronounce the church or tower to be Norman or Early English. It was this approach that led John Gage in 1829 to declare all round towers post-Conquest because he simply looked at the windows. On the other hand Shereford and Framingham Earl, both with Norman doorways but where the nave walls are admitted Saxon by almost every writer. At Shereford three of the four nave quoins consist of large flints and conglomerates albeit with some repairs, while a double splayed round-headed window still lights the nave from the south (plate 27). At Framingham Earl the four corners of the nave are all very large flints cut to give a sharp corner, and three circular double-splayed windows still show in the church walls.

If we look carefully at all the features in these East Anglian churches it soon becomes clear that almost all the dressed stone was cut after the Conquest. It is an easy matter to list the dressed stone of pre-Conquest date we can see in the round tower churches. It is probably this feature that prompted the belief that the churches must have been of wood until the influx of dressed stone after the Conquest. We know of many circular double-splayed windows that were built without any dressed stone, and also round-headed windows likewise constructed entirely of flint rubble. Add to this the number of belfry windows, mainly double-light, with triangular heads (ignoring for the moment any later dressed stone in them) and other belfry windows of flints, such as those at Burnham Norton, Burnham Deepdale (plate 6), and Risby (plate 23). There are a great many more however, lower down in the towers and now blocked up, that can be plainly seen within the tower, that prove these belfries never had a piece of limestone in them at the time of their construction.

If windows could be built so well without dressed stone, then why not doorways? The Taylors tell us that although the Saxons readily built their windows of flint rubble, they would not trust their doorways to this treatment, but used blocks of stone for this purpose. I disagree here with the Taylors, whose work I admire, because they have obviously not seen the five examples of Saxon doorways in flint and conglomerates that have escaped the attention of later builders. Those at Hardwick (plate 21), and Taverham are built of flint rubble, while those at Morton-on-the-Hill and Great Hautbois are built mainly of conglomerate. Aylmerton tower doorway (plate 22) is built of large flints and two large pieces of erratics. All these doorways are in Norfolk and it is very noticeable that none of them constitutes the main entrance, which has in every case had more elaborate doorways inserted. It is clear that these churches and towers were built of local stones well before the Conquest.

What dressed stone then can we assign to pre-Conquest days? In Hasketon nave wall, there are three pieces of dressed stone that were cut and drilled for a Saxon double-splayed window (plate 28). Yet the whole church is certainly Norman, and these pieces of stone are purely preserved remnants. Whether they were brought from outside the county we do not know. It is a mystery that is still unresolved. In the Saxon belfry windows of Beachamwell, near Swaffham, (plate 5), there are two or three pieces of re-used dressed stone. From their shape they appear to be either tomb stones or more likely parts of a broken churchyard cross. At Aldham in Suffolk there are two pieces of stone carved with the cable pattern generally called Saxon. These appear to have come from a memorial, which could well have been a churchyard cross. The only other round tower church that I can recall having any pre-Conquest dressed stone is Cranwich near Thetford. Here there are four circular windows in the tower with a knot design that are regarded as Saxon. These four small slabs of stone could well have been brought into the area from outside, but I cannot explain why only these, which are of a purely decorative nature, were brought in.

Knowing something of the materials available to the Saxons we can now turn our attention to the method of building these towers and churches, and in doing so understand more fully why we so often see large sections of walls of differing or contrasting materials that seem to have no decorative purpose. One building method suggested by some writers, including Stephen Heywood, is that shuttering was used and the flints and mortar poured in and allowed to set. But to make any savings in time, surely sections of at least three feet in height would have had to be built, because the mortar would contain more water and the walls would be hemmed in by boards restricting the drying out. The tower or church wall would need to have a wall of wooden planks built for the outer and inner face saving a space say of three feet for the wall. This shuttering would have to be sturdily built to take the weight and thrust of the mixture going inside. It is for these reasons that I reject shuttering as a method of building with flints. Boards were not so easily obtainable as they are today, and in no case have I found any board marks left in the mortar on the inside or outside of any of the main walls, although I have seen board marks left in the mortar of many windows and upper doorways. If flints and mortar were poured in they would never have settled in the patterns they now show.

The most likely method seems to be as follows: using as stiff a mortar as possible the wall would be built to a height of nine inches. This seems to have been the highest that could be built with flints before the flints started to slip or slump. The builders then had to wait a number of days for the mortar to set before another nine-inch layer could be built. Owing to the slow setting qualities of the mortar used there had to be no frost before it set, so all building ceased at Michaelmas and did not start again until Easter or Lady Day. One season's work could not construct more than 10ft, and this is why churches, towers and castles often show distinct changes of materials from one season to the next. (See plate 14). Saxons, I believe, built their walls of solid flints right through, while the Normans built a solid inner and outer skin and filled in between with small flints or rubble. This was probably why Norman walls had to be much thicker than Saxon walls.

The absence of limestone, sandstone, granite and other stones that can be split and worked for building puts East Anglia in a special position. However, it is an aid to dating these early churches, and the lack of ashlar gives another key to unlocking the dates of round tower churches. The constant assertions that churches with Norman doorways must be post-Conquest churches. The constant assertions that churches with Norman doorways must be post-Conquest is not borne out by other features, which include Decorated or Perpendicular windows or doorways. Once we can understand that these features could have been inserted into walls already standing , we can see that these features only tell us that the walls cannot be later than this feature. From the earlier details of building walls, it is plain that they were a very lengthy process to build, and so were never indiscriminately demolished unless a much larger building was contemplated. We know that limestone was almost absent from any building in East Anglia before the Conquest, but that does not mean that any building containing limestone is post-Conquest. The apparent crudeness of flints and conglomerates as corners, doorways or windows, would seem to prohibit their use once dressed stone was available, Therefore, when flint features are seen in a wall that also has dressed stone, it surely means that the wall is earlier than the dressed stone. The time it would have taken to build a church in those days means it must have been impossible to build all the churches with a Norman doorway in the 100 years from the Conquest to the Early English period. It would have been far quicker to insert windows and doorways into flint walls than to build the walls themselves, and this I am sure is what occurred.

Chapter 7

EARLY PLANS

In Chapter 5 I expressed my firm conviction that stone churches soon replaced any built of wood and that these stone churches were often built several centuries before the Conquest. I would like now to take a look at how we can tell an early church from a later one. Leaving aside for the moment the various Saxon features such as windows and long-and-short work I would like to dwell on the basic plan. North Elmham and Dunham Magna in Norfolk and the Minster at South Elmham in Suffolk are quite probably the only great Saxon churches in East Anglia. By this I mean a church with aisles or transepts and of more importance than one serving a small parish. So what plan should we expect to see in the small parish church?

The four simple and basic plans of our early churches were like the plans figs 1 to 4 (below). Many early writers agree that these were the plans of the early churches of the villages. I believe that these stone churches were built soon after the missions of St. Fursey and St. Felix. Baldwin Brown told us that we could generally get a good idea if a church was Saxon if it was long, narrow and tall. But he then modified this rule by giving a list of Saxon churches that were not narrow. Looking at this list, we can see that all the wide churches were major churches and probably of cathedral type, but the parish church was generally very narrow.

Fig 1 Nave and Chancel same width

Fig 2 Nave and Chancel same width apsidal east end

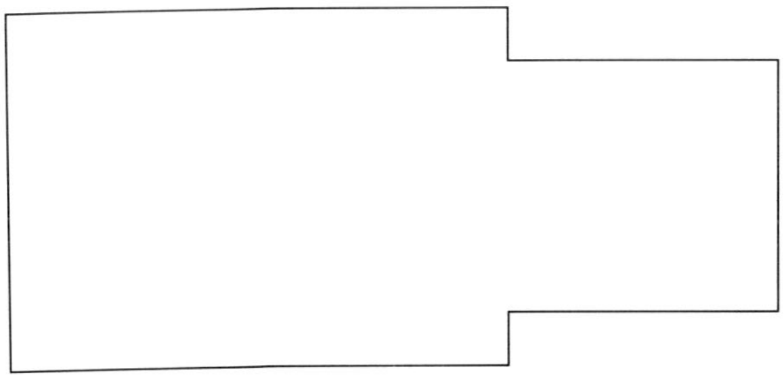

Fig 3 Nave under 20ft. wide with narrower Chancel

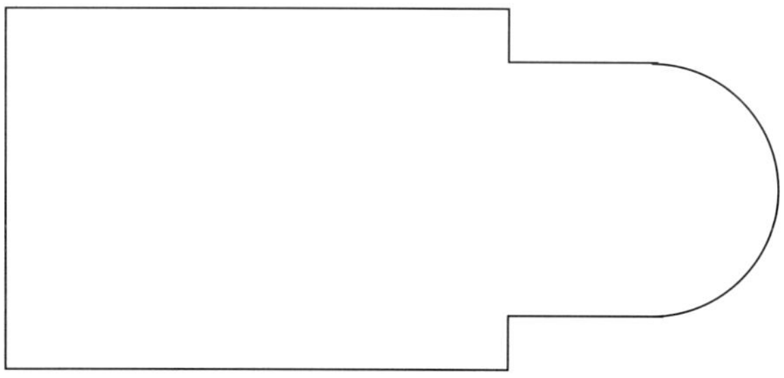

Fig 4 Nave under 20ft. wide with narrower apsidal Chancel

Note that two of the plans have apsidal east ends. Many writers assert that the apsidal east end was a strictly Norman feature. While the Normans used an apsidal east end it was by no means previously unknown in this country, as seen at Worth in Sussex as well as at least four East Anglian round tower churches that survive in this form today. There are also a number that we know have been altered in later years. The four surviving apsidal round tower churches are Fritton St. Edmunds, Hales and Heckingham, all close to each other on the Norfolk-Suffolk border and Pentlow in Essex. The square east end was also used and in the Early English period it became almost universal.

Most of the early churches had naves and chancels of about the same width. Some were built with a narrower chancel some time before the Conquest and there are several early examples in the round tower church group. Although our dating is not at present precise enough to give a definite date to each and every church, we can get to within 100 years in most cases.

Most of these early churches, however, have later had aisles and or transepts added to their original plan. Many large churches have within their apparent late-medieval building a small early church which has been enlarged rather than rebuilt. Careful study can often discover these early churches within the later buildings. The width between the arcades often gives the original nave width which, if under 20ft., should give us our first clue. If we can then find a return nave wall, (see fig.6). of the original church, the thickness of this wall can give a good idea of its age. These early plans were in use before towers began to be built and the number of round towers added to these early churches is an indication of the number of East Anglian churches that were built before towers became the norm.

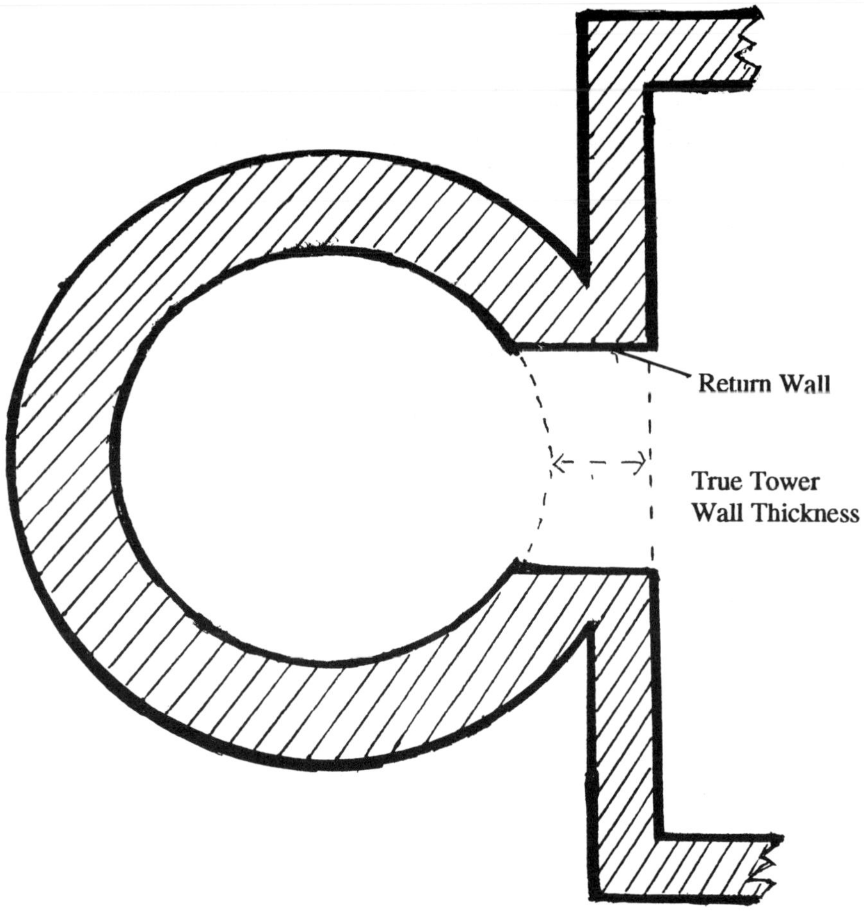

Fig 5

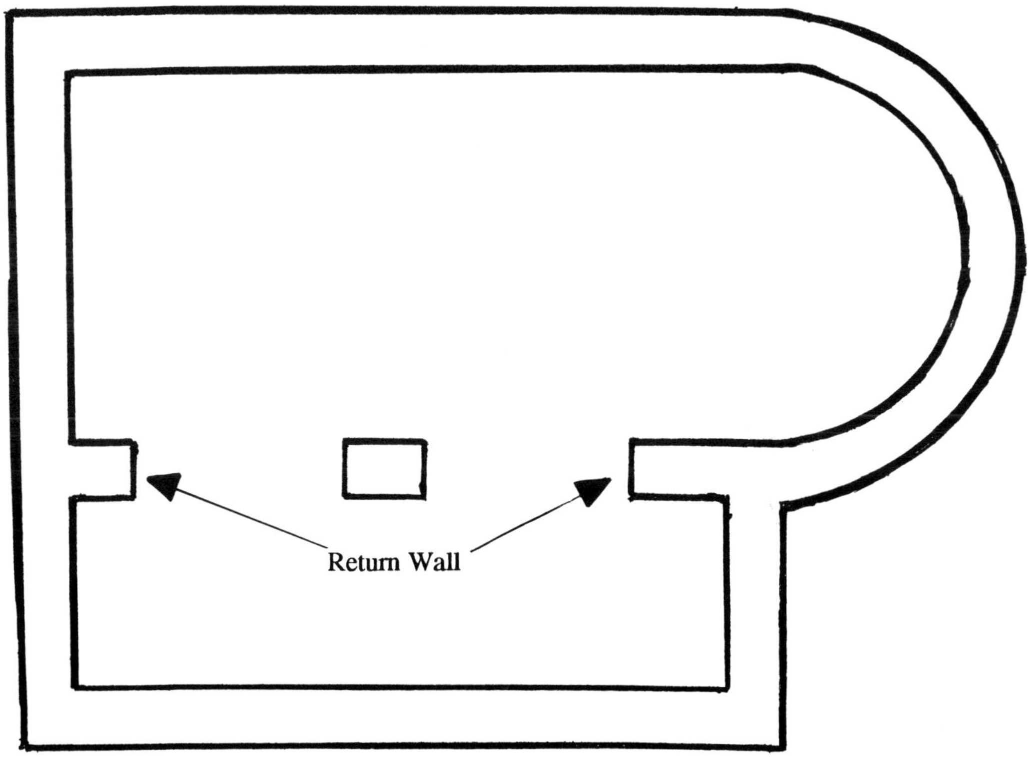

Fig 6

Chapter 8

CHURCHES BEFORE TOWERS?

In his *"Norfolk Churches"* Munro Cautley outlined his belief that the towers were built before the churches as this fitted in well with his Defence theory. In chapter 7 I gave the plans of our earliest churches which did not have a tower. I believe that it will pay us now to look at this aspect to see which of these concepts is correct. If Munro Cautley is correct, then it is certain that flint buildings were in being well before the Conquest. Like Munro Cautley, most writers take it for granted that these round towers were built before their churches, while at the same time failing to recognise that there are Saxon churches remaining in East Anglia.

Throughout my studies of these churches I have found myself at variance with the long-established views on this subject. If the towers were built first and free-standing then building in flint must have been much earlier than the writers would have us believe, and churches of wood would hardly have been built right up to the Conquest. Domesday records at least 390 and possibly 448 churches in Suffolk and 243 in Norfolk in 1086. Yet most of these towers are still classed as Norman by experienced writers. However, if the churches were built first, then the towers might well have been the first bell towers built for these churches. Fixing the date for early church bells, or the earliest towers, could well help in dating these bell towers. I have often mentioned in my writings of towers being added to existing churches, although Munro Cautley refers only to Little Bradley as being in this class, and the Taylors list but six.

Looking first at the towers in the Taylors' list, the feature that dates them as later than their churches, is a flat east wall internally. This represented the outside of the nave west wall.
Quite often this flattened east side continues on the upper floors and in a few cases, as at Gayton Thorpe in Norfolk and Gunton in Suffolk, even the east side of the tower above the nave continues in this flattened mode.

Looking at each of these plans to see how we can check them and understand how they prove that the tower and church were built in the order I am certain they were; fig 7. shows us the flat east side of the tower, which in itself should be quite convincing. In a number of cases we can also see clearly that the two walls are not in bond and were therefore built at different times. The tower could never have been built with only three-quarters of a circular wall. Finally, if we measure at the west window, we find the true thickness of the tower wall, but over the head of the tower arch (or doorway) as is often the case in these churches, we find it measures much less, the thickness of the nave walls in fact.

TOWER PLANS

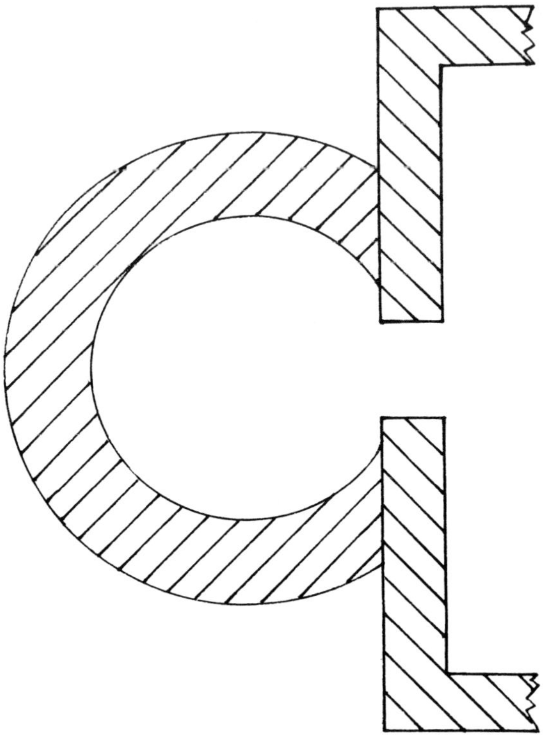

Fig 7 Tower built on to church

Fig 8 Tower and church built together

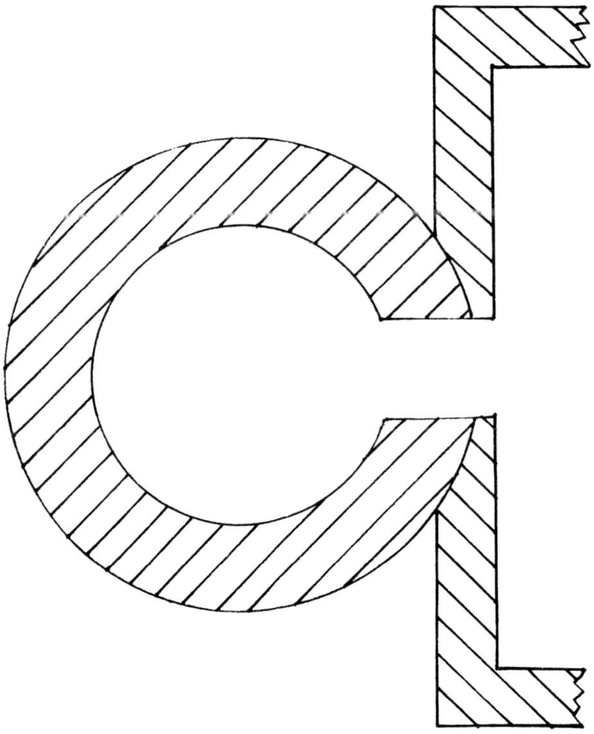

Fig 9 Tower built before church

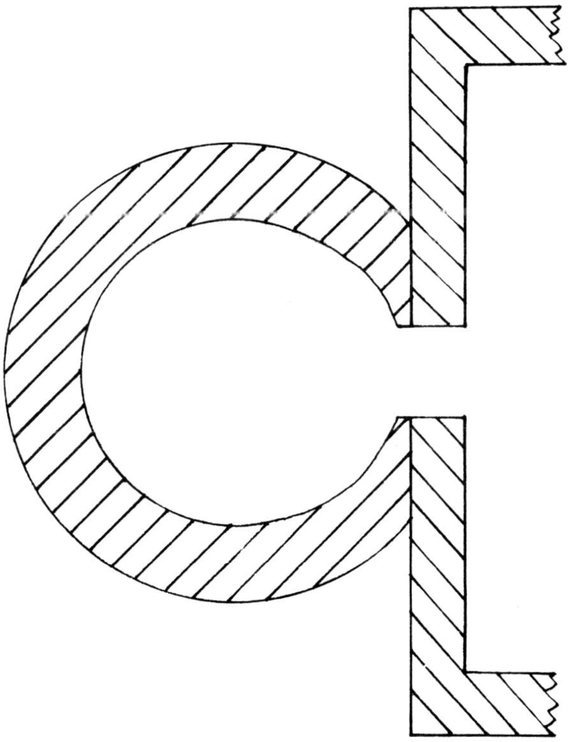

Fig 10 Tower built on to church but inner wall curved

TOWERS WITH A FLAT EAST WALL

NORFOLK
Ashmanhaugh Rebuilt (1849)
Bawburgh
Beachamwell
Brampton
Brandiston
Clippesby
West Dereham
Gayton Thorpe
Hales
Hassingham
Great Hautbois
Intwood
Letheringsett
Merton window can be seen
Morton-on-the Hill window can be seen
St. Mary Coslany Norwich
Quidenham
Repps-with-Bastwick
Runhall
Rushall
Syderstone
Tasburgh
Thorpe-next-Haddiscoe window can be seen
East Walton
Weeting Rebuilt (1868)
Worthing

SUFFOLK
Aldham
Belton Rebuilt (1849)
Beyton
Little Bradley
Bradwell
Herringfleet
Mettingham
Spexhall Rebuilt (1910)

ESSEX
Great Leighs
South Ockendon
Pentlow

CAMBRIDGESHIRE
Snailwell

TOWERS WITH THINNER EAST WALL BUT CURVED

NORFOLK	DIFFERENCE
Aslacton	1ft. 9"
Bexwell	6"
Burnham Deepdale	8"
Old Catton	1ft.4"
Cockley Cley	10"
Colney	8"
Croxton	8"
Eccles	2"
Edingthorpe	1ft.5"
Fishley	3"
Forncett St. Peter	5"
Haddiscoe	1ft.6"
Kilverstone	1ft.3"
Matlaske	1ft.2"
South Pickenham	4"
Stody	1ft.0"
Surlingham	2"
Swainsthorpe	10"
Tuttington	4"
Taverham window found	1ft.2"

NORFOLK	DIFFERENCE
Threxton	2"
Yaxham	4"
SUFFOLK	
Brome tower recased	11"
Bruisyard	11"
Bungay	3"
Barsham window found	
Fritton	4"
Gisleham	7"
Holton St. Peter	3"
Ramsholt	2"
Risby	1"
Rushmere	6"
Syleham	1ft.8"
Theberton	3"
Thorington	6"
ESSEX	
Lamarsh	3"

Fig.8. illustrates where the tower was built at the same time as the church. Here we can see by the plan that the tower has the same wall thickness all round. The tower is circular internally, but it may not always be a perfect circle, for not all village builders were so skilful and the age of the church has a lot to do with the skill of its builders. Fig.9 illustrates how Munro Cautley believes all these towers were built before their churches, with the nave wall six inches in advance of the tower to be certain of a flat west wall. Here the only indication we have that this might be one of those towers, is that the tower wall at the west window, measures about six inches less than the tower east wall, but this must be measured under the tower arch at the centre of the head. This is most important, for as can be seen in fig. 5. if, as most scholars have done, we measure this wall at the tower return wall, we get a false measurement. This is what Munro Cautley may have done, for a number of other writers have done this, and called some of these tower walls six feet thick, which none of them are. From all my measurements, only twelve towers show a tower wall thicker on the east than at the west window. I feel certain that none of these towers was built in isolation before the church was built.

Fig. 10. This is where the tower is circular internally, but yet has a thinner east wall than at the west window. Until 1981, I had classed these towers as built with their churches. Although the two measurements were different, I had no means of knowing why this should be so. Then in January, I had a call from the rector of Taverham, where a west gallery was being built. I had told them to expect to find an upper doorway when they broke through the nave west wall. What they found was a west window. This was proved as the opening had an internal splay, and only a ten inch opening on the west. In no way could this have been a doorway. I had already proved that this church and tower were Saxon, but this discovery showed that the church stood here first. The head of the west doorway into the tower measured only 2ft. 10", the nave west wall in fact. Later, my figures and observations revealed that Barsham in Suffolk was another tower in this class. Here a fire destroyed the thatched roof in 1979, and the heat had destroyed the plaster at the top of the nave west wall. It revealed a double-splayed window in flints, as seen at the church of Morton-on-the-Hill, and proved once more, that this window looked out upon the churchyard before the tower was built. Since then, in August 1991, the tower of Cockley Cley collapsed (plate 13). and the exposed west wall of the nave showed clearly that the tower and nave were not in bond. Once again, there was a difference in the measurements of east and west, although the tower was circular internally. With three examples in damaged towers, the conclusion is obvious. We must place towers with these measurements almost certainly in the same class as those built after the churches or at any rate after the nave west wall. The only remaining question is how much thinner must the east wall be compared to the west, before we can say the tower is later? We must always allow for slight differences in measurements in flint walls so I leave it to the reader to decide how many of the listed towers were built later.

Chapter 9

DOORWAYS AND PORTICOS

The earliest Saxon churches in East Anglia were built without towers. However, we are told that porticos or porches were known in other parts of the country. The church and west portico at Monkwearmouth in the north were dedicated in 674. This portico, which originally had one upper floor, was later raised twice to form what is now the fine Saxon tower 59ft. high. Evidence that these porches or porticos with one upper floor could be built as early as the 7th century contrasts with the date of towers first known in Italy in the 9th. century, which were higher.

Although church towers were unknown before the 9th. century, the Roman circular bastions of Burgh Castle were an example of what could be built with the local flints. They are still standing today and their walls are as strong as ever. There was therefore no reason to look to the continent for the prototypes. Early East Anglian towers were never more than of nave ridge height, so they could originally have served as porches: a porch no higher than the nave roof cannot really be called a tower.

At Acle in Norfolk, the circular tower stops short of the nave ridge and is surmounted by a 13th. century octagonal stage. We are so used to seeing porches against the south or north nave doorways that we tend to believe that they were always in this position. In fact the nave doorways were not always in the western end of the nave wall. H.M.Taylor, writing about Thorpe Abbotts, says, "Towards the west is a simple Transitional Norman or Early English pointed doorway wholly faced in wrought freestone; while near the centre of the wall is a blocked earlier doorway, whose jambs and round-headed arch are wholly formed in flints and seem to us good evidence for assigning a late Saxon or Saxon-Norman date to the part of the north wall in which they stand."

It was a long time later, at Barney church in Norfolk, when I noticed another Saxon blocked doorway in the centre of the nave south wall. Further examples were then seen and noted, outside East Anglia as well as within. In three years the following examples were found in East Anglia: Darsham, Friston, Henstead ,Snape, Thornham Magna and Thwaite in Suffolk; Barney, Belaugh, Swanton Novers and Thorpe Abbotts in Norfolk. These examples prove that church entrances were not always in the west end of the north or south nave walls. Many churches were entered by a west doorway and some still are. Looking first at those churches which were built before their round towers, we notice that most of these have a normal doorway-sized entrance into the tower from the nave instead of the usual tower arch. This strongly indicates that the main entrance was at the west end of the church in early days. At Pentlow in Essex the Saxon west doorway was altered in Norman times, as can be seen by the typical chevron mouldings. It is plain to see that the tower was built on later as it overlaps part of the Norman moulding of the doorway. This highly decorated west doorway is proof that this was the main entrance to the church in Norman times. Other examples of where a normal doorway is still the entrance to the tower that has been added to the church are at Great Hautbois, Letheringsett, Runhall, Taverham, Thorpe-next-Haddiscoe and Worthing in Norfolk, and at Aldham, Little Bradley and Herringfleet in Suffolk. In addition, many round towers have, or had, ground floor doorways that must have been entrances to the nave, for in some, beside the doorway, there is a recess or alcove for a holy water stoup, as at Bedingham near Bungay.

What has all this to do with porticos? We have seen that there are no Saxon porches left in East Anglia although the early writers assured us that they were built in some parts of the country. Looking at the round towers of East Anglia it is clear that most have been raised at least once, but a large number, as seen from the inside, have been raised twice, from their original very short towers. It matters little whether you call the early round towers porticos or towers, the Saxon builders of those early days did not need to look to Italy for their inspiration. Monkwearmouth and other major churches in Britain showed that these low structures could be built to the west of their churches as early as the seventh century, and there was Burgh Castle on their doorstep as a fine model.

Fig 11 Norman stones facing a Saxon Opening
Note SET-BACK Arch

Fig 12 Norman Doorway or Tower Arch

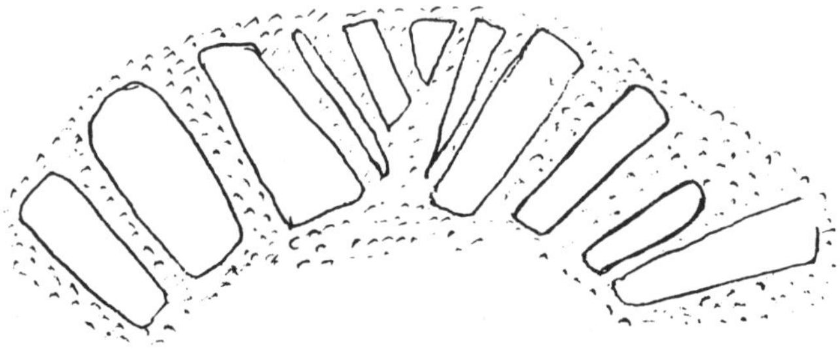

Fig 13 Tredington Church
Tredington Fashion by Baldwin Brown
Non Radial Voussoirs

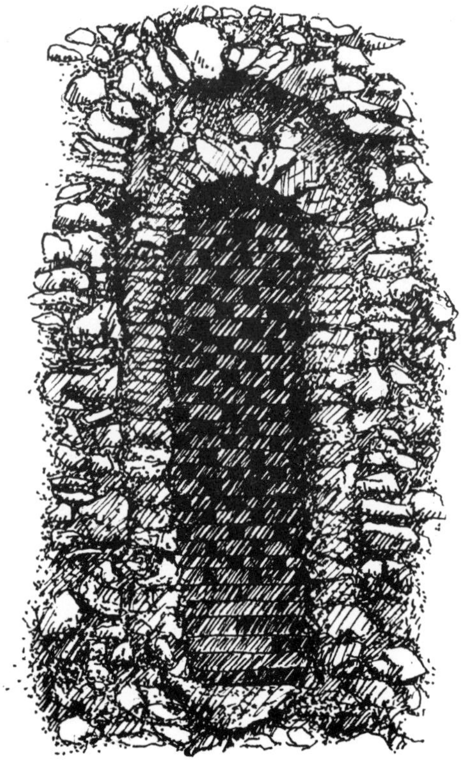

Fig 14 Burnham Norton
Non Radial Voussoirs

Chapter 10

SAXON FEATURES

It is now time to examine the features we call Saxon, and try to determine how far they can be relied upon to date a church or tower. Except where I have indicated otherwise I have relied upon *"The Arts of Early England"* Vol.2. *"Anglo-Saxon Architecture"* by Baldwin Brown published in 1925 and also H.M. and Joan Taylor's *"Anglo-Saxon Architecture"* of 1965. I have added some local information of my own. The features mentioned have particular reference to round tower churches.

In all cases, I have studied on the ground the feature described before including it in this section. As my notes will show, I place much more reliance on the materials used than on the shape of the feature.

Although the Taylors mention, from time to time, the absence of building stone in East Anglia and quote the ability of the local builders to construct corners and windows with flints, yet in other parts of their work they ignore their previous assertions to say, "Triangular headed windows and doorways indicate an Anglo-Saxon date. The indication becomes much more reliable if the heads are formed of pairs of large stones which pass through the full thickness of the wall." There are not many instances of this in East Anglia for here these triangular-heads are usually formed with the same flints as the walls themselves, as at Forncett St. Peter, (frontispiece), and Hales (plate 17).

We have already partly dealt with the shape of Saxon churches in chapter 7. The earliest churches would have been very narrow, their width increasing as the builders' skills improved. But up to the Conquest few if any East Anglian naves were over 20ft. wide. My list of measurements supports this. From Norman times onward few if any were built under 20ft. wide. I have based my measurements for dating purposes on the nave width rather than the chancel, as the chancels have been altered much more that the naves. They have been lengthened, shortened and rebuilt, whereas, if a nave was altered, it would almost certainly have been done by adding one or two aisles. The original nave width can still be found by measuring between the arcades which separate the nave from the aisles.

The next feature to check is the wall thickness. We are told by the Taylors that the thickness of Saxon walls is rarely 3ft. and usually much less. In East Anglia with flint walls we must expect to see some above this measurement. In fact, for church walls, 2ft. 6" is quite rare, and increases to about 3ft. while tower walls average 3ft. 9". While the wall thickness is recognised as a reliable guide in separating pre-Conquest from the much thicker Norman walls, yet from the Early English period onwards builders reverted to thinner walls.

Having checked on the wall thickness, what can we learn from the wall surface? Many writers dismiss any attempt to date a flint wall from the surface. I must admit, that in a great many cases this is reasonable, as the walls have been repaired, patched, refaced and old openings filled in. Saxon walls are the oldest parts of the churches, and so they have received many alterations to their surfaces. There are nevertheless a large number of walls, or sections of walls where the original surface shows distinctly its date of building.

The earlier Saxon walls are the easiest to recognise, for their general surface contains flints of all sizes, laid randomly in masses of mortar. There is no general knapping of the flints, but some large ones may be cut to keep the wall flat and generally the larger flints are lower down. Sometimes repairs hide the large mortar gaps by galleting.(See Chapter 12). In later Saxon walls the flints are more often selected and tend to be coursed; sometimes they are laid in decorative bands of differing flints and other materials. These are more difficult to distinguish from later refacing work.

It is well known that many Saxon walls have a plinth or thickening at their base although it is not fully understood why. It may have been to give the wall a wider base on soft ground, but as it is often difficult to distinguish between a Saxon plinth and one of later days a plinth on its own is not sufficient evidence to date a wall as Saxon. I have seen a number where the wall was definitely later. The reason why many more plinths are being discovered is because architects are now digging down to the original churchyard level in order to combat dampness.

In a large number of Saxon churches the awkward corner, where the tower joins the nave west wall, is filled with a fillet of flints or other material. They are generally a quarter-round section, tapering off at about eaves height, though a few have a decorative top to finish them off (plate.8). They all appear to be of Saxon date, although as there are so few Norman towers, we cannot be certain that there never were any later fillets.

Saxons never built deep buttresses seen in later years and very rarely in our small churches did they thicken their walls at all by adding pilasters. Pilasters in flints can be relied upon as Saxon, because the only other pilasters of this shallow type are Norman and they are always faced with dressed stone. The only unaltered pilasters on the round tower churches are at Framingham Earl; but at Hales, Heckingham and St. Etheldreda in Norwich there are pilasters that have been refashioned with dressed stone. They are very shallow buttresses standing about three inches proud of the wall and about nine inches to one foot wide.

Ledges caused by thinning of the walls is a feature that I have often noticed and recorded, and I consider to be a Saxon feature. One of the most common places where walls are thinned is the nave west wall, sometimes at eaves height, but hardly ever below. I have never seen this feature in any Norman church and therefore feel it is pre-Conquest representing the Saxon builder's confidence in the strength of his mortar. The tower walls are also often thinned in this way, sometimes outside, as at Matlaske, but more often internally at one or more levels. Sloping walls, whether internal or external I do not regard as a reliable guide as I have seen examples in later as well as Saxon walls.

Rebates at the tops of jambs of both windows and doorways are a reliable Saxon feature. They were necessary when building such an opening in flints because there were no larger blocks of stone to support the wall being built over the arch. To do this, the arch was shuttered from the imposts and the wall built over the boards. When the mortar was set, the boards were removed leaving the rebate of about two inches. In some cases these rebates have disappeared due to replastering. In a few cases we can see that tower arches faced with Norman dressed stone actually face a Saxon opening as they show a rebate at the base of the arch where the later stones have followed the shape of the original opening. Examples of this are at Gisleham and Gunton in Suffolk and Ingworth in Norfolk. There is no need for these rebates when using dressed stone and I do not know of any other examples. See fig. 11.

The quoins or corners of these walls deserve attention before we examine the windows and doorways. Let us start with the well-recognised long-and-short work. These quoins are regarded as the most reliable of Saxon features. We must note these because a few of the round tower churches have them, although flint corners are far more common in the stoneless countryside. Little Bradley, (plate 33), in the west of the region, may have had easier access to the dressed stone of the Midlands, or more probably they are Saxo-Norman, for the stones are far too small to be Saxon work. Plate 33 will explain clearly what is meant by the term long-and-short work. The odd sections of long-and-short work in other round tower churches are not dressed stone (limestone), but odd blocks of erratics (plate 34) and sometimes blocks of conglomerate from surface soil as seen at Great Ryburgh in Norfolk (plate. 37). Other Saxon quoins, probably only met with in the stoneless areas of East Anglia Sussex and Berkshire are of flints. When used for corner stones flints are selected either for largeness, when they are cut to give a sharp corner, or for flatness to give a good depth in the wall, (plates 39 and 40). Roman tiles or bricks and conglomerates are also sometimes found in these corners as well as in the walls. Some corners contain flints of the same size as the general walling, probably because no larger flints were available.

Before we leave flints, I would like to mention herringbone work. This has caused much controversy since Baldwin Brown called this feature Saxon. Herringbone work can be seen at times in much later walls than Saxon, but it was used to a great extent before the Conquest, so this style does not exclude the wall from a pre-Norman dating. It does mean that we should not use this feature for calling the wall Saxon unless there are other factors to provide more proof.

The Taylors tell us that Megalithic (very large) stones for the corners are a sign of Saxon work. They may be laid side alternate, or face alternate, but even more likely laid randomly. The stones used for such corners are either erratics or conglomerates.

After flint, conglomerate is the most common stone used as quoins in round tower churches in pre-Conquest times (plates 14, 37 and 38). In a great many cases, these have been replaced in later times by dressed stones. Although Saxon corners were usually constructed of very large stones, often quite small blocks of conglomerate were used where no large blocks were available. Even then the conglomerates were no doubt larger than the largest flints to be found. Roman tiles are sometimes used in the corners. Generally they are mixed with flints or conglomerates but occasionally they are used on their own for the whole corner or other feature (plate 35).

In East Anglia we can recognise a Saxon window mainly by its construction of flints or conglomerates as well as its distinctive shape. Also many of them are of the double-splayed type, although single-splayed windows are also seen. As with quoins these have usually been improved with dressed stone by Norman or later builders.

Circular double-splayed windows are probably the most common early type throughout Norfolk and Suffolk. So common, in fact, that most writers believe that they must therefore be Norman! They were constructed with two cones of basket-work laid end to end on the partly constructed wall, with the smaller openings together in the centre of the wall. The wall was then built round these cones, and when the mortar was set, the cones were removed. Only two inner splays of these windows remain with the basket-work pattern still visible, and they are in the tower at Hales in Norfolk (plate 26). A great many more are visible, but in every other case, the windows have been replastered and so the basket-work pattern has been lost.

Round-headed double-splayed windows are not so prolific, but many are still to be seen. The heads of these were shuttered with boards while the wall was built over them. Once again only a few retain the board marks of their construction because many have been replastered in later days, (see plate 27).

Other types of Saxon windows are the familiar single-splayed, triangular or round-headed windows. These are single openings below the belfry, and in this area are formed either in flints or conglomerates. Beeston St. Lawrence is a good example of these windows fashioned in conglomerate, and although now blocked they are plain to see. Sedgeford and Titchwell are small examples in flints of triangular-headed windows, while Clippesby has a blocked round-headed flint window in the north wall.

Double-light triangular-headed belfry windows are the most easily recognised Saxon feature in any tower, (plate 7). But while sources suggest they should have long stones for the triangular heads, and a long through-stone to support the centre and a baluster in the centre of the wall to support this, in East Anglia we generally find that though a baluster and through-stone to support the heads are there, the jambs and even the triangular-heads may be of flint rubble. While these are recognised, little if anything has been said of the other types of Saxon belfry windows.

At Cranwich, we can see a large round-headed Saxon belfry window constructed of flints, with a few pieces of dressed stone used in repairs. Generally, in the early towers, the belfry windows were narrow round headed. There might be just four, as at Rickinghall in Suffolk; only seen within the tower. But some time later these windows were increased in number to become a ring of six to ten. The best example is at Bexwell in Norfolk, where there is a ring of nine, (plate. 4). In almost all other towers, however, since most of the flint faces have been replaced with dressed stone, writers have called these towers Norman, although the flint interiors of these windows show them for what they are. Examples of these improved windows are at Blundeston, (plate 9), Holton St. Peter (plate 12), and South Elmham All Saints in Suffolk. These rings of round-headed belfry windows continued until late Saxon times, probably until the Conquest, for a late Saxon tower at Risby in Suffolk has retained its original flint facings. Here we can see the only remaining double ring of these windows, (plate 23).

Very few Saxon doorways are left in East Anglia, mainly due to their crude appearance without dressed stone. I have seen only five that are virtually unaltered in the round-tower churches. Hardwick, (plate 21), and Taverham each have a north doorway built entirely of flint rubble with the exception of two pieces of erratics as imposts. The arches are round-headed. Great Hautbois and Morton-on-the-Hill both have north doorways that are round-headed and built of local conglomerates. All these doorways are on the north side and do not form the main entrance, which is probably the reason why they have not been altered. Aylmerton tower has what was a triangular-headed example (plate 22). The jambs are selected flints, and two long slabs of erratics form the head.

There are a variety of upper doorways in towers both round-headed and triangular-headed. Many have been altered, and some have been either blocked up and forgotten or destroyed during alterations. The feature itself is not entirely pre-Conquest, for there are examples as late as the 14th. century, many of them in square towers. Examples are at Acton and Brandeston in Suffolk and Great Melton and Tilney All Saints in Norfolk.

As previously explained, I believe the introduction of seats into churches in the 15th. century meant the staircase to this upper doorway interfered with the seating layout, and from then on stair turrets were built to reach the upper floors. The same rules apply for upper doorways as for ground floor doorways; construction is of flints, and/ or conglomerates for the main building materials with sometimes a triangular head, (plates 17,18,19 and 20).

In connection with windows and door arches, it may be worth while to examine the feature of non-radial voussoirs in detail. Baldwin Brown in his *"Arts of Early England* Vol.2. *Anglo-Saxon Architecture"* says of them, "Some Norfolk churches with others in different districts, supply curious illustrations of this in the form of arches constructed generally of re-used Roman bricks put together in quite blundering fashion." He says Saxon masons appeared to have no idea of how to construct a round-headed arch, for example the first blocks above the imposts were set at the wrong angle and a similar incompetence in finishing it at the crown meant that the two sides met at the wrong angle and left a wedge-shaped space between them that had to be filled up anyhow. This construction is totally foreign to any Norman or later builder, and Baldwin Brown asks the question, "Would any Norman mason ever make such a mistake in the art in which he was so thoroughly schooled?" (See figs 12, 13 and 14.)

In fact these arches are no mistakes made by some slip-shod worker, for we can see them in a great number of our Norfolk and Suffolk churches. Baldwin Brown was able to prove this feature in Tredington church, Worcestershire, and gave it the name "Tredington fashion." The Taylors include this feature as Saxon and record the credit for it to Baldwin Brown. Examples of it in round tower churches are at Bexwell, Burnham Norton, Clippesby, Hales, Haveringland and Merton in Norfolk, and Mettingham, Mutford, Rickinghall Inferior and Risby in Suffolk. The details of these features will be found in the "Church Notes".

Chapter 11

SAXO-NORMAN OVERLAP

It is universally recognised that the Early English pointed arch was replacing the rounded Norman arch from about 1175. A small overlap obviously occurred. Many of these features can also be corroborated by wills and other documents. Prior to the Conquest, very few records were kept, and even in those cases the very general account available may not be enough to convince us that the church seen today is the one in the records. We have therefore, to seek to date early churches by their features alone, but this should not deter us from trying to put a date to their age, even if it can be only approximate.

In chapter 2. I recorded the statement by Sir Alfred Clapham, that the Normans arrived with a very strong system of government that deposed the Saxon thegns and clerics within a very short period. The whole structure of government, both secular and ecclesiastical, was changed in a manner never known before or since. How in these conditions could Saxon architecture be expected to survive?

Some writers have suggested that the overlap or Saxo-Norman period lasted a long time. But I believe it was very short indeed, if it ever in fact existed in church architecture. Before any churches could be built with the dressed stone that the Normans were used to seeing in their churches, supplies would have to be brought either from the Midlands or from Normandy. The amount of Caen stone in East Anglia seems to show that it was easier to ship it from Normandy than to bring it overland from the Midlands. However, only after the military needs of the conquerors had been satisfied would there have been the ships available to bring over this stone. Thus it was not until 1096 that Caen stone began to be imported for building Norwich Cathedral. Then the quarries and the shippers would quickly have recognised a ready market for their stone to update the many village churches with the wonderful Norman carved doorways which could easily be inserted. In a number of cases this can be proved to have happened. Windows and doorways have been changed in these churches many times over the centuries.

All writers refer to the period of the overlap as though church building carried on without a break after 1066 and even increased. I believe that after the Conquest, which only just began at Hastings in 1066 and took years to complete, all available builders would have been conscripted to construct encampments. Wood would have been used because speed was essential and even masons and 'wallers', the early name for bricklayers, would have been enlisted for they could erect the posts ready for the carpenters. I feel certain that no churches were built in the years immediately after the Conquest, because all available builders were required for military work.

While the Norman masons were busy building both Norwich Cathedral and castle in the first half of the twelfth century there may well have been the first regular shipments of stone from Caen. This not only implies that dressed stone was not widely available, but that a great number of builders would be required on this and other castles urgently needed by the Norman overlords. It seems unlikely that there would be either material or labour free to build village churches until these major buildings were well in hand.

By this time many of the established Saxon builders would have died and any youngsters would have been trained according to Norman practices. Before 1066 no East Anglian builder could be termed a mason, and so the artisans would have had to be trained in the skill of working in stone. It is inconceivable that the old Saxon features would have continued to be constructed of flints since Saxon builders preferred much larger stones for the important structural parts of a building than did the Normans. We should remember that the Saxon period lasted for 450 years, during which time undoubtedly many churches were built of stone. How can we account for the number of complete churches once thought to have been built in the 85 years from 1090 to 1175? Does the large number of Norman doorways in Norfolk and Suffolk really mean that all these churches were completely rebuilt by the Normans?

Surely the explanation of this apparent massive church building programme, that so puzzled Munro Cautley, must be that in reality there was simply a massive insertion of Norman doorways, windows and quoins into Saxon churches, and that chiefly in the twelfth century. Remember, we are assured that none of the more elaborately carved doorways was built before 1140, far too close to the Early English period to enable all these churches to have been rebuilt. The only alternative is that most were insertions. Moreover, these fine carved doorways could not have been inserted into wooden church buildings but must have been inserted into stone churches already there. This presupposes that the parish churches of Saxon East Anglia already existed as flint buildings, and I conclude that many of their walls still remain, their antiquity unrecognised because of the insertion of later windows and doorways.

Chapter 12

SOME INTERESTING FEATURES

Many interesting features are missed in a hurried visit to a church. In this chapter I want to describe features I have noticed and that are not often mentioned in church guides and some that I believe have not been recorded before. Some of these I feel certain I understand, and know what they are and why they were made, but of others I am less certain.

WALL TIES I noticed these first in Fritton St. Edmund, Suffolk, where the masonry ties consist of blocks of dressed stone about 14 inches by 4 inches. For some time I could discover no obvious reason for these blocks of stone, but after seeing many in other churches I realised they were an early form of wall tie, used to repair cracks in round towers long before the later builders' steel rods. Later, in the tower of Matlaske church, I saw another form of these ties, made of many flat red-brown tiles but about the same dimensions as the blocks of stone. It was the position of these masonry blocks that first gave the clue as to their use. They were placed one above the other over the tower west window or the tower arch, two of the weakest points of a round tower where most cracks develop. Internally, we sometimes see a complete ring of these blocks round the tower in order to hold the whole structure where there has been considerable weakness.

TOWER ARCH NOTCHES I had already completed a considerable amount of my round tower study when I became aware of the notches on many of the tower arches. At first I thought they might have been scribed by the builders who plastered the arch either to signify what was beneath the plaster or to give early warning of a crack developing. Both these ideas were very tentative and I continued to record these notches. At least two arches had notches cut in their dressed stone facings and so these tended to disprove the idea that they signified flints beneath the plaster. It was while pointing them out to a group I was showing round a church that one of the party suggested that the notches might have been caused by the rub of a bell rope over the centuries. This theory seemed much better than my idea and could well account for the number of notches seen from one or two to over a dozen. The Sanctus bell may well have been rung from beneath the tower arch and not from the upper doorway as is often suggested. I have since been told that at Mendlesham in Suffolk the old practice is still kept whereby the bellringer continues to toll the bell while looking through the nave doorway to check that all the congregation has entered the church. So the bell rope rubs the head of the tower arch and would of course in time and over many years make the grooves I had noticed.

CONICAL TOPS. The conical top in red-brown tiles on some of the round towers is very attractive but otherwise has provoked little interest. It is only when one climbs these towers to measure them that one becomes aware of the large number of conical tops hidden behind later parapets. Add to this the number of Victorian prints showing conical roofs that have now been replaced by flat roofs and it becomes clear that this was their original shape. As there was no slate or stone in the area the early roofs must have been of thatch or clay tiles. The stump of Ingworth tower has had a cone of thatch to roof it for some years, and I feel certain that this was the original roofing of these towers.

BATTLEMENTS These are often mentioned or shown in pictures of round towers when early writers call them defensive towers. They are always, however, much later than the towers themselves and are purely decorative in their use although copied from the defensive battlements of castle keeps. The earliest battlements on round towers are of the 13th. century, but it was in the 15th. century that most of the towers received their crenellated parapet. Many of these have fine flushwork decorations.

PUT-LOG HOLES Many towers and church walls have this feature and they are by no means restricted to either the round tower churches or the Saxon period. They are the square holes, left in the walls, which held the ends of the horizontal scaffold poles. They may be framed with either bricks, tiles or thin pieces of wood. Named after the horizontal scaffold poles, they were useful in flint walling because they could either be left open or filled in with a weak mortar when the scaffolding was removed and easily opened up again when repairs were needed. Internally, they were mostly left open. This further points to a roof of thatch as this material needed more frequent attention than the walls.

STEPS IN TOWER WALLS Nothing is said about these by the early writers who rarely studied the towers closely. The steps, usually about four inches in depth, were used to thin the walls as the height increased, and I have formed the opinion that this method of tower building was Saxon. The Norman method seems to have been to taper the walls either within or without or both. Advantage of the step is often taken to lay the joists of a floor, and whenever this is done the step is concealed. Steps are usually on the insides of the towers, but not always, for at Matlaske the step is outside at a height of about 15ft. and is about four to six inches deep.

STEPS OR REBATE IN NAVE WEST WALL This, I feel certain, is a Saxon feature to thin the wall where less strength is required as in tower walls. I have noticed this feature only where I have been able on other evidence to date this part of the church Saxon. The rebate is usually four to eight inches deep and above the tower arch at about 12ft. to 15ft .from the ground. In a few cases it can be seen in other walls.

SLOPING NAVE WALLS Here we have a feature that causes me some uncertainty for while there are some that I can confidently call Saxon, there is the case of Hemblington where the north wall is vertical while the south wall that slopes has apparently been rebuilt further south to widen the church. This is indicated by the way the tower is offset; and as the north wall is vertical, we cannot say the rebuilt wall was built to match up with the other.

TOWER PROJECTING INTO CHURCH There are only two such round tower churches and both are Saxon. But why the tower projects into the nave in this way is something that I cannot at present understand. They are at Fritton St. Edmund and Holton St. Peter, they are only about 20 miles apart and both in Suffolk. They each project about 18 inches into the nave, but beyond that they have very little in common.

TOWER STAIRCASES Bardfield Saling, Spexhall and Higham must surely be the only round towers with staircases built with the towers. These were three of the latest round towers to be built. However many others have had staircases built on at a later date. All of these seem to be of the 15th. century, but some of the most interesting are staircases built within the tower wall itself. While the majority conform to the general pattern of a stairway spiralling in a clockwise direction from the days of defence building, in just one case, Yaxham, the stairs go anti-clockwise. There are a few staircases within the tower itself, and while some may be of wood or cast iron the staircase at Forncett St. Peter is well worth a close study. It is of triangular blocks of oak laid to form a circular staircase round half of the interior of the tower to reach the first floor.

GALLETING. This is the insertion of small pieces of flint into the surface of a flint wall. It is generally done when the wall is being repaired or repointed. It is therefore not a Saxon or even an early feature. Galleting may well be used to cover the large mortar gaps in a Saxon wall, as this method of surfacing a flint wall has often been adopted with the idea of presenting a solid flint shield to the weather.

Chapter 13

DATING FLINT CHURCHES

Writers have so far tended to rely on windows and doorways in order to date East Anglian round towers and their churches. While dating the window gives the latest date at which the wall could have been built, it should be understood that the wall containing the window or doorway could easily be much older. This can be readily understood when we consider how many old houses now have modern picture windows. We all know of the many churches that were restored in Victorian times with new windows and doorways, though the fabric remains basically Medieval. While we must always remember that sometimes a doorway or window might have been reset in a later wall, this can nevertheless generally be detected fairly easily.

After an extensive study of the round-tower churches, I feel confident that a great number of Saxon churches were built either with flint or conglomerate quoins but have had their quoins replaced with dressed stones after the Conquest without the walls being demolished. Otherwise their basic shape would have been altered to a wider church as was favoured in later years. However, the builders obviously saw no sense in levelling and rebuilding a narrow church for the wall thickness still conforms to Saxon and not Norman dimensions.

Looking at this from another angle, it is recognised that the Saxons used a much better mortar than the Normans. Therefore, barring fire or storm, there would have been no need to demolish and rebuild a Saxon church unless the Normans required a more prestigious church. Churches most likely to be rebuilt would be those of fast growing and richer communities who wanted a larger church. The smaller villages and hamlets were more likely to retain churches with far less alterations and rebuilding of the walls. By this I mean the main walls and not the facings of quoins or buttresses.

Most writers state that flint churches cannot be dated, but then they proceed to date them by their windows and doorways. Indeed, it is quite common for these churches to be called Decorated or Perpendicular with a Norman doorway. As we have already stated, in some cases a doorway has been re-set in a later wall, and ruined walls have been rebuilt with later windows, but the large number of churches called Medieval with Norman doorways cannot all have re-set doorways. It seems obvious that because it has been said so often that flint walls are not dateable, no one has attempted to date them. Let us look at this aspect of dating a church or tower. Churches were built to last, and they were not often demolished and rebuilt as some writers allege, unless they were to be enlarged. Even the enlargement was often done by adding one or two aisles or extending the chancel. I believe that total destruction in order to rebuild was usually confined to the 15th. century during the prosperous times in the wool trade, or when a village developed into a town and the church became too small for the population. But even then it is more probable that great enlargements, or churches on new sites were far more usual than demolition and rebuilding of a similar size on the same site. Witness the 15th century church of St. Mary in Bungay, quite close to the Saxon round tower church of Holy Trinity. A great deal has been written about the vast amount of church building by the Normans but the truth now appears to be that there was a massive amount of alteration to the many existing Saxon churches.

Saxon windows were also replaced with the dressed stone which was flooding into the area after the Conquest and in many cases replacing the flints and conglomerates of the corners with the smarter looking dressed stone. The vast amount of Caen stone used in East Anglia demonstrates that transport of this heavy material was far easier by sea and it was still very difficult to bring it from the Midlands. Whatever may have happened in other parts of the country, East Anglia, from its unusual position of having no building stone except flints and conglomerates, must be looked at entirely differently. First of all, this was a prosperous and relatively well populated part of the country. Also Christianity was established and being organised in the seventh century. Parishes and Hundreds had been formed, and this would not have been easy without a significant distribution of church buildings.

In chapter 5. I discussed the development of these churches from timber to stone, and so we can commence our efforts at dating from the churches now standing or in ruins. All attempts at dating should start from the later and work back to the earlier periods. Squared knapped flints are 15th. century or later. These are mainly seen in the flushwork of battlements of this period and sometimes in porches added about this time, but also in rebuilt or restored chancels. They may often be of Victorian date.

Cut flints that have not been squared can be of any date from the 13th. century onwards. With regard to whole flints, these can be of all periods, but there are often indications that can give a positive dating to a particular period. My studies so far have concentrated on the earlier periods (Saxon and Norman), but there must be signs also of the later periods and useful work waits to be done by those who visit these churches and who are prepared to study and record their findings. The main types of walls are of flints of selected sizes placed neatly in rows (i.e. coursed), and flints of all sizes placed without regard to coursing and with large mortar gaps and also very small flints or rubble with large amounts of mortar. Mixtures of flints, sometimes with Roman bricks and conglomerates, are also to be found. Some walls are built almost entirely of conglomerate or carstone. We have to remember that all these churches and towers have been repaired and altered to some degree, and have had windows and doors blocked up and others inserted, but the surprising thing is that after about a thousand years the main surface of so many of these walls has remained unaltered. Large flints have been cut to give a sharp corner where they have been used for quoins. In round towers or their churches, I have rarely found carstone or conglomerate used in a wall later that the Saxon period. However, where aisles have been added, the materials including these two stones have often been re-used from the old nave walls for rebuilding the new aisle wall.

In order to discover the age of these churches we must refer to features that we can be sure of. We shall then have some relevant facts for comparing one period with another. In two towers that we can date accurately as early Norman (Haddiscoe and the top of Herringfleet tower), we find that in both cases selected flints, neatly coursed were used, and some larger flints, again selected for size and shape, used as bands of decoration at Herringfleet. In every case of early Saxon workmanship no such selection has been made. However we can see the first examples of this technique in a few later Saxon towers such as Forncett St. Peter and Bungay both about 1,000. In all early Saxon churches or towers, 800 to 1,000 flints of all sizes have been used with large mortar joints and often very large flints are used at the base. Large blocks of erratics are often seen as well in these walls though they are often mistaken for dressed stone. Odd shaped flints may have a cut surface, but these are cut only in order to give a more even surface and they are not a methodic knapping of flints.

This is the clear pattern that is seen from my study and covers the Saxon period from 800 to 1,000. The height of the round towers in these early years was never over 35ft. Approaching the year 1,000 the general aspect improves nearing the quality of workmanship seen in the tower of Forncett St. Peter (frontispiece) where the tower height also increased up to 60ft.

But is it possible to date these churches any more closely? I believe it is. In chapter 8, there is a list of churches that were built before their towers, and a further list of possible such churches. Although we may not have conclusive evidence to say with certainty that such and such a towerless church was built between 800 and 900, when we know it is early Saxon, we can be fairly certain that this dating is reasonably accurate.

As I pointed out in chapter 7. my tables of nave widths can place naves that are narrower than 20ft. (without aisles) as prior to 1,000 and if wider probably later. We can confidently call any quoin, window or doorway built without dressed stone as Saxon and pre-Conquest. The criteria are different in other parts of the country because of the nature of the building materials available. Of course we must look for the Saxon features (detailed in chapter 10) and if we see them in flints we can be certain they are pre-Conquest. The main point I wish to emphasise is that the Saxon period of church building lasted for 450 years while the Norman period was at most 100 years, but more likely only 75 years due to the unsettled conditions in the 11th. century. Far from Norman doorways being signs of complete Norman churches they serve only to prove the churches are not later than Norman, but may be insertions.

In the early Norman period, the walls alter little from the late Saxon except for being thicker. From then, however, dressed stone is used in all windows and doorways both inside and outside, which none of the previous periods possessed. String courses also begin to appear.

Briefly we can date towerless churches with a narrow nave and thin walls as early Saxon or 800 to 900. Short towers, whether added to a towerless church or built with the church as middle Saxon or 900 to 1,000. Tall well-built towers belong to the late Saxon period, 1,000 to the Conquest.

Although most of these towers are Saxon, some were built later. These were generally of the taller style, and the walls were much thicker than those of pre-Conquest date. One final point to establish a Norman date is that the windows would be finished off inside as well as outside with dressed stone.

Chapter 14

NEED FOR PRESERVATION AND FURTHER RESEARCH

From this survey it will be seen that about 85% of East Anglia's round tower churches are pre-Conquest. Others may be too and proof may be found at some later date if repairs are done carefully and searches conducted when repairs are made. Unfortunately, some of these villages where round towers are sited have not the resources to put repairs in the hands of experts and have to rely on a local cost-conscious builder. This is not always the best way to discover hidden features. Even more important, features already on view may be lost because funds to restore them cannot be found and those responsible may not be fully sensitive to the historical significance.

I believe round tower churches are the earliest that can be studied as a group. They are also conveniently close to one another for detailed study by the same team. What better opportunity could there be for a study in depth to reveal their history and their secrets? The history of the buildings, parish records, wills and court rolls may well shed more light on them. Furnishings are still only partly known and written up. Much can be done both by studying these churches and by searching parish records and record offices.

Regarding the maintenance of these churches, it is a great pity that such a wealth of heritage lacks the necessary finance to make it safe for posterity. Because they are small village churches vast sums are not required; and because their materials are mainly flints, stone masons would be required only for work on doorways, windows and quoins. The small communities, however, cannot always raise the money needed to maintain these buildings, and although grants help to keep them open, neglect and postponement of repairs leads to the loss of entire towers as at Cockley Cley and others. Within the past forty years three of these towers have fallen. Morton-on-the-Hill in 1959, Onehouse, a gradual collapse between 1986 and 1990, and Cockley Cley in a sudden collapse in 1991. Careful restoration could not only save these churches and their heritage for the nation, but it could reduce the cost of their maintenance.

These churches should be repaired as they are, and not made into elaborate show pieces or their beauty and significance would be destroyed. Vast sums are not needed, indeed it could spoil them, but enough should be found to preserve them whether they are used for worship or for aesthetic appreciation or historical interest. The kind of sum required is spent quite casually on ruined castles or town walls that serve no purpose to the community other than as a token of past history. I would not like to see these towers, marks of faith as well as history vanish. Surely these buildings, most of which are still serving the community, should be preserved when it would cost so little. To those who say the villages who want them should repair them, let me reply that they should study some of the church visitors' books and they would see that people come from far away to visit these churches.

Repairs and heating are both more costly than in a modern building, but what a loss it would be to us all if they disappeared. To those who would argue that we could lose a few without their being missed, may I point out that each one has something special to offer. Once there must have been nearly 1,000 of these churches in East Anglia. Now that their number has been reduced to 175, can we afford to lose even one?

If I were to permit myself a look into the future it would be to predict that in due course, perhaps by the turn of the century, the Round Towers of East Anglia will become a major attraction for scholars and tourists alike. A nucleus of such interest is already in being in the form of the Round Tower Churches Society, based in Norfolk.

1. East Lexham, Tower south, Norfolk

2. Howe, Tower with Saxon windows, Norfolk

3. Gayton Thorpe, Tower west view, Norfolk

4. Bexwell, With upper doorway, Norfolk

5. Beachamwell, Tower with Saxon windows, Norfolk

6. Burnham Deepdale, West view, Norfolk

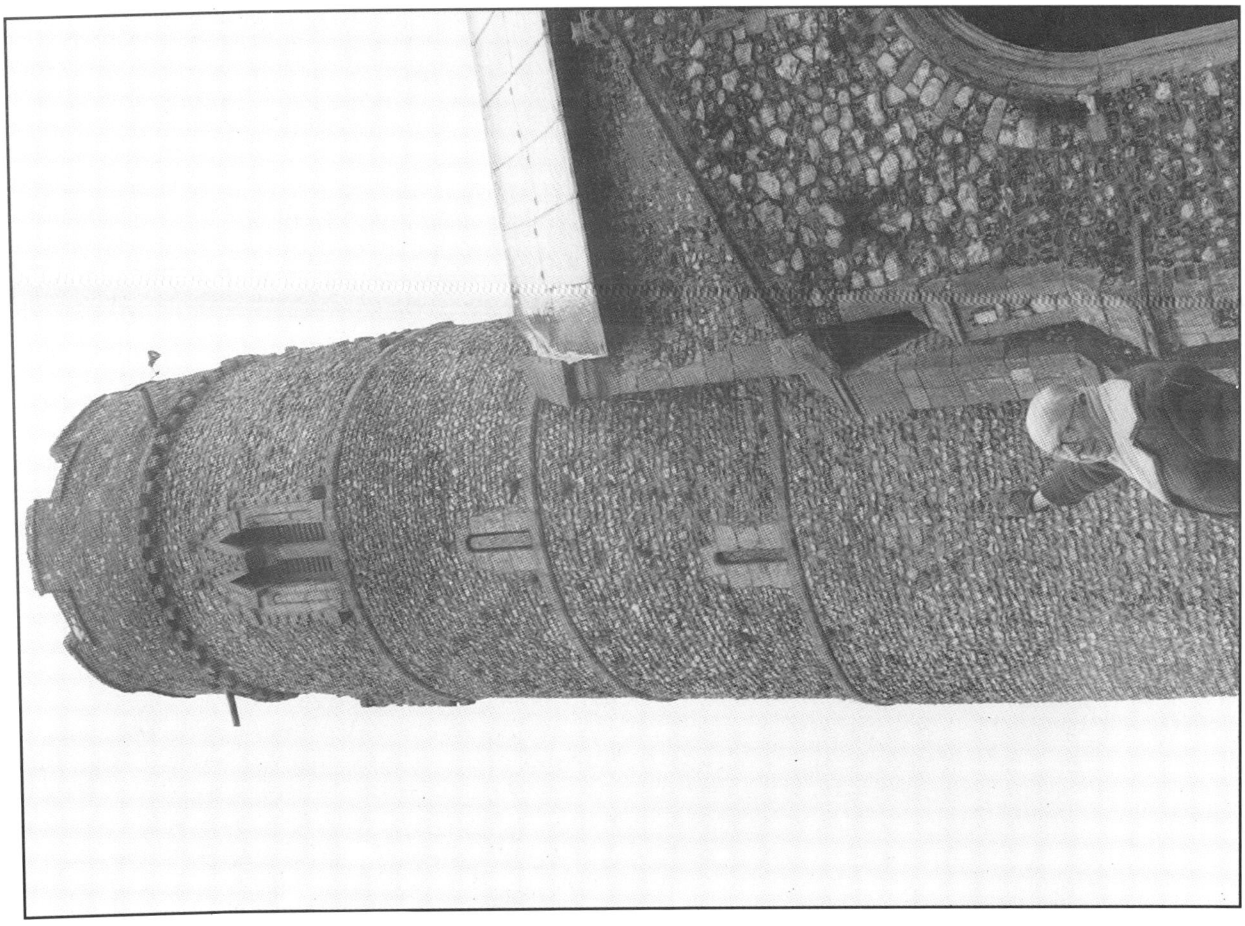

7. Haddiscoe, Tower south view, Norfolk

8. Thorpe-next-Haddiscoe, Tower south view, Norfolk

9. Blundeston, Tower west view, Suffolk

10. Ramsholt, Church south west, Suffolk

11. Ashby, Tower south view, Suffolk

12. Holton St. Peter, Church south east, Suffolk

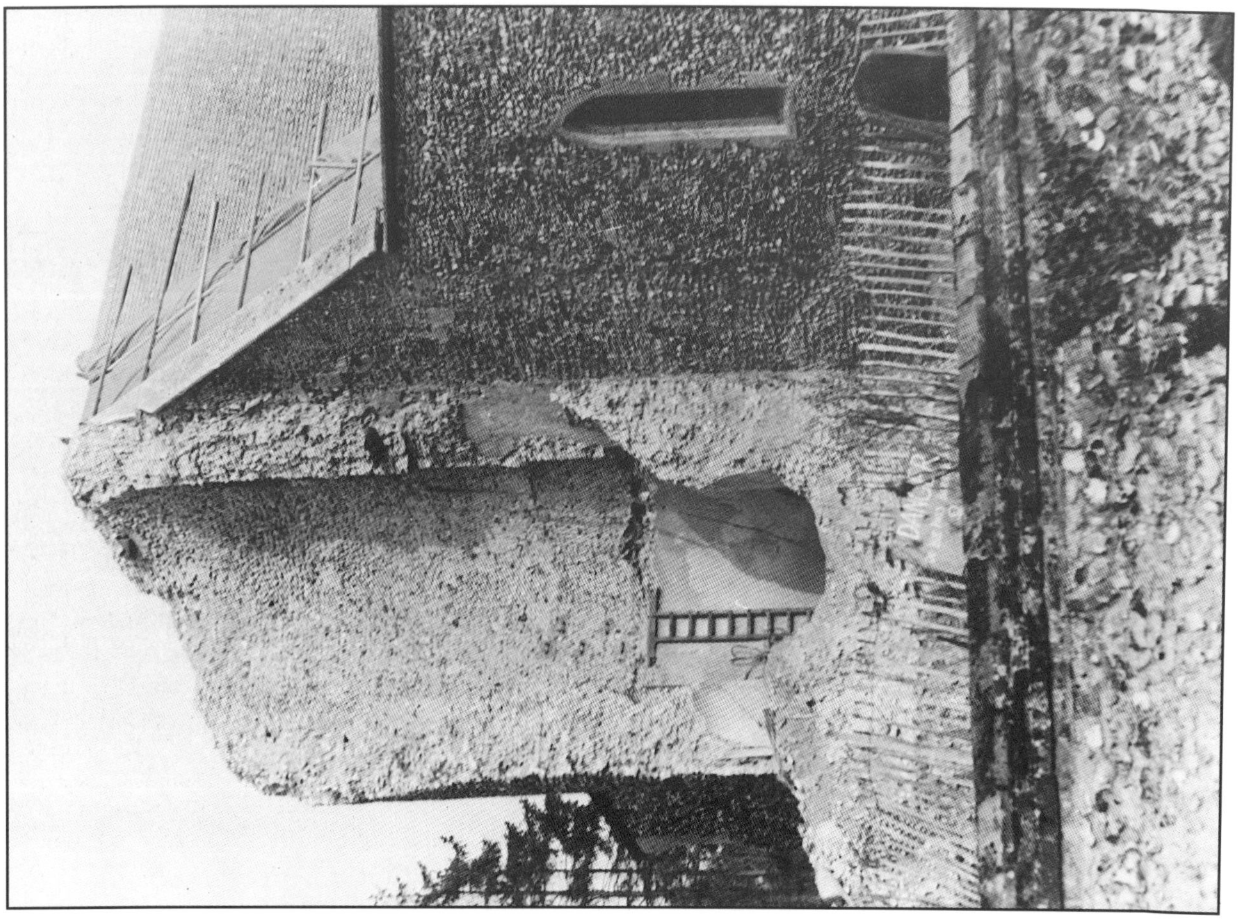

13. Cockley Cley, Ruins of tower, Norfolk

14. Bessingham, Base of tower differing materials, Norfolk

15. Gayton Thorpe, Base of tower, Norfolk

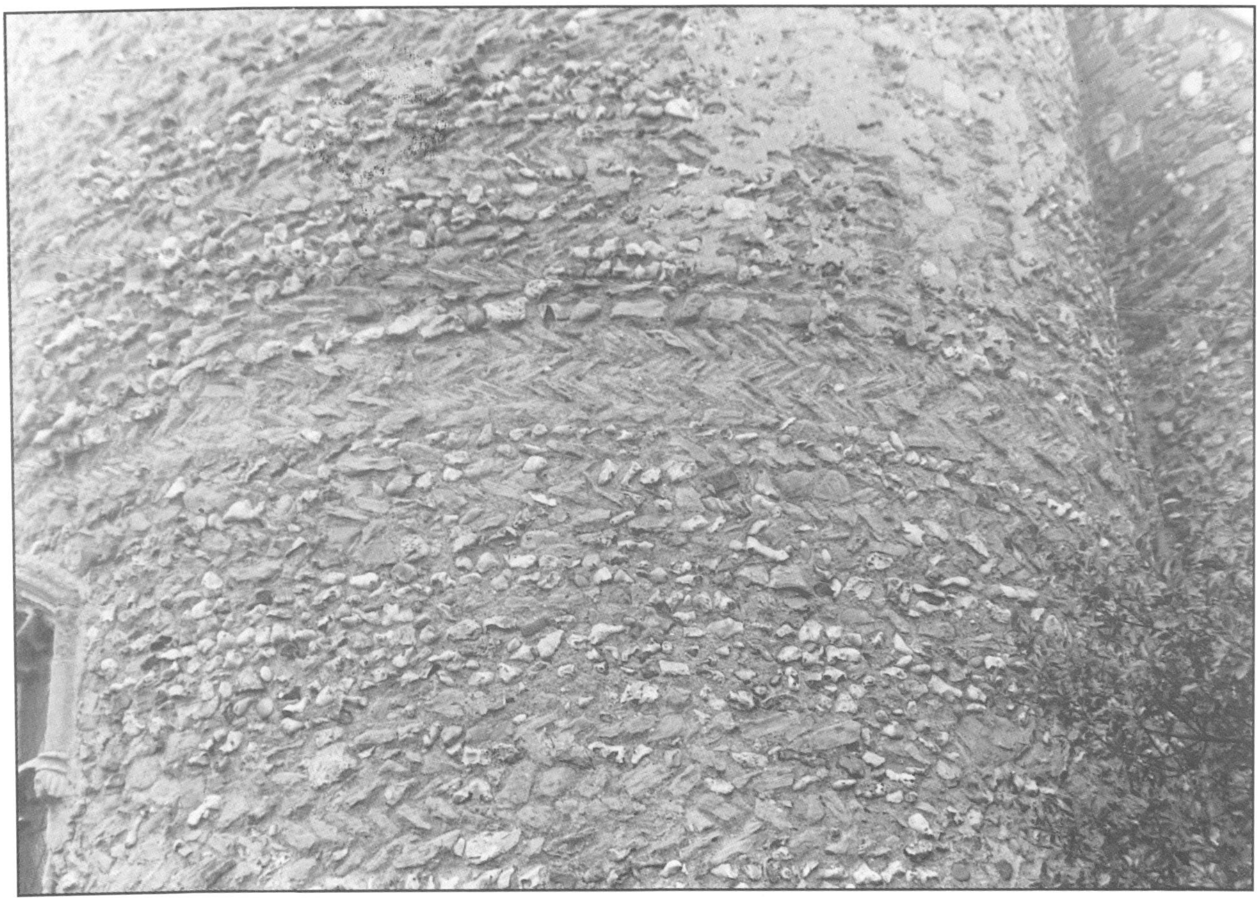

16. Bungay, Herringbone work, Suffolk

17. Hales, Upper doorway of flints, Norfolk

18. Mutford, Upper doorway; rebates, Suffolk

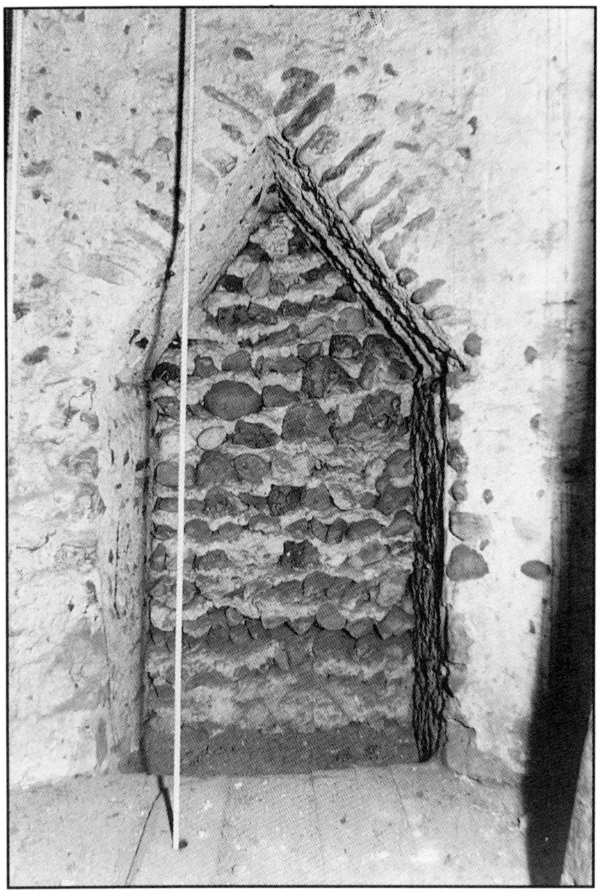

19. Gisleham, Upper doorway flints, Suffolk

20. Gayton Thorpe, Upper doorway, Norfolk

21. Hardwick, Saxon north doorway flints, Norfolk

22. Aylmerton, Saxon tower doorway, Norfolk

23. Risby, Saxon belfry windows, Suffolk

24. Haddiscoe, Saxo-Norman belfry, Norfolk

25. East Lexham, Saxon belfry window, Norfolk

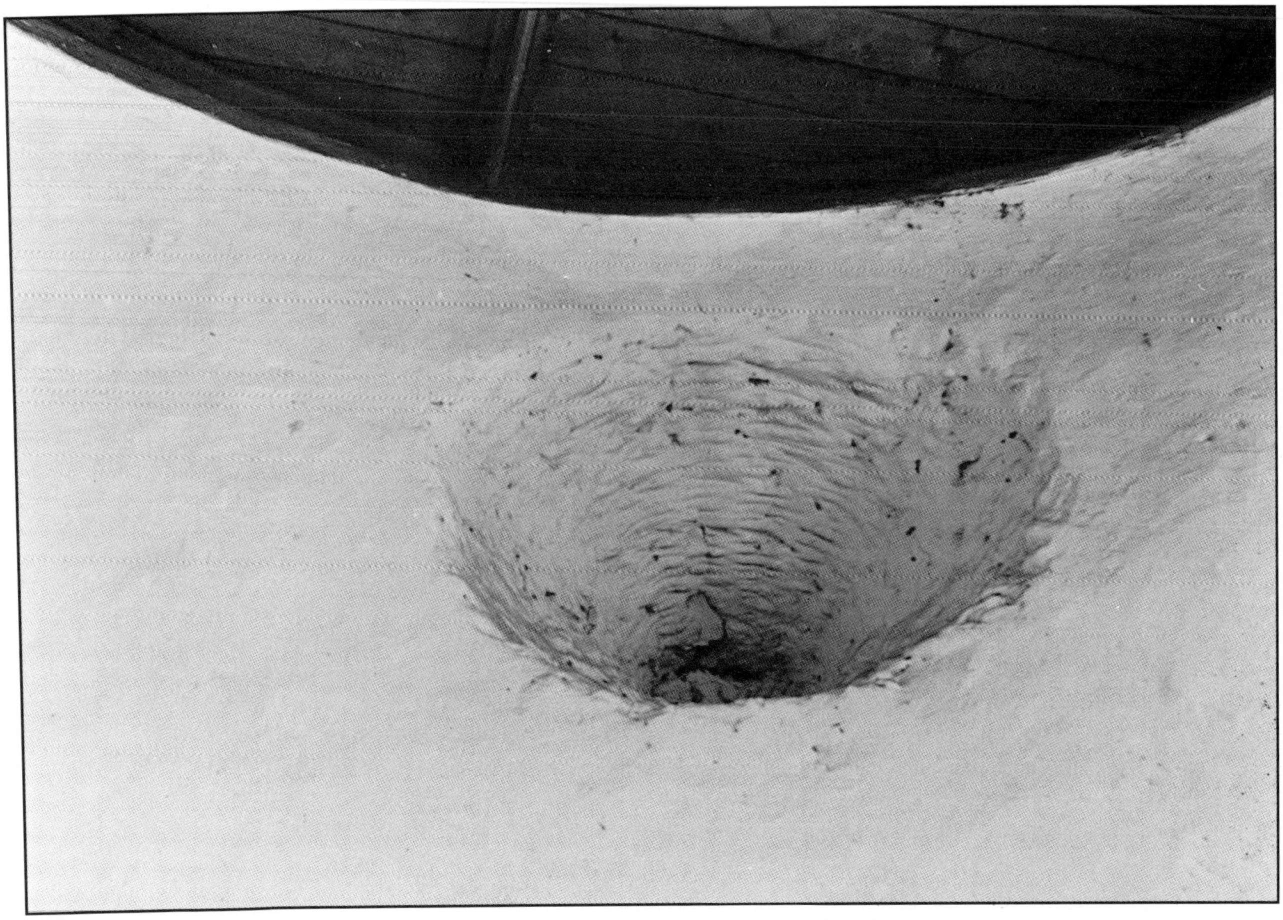

26. Hales, Saxon circular window, Norfolk

27. Shereford, Double-splayed window, Norfolk

28. Hasketon, Saxon window preserved, Suffolk

29. Haddiscoe, T/Arch and upper doorway, Norfolk

30. Little Saxham, T/Arch and upper doorway, Suffolk

31. Bedingham, Saxon tower arch, Norfolk

32. Horsey, Tower arch, Norfolk

33. Little Bradley, Saxo-Norman L&S work, Suffolk

34. Syleham, Saxon L&S work, Suffolk

35. Broomfield, S/W corner Roman tiles, Essex

36. Ingworth, Altered north east corner, Norfolk

37. Grt. Ryburgh, Conglomerate L&S work, Norfolk

38. Morton-on-the-Hill, Conglomerate corner, Norfolk

39. Swainsthorpe, Flint S/W corner, Norfolk

40. Pentlow, Flint S/W corner, Essex

CHURCH NOTES - NORFOLK

N1. ACLE. St. Edmund, King & Martyr

K6 Sheet 134. Map Ref. T.G. 401 103
Tower Middle SAXON

Tower Height	54ft.
Height of Circular part.	38ft.
Internal Diameter Grd:	10ft 6"
Tower Wall Thickness	3ft. 5"
Nave Ridge Height	43ft. 6"
Bells 6	
Chancel Width	18ft. 5"
Nave Width	28ft. 1"
Chancel Length	40ft. 11"
Nave Length	69ft. 3"
Nave Wall Thickness N. & S.	3ft. 3"

St. Edmund's Church stands in the centre of the village on an elevated site. It has a round west tower with octagonal belfry, nave, chancel, north and south porches.

The earliest part of this church would seem to be the circular section of the tower, which is constructed of uncoursed whole flints of varying hues. At present the height of this section is 38ft. although one cannot be certain about this, because of subsequent alterations when the octagonal belfry was added.

There are but two openings in the circular portion; a large three-light traceried west window, which is obviously a Victorian insertion, as Ladbrooke, 1824, shows a much smaller square-headed one; and a tiny rectangular opening somewhat higher, which is not shown by Ladbrooke, and this, too, is probably an insertion. In the southern re-entrant angle is a stair turret, which is probably contemporary with the south porch, but in the northern re-entrant angle no quarter-round pilaster is visible, so it would not seem that the alteration on the south has destroyed this feature.

The octagonal belfry, springing from a string course crowning the circular section, is 13th century, as witness the plain lancet windows not only on the cardinal sides, but also in the diagonals, a novel conceit. The battlements, however, were not added until 1472, at a cost of £16, according to Blomefield, who adds that they were made by the "Church reves". He does not state whether this included the figures at the angles, which form pinnacles. A central shield decorates each side of the battlement.

The south porch, with its upper room and stair turret, is probably contemporary with the battlement, but has been altered, for Ladbrooke shows the west window with a pointed head, and a large sundial over the south doorway. The window to the west of the porch, in the nave, has been partially renewed, for in 1824 the bottom section was blocked up. The remaining windows on the south of the nave, which are early 14th century, and the rood stair turret at the east end of the nave appear to be unaltered.

All the windows of the chancel are in the Decorated style, probably early 14th century, except the east window, which dates from the restoration of 1860. It does not represent what was there before, according to a pencil sketch of the church c. 1820. This shows a three-light pointed window with mullions running up to the arch. From this sketch, also, it is apparent that the north nave windows, likewise early 14th. century, are largely unaltered in appearance even though they have suffered restoration. The fine 15th century north porch, with upper room, stair turret, flushwork panelling and a pointed niche flanked by two small windows of similar design, appears to be largely unchanged. The material here are cut black flints and dressed stone.

Turning to the interior, a little more evidence of an early date comes to light. There is an upper doorway or opening at first floor level in the tower, with jambs of selected flints, but the lintel and step appear to be modern. The wall of the tower at 3ft. 5" as noted above, appears to be a little under the average, which points to a Saxon date. Of Norman work, only some carved remains of a doorway, found in 1927 when the rood stairs were re-opened, now appear, so thorough were the subsequent alterations of the 14th century and later.

Looking at the material before us, the Saxon evidence is entirely in the tower, consisting of the relative shortness of the tower, the below average thickness of the wall and the jambs of the upper doorway. It is interesting to note that Munro Cautley says the tower is "probably pre-Conquest", though he gives no reasons for this statement. The tower and parts of the nave west wall are therefore the only parts that can claim a pre-Conquest date.

N2. ASHMANHAUGH. St. Swithin.

J5 Sheet. 134. Map Ref. T.G. 314 212
Tower 1849 Church Middle SAXON

Tower Height approx.	32ft.	Nave & Chancel Width	14ft. 9"
Internal Diameter Grd.	6ft.	Chancel Length	20ft. 4"
Tower Wall Thickness.	2ft. 7"	Nave Length	37ft. 6"
Bells 1		Wall Thickness. N & S. Nave	2ft. 6"

Two miles north of Wroxham and the Broads, this church stands in quite flat countryside and serves only a small scattered village. It has a round west tower, nave and chancel in one, and south porch.

The one bell is inscribed *"Wm. Dobson Founder, 1828"*. The round tower we are told fell into ruins and was rebuilt in 1849.

The present tower is entirely of knapped flints, and tapers slowly all the way to the top, which is finished with battlements. There are no fillets to north or south, and the belfry windows are single-light lancets, as is the ground floor west window, the only other window in the tower. The west nave wall is also in these knapped flints, a sign that this wall also was restored with the tower. It is said that this tower replaced a Saxon tower, which may well be correct, for as we shall see, the church appears to be of this period.

As the tower is firmly of the date given, and has no important features other than having the smallest diameter of them all, we will now examine the church. This is a plain rectangle only 14ft. 9" wide internally, with walls only 2ft. 6" thick, and with ample evidence of Saxon workmanship in the materials used and in the walling. There is no sign of the early quoins that have been replaced by dressed stone. The south nave wall is the only one free of conglomerate although there are major signs of repairing. But the south and east chancel walls contain much of this material, while the north chancel wall also has several blocks and there is a curious blocked arch of early brick. In the north nave wall, much conglomerate again, and there is much mortar between the whole and cut flints in all the walls. The band of conglomerate in the north wall, and the two blocks below at the western end, correspond to the cut-away section within the church. This is often referred to as the height and length of the original church, but I feel the evidence is very inconclusive. I have never seen a Saxon church so low or as short, and the wall further west does not change in character, so it all appears as one.

Going into the church we see the section referred to where the plaster of the north wall has been removed to show a long band of conglomerate and large flints, obviously of early date. There are no Saxon features such as are required by the early writers, but the shape, wall thickness, and materials used, must surely outweigh the lack of these signs. Without the original tower, dating is difficult, but I feel sure it was pre-1,000 probably nearer 900. Two 13th. century Early English and three 14th. century Decorated windows still survive with some restoration, but there is nothing from the Norman period.

N3. ASLACTON. St. Michael.

H8 Sheet 144. Map Ref. T.M. 156 911.
Tower Nave and Chancel Late SAXON.

Tower Height	53ft.
Internal Diameter Grd:	11ft. 4"
Tower Wall Thickness.	3ft. 9"
Nave Ridge Height.	32ft.
Bells. 5	
Chancel Width.	11ft. 6"
Nave Width.	14ft. 5"
Nave & Aisle Width.	27ft 3"
Chancel Length.	18ft. 10"
Nave Length.	27ft. 7"
Nave North Wall Thickness	3ft.

St. Michael's stands on a small mound with a cluster of houses nearby. It is situated where the concentration of these churches is greatest, and about 12 miles from Norwich. It has a round west tower, nave, chancel, south aisle and south porch.

Most writers acknowledge this tower as pre-Conquest solely on account of its typical belfry windows; but are these the only surviving Saxon features? The tower, which is 53ft. tall and finished with battlements of the 15th. century must have been over 40ft tall originally, and therefore late Saxon (1,000 to the Conquest). The construction, although not coursed flints or selected for size, nevertheless has the appearance of skilled work, and is a good shape, although slightly oval, so it may be early in this period. The double triangular-headed belfry windows, have flint rubble jambs and heads, and are supported in the centre by a long through stone on a rough baluster. Below these, are only two later windows. There are no fillets between church and tower.

Inside, the tower arch is tall, but it has been opened out and dressed stone facings have been added at the springing, the jambs may however remain original under the plaster. On the first floor, at a height of 18ft. is an upper doorway. It is 5ft. 8" tall by 2ft. 2" wide, and rectangular in shape, with flint jambs and a wooden lintel that is undoubtedly later. The internal east wall of the tower is curved, telling us that the tower was built with the church. In 1985, while workmen were checking cracks in the west wall of the tower, a ground floor doorway was found with a flint frame, showing that it was of Saxon origin.

Is this the church that was built with the tower? There is no impression of a Saxon church as we stand in the nave, for it looks almost as wide as it is long. But when we start to measure it we find that the wide aisle gives us this impression. Note that the chancel and the nave widths are under 15ft., quite narrow even for Saxon work, while the north wall thickness at 3ft. is also of Saxon proportions. Pevsner, we note, records traces of Saxon long-and-short work at the N/E corner, but I would disregard this feature for the following reason. The four corners, and also the N/W buttress, that must at the earliest be 14th century, but more likely 15th., also have their stones laid in the same style. The stone itself looks the same. This is not to say that I think the walls have been rebuilt, but I feel certain that all the corners have been renewed.

The five bells were overhauled and rehung during 1977/78. All the work locally being done by voluntary labour.

N.4. AYLMERTON. St. John the Baptist.

H2 Sheet. 133. Map Ref. T.G. 182 401.
TOWER Middle SAXON

Tower Height	49ft.
Diameter at Grd:	7ft. 11"
Tower Wall Thickness.	3ft. 8"
Bells 2	
Chancel Width.	14ft. 7"
Nave Width.	24ft. 11"
Chancel Length.	28ft. 4"
Nave Length.	47ft. 7"

This lofty church stands on a steep knoll over 200fteet above sea level and only two miles from the coast. Messent refers to this position as fulfilling the romantic theory of the "Defence Towers", but no writer has yet called it earlier than Norman. It has a round west tower, nave, chancel, and south porch. The first appearance is anything but ancient, but many alterations and restorations have left their mark and covered the evidence of its bulders. The tower is constructed of whole flints with 13th century belfry windows, and is circular for its full height, having battlements of the 15th century. The first early feature to notice is the tower south doorway (plate 22.) Although the pointed head has misled many writers, a close examination will reveal its true antiquity. Note the selected flint jambs, that would never be built when dressed stone was available, and the head, not constructed of small voussoirs, as was usual in the Early English period, but of two long stones to make a triangular head in the Saxon fashion, and to set the seal, they are set back on the jambs, although this would not be necessary with the stones to support the head. Further confirmation is to be seen inside the tower, where the crude finishing with flints was altered to a normal 13th. cenury doorway constructed entirely of dressed stone in small blocks. The head of the doorway, through the wall thickness, has no dressed stone and its only strength is found in the flints and mortar of the builders. The two stones of the outer head, I believe were from a large erratic split in two and not the usual dressed stone. Whether the stones were shaped at the time of building or when the inner door frame was fitted, does not alter the fact of its age. By examining the inner and outer door frames topgether, it is plain to see that the inner is later, for if both were the same age, the finer workmanship of the inner frame would have been on view outside.

Inside we can see the tower is curved on its eastern side indicating it was built with the church, but the nave width at 25ft. as well as the style of the church walls does not suggest pre-Conquest work. The tower arch and the upper doorway, are not as would first appear pointed, but correspond to what the Taylors called *"Cruck shaped"* that were shuttered by timbers of natural shape during their building. Note the lopsided aspect of the arches, and the rounded edges.

The ledge in the nave west wall at a height of about 14ft. has been noted in too many pre-Conquest churches to be dismissed as the original height of the church.

On the north side of the nave at the east end we can still see the ruins of a transept or chapel. The archway at the S/E corner was the doorway to the Rood Loft. In the blocked up archway that led to this chapel, is a double-light Y-traceried window, that was inserted when the chapel became disused, and may date the chapel itself.

Some brick foundations that extend to the east, beyond the present chancel, suggests that the church was much longer in early times. The present width ties in with Saxon measurements, and the walling seems earlier than the nave., but there is no more tangible proof. It appears that the chancel at the very least, was extended from its first shorter version, and then later reduced to its present size.

N5 BARMER. All Saints.

D3 Sheet. 132. Map Ref. T.F. 809 337.
Tower and Nave Middle SAXON

Tower Height approx.	28ft.
Internal Diameter Grd:	8ft. 6'
Tower Wall Thickness.	3ft. 9"
Bells 1 small	
Chancel Width.	14ft. 1"
Nave Width.	16ft. 7"
Nave & Aisle Width.	25ft. 11"
Chancel Length..	24ft 1"
Nave Length.	27ft. 1"

This remote church, now vested in the *"Norfolk Churches Trust"*, is called Early English, with a Norman tower, by most writers, but although neglect and restorations have left their mark, there is plenty of evidence to prove the Saxon date of the building.

Consisting of round west tower, nave, chancel, and north aisle, this small church is one of those rarities, standing as it does in a circular churchyard, which almost certainly means it stands on the site of a pagan temple. This site, therefore, we know has been used for worship from the earliest times. That the church and tower are pre-Conquest must surely be beyond dispute, for three of the four nave corners are built of flints. The N/E corner, disturbed or covered by the 14th century north aisle being the only one missing. This undoubtedly places all the nave walls firmly in the pre-Conquest period, and the nave width of 16ft. 7" gives us more evidence that early Saxon naves were narrow. No positive evidence is seen about the chancel's date, and the walls are now faced with cut flints. But have they been rebuilt? Or merely refaced during the many restorations?

The tower is circular over the tower arch, and that implies being built with the church. The height of about 28ft., although we know it may have been lowered, points very strongly to the very early period of 900 to 950. The step to thin the tower walls internally at 16ft. 5" is further confirmation of its Saxon dating. There are no fillets between tower and church, but the uncoursed whole flints of both tower and nave show once again the Saxon technique.

The north aisle is 14th century, with three arcades of octagonal piers, the pointed arches having single chamfers towards the nave and double chamfers towards the aisle. The south side of the nave still preserves its corbel table, while inside the wooden south door is a cast iron door dating from 1870 when Thomas Kerslake re-roofed the church and used it for the burials of his family. The iron door was an insurance against the prevalence of body snatchers at this time.

All the windows in this church are Victorian in the Early English style; but dare we think that they are copies of the windows they replace? This delightful church, although rather remote, would welcome a band of people to adopt it.

N.6. BAWBURGH. Sts. Mary & Walstan.

H 6.Sheet 144. Map Ref. T.G. 153 086
Tower and Nave West Wall Middle SAXON

Tower Height to top of Cap approx:	45ft.
Height of Tower approx:	40ft.
Internal Diameter Grd:	9ft. 6"
Tower Wall Thickness	3ft. 6"
BELLS 1.	
Chancel Width	18ft. 3"
Nave Width	24ft. 6"
Chancel Length.	24ft. 6"
Nave Length.	39ft. 10"
Nave Wall thickness N & S.	2ft. 2"

This church with its dedication to St. Walstan, denotes its close association with this Norfolk saint, and the well, noted in medieval days for its healing powers, is in the farmyard close by. The church stands in a very prominent position above the nearby farm, but not on high ground relative to the surrounding countryside. It consists of a round west tower, nave, chancel, and south porch.

The tower tapers gently towards the top, rather like a nineteenth century tower mill, and is finished with a conical cap of red-brown tiles. This is crowned with the symbol of a flaming torch. Four single light lancets provide the belfry windows for the single bell that was not seen, and there is no string course or dividing line at the base of the belfry section. The ground floor west window is Perpendicular and no other windows are in the tower. Flints of all sizes, some quite large and of various hues have been used in its construction, while large amounts of straw coloured brick or tile were used from the belfry to the top, but below this, there is only some used in filling below the west window. Three pieces of conglomerate, were seen, although there may be more, for this tower was cement rendered, and it has only partially flaked off. The tower looks a poor circle at the top, and internally at the base appears to be oval and slightly flattened on the east.

Externally on the east, the tower is splayed into the nave west wall, but without fillets, so there is good reason for believing it was built against an earlier church, as the tower east wall measures barely 2ft. 8".

Little of the early church remains however, for although we can see the nave west wall is not straight, but curves westwards, outside, we can see the Saxon flint quoins as a vertical line that besides confirming the Saxon west wall, shows us that the nave has been widened by about 3ft. both to north and south. The present north and south walls therefore are too thin to be Norman, and the uncoursed flintwork places them in the Early English period. In the north wall of the nave can be seen the blocked up archway that led once to St. Walstan's Chapel, the patron saint of farmworkers. Although little of the ruins of this chapel remain, we know that it was built after the nave was widened in the Early English period, and therefore was not the chapel referred to in the History on view in the church.

The chancel could well belong to the Saxon church, as the walling appears early, and the wall thickness is 2ft. 5" more like a Saxon wall. However, there are no Saxon features to give any proof of this, so once again we can only conjecture.

N7. BEDINGHAM. St. Andrew

J8 Sheet 134. Map ref. T.M. 285 934
Tower and Nave West Wall Middle SAXON

Tower Height.	61ft. 6"	Nave Width	18ft. 7"
Circular part	42ft. 6"	Nave & Aisles Width	47ft. 11"
Tower Internal Diameter Grd:	10ft. 5"	Chancel Length	36ft. 1"
Tower Wall Thickness	3ft. 10"	Nave Length	74ft. 7"
Bells 5		Arcades (Original Nave Walls)	2ft. 6"
Chancel Width	18ft.		

In flat open countryside, among a group of round towered churches to the north of the river Waveney, Bedingham Church consists of a round west tower with an octagonal top, nave, chancel, north and south porches, north and south aisles and north and south transepts.

For such a small and scattered village, this church has almost cathedral proportions. Probably only Sedgeford of the round towered churches, in the north of Norfolk can come anywhere near to it for size.

Forty two feet of this sixtyone foot tower is Saxon, but it has none of the usual fillets. Flints of all sizes and colours are to be seen in this tower, and there are no signs of coursing of the flints. Steel ties have been put through the tower to hold it together. The octagonal belfry stage is Perpendicular, as are the belfry windows and also the ground floor west window. above this window is a round-headed slit window, and these are the only windows in this tower. The circular part of the tower conforms to the expected Saxon height, but it is the tower arch (plate 31) that really shouts Saxon at you. It is identical to the one at Tasburgh; tall and narrow and built entirely without dressed stones, and with a very rough round head. The whole is plastered over but the construction can be readily observed. This tower is very unusual in having two upper doorways, but I believe that the upper one was built later as a Sanctus Bell window, as dressed stone has been used in the frame.

The tower arch is 12ft. 10" tall by 3ft. 6" wide, and the tower wall thickness is almost the same at east and west, that implies the tower being built with the church. The church then, however, was much different than what we see here now, for the width would have been 18ft. 7", or the nave without the aisles. Confirmation of this can be seen outside in the nave west wall. The old N/W and S/W quoins of flints can be seen against which the aisle walls were built. The south aisle was built first with quatrefoil piers to the arcades, while the north arcades have octagonal piers which are later. Whether any of the old Saxon walls remain above these arcades is open to doubt, although it is surprising what the early builders managed to do without demolishing the old walls.

The chancel remains at its old width, but we have no features to prove they are the same walls, but the Early English and Decorated windows there now, only confirm the latest date that they could be built.

This church has been altered and enlarged many times during its long life, and in seeking for the early dating of these churches time has not allowed for the detailed work involved in this further study. This church however has so much interest and history that it should be thoroughly studied and documented as soon as possible.

N8 BEACHAMWELL St. Mary

C6 Sheet 143. Map Ref. T.F. 750 053
Round West Tower Late SAXON. Nave and Chancel Middle SAXON

Tower Height	53ft.
Height of Circular part	34ft
Tower Diameter Grd:	8ft. 9"
Tower Wall Thickness	3ft. 1"
Nave Ridge Height	27ft. 3"
Bells 2	
Chancel Width	13ft. 10"
Nave Width	14ft.
Nave & South Aisle Width	26ft. 2"
Chancel Length	20ft. 6"
Nave Length	37ft. 5"
North Nave Wall Thickness	2ft. 7"
South Arcade Wall Thickness	2ft. 7"

Beachamwell St. Mary's stands beside its village green on quite flat ground just five miles from Swaffham. It has a round west tower with an octagonal top, nave, chancel, south aisle and north porch.

A complete long-and-short quoin at the N/W corner of erratics, and the two eastern quoins, although these two, appear to have been altered in later years, to give us grounds for calling the nave and chancel of this church Saxon. I am dating this church earlier than the Taylors, because (a) the tower seems certainly to have been built against an earlier church, and (b) the height of the circular portion, 34ft. seems to belong to the earlier Saxon towers. The 15th century octagonal belfry has Y-traceried bell openings on four sides and flushwork replicas on the other four (plate 5).

The Saxon belfry windows are worthy of close study, in as much as they show us (a) that their mortar was very good indeed, to last as most of it has, to the present day; and (b) the re-use of stones to form their windows, and using them only where it was considered essential. Taking them in turn:- starting with the north window which is the only one that has not been blocked up. The vertical shaft at the centre is carved on its eastern face, and looks extremely like a churchyard cross. It is rectangular in section and tapers as would a cross towards the top. The triangular heads are set back two inches to three inches on their jambs and only four stones are used to form the two triangular heads at the front of these windows. The remainder of the heads of these windows are in flint rubble. There is no splay to these belfry windows. I could not determine what kind of through-stone was used to support these heads. East windows:- These are the words of H.M. Taylor which I have checked and agreed are correct. "In the east and south faces of the tower, the individual openings of each double window have round heads arched in flattish flints:- and the mid-wall supports are in the form of piers rather than thin shafts; that on the east showing traces of carving like a re-used grave-slab. South windows:- This differs from H.M. Taylor's account in the details of the centre column as follows:- The south window has a bulbous column that appears to be made of two flat slabs, one on the outer face and the other on the inner face of the tower. This inner slab can be seen inside the tower. In between these two slabs is flint rubble. The north and west windows have the typical triangular heads. The west window has a cylindrical centre shaft, that swells at its centre.

Below the south belfry window is a slit window made of flint rubble without any other frame. The slit window in the west face has been cemented over. so most probably this is the same as the south window under the cement. The north face now houses a clock where once, no doubt, another slit window lighted the first floor. There are no fillets between tower and church.

The upper doorway is slightly to the north of centre, and measures 2ft. 6" wide by 5ft. 6" tall, and is 18ft. above the ground. This tower was built against, and not with the present church, as the straight east side to the tower over the tower arch shows us. If the upper doorway was a west window, opened out to its present shape, it may be the reason why it is not central.

The piscina near the centre of the south aisle, implies that this was lengthened at some time. In fact, it was in the last century that two more bays were added to the old aisle, while Perpendicular windows were put in, in the 15th. century, which the 19th century addition copied. The tower contains two uninscribed bells, and the most interesting treasures are a delightful carved angel over the vestry door. and some fine graffiti on one of the arcade columns.

N9 BEESTON St. Lawrence.

J4. Sheet 133. Map Ref. T.G. 328 219
Tower, West & North Nave Wall Middle SAXON

Tower Height approx.	50ft.
Tower Diameter Grd:	9ft.
Tower Wall Thickness	2ft. 10"
Bells 1	
Chancel Width	19ft. 1"
Nave Width	19ft. 1"
Chancel Length	38ft.
Nave Length	51ft. 7"
Nave North Wall Thickness	2ft. 6"
Nave South Wall Thickness	2ft. 4"

The village of Beeston has now disappeared and the church stands in the grounds of the Hall beside the Norwich to North Walsham road, and nine miles north east of Norwich. It was recognised as Saxon by Rev. John Gunn M.A. and was published in *"Proceedings of the Archaeological Institute Norwich 1847"*.

Very large flints were used in the construction of this tower, and also a large amount of conglomerate. The stones are not coursed, and there are no fillets between tower and church. About 20ft. up on the north side there is a triangular-headed window with a frame of conglomerate, and at the same height on the south and west are similar windows now blocked up. What was probably a similar but smaller window now blocked up can be seen below the present ground floor west window, and this is only about four feet from the ground. The four belfry windows are single-light Gothic that appear to be the same date as the present west window, probably 14th century when the battlements which used to crown this tower were built. These however were removed some years ago as being unsafe. The tower batters above the blocked up windows and below the belfry.

The internal diameter of the tower is 9ft. with walls under 3ft. thick, which is quite thin even for a Saxon tower. There is a very curious tower arch with the return walls of such differing measurements. The north measuring 3ft. 7" while the south is 4ft. 7". Not only is the opening off centre with the tower to give this oddity,but it is also off centre with the nave. The only explanation I can give, is that when the nave was widened by 4 feet to the south, the tower arch was moved towards the south to bring it nearer the centre to assist the processions. Although the tower arch seems to have been altered in this way, it still appears to be Saxon, as it is very tall and narrow and the jambs seem to be of flints, although they are rendered, so one cannot be sure what lies beneath. There is only a slight chamfer towards the nave.

The Rev. Gunn says; "The size of the rectangular-headed windows is 5ft. tall by 2ft. wide outside, and 18 inches inside the tower. "This is the reverse of Norman splays. Conglomerate is much in evidence he says inside the tower. This I must accept until I have been able to ascend the higher levels.

Herringbone work in conglomerate can be seen in the north nave wall about 10ft. up. This wall is only 2ft. 6" thick, and besides showing the N/W quoins of conglomerate partly hidden behind a later buttress, the original eastern quoins of the nave can be seen as a vertical line of conglomerate blocks about 28ft. from the N/W quoins. This is quite short for a Saxon church, unless the chancel was narrower at first and later made wider to the north wall of the nave, but there is nothing to support this idea above ground. There is one bell in the tower, but this was not seen.

The nave has been widened towards the south, and the ceiling is in Georgian panels, the same motif as is used in the nearby Hall.

N10. BESSINGHAM. St. Andrew.

H2. Sheet. 133. Map Ref. T.G. 166 370

Tower, Nave West and North Walls Middle SAXON. Tower raised Late SAXON

Tower Height	50ft.
Internal Diameter Grd:	7ft. 3"
Tower Wall Thickness 1st. floor	3ft. 2"
Bells 2	
Chancel Width	16ft.
Nave Width	16ft.
Chancel Length	16ft. 8"
Nave Length	33ft. 3"
Nave Wall Thickness N. & S.	2ft. 6"

This church is situated on a high point about four miles from the coast. It consists of round west tower, nave, chancel, and south porch.

The most interesting early feature of this church is the Saxon tower that has not undergone too much restoration. Outwardly, the first ten feet is constructed almost entirely of conglomerate in quite large blocks with only a few flints, followed by one course of flints and then a course of conglomerate. Then another ten foot section, this time of whole flints with almost no conglomerate. From there to the base of the parapet is again almost entirely conglomerate. The battlements, of whole white flints are later; probably late 13th. century. There are no fillets between tower and church. (Plate 14).

The twin-light Saxon belfry windows at the cardinal points are constructed entirely of conglomerate. The jambs, using small pieces, and the inverted Vs, of the heads having flat slabs. These rest at their centres on massive through -stones which in turn are resting on plain cylindrical shafts roughly hewn from this intractable stone. They have no bases or capitals. The windows are outlined with minor decorations in the same stone.

The tower was restored in 1986, and the architect advised me that they had discovered some more Saxon windows that had been blocked up and forgotten. There was a ring of eight circular double-splayed windows at the top of the tower, as at Forncett St. Peter.

Below the belfry, at 27ft. are four round-headed windows, framed in conglomerate. The north and south ones are still intact and are blocked with bricks to prevent birds getting in, but small spaces have been left to allow a little light to reach the second floor. Inside the tower these windows have their heads arched with flat flints laid non-radially. Internally also at this height is a ledge to thin the tower wall by 3 to 4 inches, which is seen in many Saxon towers. Lower down, at 19ft., in the west face we can see a round-headed window, with its head formed by thin pieces of conglomerate, while inside the tower, at the same height, to the north and south blocked circular windows are visible. There is a good series of put-log holes from the first floor upwards.

At first floor level, 16ft. 9" there is an upper doorway facing east, with a triangular head, but I was not able to measure this, as it was enclosed beyond the head and jambs with plaster board. The tower arch is tall and narrow, and unmoulded except for the imposts; with the round-headed arch set back on its jambs in true Saxon fashion.

The church walls seem to have been mostly rebuilt. Those surviving Saxon walls being the nave west wall, and south wall as far as the south porch; (plate 14). The quoins are seen as large blocks of conglomerate. Also the north wall as far as the chancel; the large blocks of conglomerate forming the nave N/E corner can be seen as a vertical line against which the later chancel wall has been built. The Saxon church was therefore either quite short, the length of the present nave, or the chancel narrowed at this point, with the possibility of an apsidal chancel which seemed quite popular.

The windows are all Perpendicular, and have been restored to some extent, and the piscina, strangely in the north chancel wall, must have been reset when the large Perpendicular window took its place in the south wall.

N11. BEXWELL. St. Mary.

A7. Sheet. 143. Map Ref. T.F. 631 034

Tower and Church Middle SAXON

Tower Height	52ft.
Circular Part.	39ft.
Internal Diameter Grd:	10ft. 7"
Tower Wall Thickness	3ft.
Bells 1	
Chancel & Nave Width	18ft. 8"
Chancel Length	22ft. 9"
Nave Length	43ft.10"
Nave Wall Thickness N.	2ft. 6"
Nave Wall Thickness S.	2ft. 5"

In the N/W corner of Norfolk, well away from the Snettisham carstone quarries, are two distinctive round tower churches, West Dereham and Bexwell. Both appear at first sight to be constructed almost entirely of carstone, and this is what most text books would have us believe . On closer examination we find that while Bexwell is built mainly of carstone with an occasional block of conglomerate and some flints, West Dereham church and tower are almost entirely of conglomerate. These two stones are explained in Chapter 6. Building Materials and Methods . Why then, we are forced to ask ourselves, were these two ancient churches, two of only four round tower churches to be built predominantly of these two materials, so close together, and yet each one with a different stone. My research into these churches has led me to believe that villages in Saxon times were almost self sufficient; building materials were certainly not the things to be bought outside the parish and carried at heavy expense. Therefore, when I read about the exhausted carstone quarries at Bexwell, and was told that conglomerate was still being unearthed on the farms at West Dereham, my theory gained more strength. Both these churches I feel certain are of Saxon origin, and the tower and church walls are still mainly original.

Turning now to Bexwell, which stands on a small mound in a circular churchyard overlooking the fens, and on the south side of the Downham Market to Swaffham road. It consists of a round west tower with an octagonal top, nave and chancel in one, and a later south porch.

The tower is curved inside at the east, showing that tower and church were probably built together. Dealing first with the tower which has many Saxon features left to place it before the Conquest; the first is the original height of 39ft. This places it with the church in the middle Saxon period, between 900 and 1,000. The later octagonal stage, built thankfully also in carstone, raised the height to 52ft., but here dressed stone was used for the quoins and window facings. This seems to be of the 15th. century. There are no fillets between tower and church but these were by no means always used on Saxon towers. One interesting point to note is that this is the only round tower with a west upper doorway, (plate 4), but it was exciting to find that there was also an east upper doorway as well. They are the same dimensions 3ft. 5" wide by 7ft.10" tall, but while the east doorway is at first floor level of 17ft. 6" the west doorway is 2ft. 3" higher. These are both definitely doorways and not windows, for they are cut straight through the walls with no splay whatever . The west doorway still has its old door. Inside the tower the jambs and round-headed arches are constructed of medium sized blocks of carstone, but these are rectangular and not wedge-shaped. They are also laid in a non-radial fashion. Outside, the west upper doorway is constructed of quite small blocks of carstone, almost flint like in size. On the same level, there is a north and south round-headed window of about the same size internally, but these have decided splays and they appear to be original. Below these features, at 10ft. from the ground, are two circular double-splayed windows, now blocked, and only found and showed up by the tower restoration of 1988. The ground floor west window is a double-light of the Perpendicular period.

30ft. from the ground, at the top of the circular stage, is a ring of ten round-headed windows, now blocked up with flints, that were the original belfry windows. The construction was similar to those on the first floor but with little or no splay. The tower arch is round-headed, and has only simple chamfered imposts The floor of the tower is on two levels; the west is of early brick and is nine inches lower than the east, which was re-floored by the Victorians in 6" black and red-brown tiles. We descend one foot to enter the church, and this makes the churchyard about two feet higher than the early church floor. One wonders if there are still earlier floors beneath the one we stand on. There is one bell in the tower. John L'Estrange, 1874 in "The Church Bells of Norfolk" writes:- Bexwell has one bell, 28" diameter inscribed MAGISTER JOHANNES RISTON ME FECIT. It came from the Lynn Foundry.

The nave and chancel are one without a chancel arch, and the dimensions 66ft . 7" by 18ft . 8" indicate the probability of its being Saxon. Pevsner tells us there is a Norman double-splayed window in the nave, which does not agree with the Norman features we are told to expect by other experts. The Saxon double-splayed window is in the north nave wall just east of the north doorway. Opposite this in the south wall is another; but in this case the outer splay is blocked up. So we have two Saxon windows to positively identify the nave walls as Saxon. Next to these Saxon windows are two very tall lancets, with what appears to be Victorian frames; but they might be restorations. Further east along the north wall is a double-light window in the Decorated style, but again this is Victorian; but here, much of the stonework is older. In the north of the chancel is a three-light Perpendicular window that has been partly restored, while the east window of three separate lancets in Early English style is certainly Victorian .

Further discoveries on later visits included a squint in a very unusual position at the S/W corner of the chancel. Although sceptical at first, it looks directly to the altar and could not be a position for a put-log hole. The chancel contained the first cast iron poppyheads that I had seen. There were two varieties of the design which showed the aim of the makers was to continue the practice of variety in these decorations .

There are a great many interesting and early items in this church and tower which has been said to have little value. The church and tower are very definitely of the middle Saxon period as proved by the many early features detailed here. The ring of Saxon belfry windows, first recognised here, can also be seen at Holton St. Peter and South Elmham All Saints, and in double rows at Risby; all in Suffolk.

N12. BRAMPTON. St. Peter

I4. Sheet. 133. Map Ref. T.G. 220 247

Nave Early SAXON, Tower Middle SAXON

Tower Height approx:	55ft.
Circular part approx::	40ft.
Internal Diameter Grd:	7ft. 5"
Tower Wall Thickness	3ft. 4"
Nave Ridge Height approx:	35ft.
Bells 1	
Chancel Width	15ft.
Nave Width	28ft. 1"
Chancel Length	35ft.11"
Nave Length	26ft.

This ancient church lies a quarter of a mile south of the river Bure and two miles S/E of Aylsham. The village has moved away and only a few houses are now near the church. The church consists of round west tower with an octagonal top, nave, chancel, south porch and south vestry.

The Saxon indications are few but conclusive. Starting with the tower arch, which is quite tall and has Saxon indications. Although the head has been altered, there are good signs that the jambs are still of flints. We can see on entering the ground stage of the tower that the eastern face is flat and not curved. This tells us that the tower was built against the earlier church. My measurements show that the west nave wall and especially the tower walls are much too thin to be Norman. There is no sign of an upper doorway, or of any blocked up windows.

Outside, the construction of the tower shows the Saxon influence. The flints are whole and mainly large, and with no coursing. There are two bands, mainly of conglomerate, near the top of the west window, as decoration. There are also other pieces of conglomerate scattered throughout the tower. At about 30ft. are three round-headed slit windows, framed with dressed stone, that should be examined from within the tower. The tall octagonal belfry stage of the 15th. century, with double-light openings is faced with early brick, and has brick frames for the openings and battlements, but dressed stone for the corners. There are no fillets between tower and church.

It is at the N/W quoins that we get our most positive Saxon feature. There is no buttress here, and the lower part of the corner is Roman tiles, and above this are several pieces of either sandstone, or a pale carstone; They are definitely not conglomerate or the usual limestone used for quoins. This is a very definite Saxon feature and includes the north wall.

The rest of the church looks at first sight to be quite a hotch potch of additions and alterations. Further investigation however, shows up a pattern that seems quite logical. The tower is off centre to the north of the nave, and the chancel is also off centre towards the north. It can be seen however, that the chancel is in line with the tower. There are blocked up arches of dressed stone in the south chancel walls and also at the east end of the nave.

This is what must have happened:- The original church was the present length, and the width of the chancel. Later, probably after about 50 years, the tower was added; this is indicated by the flat side to the east of the tower. Later a south aisle was added with arcades. This is accounted for by the dressed stone arch at the east end of the nave. Later still, a south transept was built, now showing as a blocked up arch in the south of the chancel. Some time after this, probably when the roof needed some drastic repairs, the south aisle arcading was removed, and the new roof covered the nave and aisle in one .

The transept was removed either then or later. In Victorian times a vestry was added to the present chancel, quite near the old transept, but slightly further east. There is now no sign of a north door, a window occupies its position, but surely at one time a door was there.

N13. BRANDISTON. St. Nicholas.

H4. Sheet. 133. Map Ref. T.G. 142 214

North Aisle Early SAXON. Tower Middle SAXON.

Tower Height approx.	30ft.
Circular Stage approx.	20ft.
Internal Diameter Grd:	10ft. 7"
Tower Wall Thickness	3ft. 4"
Bells 1	
Chancel Width	20ft. 3"
Nave Width	20ft. 3"
Nave & Aisle Width	33ft. 7"
Chancel Length	11ft. 3"
Nave Length	38ft. 2"
Nave Wall Thickness S.	2ft. 9"
Original Nave Wall Thickness N.	2ft. 4"
Original Nave & Chancel Width	11ft. 6"

This church is very isolated, and when visited in August 1979 a notice on the door stated the church was being made redundant. It is now in the care of the *"Redundant Churches Fund"*. It has a round west tower with an octagonal top, nave, chancel, north aisle and south porch.

The layout of Brandiston Church is very confusing at first, especially as Messent tells us that the tower was completely rebuilt on its old foundations in 1890. I would think that in the main it was a rebuilding of the octagonal belfry stage, for the lower part looks like early work and is not in the building style of the Victorians.

The concept of an early tower of a village church being built against its aisle is so remote that I looked to find an explanation. It is there and quite plain to see. If we look at the components on their own, we find that the nave is 14th. century Decorated, see the windows with flowing tracery, also the arcades leading to the north aisle of quatrefoil piers, also of this date . So if the arcades are the same date as the nave, the north aisle was here before this, and was therefore the original nave .

The north aisle, (original nave), being very narrow at 11ft. 6" and with a wall thickness of 2ft. 4" appears to belong to the Early Saxon period although there are no windows to confirm this for us. The tower with its flat east side, we can see was built against the earlier nave, and although no reliable Saxon features have survived, there are a number of factors that imply pre-Conquest work. The tower is constructed of whole and cut flints, many quite large, and at the base is a plinth of flints, often found in Saxon work. Flat fillets or pilasters in flints are to be seen between tower and church, although the usual practice in Saxon times was for quarter-round fillets . The tower wall thickness at 3ft. 4" is another strong point for a pre-Conquest dating. Above the circular section, is an octagonal battlemented belfry with three belfry windows, and it appears to be this section that was rebuilt in the restoration of 1890. The plan of the tower is distinctly oval .

The present nave is firmly in the Decorated period, with large east and west windows, and the south porch a century later. Outside the east end can be seen the demolished chancel outlined by two or three courses of red bricks 20ft. by 13ft .

N14. BRECCLES MAGNA. St. Margaret.

E7. Sheet 144. Map Ref. T.L. 958 946

Tower and Church Middle SAXON.

Tower Height	45ft. 9"	Chancel Width	19ft. 9"
Height of Circular Section	35ft.	Nave Width	19ft. 9"
Internal Diameter Grd:	11ft.10"	Chancel Length	28ft. 5"
Tower Wall Thickness	3ft. 4"	Nave Length	42ft.11"
Nave Ridge Height	33ft. 6"	Nave Wall Thickness N. & S.	2ft. 7"
Bells 1			

Breccles Magna stands beside the East Harling to Watton Road, and with few houses nearby; it consists of a round west tower with an octagonal top, nave, chancel and south porch.

The fine carved Norman font, and the tower arch, which is Norman in style, would help place this church and tower at least to Norman days, but are there grounds for considering an earlier dating?

Starting with the tower, internally there was nothing to show beyond what could be seen from outside. The height of the circular section is 35ft., too low for Norman. Its octagonal belfry stage, 11ft. tall was added in the late 15th. or early 16th. century. It has double-light windows on the usual sides and the alternate sides have a chequered pattern of black and white knapped flints. This octagonal stage looks extremely squat as it has a plain parapet without the usual battlements. There is a square-headed Perpendicular window on the ground floor to the west, and above this, a rectangular slit window with a dressed stone frame. There are possibly five other windows in this tower that are blocked up, three of which give the impression that they may have been circular. They are stone rectangles at north, west and south, at the height we expect to see Saxon circular windows, but there are no further signs within the tower to confirm this. There is one bell in the tower.

The tower arch is Norman in style, but the imposts of a single stone on each side is decidedly unusual to say the least of this period. These imposts too, are different in their carving and seem to have a Saxon influence. Could they be the work of the Font mason, or were they split from a churchyard cross? The diameter of the tower internally at 11ft. 10" is large for a Saxon, but by no means unknown, while the wall thickness measured at the west window and over the tower arch is 3ft. 4", surely too thin for Norman workmen. The north and south nave walls are both only 2ft. 7" thick, and this certainly indicates a Saxon dating.

So we have a number of good Saxon indications, and I have yet to see a Norman church with walls as thin, or nave as narrow as we have here. None of the original quoins have remained, but the nave width gives us a further pointer to pre-Conquest work. The length of the church inside is 71ft. 4", and it is 19ft. 9" wide, with the nave and chancel the same width, another early feature. The east window is Decorated in style and possibly has some of the original stonework. The rest of the windows are Perpendicular and all have had some restoration, some a great deal. The nave and chancel walls were raised when these windows were installed.

Near the priest's door in the chancel is an oval floor slab inscribed in Latin *"Status visit erecta"*. Beneath it is the body in a standing position of Ursula, the daughter of the Lord Chief Justice of England, Sir Thomas Richardson. Ursula died in 1658. This floor slab is linked to another, strangely, that of her father, not of her husband, Sir William Hewyt, Kt., who lies in the chancel further north.

N15. BROOKE. St. Peter

J7. Sheet. 134. Map Ref. T.M. 294 996
Tower and Church possibly SAXON

Tower Height	55ft. 6"
Internal Diameter Grd:	12ft. 8"
Tower Wall Thickness	3ft.10"
Nave Ridge Height	44ft. 6"
Bells 6	
Chancel Width	22ft
Nave Width	21ft. 6"
Nave & Aisle Width	35ft. 9"
Chancel Length	29ft. 8"
Nave Length	49ft. 6"
South Nave Wall Thickness	3ft. 1"

This church is situated in fairly flat countryside . It was originally near the centre of the village; later the population moved towards the main Norwich road, leaving the church rather on the outskirts. Now however, another shift of the population is taking place, as a new residential estate is being built near the church bringing it once again to the centre of the community. It has a round west tower, nave, chancel, north aisle and south porch,

The tower is constructed mainly of whole flints of medium size and well coursed. There are no fillets between tower and church, and the four belfry windows of the 13th. century in the diagonals are below a later 12 sided parapet, which Messent called 16 sided, and Pevsner octagonal. Early bricks and cut flints have been used to give this parapet a chequered effect. The upper doorway, 15ft. 3" above the ground is 1ft.10" wide by 5ft. 6" tall, but alterations have left nothing by which to date it. The tower was originally about 40ft. high, as the old belfry windows can be seen below the present ones inside the tower; but as they are not Norman in character, Saxon work is implied. Also, there is a 4 inch step to thin the nave west wall, about 13ft. up, and this is usually a Saxon feature.

The south doorway has remained almost unaltered since the 13th. century, which with the south nave wall looking early and unaltered, gives good grounds for believing that this wall is not later than the south doorway. The chancel windows are of the Decorated period, but the walls are almost certainly earlier. The puzzle is the north arcade, with the two western bays cut straight through the wall and with only simple chamfers; while the two eastern bays are of late Perpendicular style, with octagonal piers and Tudor arches, the western end must be of early date, but was the aisle lengthened, or just restored in Tudor times? But if so, why not all of it?

The Victorians restored this church so much that many of its features have been altered since Ladbrooke sketched it in 1822. I list the obvious alterations on the south side since that sketch was made. Two table tombs have disappeared from near the south porch. Buttresses against the south wall have been repaired with red bricks and their shape altered. There are now windows in the south porch where Ladbrooke shows none. The nave roof is now of slates and not thatch, and Ladbrooke shows both gable crosses missing, but these have now been replaced. The Victorians added two more buttresses of red brick to the east wall to stabilise this end, and the four-light intersecting window has been replaced with a three-light in the Decorated style. Two nave windows that had pointed heads, now have Tudor heads and the lights are entirely different. The east window in the south wall of the chancel has been altered and the west window has been replaced with a priest's door. All these features have been altered since 1822 by restoration work, and while drawings may not be 100% accurate, they do give a very good idea of what has been altered since they were made. Although no definite Saxon features were seen, the measurements show clearly the walls could not have been later than Saxon.

N16. BURNHAM DEEPDALE. St. Mary.

D1. Sheet 132. Map Ref. T.F. 804 443

Tower, West and South Nave. Middle SAXON

Tower Height	41ft.
Tower Height to top of Cap	44ft.
Internal Diameter Grd:	9ft. 3"
Tower Thickness on East	4ft. 3"
Tower Thickness at W. Window	4ft.10"
Tower Thickness on First Floor	3ft. 9"
Nave Ridge Height	35ft.
Bells 1	
Chancel Width	17ft. 8"
Nave Width	19ft. 9"
Nave & Aisle Width	31ft. 6"
Chance Length	22ft. 9"
Nave Length	42ft. 9"
Nave North Wall Thickness	2ft. 3"
Nave South Wall Thickness	2ft. 4"

This church on the north Norfolk coast, consists of a round west tower, nave, chancel, north aisle and south porch.

There are a number of questions that we cannot answer at present. We see the tower (plate 6), faced in well coursed and selected flints, too even, I would think, to be Saxon or even Norman. It has a shallow lead cap, three Saxon round-headed belfry windows below this, at north, south and west, while the fourth at the east is only seen inside the tower because the higher Victorian roof line blocks part, so it was blocked up and shows as an alcove within the tower. Lower down are three more similar windows, again at north, south and west, and here the north window is blocked, leaving an alcove inside the tower. All these windows have selected flat flints for the heads which are set back on the jambs, which have larger flints. These windows are closed with trellis and wire netting. Below them on the first floor is a round-headed double-splayed window of Saxon date constructed again entirely of flints. This faces west, and opposite, at 14ft. 6" above the ground is the triangular-headed upper doorway 6ft. 3" tall by 2ft. 3" wide. The head is set back in Saxon fashion by 3". This is seen from the nave and the tower, and is fitted with a door, one of very few to be so complete.

Below this, is the round-headed tower arch, 12ft. tall by 4ft. wide, and the head set back once more by 3" to 4". The tower is curved inside towards the east, which implies the tower and church were built together. Inside the tower, a great deal of conglomerate shows that most of the inside was lined with this stone.

Outside, the base of the tower is thicker by 6" up to a height of about 10ft; and although this seemed at first to be Victorian, it is to be seen on the Ladbrooke's sketch, so it was here in the 1820's and so may well be early. As the tower at Matlaske, (also Saxon), has a similar thickening, there is a distinct probability that this feature may be original with the tower. There are flint fillets between tower and church to further strengthen our case, but the pointed west doorway that Ladbrooke sketched has been blocked up and a simulated Saxon window inserted.

None of the Saxon windows now showing in the tower were to be seen in Ladbrooke 's day, when the tower was plastered over, and it had only four square windows with quatrefoil openings, and a west pointed doorway. The present Victorian north aisle, has four arcades, although the old one that had been removed and blocked up only had three. So it is entirely new and not a reconstruction.

The Norman north doorway, which looks original, was most probably moved out to the original aisle, back when this was removed, and out to its present position when this aisle was built.

So we know that the tower and west wall are Saxon, and although the north wall has disappeared into the arcades of the north aisle, the south wall appears to be original, and so most of this church dates from pre-Conquest times. The selected, coursed flints of the tower, must be a refacing in the Victorian restoration, and this accounts for the thickness of the wall which is 4ft.10" below the ledge and 4ft. 3" above. The west side, we can also see is about 7" thicker than the east, which another layer of flints would account for.

N 17. BURNHAM NORTON. St. Margaret.

D1. Sheet. 132. Map Ref. T.F. 835 428
Tower, Nave West Wall and Chancel Late SAXON

Tower Height	55ft.
Internal Diameter Grd:	11ft. 2"
Tower Wall Thickness	3ft.
Bells 1	
Chancel Width	16ft. 6"
Nave Width	17ft. 5"
Nave & Aisles Width	42ft. 3"
Chancel Length	21ft. 5"
Nave Length	59ft. 2"
Arcade Wall Thickness	2ft. 1"

Standing on high ground in otherwise flat countryside, this tower shows once again the preference for building churches in a commanding position. It comprises a west tower, circular for its full height, nave, chancel, north and south aisles and north porch.

Quite a large church for this sparsely populated area, but the aisles were added when the Carmelite Friary, which was close by, probably influenced the importance of this country church.

We are again discussing a Saxon church, although the Taylors visited it and pronounced that it was not Saxon. Their reluctance is hard to explain, as they noted most of the Saxon features, but it seems wanted Saxon belfry windows of the accepted shape and style before agreeing to a pre-Conquest date.

All the tower windows I feel certain are Saxon, and agree to Baldwin Brown's, and the Taylors' requirements for pre-Conquest work, namely, built of flints, and with heads of flints not laid radially.

Starting once more at the tower, we can see that it was built in sections, from the differing types of flints used. The later battlements are the only additions to this tower which has remained substantially the same throughout its life, which started I believe between 1,000 and the Conquest. The height of the original part of the tower must be about 50ft., which places it among the later Saxon towers. It is curved inside on the east, which says it was built with the church, and there are no fillets between church and tower.

The belfry stage, which contains one bell, has a ring of six belfry windows, all single-light, round-headed, and built entirely of whole flints. They are recessed, which is why the Taylors have rejected the whole tower, but why this rejection of Saxon workmen who have left a whole range of one off experiments? The heads have their flints laid in a non radial fashion, (fig. 14) found by Baldwin Brown, and accepted by the Taylors as a certain sign of Saxon work. There were signs above these belfry windows that suggested the possibility of blocked up circular windows in the fashion of those at Forncett St. Peter and Bungay. But when the tower was restored a few years ago, although the builders agreed that these were indeed circular windows, they were not opened out, or even repointed to make them more visible.

On the first floor there are three more round-headed windows built in the same fashion with flint frames, but the openings are narrower. They are at north, south and west. A similar window is at ground floor level to the west, and must be one of the very few that are original at this position. All the windows seem original with just a few pieces of dressed stone inserted as repairs. There is no sign of a ground floor doorway to this tower.

The tall and narrow tower arch, which is plastered, is almost certainly constructed of flints, and the round-headed arch is set back 4" on the jambs. It is 12ft. 9" tall by 5ft. 5" wide. Above this, 17ft. 9" from the floor is the clear outline of the upper doorway. This is round-headed, but the arch is not set back, though of course the plaster may hide this feature.

Turning now to the church, in the nave west wall we can see the original flint quoins to north and south of the Saxon nave, and the later Early English aisles have been built against these, in the usual practice without bonding. The original nave walls were cut through during the 13th. century, for the aisles to be added. The two west aisle windows, (one in each), show by their Y-tracery that they were from this period. . The nearby Carmelite Friary, founded in 1241 may have been the reason for this enlargement. The south chancel also has two single-light windows, but their heads are not true lancets and they may have been altered later in their life. At this period, probably all the arcades were as the two S/W ones are still, but in the 15th. century much restoration, called rebuilding, renewed the other arcades, put Perpendicular windows in the clerestory (four double-lights with square heads to north and south), and also inserted three-light Perpendicular windows all round the church except the chancel. These windows all have small embattled transoms across each light. The chancel has Decorated double-light windows, two to the north and two single-light pointed windows on the south.

Many interesting features of great value and beauty are in this church, and the churchyard contains the grave of Captain Woodgett, the last Master of the *Cutty Sark.*

N18. BYLAUGH. St. Mary the Virgin.

G5. Sheet. 133. Map Ref. T.G. 037 183
TOWER SAXON

Tower Height	51ft. 9"	Bells 1	
Internal Diameter Grd:	8ft.11"	Nave & Chancel Width	19ft. 1"
Tower Wall Thickness	3ft. 9"	Chancel Length	7ft. 7"
Nave Ridge Height. approx.	30ft.	Nave Length	22ft. 8"

This mainly Georgian church lies about half a mile south of the old Hall and on the bank overlooking the river Wensum, not far from East Dereham. Apart from the romantic theories of Watch Towers overlooking the waterways, there is little evidence left to date either of the tower

or the parts left of the church. The church was mainly rebuilt by Sir John Lombe in 1810 with transepts and octagonal angle turrets that are quite out of placc on these ancient churches. Only the circular part of the tower shows any sign of antiquity,

The 14th. century octagonal belfry stage with battlements must be mentioned because Charles Cox in 1910 called this hexagonal. Whcthcr this was a printer's error or his own I know not. The one bell in this stage is inscribed *"Mears and Stanwick Founders London 1865."*

There are only two windows below the belfry stage, and many writers ascribe this lack of windows to the Saxon period. My studies however, show a large number of small windows in most Saxon towers although many have been blocked up over the years. These two windows are:- a ground floor west window of late date, and a small slit window in the north to give light to the first floor, about 20ft. up. This window is also of uncertain date. The very large batter at the top of the circular part is mostly on the east side and gives the tower a truly early appearance, but I believe that this was done when the octagonal belfry stage was added and owes nothing to the original builders. We are left therefore with nothing but the measurements and the wall thickness, which have shown their worth in separating Saxon from Norman work.

The diameter of the tower at ground level is 8ft.11" and is the same on the first floor, while the thickness of the wall is 3ft. 9". The height of the circular part is 37ft. 3" These measurements are all within the usual Saxon range, and they enable us to call this tower Saxon. We cannot call it Norman, for the walls are too thin, and the tower too low for such a dating.

N19. OLD CATTON. St. Margaret.

I5. Sheet 133. Map Ref. T.G. 231 123

Tower, Chancel and Original Nave. Middle SAXON

Tower Height	46ft.
Height of Circular part	38ft.
Internal Diameter Grd:	10ft. 7"
Tower Wall Thickness	3ft.10"
Nave Ridge Height	40ft.
Bells 1	
Chance Width	16ft. 1"
Nave Width	17ft. 3"
Total Width with aisles	53ft. 3"
Chancel Length	22ft. 9"
Nave Length	39ft. 6"
Arcade Wall (orig. Nave)	2ft. 6"
Aisle Walls Thickness	2ft. 2"

This much restored church stands in the middle of a residential area of the suburb to the north of Norwich. It consists of round west tower, with octagonal top, nave, chancel, south aisle, two north transepts, north chapel and south porch. Picture on front cover.

So good is the history of this church written by Noel Boston MA, Vicar, and on view in the church, that I follow his dating; largely because he has researched into the church records and can give dates for many features. These then are his datings:- South aisle 1850, two north transepts a little later, replacing a north aisle. North wall of Choir aisle (also called Chapel of our Lady), rebuilt in 1867, west gallery 1773. During the 15th century, the following were added. Octagonal belfry stage to the tower, south porch with upper room, north aisle, (where the two transepts are now), and clerestory with the raising of the roof. The Chapel of Our Lady was built about 1350. Before this, there was our simple church with a west tower, nave and chancel which Rev. Boston calls Norman, but which I am certain stood here in Saxon times.

The first Saxon feature is the S/W quoin which is of large flints cut to give a square corner, to a height of about 15ft. Above this, repairs and the heightening of the nave walls shows as 15th century squared black flints and brick quoins. The N/W quoin has been entirely replaced with dressed stone, and the west wall refaced with cut flints. This stone seems to be Victorian and from the time when the north transepts replaced the north aisle. There are no fillets to this tower. The base of the tower is of cut flints and spreads out to a slightly larger diameter. Above this, to about the height of the first floor, or 16ft. the tower is faced with a patchwork of cut flints and early brick. This and the base, which has deceived most writers into thinking of this as a later tower, appears to be a refacing of the lower half of the circular part in the 15th century when the octagonal stage was added. Above this level, whole and cut flints are used without any coursing in true Saxon fashion until about one foot from the top of the circular part. Here, there are average sized whole flints, used no doubt to tidy up the top ready for the octagonal section.

Going inside, we find that the east side is curved, implying that the tower was built with the original church. On the first floor facing east is the upper doorway, with flints specially cut for the jambs, although the head has been repaired with brick, probably when the tower was raised. Many large flints, some cut because of their size can be seen here on the first floor up to the height of the head of the upper doorway, and this is only three feet from the top of the circular part. There are no signs of blocked up windows or put-log holes either inside or out. Only two windows are in this tower below the belfry and they are of the 15th century.

The one bell in this tower is inscribed *"ANNO DOMINI 1620"*. There are no scratch dials but one votive cross was seen on the L/H jamb of the south doorway.

N20. CLIPPESBY. St. Peter.

K5. Sheet 134. Map Ref. T.G. 428 145
Tower Middle SAXON. Church Early SAXON.

Tower Height.	48ft.
Height of Circular part	29ft.
Internal Diameter Grd:	11ft. 11"
Tower Wall Thickness	3ft. 5"
Nave Ridge Height	28ft.
Bells 1	
Nave & Chancel Width	16ft. 9"
Chancel Length	23ft. 8"
Nave Length	48ft. 4"
Nave Wall Thickness. N. & S.	2ft. 9"

Standing well off the main Acle to Martham road, (B1152), on flat ground, this church can easily be missed. It has a round west tower with octagonal top, nave and chancel in one and south porch.

Few Saxon signs have remained, but I would place it in the middle Saxon period. The clear pointers are the long and narrow church and the Saxon style of walling. The nave and chancel as one rectangle is another sign of an early church. The one remaining Saxon window is in the north wall; it has a frame of selected flints, and is a narrow slit window.

The tower, that usually holds many early signs, fell into disrepair in Victorian times, and was heavily restored. Most of the internal surface from first floor level at least is brickwork, and so no early features are left. The three circular windows are Victorian, with dressed stone facings, and brickwork inside the tower. Can we believe that these replaced Saxon circular windows? The thought is there, but perhaps further research into records will give us a clue. The tower, showing a flat side internally to the east, tells us that it was built against an earlier church, which points once more to a pre-Norman dating. While we know that it was in very bad shape before the Victorian restoration, there is nothing to suggest that it was entirely rebuilt. Indeed, there is ample evidence that the base, up to the first floor is original. The wall thickness at the west window is only 3ft. 5" which is under the average for these towers, and so is another indication of Saxon age, while the diameter at ground level is just under 12ft . The circular section is 29ft. tall, but knowing the poor condition of the tower at this time, we cannot place any reliance on this as the original height of the tower. The modern octagonal top with heavy stepped battlements is obviously Victorian, and detracts somewhat from the character of the early church.

The main entrance in early days was on the north, and the road is still on that side. The stoup is still just inside the north doorway, and the Norman north doorway is the richer of the two, confirming this . The jambs of this doorway have an engaged column on either side, and a square section with three-quarter-round moulding inside these. The capitals are fluted, but this is restored work. The bases of these columns are carved and they rest on a plinth peculiar to many churches in the Waveney Valley. The arch has zigzag moulding and a restored arch of billet moulding.

All the external wall facings appear to be of a similar date and show little signs of alteration over the years, which gives good grounds for believing that all the walls may belong to this period.

The one bell is dated 1838, but it has no other inscription. There are 11 votive crosses, 3 on the L/H jamb and 8 on the R/H jamb of the south doorway. Two scratch dials were seen at the porch entrance, one only 2 inches across.

N21. COCKLEY CLEY. All Saints.

D6. Sheet. 144. Map Ref. T.F. 791 042
Church Early SAXON. Tower Middle SAXON.

Tower Height (before fall)	48ft. 6"
Height to Base of Parapet	44ft. 6"
Internal Diameter Grd:	8ft. 6"
Tower Wall Thickness	3ft. 8"
Nave Ridge Height	35ft. 6"
Bells 1	
Chancel Width	18ft. 5"
Nave Width	18ft. 7"
Nave & Aisles Width	50ft.
Chancel Length	32ft. 3"
Nave Length	34ft. 11"

On a small knoll overlooking the river, All Saints is one of three churches that were in this village. St. Peter's at the east, All Saints at the west, and S/E of All Saints is the small chapel of St. Mary, now unused. All Saints consisted of a round west tower with octagonal battlements, nave, chancel, north and south aisles and south porch.

Prior to 29th.August 1991, the tower was constructed almost entirely of flints of average size, mainly from chalk beds. There were two bands of cut flints as decoration at about 10ft. and 20ft. from the ground. Otherwise, the flints were whole. The battlements were octagonal of 1866, but below them the tower was circular. The four belfry windows had Y-tracery, but these were also a reconstruction from the 1866 restoration, although much of the early stone was reused. Below the belfry stage, near the top decorative band of flints, on the west, was a round-headed slit window. Below this, on the ground floor was a 14th. century ogee-headed single-light window, and on the south, a similar but smaller window .

Not noticed by me, or recorded by any writer, is the possibility that there were one or more Saxon circular windows in the tower. My photo of 1976 shows fairly clearly, that just above, and slightly to the left of the upper slit window, a circle of flints, laid differently from the general pattern, and round this is another circle of longer and selected flints. The height is where we would expect to see Saxon circular windows. Further to the south, there was another possible blocked circular window. Unfortunately, none of these sections were recovered to give us positive evidence of the windows.

Inside, the tower was circular, but like a number of others, it was built against an earlier church. The measurement over the tower doorway was 2ft. 7" against 3ft. 8" at the west window, which helps to prove this point.

The tower fell without warning at 9pm. on 29th. August 1991 with another fall three-quarters of an hour later. On the south, only about 2ft. of the wall remained, while on the north, very little fell. It was found to be so unstable, that it had to be removed to the height of the nave ridge.

Examination of the remains showed clearly that the tower was indeed later than the nave west wall. At eaves height on the south, an area of about one square yard was completely flat as if troweled, and just above and below this area, the flints had come away in a straight line, indicating different building dates of church and tower.

CHURCH:- The roofs are of tiles and the walls are constructed of whole flints, with the quoins and buttresses faced with dressed stone. How much of the original walls remain beneath the Victorian facings it is hard to say. The rector told me that the church was almost rebuilt round the 14th. century arcades in 1866 to 68. In most cases where records talk of a rebuilding, they mean a major reconstruction and not a demolition of the walls.

The nave and chancel conform to Saxon widths, so the walls might well be that early, although refaced. The chancel appears to have been restored in Early English times with five lancets to the north and five to the south. They have been restored on the outside, but can we trust the inner frames to be original? Both aisles appear to be 14th. century with quatrefoil piers and fillets, but only the south is genuine; the north is a copy from 1866. The 15th. century gave the church a clerestory and south porch, but the clerestory was removed and new roofs put on in 1866 and the porch restored.

We can see that the tower doorway and the tower are not central with the nave, but are slightly (about 2ft) to the north. Was the nave widened by such a small amount, or was the tower, for some reason, built off centre originally? While Gayton Thorpe, only 10 miles away had its nave widened on the north by 3ft. to get more room, it was then made 22ft. wide. It seems very unlikely, that a nave would have been widened by so small an amount to finish under 19ft. wide. We are left therefore, to conclude that the church was NOT widened, but the tower and doorway were built north of centre.

N22. COLNEY. St. Andrew.

H6. Sheet 134. Map Ref. T.G. 181 080

Tower and parts of Nave Walls Late SAXON.

Tower Height approx.	55ft.
Internal Diameter Grd:	12ft.
Tower Wall Thickness	3ft. 5"
Bells 2	
Chancel Width	20ft.
Nave Width	18ft.11"
Chancel Length	24ft.10"
Nave Length	41ft. 9"
Nave Wall Thickness	3ft.

On quite flat ground, with few houses close by, the church is now in a slip road since the B1108 road has been widened. It has a round west tower, nave, chancel and south porch.

This is another church where the zeal of the Victorian restorers has removed or covered many of the early features. The tower is battlemented and circular for its full height of about 55ft. The internal diameter is 12ft. and with walls only 3ft. 5" thick, there are good grounds for thinking of it as a Saxon tower. The proof of its Saxon origin are the three round-headed double-splayed windows at first floor level, at north, west and south. Only the outer splays remain open, but these show clearly that they were built entirely of whole flints. The four belfry windows are single-light Early English, and the ground floor west window is a modern round-headed window. The tower is constructed of whole and cut flints, but the surface does not appear to be original, as many small pieces of cut flints have been added to the surface. The tower is not sectionised in any way. There are fillets here between tower and church, but they are not of the usual quarter-round shape, more like pilasters, being 25 inches long and 5 inches deep. There appears to have been a 4 inch plinth round the base of the tower, for the flat pilasters seem to rise from this plinth which shows beside each of them, although it has disappeared from the remainder of the base of the tower.

The tower arch, 6ft. 4" wide by 15ft. 6" tall, is Saxon in shape, but what we see is a modern pseudo Norman arch of the Victorian restoration, for John Gunn in 1849 saw a very different opening formed of flints, and some very rough pieces of stone to form the abacus.

No upper doorway is visible from the nave, but the carved eastern wall of the tower on the ground floor shows that the tower was built with the church. Looking for confirmation of this, we see that the S/W quoin is modern dressed stone, but the N/W corner appears to be original and built of flints and brick, with some pieces of sandstone, now dark grey, which may be discoloured carstone. This confirms the nave west wall and at least part of the north wall are Saxon. Looking at the south wall, we can see a blocked up window just to the east of the south porch roof, with its head arched in early brick. This is where a number of Saxon circular windows have been found. The Taylors noticed a vertical line at the buttress to the west end of the chancel where a later chancel was built on to the Saxon nave.

The north wall of the nave contains one Y-traceried window of Early English date, while most of the remaining windows of the nave and chancel are from the Decorated period (14th. century) although much restored. The east window however is Victorian in the Perpendicular style .

More evidence of Saxon work might be found if we could ascend the tower .

N23. CRANWICH. St. Mary the Virgin.

C7. Sheet 144. Map Ref. T.L. 783 948

Tower and Church Middle SAXON

Tower Height	47ft. 6"
Internal Diameter Grd:	7ft. 6"
Tower Wall Thickness	3ft. 2"
Bells 1	
Chancel Width	15ft. 2"
Nave Width	15ft. 3"
Chancel Length	31ft.
Nave Length	34ft. 8"
Nave Wall Thickness N. & S.	2ft. 9"

This church, in a circular churchyard, places the site almost certainly in the pre-Christian era. It is situated in open countryside, but curiously hidden from the main road by a group of trees. Very few houses are near, in fact the population of the hamlet is only about 40 people. The church consists of a round west tower, nave, chancel and south porch .

This church is recognised by all as Saxon, so our efforts will be directed towards dating it closer, and recording the Saxon features more fully. This tower is constructed of whole and cut flints and is uncoursed. It tapers slightly as it rises, and inside is a very poor circle, indicating it is one of the earlier towers. There is a decorative band of conglomerate (not carstone) as noted by most writers, just below the west window at about seven feet up. the battlements are later, but all below these are of pre-Conquest date.

In all, there are four belfry windows, four circular with a knot design, one west window on the first floor, now with a dressed stone frame, and a west Bull's-eye window on the ground floor. The four belfry windows are round-headed and built entirely of flints, with the exception of some pieces of dressed stone that have been inserted for repairs. It can be seen on close inspection, that the triangular-headed eastern window noted by the Taylors, is really round-headed like the rest, but it is a piece of dressed stone inserted for repairs that gives this impression. Inside, these windows are entirely flint with no splays. The four circular windows with a knot design, just below the belfry windows, are interesting, because inside, they are not really circular, but round-headed measuring 1.1m. by 1.1m. They are constructed entirely of flints, and their heads are set back on their jambs in true Saxon fashion. Were they the forerunner of the circular double-splayed window? Or just another of the Saxon builders 'experiments? The outer faces of these windows, which are circular, are closed with a single dressed stone slab carved with a knot design, that is called Saxon by all writers. Being always sceptical of Saxon carving in this area, I wonder if they could be later insertions of late Saxon or Saxo-Norman date? For dressed stone must have been very rare in this area when this tower was built. At first floor level, 20ft. up in the west face is a round-headed window, built like the others with a set-back head, but taller; this now has a dressed stone frame to the outer face.

On the same floor, is the church clock which has a diamond face coloured blue. It was restored between 1975 and 77 and is now working. The clock bell and striker, now repainted and mounted on the roof no longer chimes the hour. The circular Bull's-eye window on the ground floor, which up to 1977 had three steps to its sill, now has a steeply splayed sill after the 1977 tower restoration. Inside, the tower is cement rendered to a height of 5ft. 6", and above this is the rough flints. The tower arch is round-headed and once more is built of flints; it measures 12ft. 6" tall by 4ft. 3" wide, and the return wall is 4ft. 2". It is partly closed in and plastered on the nave side, and fitted with a modern door. There are no steps or ledges to thin the tower walls inside or out, and no fillets between tower and church. The tower walls however, splay into the nave west wall giving a horseshoe plan.

The one bell is inscribed "THOMAS NEWMAN OF NORWICH MADE ME. 1744." Below the belfry windows are two beams of an old bell frame. One is inscribed:- "THOMAS ADAM LADMEUP 1682". The other has at the L/H end:

RICH[d]) CW
NEWELL) 1719
and at the R/H end:- WILL MAIER AND
ROB POLLE CW

The build of the walls is very similar to that of the tower, being uncoursed whole and cut flints. The measurements given for the nave walls at the head are those at ground level, but these narrow by steps or ledges. The south nave wall has a 5" ledge at 4ft. 4" from the ground, reducing the wall to 2ft. 4" . To the west of the south porch there is a second ledge slightly higher up. On the north wall this ledge is only 2ft. 9" from the ground, and one can speculate as to why these should be at different levels. The tops of these ledges are covered with dressed stone, but we can regard this as later treatment to keep the walls dry. There are no ledges to the chancel walls which are only 2ft. thick.

The Taylors regard these offsets as added features, probably because of the dressed stone quoins, and the capping of these ledges. However, they regard the S/E quoin as probably original above the offset. It is here that I differ from their assessment. for I believe that ALL the dressed stone quoins were fitted later to the original flint walls that had their ledges from the time of their building. Evidence of this can be found at the base, where the corners are of flints.

The nave has two double-light Perpendicular windows on the north, while on the south are Decorated windows, one of three-light, one double-light and one single-light. The chancel windows are all Early English with Y-traceried heads to north and south, and a three-light intersecting window at the east. Although no Saxon or Norman windows remain in these walls, the thickness and construction alone is sufficient to class them as pre-Conquest. The north nave door is blocked, but has a Gothic head, the south doorway inside the porch is Norman of a simple style but with dog-tooth moulding on the outer arch.

The church clock was made by Tucker renowned for his clock making, and another of his clocks is in the tower of Great Leighs in Essex. In 1972 the church roof of slate was in very poor condition. The hamlet is very small, yet they decided to return the roof to thatch. Now this delightful church looks even more splendid with its traditional roof, completed in 1974.

N24. CROXTON. All Saints.

E8. Sheet 144 . Map Ref. T.L. 874 866

Church Early SAXON. Tower Middle SAXON. on Measurements only.

Tower Height approx. with spire	55ft. 6"
Tower Height approx. without spire	40ft. 6"
Height of Circular part	30ft. 6"
Internal Diameter Grd:	8ft.11"
Tower Wall Thickness	3ft. 9"
Bells 1	
Chancel Width	16ft. 6"
Nave Width	15ft. 9"
Nave & Aisle Width	29ft. 1"
Chancel Length	25ft. 9"
Nave Length	37ft. 7"
Nave North Wall Thickness	2ft. 7"

This church stands quite high in relation to its surroundings, but like so many more, it is not on the crest of the hill. It is on the north side, just below the top with the village below it. It has a round west tower with an octagonal belfry and spire, nave, chancel, south aisle, north transept and south porch.

The tower is constructed of whole and cut flints with a few pieces of stone inserted as repairs, or they may be erratics. There is a plinth at the base of the tower about 4" deep and 2ft. 6" high; and only one window below the belfry stage. This is a lancet window on the ground floor in the west face. The octagonal belfry has four double-light Y-traceried windows which seem to be of late 13th. century date. There is also a clock with one face that looks northwards towards the village. Above the octagonal section is a tall octagonal spire covered with slates in the Essex style, and I believe the only one like it in Norfolk. This tower had a shallow slate cap in Victorian times so the spire is quite probably a late Victorian restoration. There is no stair turret or fillets to this tower, which has a straight eastern side, and this implies that the tower was built against an earlier church. There are no definite signs of an upper doorway, but there is some disturbance at first floor level, and the clock mechanism is close to the east wall, so we cannot be sure on this point. The tower arch is tall with a pointed head.

The external roofs which were slate were changed to tiles on the nave in 1978. The walls are of whole flints and the S/W quoins are of dressed stones, but the other corners are now covered with buttresses. The clerestory windows with brick frames over the south aisle are 15th. century, but the aisle beneath it is Victorian, as the earlier aisle was removed many years before. No scratch dials or votive crosses were seen.

There is a south nave and south priest's door, but strangely not a sign of a north doorway, although the village lies that way. The nave has a single hammer-beam roof' which Cautley tells us is late, and in the north transept is one of Ladbrooke's etchings of the 1820's that shows the great alterations since his day.

The chancel here is again wider than the nave by 9". The tower is quite narrow with an internal diameter of 8ft. 11" and the wall thickness of 3ft. 9" is about average. No early signs have been left here before the late 13tn. century, but the measurements tie up with those of the Saxon era so well, that there is little doubt that it belongs to the date given.

N 25. DENTON. St . Mary.

J8. Sheet 156. Map Ref. T.M. 286 873

Tower Norman and Victorian, Church Decorated

Tower Height	57ft.
Height of Circular part	40ft.
Internal Diameter Grd:	12ft. 6"
Nave Ridge Height	40ft.
Bells 3	
Chancel Width	21ft. 1"
Nave Width	21ft. 1"
Nave & Aisles Width	45ft. 2"
Chancel Length	46ft.10"
Nave Length	49ft. 2"

From the lych-gate at the west, this church shows a Victorian square tower of red brick. There is no sign from this angle of the original round tower, part of which can be seen from the north and south. The church consists of a west tower, nave, chancel, north and south aisles, north porch and south vestry .

The round tower that was here fell and was replaced with a square tower of brick in Victorian times. The east side of the round tower however remains, but it has no distinguishing features, so presumably it is Norman, for we can tell that it was wide, though not as wide as Wortham. The diameter given at the head is in the square section, and we can see that the round tower would have been wider than this, but there is not enough left to give a definite diameter. There are three bells in the tower and a clock that faces north and west in the square section. The three belfry windows at north, south and west are double-light with ogee heads. There is a round-headed slit window in the east side of the upper square section, and a three-light Gothic/Victorian window in the west face over the west doorway. There are battlements but no spire or weathervane. No upper doorway remains, but the tower is curved towards the east, so it was built with the church of its day.

The whole church would seem to have been completely rebuilt, for there is no sign of any features before the Decorated period, and very few alterations after this until the Victorian restorations, which appear to have done little beyond repairs. The arcades and chancel arch are apparently the same age and would seem to be 14th. century Decorated, with the windows of both aisles being of this style with the exception of two three-light windows in the south aisle which were altered in the following century. The chancel has five double-light Y-traceried windows, again of the 14th. century, but all these windows have undergone severe restoration and some may be Victorian copies. No scratch dials or votive crosses were seen.

N26. WEST DEREHAM. St. Andrew.

B7. Sheet 143. Map Ref. T.F. 667 021

Tower Middle SAXON. Nave west wall Early SAXON .

Tower Height	47ft. 6"
Height to top of cap	50ft.
Height of Circular Part	33ft.
Internal Diameter Grd:	17ft. 4"
Tower Wall Thickness	3ft.11"
Nave Ridge Height	34ft. 6"
Bells 5	
Chancel Width	20ft. 6"
Nave Width	23ft. 3"
Chancel Length	33ft. 3"
Nave Length	51ft.10"
Nave Wall Thickness N. & S.	2ft. 6"
Nave Wall Thickness West	3ft. 3"

This unique and interesting church stands on raised ground, but away from the present village. It has a round west tower with octagonal top, nave, chancel, south porch and north vestry.

This church and tower have no remaining Saxon or Norman features to point to, but only the wall thicknesses, and the Saxon workmanship and the instinctive feel when one has seen so many of these churches. I must however admit to some uneasiness at the width of the nave and chancel, for this is very unusual except in late Saxon times.

The tower and church are almost entirely constructed of conglomerate and not carstone as other writers tell us. This conglomerate is still turned up by local farmers when ploughing and explains why the carstone from near by Bexwell was not used. The Saxons were adept at using very local building materials and raising very sturdy and long lasting structures. Although none of the regular Saxon features show in this tower or church, and the diameter of the tower is quite large, I feel certain that we have here a Saxon tower built against an even earlier church .

On my second visit, the tower was being repaired and the two workmen who had just finished the octagonal belfry and had started pointing the circular part told me that the core of the tower walls was clunch (hard chalk).This was interesting, because I had seen this material used as a core in the walls of the tower and nave of St. Nicholas, Feltwell. I am certain that these building materials, conglomerate and clunch, being the main stones used, are sufficient to date this tower and church as Saxon. I doubt if the Normans would ever have built or allowed a church to be built with this crude material. Later buttresses have been added using this stone, but by then, men were willing to keep the character of this building.

The tower is built of large blocks of conglomerate, the Normans preferred small blocks, and it is quite large for a Saxon tower, having an internal diameter of 17ft. 4". There are several Saxon towers however at 12ft. 6". The tower wall is 3ft. 11" thick measured at the west window, which is only slightly over the average thickness. The circular part, which is 33ft. tall, would hardly have been tall enough for a tower in Norman or later times, as the later Saxon towers were already approaching 60ft. This tower shows clearly that it was built against an earlier church, by this I mean that the present church, or at least the nave west wall was here before the tower was built. Inside the tower, on the eastern side, it is flat as in other towers built on to an existing church. In this case, however, the flat wall extends to a much greater height. We can distinctly see the inverted V in the wall which was the outline of the original roof. This shows that the nave roof is now higher than the original building. Inside the octagonal parapet is a cap of red-brown tiles, another tower that keeps its conical shape in spite of its octagonal belfry. There are eight single-light windows, one in each face. Five bells are here, the large one is inscribed:- *"Robert Skelton Ch. Wlarden T. Osborn Fecit. 1785"*. The west belfry window has "Fred Robertson" nicely cut into a stone in the head of it This must have been an earlier mason working on the internal restoration, as the recent ones were only on external work. There are two other windows in the tower, the ground floor west window and one of the original belfry windows, again in the west face. The original north and south belfry windows are now blocked up, but inside the tower, the south window shows as an alcove with a round head, and the north window can be seen in outline.

Walking round the outside of the church, we can see that there are no fillets between tower and church and no stair turret. There is ample evidence of large restoration work in the 15th. century, for all the church windows are in the Perpendicular style. The nave windows have transoms, and the buttresses, also built at this time, are in conglomerate with dressed stone facings. The east wall is very much repaired, but when this was done is very hard to determine. The south priest's doorway was probably inserted in the 15th. century, but the head and some of the jambs are Victorian repairs.

No scratch dials or votive crosses were seen, but most of the church furniture is 17th. century.

N27. DILHAM. St. Nicholas.

J4. Sheet 133. Map Ref. T.G. 326 259
Tower and Church 1931

Tower Stump	
Internal Diameter	9ft. 2"
Tower Wall Thickness	2ft.11"
Bells 1	
Chancel Width	24ft. 3"
Nave Width	24ft. 3"
Chancel Length	26ft.
Nave Length	45ft. 3"

Well outside the present village, this rebuilt church stands on its old site, and rather isolated in quite flat countryside. It consists of a stump of a round tower, continuous nave and chancel, south porch and north vestry .

This church has had an eventful history and a surprising summary of it is told on two lead tablets and the account by Charles Cox in 1903.

A lead tablet on the return wall of the tower arch reads thus:-

TURRIS. ANTIQUA. DILHAMENSIS. QUADRATA. A. °DNI. MCCCLXXV AEDIFICATA. VETUSTATE. TANDEM. RUITURA. A. °DNI. MDCCCXXXV. DEMULITA. EST. ET. TURRIS. HAEC. ROTUNDA. A. EODEM. INCHOATA.
HICKS, DEACLE. AM. VICARIUS.
GUL: T: SPURDENS. LLB . CURATUS.
SHEPHEARD. THO. TAYLOR. AEDILIS
DIRUIT AFDIFCAT MUTAT QUADRATA ROTUNDIS=
A. TAWKE PERCUSS.

The translation by Revd. Dr. Edward Brooks, is as follows:"(This) ancient square tower of Dilham was built in 1375 on the pattern of the old, and at last fell into ruin in 1835 when it was demolished, and this present round tower begun in the same year.
Hicks Deacle MA Vicar
William T. Spurdens LL.B. Curate
Shepheard Thomas Taylor, builder; he demolished, rebuilt, and changed the square tower to round.
Tawke, Bellringer. (or Striker)"

Charles Cox tells us in *"County Churches Norfolk"* Vol. 1 . "The church of St . Nicholas is merely a small parallelogram of red brick with a line of flints at the base, and with windows that have wooden tracery .... Over the entrance is a tablet inscribed James Taylor, William Lyall, churchwardens, MDCCLXXV. (1775). The old church was rebuilt on the meanest lines, both within and without in 1775."

So this year the church was rebuilt in brick against the square flint tower. Within 100 years at 1835 the tower was in ruins, but a round tower replaced it; but by the end of the century this had also collapsed. We hear that the tower was used as a chimney for the church heating system, and perhaps this contributed to its downfall.

In 1931 the present church replaced the whole of the old building, including the stump of the round tower. A brief note in the *"Eastern Daily Press"* of 11th. July 1931 read:- "The present church is built of Clipsham stone".

The whole church is built of whole flints of even size, and Clipsham stone has been used for the facing of windows, doors, and corners. It is in the Perpendicular style. Munro Cautley tells us that some parts of the old roof have been retained.

So with the help of a number of people, the unusual history of this church has at last been told.

N28. ECCLES. St. Mary.

F8. Sheet 144. Map Ref. T.L. 019 894
Tower and Church Middle SAXON

Tower Height.	51ft.
Stone Course base of Belfry	36ft.
Internal Diameter Grd:	10ft. 2"
Tower Wall Thickness	3ft. 8"
Nave Ridge Height	29ft.
Bells 3	
Chancel Width	18ft. 6"
Nave Width	18ft.
Chancel Length	34ft.
Nave Length	51ft. 1"
Nave Wall Thickness	2ft. 2"

St. Mary's Eccles, near Attleborough, is in open and very flat countryside and quite near the Hall. It has a round west tower, nave, chancel, and north porch now used as a vestry .

There are three inscribed bells in the tower which is 51ft. tall. The top is circular with a flat lead roof and circular battlements. The four belfry windows are double-light with Y-tracery of the late 13th. century, but some of the tracery is broken. There are three lancets with hardly any splays at a height of 26ft. These are at north south and west, with rough stones and some very large flints used for the jambs. The inverted V heads are of two very rough stones and very large flints into the depth of the wall. These appear to be the early belfry windows, before the tower was raised in the Early English period. Internally also, in the ground stage are two fine sets of put-log holes. Outside, the tower is fairly well coursed with mainly medium to small whole flints. There are fillets to north and south of the tower, to height of about 10ft., but these could be repairs, or they may be the remnants of Saxon fillets. There is no upper doorway, but the tower is curved on its eastern wall which implies the tower and church were built together. The tower has an internal diameter of 10ft. 2" and a wall thickness of 3ft. 8" both about average for Saxon times. The tower floor is one foot higher than the nave. Inside the tower on the south side, in the ground floor stage, is an alcove with a triangular head made of two rough stones, but it is only 20 inches wide, so it seems too narrow to be a doorway, but is it a benatura? The belfry stage appears to have been added to a lower tower, as this stage is the only part to be clearly different. The lower tower, and the possibility that the lower windows were the original belfry windows, would point to a Saxon dating.

This church once had a fine Decorated south aisle, but this was removed in 1730, and the south doorway re-set into the present south wall. The church has no south porch although this is the main entrance, but the north porch is now used as a vestry. The 14th. century chancel arch has cut into the south canopied niche of an earlier period, but the north one has escaped. The upper doorway of the Rood Stairs can be seen by the Rood beam, which is carved, and the lower doorway is outside the church, in what was the south aisle . T he arches have been filled in with red brick. All the windows were renewed in the Perpendicular period, but the east window was again restored in Victorian times.

There are no Norman features, and the evidence for Saxon workmanship is slight but clear cut. Nave width, and wall thickness is now well known to be a key factor, but the remains of the fillets is another. The tower however, gives the most positive evidence. The original very short tower, and the original belfry windows that were triangular-headed, and had flint internal frames is quite clear.

N29. EDINGTHORPE. All Saints.

J3. Sheet 133. Map Ref. T.G. 323 331

Tower and Church Late SAXON

Tower Height	55ft. 6"
Height of Circular part.	36ft. 6"
Internal Diameter Grd:	11ft. 10"
Tower Wall Thickness	4ft. 3"
Nave Ridge Height	36ft. 6"
Bells 2	
Chancel Width	16ft. 4"
Nave Width	23ft. 4"
Chancel Length	16ft. 7"
Nave Length	49ft. 3"
Nave Wall Thickness N & S.	2ft. 4"

This church is in a very isolated position, approached up a narrow track and the nearest house is at least half a mile away. Although the countryside appears quite flat, the church is on a slight rise, and quite a good view can be seen all round. The church has a round west tower with octagonal top, nave, chancel and south porch.

The base of the tower appears to have a Saxon style about it, for to a height of about five feet, there are some very large flints. There is a more selective approach above this, and bands of similar sized whole flints alternate with bands of cut flints, which is unusual for early Saxon towers. Some early bricks in the lowest 5ft. suggest repairs, and a few put-log holes framed in this early brick can still be seen in the lower parts. No fillets, and no Saxon windows are to be seen

The octagonal belfry stage is dated 1400,and has brick quoins that resemble Heckingham in Norfolk, and Ashby in Suffolk. The belfry windows are partly brick and partly stone, and date from the 16th. century. All these windows have suffered badly from the weather. The faces of the octagonal section are of cut flints with brick quoins. The ground floor west window is a single-light with a squared head of the same age as the belfry windows. There is one other window in this tower, facing south on the first floor; it has a frame of brick and may well date from the building of the belfry. There is also the strong possibility that it was one of the original belfry windows and made smaller with a new frame to light this floor.

There is an upper doorway 18 inches above the first floor, which places it 23ft. 6" above the ground. It is 7ft. 6" tall by 1ft. 9" wide. The jambs are a mixture of flints and early brick and the head is much later brick, so it has been drastically repaired. However, the presence of flints in the frame, and the very tall and narrow size of the doorway, point very firmly to a Saxon opening. The tower diameter at the ground is 11ft.10", while the wall at the west window is 4ft. 3" thick. Although this thickness appears to be Norman, there must always remain the possibility of refacing. This seems to be the answer, when we find that over the tower arch the wall is only 3ft. thick.

Turning now to the church, which Charles Cox says was rebuilt about 1400, giving as his reason the windows of the nave. I have repeatedly stated that far too much reliance has been placed on dating the walls from the windows, and it can be clearly seen here in the south wall of the nave, how one writer in haste has ascribed the windows of three centuries to the one date, and later writers have copied his error. If we examine the south wall of the nave, it is plain to see that to the east of the south porch, there is a 13th. century Early English window, followed by a 14th. century Decorated, and again followed further east by a 15th. century Perpendicular window. The various periods of these windows shows how improvements and alterations were made to these churches, as and when the money was available. The poorer communities were usually left with a church showing more of its ancient features.

This fine church still has its thatched roof to the nave, but the south porch and chancel are tiles. Munro Cautley wrote that he believed the nave had a single framed rafter roof, which if correct, would be a very early type. As this is covered by matchboarding, we cannot at present confirm or deny this view.

The wall thickness of the nave to north and south is only 2ft. 4", and the walling is of uncoursed flintwork, but although both these features occur in Saxon work, they also appear in the 13th. century. The width of the nave is also against a Saxon dating. The north doorway, called by Pevsner, 1190c. seems to me to be an early Norman doorway, altered in the Transitional period. The fact that there was a Norman doorway here, is proof of the wall being at least of Norman date, and the thickness must place it earlier than Norman.

One bell is dated 1621. There is one scratch dial on the R/H jamb of the south porch. Although slight, the evidence in both tower and nave, must be enough to say that we have here a Saxon tower and church.

N30. FELTWELL. St. Nicholas.

C8. Sheet 143. Map Ref. T.L. 713 909
Tower and Nave Late SAXON.

Tower ruined stump	
Internal Diameter Grd:	10ft.10"
Tower Wall Thickness	3ft. 6"
Chancel none	
Nave Width	20ft.10"
Nave & Aisles Width	44ft. 7"
Arcades Wall Thickness	2ft. 3"
North Aisle Wall Thickness	2ft. 6"
South Aisle Wall Thickness	2ft. 2"

This Saxon church stands on a sharp knoll at the west end of the village. It is now preserved by the *"Redundant Churches Fund"* and is under the wing of the lively *"Feltwell Archaeology Society"*.

The chancel was demolished in 1862 at the same time as the north porch. In 1897, while repairs were in progress, the tower collapsed. The workmen were just returning from breakfast when the collapse occurred, and if it had happened a few minutes later, serious injury and even loss of life would have been inevitable. The tower ruins enable us to see the construction of the walls as is not possible with a complete tower. The first thing we notice is the core, which is of large blocks of clunch (hard chalk) within the inner and outer face of conglomerate as at West Dereham. While on my survey in 1976 builders were stripping the east walls of the nave and aisles, ready for replastering. The early walls were seen to be made of blocks of clunch, as was the core of the tower. This would seem to place the tower and church in the Saxon period.

We can see plainly that the original nave walls were only 2ft. 3" thick, and there are faint traces of the old conglomerate quoins. The upper doorway has its jambs of clunch, and the tower walls are thinned by a ledge at first floor level which is typical of Saxon towers. The tower wall thickness at 3ft. 6" at the west, is only 3ft. 3" over the tower arch, and the round tower is a poor circle.

The tower arch is Norman and is dated 1072 and the dressed stone indicates that it was inserted into an earlier church that had no dressed stone. The six clerestory windows are Perpendicular of the 15th. century, but most of the other windows are Victorian copies or complete restorations. The most important feature remaining from the early days is a stone bench the full length of the north wall. In the days before seating, the congregation stood for the Mass, and these benches were for the very young and the infirm.

I am indebted to Mr. A. J. Orange, late Chairman of the Feltwell Archaeological Society for deciphering the flushwork designs between the clerestory windows on the south side. They are as follows:-

1. Purely ornamental.
2. "S" entwining a small "t" "Saint" surmounted by the crown (presumably of St. Nicholas).
3. John Do.) Church wardens or principal benefactors
4 & 5. Thomas Derye) at the time the 15th. century
) clerestory was added.
6. Chequered patterns in stone and flint; supposed to be part of the Arms of the great Earl Warren.

Little of the original nave is left save the west wall and the plan in outline, but we can see how later men built on to the humbler beginnings.

N31. FISHLEY. St. Mary.

K5. Sheet 134. Map Ref. T.G. 399 115
Tower and Church Early or Middle SAXON.

Tower Height	41ft. 9"
Tower Original Height	32ft.
Internal Diameter Grd:	6ft. 9"
Tower Wall Thickness	3ft. 6"
Bells 1	
Chancel Width	13ft. 9"
Nave Width Original	13ft. 9"
Nave Width Now	20ft. 4"
Chancel Length	20ft. 7"
Nave Length	27ft. 4'
South Nave Wall original	2ft.
North Nave Wall later	1ft. 8"

Fishley church stands isolated with only the Hall and a farm near by. It stands on slightly raised ground above the Acle marshes, and hides in an overgrown churchyard surrounded by trees. It consists of a round west tower, nave (widened), chancel, and south porch.

Taylor and Taylor dismissed any idea that it could be of Saxon date, but let us view this church more closely. Originally both nave and chancel were 13ft. 9" wide, but the need for extra space in the nave decided the parishioners to increase the width to 20ft. 4". This was done, not in the usual way with arcades of wall or pillars; this aisle, (for this is what it really is), has only a large wooden beam and one steel column about the centre. Really an aisle on the cheap.

So we had at the beginning, a nave and chancel, quite narrow and the same width. All the present quoins are of dressed stone, but the original quoins were of flints, and the extension of the west wall required for the aisle was built against these, and the flint quoins can still be seen. This extension then, was built before the other quoins were altered and is sufficient evidence on its own to say that this corner is Saxon. The original south wall which is only 2ft. thick must also be Saxon and it is very thin for a flint wall.

Turning to the tower, we see that the east side is curved, so quite possibly the tower and church were built together. The tower wall thickness at 3ft. 6" is again Saxon, and outside, the wall shows no coursing of the flints which are of all sizes and some are very large. This is quite a narrow tower internally of only 6ft. 9" diameter at ground level, with a step only 6ft. from the ground, opening the tower to 7ft. 6". At first floor level there appears to be another step to thin the walls once more. We can see the four original belfry windows at second floor level, 23ft. 3", which would give an original height of the tower as 32ft . These windows are 3ft. to 3ft. 3" wide by 6ft . 5" tall. The jambs and heads are of selected flat flints, and the heads are set back on the jambs. The west window is the best preserved; the R/H impost is a roughly cut stone with a crude chamfer on the underside, and the L/H impost is a natural stone with a slightly sloping underside. There is an upper doorway 2ft. 1" wide by 6ft. 6" tall; the head and jambs are of flints and the head is set back on the jambs by about 6 inches. This has been altered with early and modern bricks to fit a quatrefoil of four stones. The doorway itself is blocked with modern bricks. The tower arch is round-headed with simple imposts on the south with a chamfer below, but no impost on the north. The head is set back on the jambs about 4 inches, and the whole tower arch has a slight chamfer towards the nave. It is now all cement rendered so further features cannot be seen.

Inside this church all early traces appear to have been covered up by cement rendering, but as we have seen, enough features have survived to date this tower and church as Saxon. The original tower height of 32ft. places it and the church in the early or middle period 800 to 1,000.

All the windows are Early English without hood-moulds, and only minor restoration has been done on them. This again shows how little money has been available at this church over the centuries. All the windows are filled with Victorian glass. An alms box was constructed from part of an old bell frame. The south doorway is simple Norman, but only the three-quarter-round engaged column on the left seems to be original. The church contains no royal arms, hatchments, wall monuments, altar tombs or ledger slabs; surely, even if money was short, some of these would have been present? One wonders when the great clearance took place.

N32 . FORNCETT. St. Peter.

H8. Sheet 144. Map. Ref. T.M. 165 928

Tower, Chancel and parts of Nave Late SAXON.

Tower Height	61ft.
Original Tower Height	58ft.
Internal Diameter Grd:	11ft.
Tower Wall Thickness	4ft. 3"
Nave Ridge Height	34ft.
Bells 5	
Chancel Width	15ft. 4"
Nave Width	21ft. 6"
Nave & Aisles Width	43ft.
Chancel Length	30ft. 2"
Nave Length	38ft. 10"
Arcade Walls Thickness	2ft. 9"
Chancel Wall Thickness	2ft. 7"

St. Peter's stands in very flat countryside and little higher than the small stream that flows about half a mile away to the south. It has a round west tower, nave with north and south aisles, chancel and north porch .

This late Saxon tower, pre-Conquest for 58ft. of its height, as witnessed by the eight circular double-splayed windows below the later battlemented parapet (frontispiece). This parapet of dressed stone and knapped flints is Victorian, for it was at this time, the upper circular windows were discovered, and the west belfry window was changed from being Perpendicular, to its present pseudo Saxon; albeit, with round heads instead of triangular. We should also note that in Blomefield's *"History of Norfolk"* published in 1736, he records, "St. Peter's Forncett, has a steeple round at the bottom and octangular at top". So this tower must at that time, have been the tallest round tower of them all.

The flints of the tower are selected and neatly coursed, a sign of the developing skills of the Saxon builders, or of a recasing of the tower. Below the ring of eight circular windows, are the four double-light Saxon windows, save the Victorian copy on the west. The other three, with double triangular heads, resting on a through stone, which in turn rests on a central baluster with simple base and capital; the jambs as usual in this area, are constructed of flint rubble. Lower down, are four slit windows, at N/W, N/E, S/E, and S/W. These windows are framed in flints, and have round heads. Below these, are three circular double-splayed windows at North, west and south. Below the west circular window is another round-headed window, with its head formed of early bricks or tiles. This is above the west doorway, and it lights the ground floor of the tower.

The tower west doorway has seen at least two major alterations since the Saxons built it, for Ladbrooke 's sketch shows a Perpendicular doorway here in the 1820's which the Victorians altered to the pseudo Norman entrance we see now. That there was a doorway here from earliest times can be seen inside where the original Saxon opening can still be seen.

There are no fillets between tower and church, but straight vertical joints in the nave west wall indicate where the original Saxon wall stops and the later aisle walls start. In spite of the evidence of the Perpendicular windows, the widening of the nave by the addition of the aisles, was the work of 14th. century builders, as the arcades and aisle roofs will show. The 15th. century windows for the whole church were inserted in another major reconstruction.

With all these alterations, the chancel appears to have escaped lightly, as it is still the same width, and hence the same Saxon walls. See the signs of the blocked up Saxon circular window over the south priest's door.

The tall and narrow tower arch, built entirely of flints with only simple stone imposts, copies the interior of the west doorway, with the occasional brick or tile laid non-radially at their heads. A word here about the stone imposts, for here, as in so many other Saxon churches of East Anglia, no stone was imported, but erratics found locally were used.

There is a round-headed upper doorway in this tower, although none of the early writers mention this. It is blocked up and plastered on the nave side, and its size has been altered inside the tower, but parts of the Saxon frame can still be seen.

N33. FRAMINGHAM EARL. St. Andrew.

J7. Sheet 134. Map Ref. T.G. 277 028
Tower and Church Middle SAXON.

Tower Height	40ft.
Tower Original Height	32ft.
Internal Diameter Grd:	8ft. 1"
Tower Wall Thickness	3ft. 1"
Bells 2	
Chancel Width at East	11ft. 5"
Chancel Width at Chancel Arch	14ft. 5"
Nave Width	16ft.11"
Chancel Length	25ft.
Nave Length	30ft. 5"
Nave Wall Thickness N. & S.	2ft. 7"
Chancel Wall Thickness	2ft. 8"

Few houses are near this Saxon church that stands in flat surroundings. It has a round west tower, nave, chancel, south porch and north vestry.

Looking first at the tower, which with its cement coating, looks rather modern, we can see a number of Saxon features. There are flint fillets to north and south; quarter-round in section, that taper off at the top. The tower itself is quite oval, as can be seen inside, rather similar to the top at Howe. The curved eastern side, appears to say that tower and church were built together, although the Taylors believe that because the eastern side is thinner, the tower may have been added later. On the first floor we see an upper doorway 2ft. 4 " wide by 4ft. 7" tall, round-headed and built entirely of flints .

Ladbrooke 's print from the 1820's showing a tower of only about 30ft. in height with a conical cap, is confirmed inside the tower, for at 32ft. the tower wall thins appreciably. No signs of early windows now show in the tower, but the tower arch, at 4ft. 3" by 10ft. 7" appears to be Saxon in shape, in spite of the pseudo Norman dressed stones .

Turning now to the church, we find that all the nave quoins are of flints, with extra large ones cut to give a sharp corner below, and smaller flints above. These place all the nave securely in the pre-Conquest period. With a tower of 32ft. in height when built, we can place the tower and church in the middle period 900 to 950. The chancel quoins at the east end are dressed stone, and here we can see a change in the construction of the walls. The chancel is rather unusual, in that it narrows steadily from 14ft. 5" at the chancel arch towards the east end, where it is only 11 ft. 5". The north and south walls have pilasters of flints about half way along, 2ft. 4" wide by 4" deep; and a little to the east of these the wall appears to curve inwards as if it was the start of an apsidal end. Although there is no proof of this, from the number of East Anglian churches that had this feature, we can count this as a distinct possibility.

We can add to these Saxon signs, features that would satisfy even the most doubtful. Near the south porch is a blocked up circular window, and in the chancel are two open windows of the same type; one in the north and the other in the south wall. They are double-splayed, about 2ft. in diameter at the wall face and with a centre opening of about 9", they are built entirely of flints .

The south doorway, although Norman, has been fitted into a Saxon opening. It can be seen that it is much narrower than the usual Norman doorway. The north doorway that leads into the modern north vestry is also Norman, as is the chancel arch, which has Victorian arches on either side .

The Taylors' comments on this church, are interesting because they, in this one church, bear out my conclusions, drawn from so many R/T churches. Namely that the Norman builders would not use flints for quoins or windows when they had sufficient dressed stone to build and decorate doorways, and other internal features. It also illustrates, how so many, apparently Norman churches, with their doorways, are in reality SAXON, with Norman additions.

N34. FREETHORPE. All Saints.

K6. Sheet 134. Map Ref. T.G. 408 055
Tower and Church possibly Middle SAXON.

Tower Height approx.	30ft.
Tower with Cap approx.	36ft.
Internal Diameter Grd:	10ft.11"
Tower Wall Thickness	3ft. 6"
Bells 1	
Chancel Width	12ft . 4"

Nave Width	13ft. 4"
Nave & Aisles Width	29ft. 6"
Chancel Length	16ft. 5"
Nave Length	32ft.
Arcades Thickness	2ft. 8"

Standing at the west of the village street, this church was very much over restored by the Victorians. Nevertheless it still has a low round tower capped by a cone of red-brown pantiles, and some Saxon indications. It consists of a round west tower, nave, chancel, north and south aisles, north transept and south porch.

Let us look closer and see if we can find beneath the Victorian restorations what the early church was like, and if possible what original parts are still here.

First, the nave we see is very narrow, 13ft. 4" and although short, would have made a very reasonable Saxon church with the chancel slightly narrower. It is also reasonably tall for its width. The north and south arcade walls are quite thin at 2ft. 8" and if they are original are distinct Saxon signs. But as all the piers and arches are Victorian, it is doubtful if any except the ends are original.

Now we come to the tower; here is a short tower, probably not much altered until the Victorian restoration, or it would surely have been raised with an octagonal belfry stage. There are three-quarter-round fillets to north and south, joining tower to church, and these are seen on many Saxon towers but not on Norman. These point very strongly to a Saxon building. The height of the tower at about 35ft. would seem to be the middle Saxon period or 950 to 1,000. The conical top shows the shape of the roof from earliest times, although then, it would have been of thatch. I have not been able to examine the inside of the tower from the first floor as it requires a ladder of at least 20ft .

Therefore, a number of pointers are here for a Saxon dating, mainly the tower fillets, and the church measurements, but more work is required, especially on the inside of the tower. All the windows are from the Victorian restoration and are in the Early English style.

N35. FRITTON. St. Catherine.

I8. Sheet 134. Map Ref. T.M. 227 933

Tower and Nave Middle SAXON.

Tower Height	53ft. 6"
Height of Circular part	38ft.
Internal Diameter Grd:	9ft.10"
Tower Wall Thickness	4ft. 2"
Nave Ridge Height	26ft. 6"
Bells 3	
Chancel Width	18ft. 3"
Nave Width	17ft.
Chancel Length	24ft.
Nave Length	50ft. 7"
Nave Wall Thickness N.	2ft. 9"
Nave Wall Thickness S.	2ft.10"

The church stands at the end of a long lane on flat ground, and one of a group of six round tower churches. It consists of a round west tower with an octagonal belfry, nave, chancel, and south porch.

Very little has survived to date this tower and church, but there is enough to tell us that the tower and nave walls are Saxon. The first indication of a Saxon origin is the tall and narrow tower arch, almost certainly of flint rubble, although now plastered over. It is remarkably like the one at Tasburgh, not very far away. Above this, and 24ft. 6" from the ground, is the upper doorway. Only the lower part can be seen from the nave, and the rest is above the ridge, and can be seen blocked up from outside the church. It can also be seen on the second floor of the tower, and is 1ft. 7" wide by 3ft. 7" tall. The original head and jambs are gone, so it is no use for dating purposes, but it indicates positively that the church was always as tall as this, and the steeper pitch of a thatched roof would bring the upper doorway inside. The church had lost its thatched roof before Ladbrooke sketched it in the 1820's.

The tower is constructed of medium sized whole flints, uncoursed, and the circular part being 38ft. high would seem to place the tower in the middle Saxon period 900 to 1,000. The 15th. century octagonal stage has quoins of medieval brick and the battlements are somewhat later. Between the tower and church are one of the strongest Saxon features, namely fillets of whole and cut flints of quarter-round section that taper off at eaves height. Near the top of the circular stage, in the west face is a slit window framed in medieval brick and glazed, that has been reduced in size from one of the original belfry windows. The blocked up south belfry window can also be seen from outside. The ground floor west window was inserted in the Tudor period. The roof was relaid at the beginning of the century, and cast in lead is the following:- "J.T. Gibson, Plumber. Norwich. 1906". The three bells are said to date from the time of Edward IV.

This church has one of those uncommon chancels that are wider than the nave, although this is hardly noticed outside. The internal roof is a simulated tie-beam and king-post construction, but the tie-beams are many, and of small dimensions, and the king-posts are flat balusters and shaped with a slightly bowed centre.

N36. GAYTON THORPE. St. Mary.

C4. Sheet 132. Map Ref. T.F. 745 185

Nave and Chancel Early SAXON, Tower Middle SAXON.

Tower Height	48ft. 6"	Chancel Width	14ft. 4"
Height to Base of Belfry	38ft.	Nave Width	21ft.11"
Internal Diameter Grd:	9ft. 2"	Chancel Length	26ft. 5"
Tower Wall Thickness	3ft. 9"	Nave Length	38ft. 4"
Nave Ridge Height	31ft. 6"	Nave North Wall Thickness	2ft. 9"
Bells 2		Nave South Wall Thickness	3ft. 3"

Situated to the east of its small green in a raised and mainly circular churchyard, this village church has a round west tower, nave, chancel, south porch and north vestry (plate 3).

One bell in the tower is inscribed:- *"John Draper Made Me. 1624"*, and another 13th. century bell is in the vestry.

While all writers call this tower Saxon, perhaps too much emphasis is given to the two double-splayed windows in the west face, and not enough to the other pre-Conquest features. Professor and Joan Taylor noted in *"Anglo-Saxon Architecture"* that the upper window was not present in Ladbrooke's print of the 1820's and even if found later did not appear to be a reliable Saxon window, although they accepted the lower window as depicted by Ladbrooke. Then, Mr. C. Farrow, writing in the *"Friends of the Round Tower Churches Magazine"*, under *"The Round Towers of Norfolk Churches Before the 19th. Century Restorations"*, quoted the Taylors' and disagreed with their interpretation of Ladbrooke 's sketch, believing the window he drew was between the two we now see. Of course it could well be that these were found and opened during the 1880 restoration, as the tower appeared to be plastered when Ladbrooke made his sketch. Bearing this in mind, I will confine myself to other features in order to date this church and tower.

Contrary to most writers, the earliest part of this building is the nave, and although the S/W quoins are hidden by a later buttress, the N/W corner shows as a vertical line against some large carstone blocks where the nave was widened by about 3ft. This also explains why the tower is off centre to the nave. The chancel is almost certainly the same date, although there are no positive signs in the walls to date them. The width is under 15ft. and the walling being so similar to the south nave wall supports this view. The main entrance at this time was the west doorway, (for there was no tower). See how the tower covers part of the west archway, that is called Norman by some writers, but if this is so, how can the tower be earlier? Note the points that dispute a Norman dating. The main stone used is a light coloured carstone in large blocks. A stone that is very unusual for Norman builders, but the size is definitely wrong, for the Normans used small stones. Next, the imposts on the return walls are single stones, a Saxon feature against the Norman practice of using a number of small stones. Finally, the arch is built of narrow rectangular blocks of carstone, and not wedge-shaped voussoirs although they do lie in radial fashion. We can therefore reasonably date the church as early Saxon, before towers were common.

The tower was built on to the towerless church, as can easily be seen by where it covers part of the western arch. It is also plainly oval, which puts it firmly in the period of the early towers, 900 to 1,000. The upper doorway (plate 20) on the first floor at 15ft. 6" from the ground, also confirms the Saxon date of the tower, for it would not have been necessary before the tower was here. It is triangular-headed and built entirely with flints that have not been selected for flatness as was the usual practice The head is set back on the jambs by about 3 inches, and it is 2ft. 8" wide by 6ft. 6" tall. Outside, the tower shows us more of its early features, for its base, for 6ft. to 8ft. is mainly large blocks of carstone and silver carr with also some conglomerate (plate 15). The ovality of the tower can be plainly seen to be carried right to the top, even of the Norman section. The silver carr, which I had previously believed to be erratics, was corrected by Mr. S. Hart, who said it was a fairly local stone, although the actual locality was unknown. The two stones now appear to be of the same family, but the silver carr lacks the iron oxides of carstone. The double-splayed round-headed windows previously mentioned, are plain to see in the west face, and I would think the upper one may have been opened out in Norman times in order to fit the dressed stone frame, and perhaps have it glazed. The lower one looks genuine, and we hope was found during restorations. In the Norman belfry stage, still circular, we can see the Transitional Norman windows, similar to earlier windows, but now with pointed heads. They are deeply recessed at about the centre of the wall, with two columns to each side and one centre column. These have capitals but no bases, and a round-headed arch with chevrons is over the complete window. The sills are deeply splayed and covered with stone or tiles as are those at Herringfleet in Suffolk.

While all the nave windows were altered in the 15th. century, the chancel retained one window from the 14tn. century and two from the Early English period. This is a very interesting church that will repay much further study.

N37. GELDESTON. St. Michael.

K8. Sheet 134. Map Ref. T.M. 395 923

Base of Tower and Church probably SAXON

Tower Height	42ft.
Internal Diameter Grd:	7ft. 2"
Tower Wall Thickness	3ft. 2"
Nave Ridge Height	31ft. 6"
Bells 1	
Chancel Width	18ft.
Nave Width	18ft. 3"
Chancel Length	26ft.11"
Nave Length	40ft.11"

The west end of the churchyard has been opened up in recent years, taking in part of the rectory garden and using this as a car park. This has opened up the west aspect of the church showing off the tower to its best advantage, where once it was hidden behind trees.

It consists of round west tower, nave, chancel, north transept and south porch. The church has been so over-restored that it is almost impossible to find any early features. The Church History states "Having fallen into dilapidation the church was extensively restored in 1864 to 66, mainly at the expense of the rector Daniel Gillett". Previous to this, in 1814 to 1815, because the tower had become dangerous, 16 feet of it was demolished and only 12 feet rebuilt. This would be the section from the base of the belfry stage. This restoration appears however to have been even more drastic, for at first floor level, 15ft. 3" from the ground, there is a complete circle of dressed stone, (masonry ties)

that obviously go deep into the wall, and this seems to be a bonding course, while an iron wall tie from north to south strengthens this belief. There is also the possibility that the tower was rebuilt from this height, yet the written evidence says it was from 30ft. or twice this height. Little wonder then, with so much repair, that there is no sign now of an upper doorway, or any Saxon or Norman features. With the tower wall at 3ft. 2" however, we can dream that it may have been pre-Conquest and hope for some early feature to come to light during some future repairs.

Two of the three bells were sold for £50, to help pay for repairing the tower in 1814. The remaining bell is dated 1513 and was from the Brasier Bell Foundry of Norwich.

The south porch was added in the 15th. century and the *"History of the Church"* again gives us a good clue to its date and probable donor, as it tells us Ralph Garney's coat of Arms is carved thereon. An unusual feature of the south porch flushwork, is that instead of cut flints, blue-grey slate is used within the dressed stone. Does this represent a Victorian restoration, or was this slate readily available when the porch was built?

The chancel was rebuilt and the north transept added during the 1864 restoration.

These then are what one can see clearly, but in spite of careful study, little of anything earlier can be found. No piscina or sedilia have survived, and all the windows are Victorian. The chancel roof is Victorian confirming a major rebuilding of this part, although the nave roof shows much earlier work. There is one interesting feature, however, from which we can read something of the earlier history of this church, and that is, the Holy Water Stoup outside the north doorway. It tells us that this was the main entrance in early days, and the roadway on this side tends to confirm this. But it poses us another question, as these features usually do. Was it built of flints to blend in with the wall? Or was dressed stone so scarce or expensive? We are left therefore with a tower only 3ft. 2" thick and a nave and chancel both narrow in the Saxon tradition, but even if they are Saxon, (and we have no proof), no identifiable parts remain.

N38. GISSING. St. Mary the Virgin.

H9. Sheet 156. Map Ref. T.M. 146 853

Tower and South Nave Wall Late SAXON.

Tower Height	54ft.
Internal Diameter Grd:	10ft. 8"
Tower Wall Thickness	4ft.
Nave Ridge Height	35ft. 6"
Bells 5	
Chancel Width	17ft.11"
Nave Width	20ft.11"
Chancel Length	27ft.
Nave Length	38ft.10"
Nave Wall Thickness N. & S.	3ft. 2"

Situated in its straggling village about 4 miles north of Diss, the church of St. Mary the Virgin consists of round west tower, nave, chancel, north and south chapels and north porch .

Its tower is considered pre-Conquest by all, except that Pevsner adds a question mark, for he says, Saxon foundations were found beneath the north porch. I do not know the extent or the description of these foundations, but unless we have definite indications that these were late Saxon, there is no reason they should alter our opinion of what we see in the tower. The Saxon period lasted from the 7th. until the middle of the 11th. century, and stone buildings were known from very early Saxon times, even if not extensive. We do not know if this church replaced an earlier one on this site, or if it was the first church on a previously inhabited site. Therefore, unless more precise information of these foundations becomes available, I consider the visible evidence to be the more important.

The tower wall thickness at 4ft. places it as one of the thicker Saxon towers, while the selection and even coursing of the flints place it in the later period, 1,000 to the Conquest. The three circular double-splayed windows built of flints, give us a definite pre-Conquest dating, while the double belfry windows are typical Norman. One point worth noting is that although we are told that all Norman windows are recessed, these, and a number of others are definitely not. There are no signs, inside or outside of any blocked up windows, so these may well be replacing the Saxon belfry windows and not a raising of the tower walls as sometimes happened. The only other window in the tower is more likely a Victorian copy than a true Norman window. The tower arch, which is tall and narrow in the true Saxon fashion, nevertheless has Norman style mouldings of the Victorian era. No upper doorway was visible from the nave or tower, although it appears one must have been here from the beginning. There are signs of a blocked up west door in the tower, another of those disappearing features.

The squared plinth of flints to tower and nave noted by the Taylors is on very few of the churches in the R/T group, unless of course they are now covered by soil, as most churchyards have risen considerably over the centuries.

The 15th. century north porch with a room over, strongly resembles the one at Roydon. The two chancel chapels, north and south, are Early English, note the two 13th. century arches leading into the south chapel, and although the north Kemp's chapel arcades have been altered to a single round-headed arch, the Early English windows with Y-tracery give us its date. Two windows of the 14th. century are in the north of the nave, while those on the south were altered about 100 years later. The nave still retains one of the finest double hammer-beam roofs to be seen in a village church and dates from the 15th. century.

Ladbrooke gives us the only proof we have of' the nave being pre-Conquest, with his illustrations of a circular window high up in the south wall. I cannot regard the long-and-short work as Saxon, because the stones are too small and there are a number of instances of similar work even in features that are indisputably 14th. or 15th century work. Therefore although I feel we can safely date the south nave wall with the tower, and most probably the other main nave and chancel walls follow the pre-Conquest line, how much is original we cannot say.

The south nave door is Norman, and over the arch is the carving of muzzled bear. At Pentlow in Essex there is also a muzzled bear over the Norman west doorway, and there is also a Kempe's chapel on the north side of the chancel. Charles Farrow, answered my query in the *"Friends of the Round Tower Churches Society Magazine"* Vol. 7 No. 6. by a reply in the following number to say that the muzzled bear was probably a Norman feature, as it appeared on a number of Norman doorways, and the two Kempes were entirely different families.

There is one scratch dial on the L/H jamb of the south doorway.

N39. GRESHAM. All Saints.

H2. Sheet 133. Map Ref. T.G. 167 386

Tower and West Wall Late SAXON.

Tower Height	50ft. 6"
Internal Diameter Grd:	7ft. 5"
Tower Wall Thickness	3ft. 8"
Bells 2	
Chancel Width	17ft. 7"
Nave Width	21ft.10"
Chancel Length	23ft. 8"
Nave Length	50ft.10"

This is one of the group of R/T Churches in the Cromer area, which for all its ancient past has very few cottages nearby. It consists of a round west tower, nave, chancel and south porch.

The tower is circular to the top with double-light Y-traceried windows in the 13th. century style, and Victorian battlements above. The flintwork is sectionised, showing the different materials used each season. We cannot however come very near to it actual date, as its original height and windows are no longer visible. Inside to the south can be seen an alcove where the original south doorway has been blocked up. The tower is circular inside, indicating that tower and original church were built together, so we can say after 950. But above the first floor, at 30ft., the tower has been strengthened internally by lining it with Victorian red bricks. No sign of an upper doorway is to be seen. The tower arch is from the Tudor period; wide, and with two engaged columns to each jamb, and fluted capitals. This is now closed with wood panels and a door.

The most interesting feature for my study was the west nave wall. This consists mainly of conglomerate with only a few flints, and the original Saxon quoins can be definitely seen about one foot in from the present corners. They are large blocks of this conglomerate and show distinct signs that they were laid in the long-and-short fashion of the Saxon builders. The north and south nave walls have much of the conglomerate from the original walls reused in them. While the nave has both 14th. and 15th. century windows, possibly dating the widening of the nave to the 14tn. century, the chancel still retains one late Early English window and one altered Early English or later window. With the chancel being under 18ft. wide, it is quite possible that this part of the building may remain at its original width.

The 15th. century south porch, faced with knapped white flints on the south, but with whole flints to east and west, has an upper room, similar to Sustead near by. Verdict:- Tower and west nave wall provides a positive pre-Conquest dating, but no other features to give the extent of surviving original walls.

There are two scratch dials on the R/H side of the porch entrance. Bells: One is large and the other is very small.

N40. HADDISCOE. St. Mary.

L7. Sheet 134. Map Ref. T.M. 439 969

Nave and Chancel Late SAXON. Tower Saxo-Norman.

Tower Height	52ft.
Internal Diameter Grd:	8ft. 6"
Tower Wall Thickness	4ft. 6"
Bells 5	
Tower Arch Width	3ft. 6"
Tower Arch Height	12ft.
Chancel Width	16ft. 9"
Nave Width	16f't.
Nave & Aisle Width	30ft. 4"
Chancel Length	36ft. 2"
Nave Length	53ft. 3"
North Arcade Wall Thickness	2ft. 9"
South Nave Wall Thickness	2ft.10"

This church stands on a cliff overlooking the marshes, on the Beccles to Yarmouth road. It consists of a tapering round tower, nave, chancel, north aisle and south porch .

In spite of its Saxon features, the tower is most definitely post-Conquest; and therefore Saxo-Norman, or Early Norman, which ever you like to call it. But it is not Saxon or pre-Conquest.

When this is fully realised, many other features of this group fall into place and we begin to be able to date them with some accuracy.

Starting with the tower (plate 7), we notice first, the 4ft. 6" walls. This is in the Norman tradition in spite of the Saxon features. The tapering shape is similar to Bawburgh although very few pre-Conquest towers use this method to thin the walls as the height is raised. The flints are all selected for evenness of size, and are laid evenly in courses, which started not from the Conquest, but from the Saxon period at the beginning of the 11th. century. We come now to the most positive and reliable factor in dating this tower to the latter half of the 11th. century, and much nearer to 1100 than the Conquest. The dressed stone, except where it has been renewed, is from Caen, and the builders were lavish in their use of it; note the stages of the tower divided by three stone string courses, almost unknown on round towers, except where an octagonal top or a parapet has been added. The 15th. century circular top is battlemented and has a chequer-board design of cut flints, separated from the belfry stage by a table course of dressed stone. The four Saxon style windows with double-triangular heads are entirely built of dressed stone (plate 24), and this is also returned on the inner face of the tower. Something never seen in Saxon work in this area. The jambs are carved with three-quarter-round mouldings with cushion capitals, and while some of the stone has been renewed, these windows are essentially the same as when the first masons built them. They have the typical double-triangular heads, with their centres resting on a through stone the length of the wall thickness. This through stone in turn rests on a baluster or column in the centre of the wall. Round the jambs and heads of these windows is the typical Norman billet moulding, and the windows rest on a stone string course. Below the belfry are two more stages, both with three round-headed slit windows. They are all identical, being of dressed stone and finished inside the tower neatly with the same material. They all have the single stone head referred to by the Taylors as Saxon, and they each rest on a stone string course. These windows are all placed neatly below the one above, at north, south and west. The lowest stage, which is about twice the height of the others, has a single-light west window, similar to, but larger than, those above, and again finished off internally with dressed stone. There are the usual fillets to north and south of the tower, once again using odd pieces of dressed stone instead of the usual flints.

A later stair turret has been added, to reach the first floor, and it is entered from the north aisle. The tower arch is built in the Saxon fashion, being tall and narrow and round-headed (plate 29), with the upper doorway above it in the same style. Both are fully faced with dressed stone. Measuring the wall over the tower arch, I found it was only 3ft. against 4ft. 6" at the west. This showed that in spite of being circular internally, it had indeed been added to a towerless church. Looking at the outside once more, it is plain to see that the tower is horse-shoe shaped, like near-by Hales.

Turning to the church, we note the narrow nave and chancel, and outside, there are dressed stone blocks in circles, where four circular windows pierced the chancel walls, two on the north and two on the south. Two can still be seen inside, but some years ago all four could be plainly seen, but either re-plastering or painting has blotted the others out at least for the present. These are not Saxon double-splayed windows, for they are too low down in the walls. They are single-splayed having a smaller circle outside. The outer stone faces have small rebates to take wooden shutters to keep out rain and wind. The Taylors write, there are signs of round-headed windows to be seen on either side of the east window. While these are no longer visible, probably through repointing, it does confirm the size and shape of this church from its earliest days.

These then are the Saxon features executed in the newly available dressed stone. The four circular windows in the chancel are not in the accepted Saxon style, the doorways are in the Norman style, although narrower than usual, and the south entrance is quite fine, with one engaged column at each jamb and a double row of stars. The inner and outer orders of the arch are chevrons with scallops in between. Over this doorway, and unique in Norfolk, is a carved tympanum, of a seated figure within a Norman arch; most probably *"Christ in Majesty"*.

The north aisle is quite early, note the five pointed arches cut through the old nave wall without the insertion of columns. Note also the arches are alternate plain and double-chamfered. Some writers believe that they were cut through at different times, but this seems very unlikely. All the windows to north and south were inserted in the 15th. century, while the east window is a four-light Decorated style window that was restored in Victorian times. The double piscina can be reliably dated around 1300, and the Norman north doorway has undoubtedly been reset in the later north aisle. We can confidently date the church as earlier than the tower on several features. The much thinner tower east wall, the nave width at 16ft. and the nave wall thickness at 2ft.10" which is Saxon compared to the tower wall thickness which is definitely Norman. The Norman doorways and the four circular windows are insertions.

N41. HALES. St. Margaret.

K7. Sheet 134. Map Ref. T.M. 383 961

Church Early SAXON. Tower Middle SAXON.

Tower Height	54ft.
Internal Diameter Grd:	11ft. 4"
Tower Wall Thickness	3ft. 8"
Nave Ridge Height	36ft.
Bells None	
Chancel Width	12ft. 11"
Nave Width	15ft. 9"
Chancel Length	23ft. 2"
Nave Length	43ft. 4"
Nave Wall Thickness	3ft.

Four miles from Reedham ferry, and 3/4 mile south of the village, the small church of St. Margaret stands on the north side of a small hill. It consists of a round west tower, nave and apsidal chancel.

This church is called 12th. century by every guide book, while Taylor and Taylor, in their *"Anglo-Saxon Architecture"* refer to it as Saxo-Norman. So what is its true age? Almost all the dressed stonework is Norman, and can safely be dated fairly close to 1150. But, with the massive supplies on hand at this time, what explanation can there be for the two circular windows in the tower (plate 26), and the triangular-headed upper doorway (plate 17), all constructed without single piece of dressed stone. Let us therefore look closer at this tiny church.

The tower is flat on its eastern side internally, and the horse-shoe shape outside also speaks plainly of the tower being added to a church already here. This simple church has kept its early identity, I believe because the parish has never been very wealthy. Its one moment of glory, must surely nave been about 1150 when the Normans, at the height of their masons' art, carried out their massive restoration.

The towerless church was doubtless built well before 950, for in 936 Athelstan ordered the building of a bell tower on the land of every Thegn. We can see clearly that the tower was added to the nave west wall, for this wall shows as a flat wall inside the tower. All the church walls are of similar construction, and apart from repairs, all show the Saxon hallmark of flints of all sizes, with no coursing and masses of mortar between the flints. Therefore, the shape, and especially the narrow church place it clearly in the pre-Conquest period, and the date is fixed by the dating of the tower.

Turning to the tower, we have more concrete evidence, for at 19ft. from the ground inside, we can see the inner splays of two circular double-splayed windows at north and south respectively. They have an outer diameter of 2ft. 6" reducing to 6 inches at the centre of the wall. The outer splays have long since been blocked up. The interesting feature of these windows is the fact they still show the basket-work pattern of how they were made, impressed in the original mortar, and are probably the only two so well preserved in the country. On the first floor, at 22ft. from the ground, on the east side, is the upper doorway. Of typical Saxon construction, it is 1ft. 6" wide by 4ft. 2" tall. Built entirely of selected flat flints, and with a triangular head. This head is set back 3 inches on the jambs, where the boards rested while the mortar set. Like the circular windows, the original mortar survives and shows the marks of the boards used for shuttering.

Three round-headed windows are on this floor, now of Norman style with dressed stone frames, while on the next floor there are three windows, showing outside as pointed heads, but inside, they are plainly, the original Saxon belfry windows; round-headed, and built without any dressed stone. This short tower then, built on to a towerless church helps us to date the tower from 900 to 1,000, which in turn dates the church from 800 to 900.

The present belfry windows are Early English, so it is reasonable to suggest that the tower was raised to its present height at this time. The belfry windows are interesting, because on the north side there is one, and this contains an odd piece of stone from an ogee arch. The east and west have two windows, and the south has none; the one here has been blocked up. The plain parapet has a pleasing decoration of chequer-work in black and white cut flints and some early red bricks.

The wide Norman tower arch was blocked in with red bricks when the gallery was built in the 18th. century. However, a little unusual billet moulding can still be seen each side at the imposts of the arch.

Moving on now to the church, the overwhelming impression is of Norman work. But if we can visualise this tiny church with flint framed windows and doorways, we can understand why the great transformation took place around 1150. The magnificent north and south doorways were inserted, see *"Anglo-Saxon Architecture" by Taylor and Taylor*. They are well documented in many other books, notably in *"Memorials of Old Norfolk"*. The Saxon pilasters round the apse were faced with dressed stone and carved. All the windows were renewed in the Norman style, and a fine arcading, pierced in places by windows round the apse; and all finely ornamented. Even the crude flint corners of the church were replaced by the new dressed stone, and they were carved too; with three-quarter-round moulding which is very unusual. Only one of the Norman windows remain in the south wall of the nave; it is now blocked, but retains its full dignity. The arcading round the apse can be followed although it has been cut through in a number of places by the later windows.

The Early English period, when the tower was raised, must be blamed for cutting through this fine arcading to insert four new and larger windows in the chancel. The nave has a double-light Y-traceried window at the S/E corner, and although the north wall near the doorway has a somewhat similar window, I believe it was refashioned from a Decorated window as seen in the south wall opposite, because of the shape of the opening. Another single-light Decorated window completes the picture of this delightful church.

This is a good example of how a Saxon Church can become hidden beneath later alterations while still retaining its original shape entirely. Apparently the only alteration to the original ground plan was a north porch that we know little about except that it was pulled down towards the middle of the 19th. century because vagrants used to sleep there. How long the porch was there we do not know at present. The meagre notes I have on this porch were obtained from E. Thornhill's *"Historical Rambles in East Anglia"*.

The church is of further interest, because it has apparently never been seated by fixed benches apart from a few choir stalls. The body of the church is seated by chairs that are usually placed by the north and south walls, leaving the nave very much as it would have been in Saxon and Norman times. This was the first round tower church to be taken under the wing of the *"Redundant Churches Fund"*.

N42. HARDLEY. St. Margaret.

K7. Sheet 134. Map Ref. T.M. 386 007

Tower, Nave West and South Walls Middle SAXON.

Tower Height	44ft.	Nave Width	23ft. 7"
Internal Diameter Grd;	10ft. 7"	Chancel Length	27ft. 4"
Tower Wall Thickness	3ft. 3"	Nave Length	40ft. 7"
Bells 3		Nave South Wall Thickness	2ft. 7"
Chancel Width	15ft. 2"	Nave North Wall Thickness	2ft. 6"

St. Margaret's is quite near the marshes on flat ground, and not far from Langley Abbey that was founded in 1198.It consists of round west tower, nave, chancel, north porch and north vestry. The church is entered by the north porch, which is rather unusual but by no means rare.

The tower is not central with the nave, but is well to the south. This again is not entirely unique as several others have had their naves widened in this way.

The tower is said to be Norman, but I am convinced that it is Saxon for the following reasons:- The wall thickness is only 3ft. 3", quite thin even for Saxon builders, and the curved eastern side, tells us that church and tower were built together. Outside, we can see why the tower is off centre, for the nave was widened on the north side. We can still see the original Saxon N/W corner made of flints and erratics. This gives us a positive Saxon dating for the west wall and consequently the tower, as it also contains many Saxon features. At 22ft. from the ground there is a ledge or step that thins the tower walls still further, a feature that I have found only in Saxon towers. There is a blocked up upper doorway, but the original shape and size cannot be determined. The tower arch has been closed in towards the nave, but inside the tower it is quite tall, and although its head may have been altered, it is entirely of flints.

The tower is circular for its full height of 44ft. and the four belfry windows at the cardinal points are single-light lancets of the Early English period. The west one has been opened out and has a frame of red brick, probably a renewing of a damaged window. This brings us to an incident in November 1970, part of the tower facing the south west, from the parapet to the lower part of the west belfry window, fell, and it was feared the parish would not be able to repair it. This may have been the area that warranted the altering of the west belfry window many years ago. Early in 1972, however, the tower was fully restored. Bryant also records that the tower was formerly surmounted by pinnacles, for in 1503, a legacy was left to purchase pinnacles for "the stepeal of Hardley". Whether they were ever purchased we do not know, but there are no signs of them now.

All the windows of the church were altered in the 15th. century, and these Perpendicular windows flood the church with light, as there there only a few odd pieces of stained glass. While the nave was widened to give more room, the chancel, which also needed more space, used another method. They cut back the walls to north and south, in four large arches, to give more room for priests and choir. We therefore have convincing proof of a Saxon dating for the portion listed above, and the narrow chancel, with no proof of rebuilding, could also be of the same date.

N43. HARDWICK. St. Margaret.

I8. Sheet 134. Map Ref. T.M. 223 901

Tower and Church Middle SAXON.

Tower Ruins	
Internal Diameter Grd:	9ft.
Tower Wall Thickness	3ft. 9"
Nave Ridge Height approx.	30ft.
Bells 1	
Chancel Width	17ft. 8"
Nave Width	16ft. 9"
Chancel Length	36ft. 9"
Nave Length	41ft. 7"
Nave Wall Thickness N. & S.	2ft. 7"

This is another church that is called Norman by everyone and yet the Saxon features are plain to see. It stands in the well kept churchyard of its small hamlet on quite flat ground, two miles from Long Stratton. It is one of the Hempnall Group, and six of the eight churches have round towers. It has the ruined base of a round west tower, nave, chancel and south porch.

With this church we will start at the nave, for the N/W and S/W corners are of large flints, that place the nave west wall and these corners firmly in the pre-Conquest period. The thin nave walls also put them before the Norman south doorway, for Norman walls were always well over 3ft. thick. The south doorway appears to date from the early Norman period, and was altered during the Transitional period, for it has billet moulding to the outer arch (an early ornament), and one piece of dog-tooth moulding on each side, (a Transitional moulding of the 13th. century). We have further evidence that the church has not been rebuilt, for the entire church looks to be in the same fashion of whole flints of all colours, and with large mortar joints with no regular coursing. At no point does this walling appear to change. At some time the walls were cement rendered and scribed to represent stone blocks. This has now flaked off in most places enabling us to see the flintwork behind. Also, in the north wall, opposite the south doorway, is the first Saxon doorway I recognised in these R/T Churches, (plate 21) and one of only five that are not blocked. It is called Norman by all other writers I know, but a careful look will show that it is built entirely of flints except for the imposts that have a simple chamfer. Note also the semi-circular head is set back on the jambs by about 1 inch in the Saxon manner. Four iron ties have been put through the nave walls to hold them, but they still stand from their original building. The eastern corners are of dressed stone and are comparatively recent. The difference in width of nave and chancel, is found in many early churches where the walls are not parallel. The whole building is a rough rectangle.

Although only a stump of the tower remains, there are still surviving Saxon features, perhaps because it was in ruins, and therefore not restored as were many others. The stump has been roofed, and now houses the one remaining bell in a small bell frame, and rehung in 1985. We can still see that the tower was curved inside, and therefore tower and church were built together. Also the tower arch was quite tall, although its actual shape cannot be ascertained, for it has been closed in with laths and plaster. But its height lends more weight to the overwhelming evidence of a pre-Conquest building. Outside we can see there are three-quarter-round fillets between tower and church to north and south. These are further positive Saxon features, while over the roof of the tower stump we can see the blocked up triangular-headed upper doorway. There is a step in the tower wall externally at about eaves height to thin the walls, yet another feature that seems to be only in some Saxon towers.

N44. HASSINGHAM. St. Mary.

K6. Sheet 134. Map Ref. T.G. 369 055

Church Early SAXON. Tower Middle SAXON.

Tower Height approx:	46ft.
Circular Part approx:	35ft.
Internal Diameter Grd:	7ft. 2"
Tower Wall Thickness	3ft. 2"
Bells 1	
Chancel Width	14ft. 6"
Nave Width	14ft. 6"
Chancel Length	24ft. 7"
Nave Length	43ft. 9"
Nave Wall Thickness	2ft.10"

Built on a small knoll, but actually in a valley, this church has a round west tower with an octagonal top, a nave and chancel of the same width, a south porch and north vestry.

In August 1970 the thatched roof was destroyed by fire that also destroyed all the woodwork in the church and the window glass. None of the stonework was damaged however, and so we see the old church and tower with an entirely new interior decoration, that somehow does not blend in with the age of the church

The first indication of an early church is the very narrow nave and chancel, but while the nave walls appear early with their uncoursed flintwork, the cut flints of the chancel indicate that the walls have been refaced, if not rebuilt. Although it is in the tower that we see the earliest work, we should look first of all at the south nave doorway. This is early Norman, with an outer order of billet moulding and outside this is chevrons. So we know that the church dates from at least Norman times, but was it even earlier?

Norman walls were never under 3ft. thick, and with the narrow nave and chancel, we have the strongest evidence that these walls were built before this doorway. The tower is circular for about 35ft. of its height, a good indication that it is one of the early Saxon towers. Then it is octagonal for about another 11ft. It is constructed mainly of whole flints, with, some very large ones near the base, much like Repps, which is also Saxon. At the top of the circular stage is a dressed stone string course, above which is the octagonal belfry of the Early English period with four lancet windows. Rather tall battlements of a later date are faced with flushwork and are surmounted by stone crosses at the corners. There is only one window below the belfry stage which is the west window on the ground floor; this is a double-light window of the Perpendicular period. At the base is a plinth, but whether this is original is debatable.

No upper doorway could be seen from the nave, but the tower was straight on its eastern side, denoting it was built on to a towerless church. This points very strongly to a church of the early Saxon period with the tower being added about 50 years later. The tower arch is 5ft. 6" wide by 12ft. 6" tall; it is cement rendered and so one cannot say with certainty that it is constructed of flints, but dressed stone invariably shows itself. There are no fillets between tower and church. Not a lot of decisive evidence, but far more than there is for a Norman dating.

The church has little to tell us, for all the furniture is new and the walls have been replastered. Although the nave and chancel are the same width, the chancel roof is higher than the nave, rather like Syleham in Suffolk. The N/W and S/W quoins appear to be Norman on account of their small size, while below the lowest dressed stone at the N/W corner appears to be a large flint . This is the strongest feature yet, and repeats what has been seen at Ashby and Ilketshall St. Andrew, both in Suffolk, where these are the last remaining Saxon features to be left. This is a positive sign that the Normans replaced the flint corners with their dressed stone, but would not trust themselves to remove the lowest corner stone. The chancel walls are of all cut flints, and it would appear that this was rebuilt or refaced when the Perpendicular windows were inserted. The nave windows however, although Perpendicular in style, seem to date from Victorian times. There is one Early English lancet, the oldest window in the church at the at the S/W corner of the nave.

N45. GREAT HAUTBOIS. The Assumption of St. Mary.

J4. Sheet 133. Map Ref. T.G. 260 205

Church Early Saxon. Tower Middle SAXON.

Tower Height approx.	45ft.
Internal Diameter Grd:	8ft. 3"
Tower Wall Thickness	3ft.
Wall Thickness over T/Arch	2ft. 8"
Bells None	
Chancel Width	11ft. 2"
Nave Width	15ft.
Nave & Aisle Width	29ft. 9"

This church is on quite flat ground and not at present near any village. It consists of the ruins of a round west tower, nave, chancel, south aisle and south porch.

Only the chancel is roofed in red-brown tiles. The tower is Saxon and was added to an earlier church, as we can see, for the tower is straight

on its eastern side, and the wall over the tower arch is only 2ft. 8", the thickness of the nave west wall. The tower tapers all the way up and is circular at the top. No steps can be seen inside the tower to thin the walls, but they are very thin, even by Saxon standards at ground level. There is no sign of an upper doorway, or a ground doorway except the tower arch. This is round-headed and has no dressed stone in its structure. Bricks of about the 15th. century and some dressed stone have been used inside this arch to make it smaller and to fit a pointed door. Note the flints laid non-radially over the tower arch. The construction of the tower in of very large flints from chalk beds, with large mortar gaps from the base up to the first window. There are only two, and these are in the west face. The lowest is 10ft. from the ground, and above here the flints are mostly average, but a few very large ones are there also. The second window is about five feet above the first; they are both rectangular with a mixture of flints and rough stones for the frames. The lintel of the upper one is a piece of conglomerate, and the lower one has what is probably a Roman brick. These appear to be authentic, but repointing leads to some doubt. The four belfry windows are round-headed and framed with whole and cut flints and some conglomerate in the west, north and east. These are of Saxon date. The south belfry window has been lost. Above the belfry, the smaller flints and smoother finish denotes repairs, and probably a little extra height added at some later date.

The quoins tell us that this was a Saxon church, and we know it was built before the tower. The N/W and N/E quoins of the nave are of large blocks of conglomerate and similar walling past this point suggests that the present chancel was also built at this time. On the south, the S/W and S/E corners of the south aisle are also of conglomerate, and it would appear that these were reused from the old nave walls, as only an odd block or two are left in the nave west wall. It seems that dressed stone was till scarce when this aisle was added. One more query, three of the buttresses at the east end have large amounts of conglomerate in them. Was this just to harmonise with the existing materials?

The walls of the church are of whole flints with very large mortar joints. Very little more could be learned from these ruins except that the south aisle had been well filled with large monuments.

N46. HAVERINGLAND. St. Peter.

H5. Sheet 133. Map Ref. T.G. 151 209

Tower. Late SAXON.

Tower Height	52ft.
Internal Diameter Grd:	11ft. 2"
Tower Wall Thickness	3ft. 10"
Nave Ridge Height	33ft.
Bells 3	
Chancel Width	16ft. 8"
Nave Width	17ft. 5"
Total Width Nave & Aisles	40ft. 5"
Chancel Length	25ft. 10"
Nave Length	55ft. 5"
North Aisle Wall Thickness	2ft. 7"
South Aisle Wall Thickness	2ft. 11"

The church stands in open countryside away from the present village. It consists of a round west tower, nave, chancel, north and south aisles, north and south transepts and south porch.

Most of the early features have been lost in the 1858 restoration, but there are enough left to give us a pre-Conquest dating for the main parts of the tower and probably of the church.

The tower is circular to the top with battlements of the Victorian period. The height and construction would place this in the late Saxon Period 1000 to the Conquest. We can see the tower is sectionised, and there are quarter-round fillets between tower and church. The four round-headed belfry windows have Saxon jambs of large flints and conglomerate, cut straight through the wall without any splay. The heads, from and including the imposts, are Victorian restoration. Inside the tower, from the top of the bell frame, has been faced with Victorian red bricks. On the first floor are three round-headed windows with jambs of flints and conglomerate . More conglomerate is seen outside than inside with the splays. The heads have flints and tiles laid in non radial fashion, though the mortar round the heads has been renewed. The upper doorway on the east, which is blocked on the nave side, is similar to, and at the same level as the three windows referred to, but it has no splay and it is slightly smaller. None have the characteristic Saxon step at the imposts. The old tower arch is tall and narrow, and apart from the imposts, appears to have no dressed stone in its construction. It is now closed in by a Victorian dressed stone doorway and a door.

The Victorian restoration of 1858 has swept away all the ancient relics of the early church. There are no wall monuments, and only one ledger slab dated 1726. All the outside walls are faced with cut black flints, but I feel certain that this refacing does not mean a rebuilding of the chancel; and even the nave with its later aisles would never have been left a mere 17ft. 5" wide. When the aisles and transepts were added, it is impossible to estimate, also whether they were added piece by piece or in one go, for while the entire wall facing appears to be of one age (most probably Victorian) all the windows of the church, although in the Decorated style, are from the 1858 restoration also. We are therefore left only with the ground plan of the nave and chancel to infer that most probably this follows the original Saxon plan.

N47. Heckingham St . Gregory.

K7. Sheet 134. Map Ref. T.M. 385 988

Chancel, Nave and Base of Tower Early or Middle SAXON.

Tower Height	39ft. 6"
Height of Circular Stage	14ft.
Internal Diameter Grd:	8ft. 9"
Wall Thickness at T/Arch	3ft. 2"
Nave Ridge Height	30ft.
Bells 2	
Chancel Width	15ft. 4"
Nave Width	15ft. 4"
Nave & Aisle Width	29ft. 4"
Chancel Length	20ft. 4"
Nave Length	40ft.
Nave South Wall Thickness	2ft. 11"
North Aisle Wall Thickness	2 ft. 4"

This church is situated on a small knoll next to a farm and sharing with the farm a narrow rutted lane. It consists of the base of a round west tower with an octagonal top, nave, apsidal chancel, north aisle and south porch.

This church is quite obviously a sister church to Hales, with their similar Norman doorways and their apsidal chancels; nevertheless they look decidedly different. St. Gregory's being so much lower and having a north aisle added, even without the question mark over the 14ft. section of the early round tower, does pose us more questions than Hales. My early notes listed this church and tower as Norman, but in later years I have come to doubt this conclusion. As well as the similarities to Hales, quite near, the quarter-round fillets between tower and church, and the narrow nave and chancel, point clearly to a Saxon date. As the octagonal section of the tower was built in the 13th. century, it seems most probable that some calamity befell this tower before then, or the circular section would have been taller. The circular base is therefore most probably Saxon by reason of the fillets, and the upper section was destroyed perhaps by a storm. In altering Ashby and Rollesby towers, the circular inner shape was kept, so with an octagonal shape inside and out, we can be certain this was later than the base . The quoins of this section are of early brick and the four lancets are also of the 13th. century. The two bells are inscribed; 1. "Thomas Newman Me Fecit 1712". 2. "ANNO DOMINI 1631 "(by William Brend) The Tenor bell (2) was split in 1763.

The nave and chancel widths at 15ft. 4" are remarkably close to the nave at Hales (15ft. 9"), and the apsidal east end is excellent proof that this was the original length of the church. One wonders if the lower than usual Saxon walls were the result of the damage to the tower before the 13th. century. The magnificent south doorway and to a lesser extent the blocked up north doorway, seems to give us a later than Saxon date for the building of the nave, but our experience with Hales, and the features we have seen, although meagre, give, with the south wall at under 3ft. thick, reasonable confidence to call the nave and chancel Saxon.

The Norman period saw the two nave doorways established, and some small windows pierced the apse, but there was not the grand restoration as at Hales. By the 13th century however, things had changed, for Heckingham appears to have become an important church to Langley Abbey. The tower we have already said was restored during this period, and the north aisle was cut through the north wall leaving the original wall as the columns and arches. E. Thornhill recalls seeing in the north aisle a floor slab to Abbot Hugo which was removed during the restoration of 1900. The south porch was added in the 15th. century cutting into the Norman doorway arch, but this does not appear to have saved the stonework, which has suffered more than Hales. The north aisle windows are Early English confirming our 13th. century dating, while the south wall windows are 14th and 15th. century. Like Hales, this church is fully thatched in the Norfolk tradition.

Our records contain Church Wardens accounts of the 19th. century, that show this church was then roofed in wheat straw. Every year, wheat straw is recorded as being bought in quantities of 2/6 to 10/- for repairing the church roof. Quite clearly, a yearly patching job was done by local farmers instead of a complete re-roofing in reed thatch This is one of the latest round tower churches to be invested in the *"Redundant Churches Fund."* Although we are sorry to lose it from those that have regular worship, we know that it will continue to be carefully preserved.

N48. Hellington. St. John the Baptist.

J7. Sheet 134. Map Ref. T.G. 313 031

Tower and Church Middle SAXON.

Tower Height	46ft. 6"
Internal Diameter Grd:	10ft. 10"
Tower wall Thickness	3ft. 9"
Nave Ridge Height	26ft.
Bells 1	
Chancel Width	17ft. 10"
Nave Width	16ft. 9"
Chancel Length	29ft. 1"
Nave Length	36ft. 10"
Nave Wall Thickness	2ft. 8"

This delightful church, situated on a slight rise, has only a few cottages near by as the small village is very scattered. It consists of a round west tower, nave, chancel and south porch.

To start to date this church, we must first look at the north and south doorways, for they are the only reminders of the Norman period. They

do give us a date by which time, the church *must* have been here. They are fine examples, especially the south doorway, which is little short of the majesty of Hales and Heckingham.

When we go on to measure the nave width and the wall thickness, however, we realise, that these do not measure up to Norman features, and must belong to the earlier Saxon period. Although no Saxon features have survived except the measurements, these are enough with the evidence of the Norman doorways to place this church in the earlier date bracket.

The tower is constructed of mainly small and selected flints, although not coursed in any way. There is only the modern ground floor west window below the belfry stage, and no blocked windows are visible. It is circular for its full height and has no fillets to join it to the church. Inside there are no steps to thin the walls, so there must be a slight taper all the way up. The four belfry windows are of the Decorated period, but the circular battlements above are from the 1881 restoration. The tower arch is round-headed and has dressed stone at the springing, but the jambs have been covered with plaster and white-washed. The arch has been closed in and a modern door fitted. I feel sure that the jambs are of flints, which would give us another Saxon feature for further proof of the early date. The one bell has no inscription.

The Decorated period was when this church received its greatest alterations, and when it must have looked at its best. The tower was probably raised at this time, when the belfry windows were built. The south porch was built then, and was a very fine example with canopied niches at the angles as well as over the entrance, which had three engaged columns at each side. All five windows in the south wall are of this period, and are mainly original. They all have slender shafts, and hood moulds with head stops internally and deep splays.

The S/E, window of the nave shows Kentish tracery, a barbed trefoil. Before the Victorian restoration, the chancel east window had intersecting tracery, then it was renewed, and now has a five-light Decorated style window. It is filled with pleasant Victorian stained glass, and still retains its Decorated internal shafts and hood mould. Rather unusual is the fact that there is only one window in the entire north wall, which is the only Perpendicular feature to be seen. The chancel arch is also from the Decorated period and shows foliated carvings on the capitals. This is a clear example of where all Saxon features have been obliterated, and yet the main walls are clearly of the Saxon era. T his church has recently been invested in the *"Redundant Churches Fund"* and is currently undergoing extensive repairs.

N49. HEMBLINGTON. All Saints.

J5 Sheet. 133. Map Ref. T.G. 353 115

Tower and church Probably SAXON

Tower Height	42ft.
Internal Diameter Grd:	8ft.
Tower Wall Thickness	3ft.5"
Bells 2	
Chancel Width	14ft. 6"
Nave Width	23ft.
Chancel Length	18ft.10"
Nave Length	41ft. 6"

Hemblington is a small simple church well outside its present village and standing on flat ground. It consists of a round west tower, nave, chancel and south porch.

Nothing concrete is visible to date either tower or church before the 13th century, although it would hardly be in this simple style unless much earlier. By the tower being off centre to the nave and in line with the chancel, we can see that the nave was widened, and therefore was early. As one Decorated 14th. century window remains in this south wall, we can presume that this was the date of the restoration that widened the church. The chancel still retains one Y-traceried window of the Early English period, while the remaining windows are from the 15th. century. My impression however, was that the church with the tower was earlier than the 13th. century window although at the moment we have no features by which we can set a date.

The tower, which has the finest set of put-log holes that I have seen, framed with 2 inch bricks, can tell us little. The tower construction is of mainly average sized flints, and evenly coursed, and apart from the altered 15th. century window on the ground floor, there are only three square windows below the belfry stage. These windows are fitted with square stone blocks having quatrefoil openings. It is tempting to think of these as being Saxon circular windows altered at some later date, but there is no foundation for this that I could see. The four double-light belfry windows are of Tudor brick, and inside the circular battlements is a small conical cap of red-brown tiles. This is therefore another tower that retains its link with the past.

The large bell with a mouth diameter of 30 inches is inscribed:- "ANNO DOMINI 1621". While the smaller has a mouth of 27 inches and has only the date "1662".

The tower arch is tall and narrow, being only 4ft. wide, and with a simple chamfer to the plaster on the nave side. This gives the appearance of being constructed of flints. If this should prove to be the case, it will be a major factor towards giving this tower and parts of the church a Saxon dating.

In the nave is one of the largest and finest wall paintings of St. Christopher in the country. It was restored in 1936.

N50. HORSEY. All Saints.

L4. Sheet 134. Map Ref. T.G. 458 231
Tower and Church Early SAXON

Tower Height	51ft.
Height of Circular Stage	31ft.
Tower Diameter Grd:	8ft. 3"
Tower Wall Thickness	3ft. 4"
Bells 1	
Chancel Width	16ft. 4"
Nave Width	16ft. 2"
Chancel Length	24ft. 1"
Nave Length	43ft. 8"

This church is in the flat coastal strip to the north of Great Yarmouth. It consists of a round west tower with octagonal top, nave and chancel in one and south porch.

Here is another Saxon church that this study has disclosed. The long Saxon shape, noted by Baldwin Brown is at once evident, and the uncoursed flintwork of the church is typical of the Saxon era. The plain rectangular building with no chancel arch is certainly a sign of an early church, but the main feature to note is the S/W corner built of flint and tiles. Although some bricks and stone have been used in repairs, this has not destroyed the feature as a means of dating. The N/W corner is partly hidden by an ugly buttress that supports this corner where subsidence has occurred; the vertical line of the original corner can however still be seen, and the corner was of flints. The other feature is the tall and narrow tower arch (plate32). The jambs are undoubtedly of flint rubble, although the head has been altered with two steps on either side of the lower centre. There are no fillets between tower and church, but the features above are enough to date this tower and church as Saxon.

In 1984 I was able to ascend the tower, where I found the four original Saxon belfry windows near the top of the circular stage, in the diagonals. They are now blocked up, but show clearly that they were built of flints. The one bell has no inscription.

The uncoursed flintwork of tower and church, place this building in the very early period, as the circular stage of the tower is very little above the nave roof. The tall and narrow octagonal stage of the 14th. century has brick quoins and single-light belfry windows. It is finished at the top with battlements. The windows of the church are mostly from the Perpendicular period, and were in very poor condition, but a change in the fortunes of this church, meant, that repairs were carried out in 1982 to these windows, as well as the tower, giving new life to this very neglected church.

The N/W corner has further evidence inside of the subsidence, as stone tie-blocks can be seen in the walls at this corner. The church roof is of Norfolk reed thatch.

N51. HOWE. St. Mary.

J7. Sheet 134. Map Ref. T.M. 275 999
Tower and Nave Early SAXON.

Tower Height approx.	38ft.
Tower Wall Height	35ft.
Internal Diameter Grd:	11ft. 2"
Tower Wall Thickness	2ft. 8"
Bells 1	
Chancel Width	17ft. 8"
Nave Width	17ft. 11"
Chancel Length	32ft. 1"
Nave Length	27ft.
Nave Wall Thickness	2ft. 6"

The small hamlet of Howe, to the S/E of Norwich, has the small and ancient church of St. Mary, which consists of a round west tower, nave, chancel and south porch. It is part of a group of several R/T Churches close by, Poringland and Brooke being the nearest.

There are several reasons why I have placed this church at least 150 years earlier than the Taylors, although it may prove to be even earlier than this. A comparison with the towers of known pre-Conquest date 1,000 to the Conquest, i.e. Burnham Norton and Forncett St. Peter, both show a careful selection of the flints, a technical ability to construct the walls straight and in a true circle, and to build to a height of 60ft. None of these features show at Howe (plate 2) and there are sufficient churches in each class to warrant a differing date period.

The curvature of the east side within the tower confirms that tower and church were built together. The short tower which has a conical top of red-brown tiles is only 35ft. to the top of the tower walls . It starts off at the base, quite oval in shape, but finishes at the top, more of a square with rounded corners. It is constructed of flints of all sizes, mainly large, with a few pieces of brick and conglomerate There are two circular double-splayed windows (Saxon) one north and one south, 13ft. 3" from the ground to their centres, and above these are three double-splayed round-headed windows (Saxon) to north, south and west. All these windows are built of flint rubble, and contain no dressed stone. Near the top of the tower on the south, is a blocked up rectangle that may possibly have been an early belfry window. There are fillets between tower and church of flints, but in this case they are not quarter-round as is usual, but flat, and more like Saxon pilasters.

The nave is defined as Saxon quite clearly by the flint corners at S/W and N/W of large flints, conglomerate and early tiles. The N/E corner of the nave is also defined by the vertical line of the original flint quoins, against which the present chancel walls are built. While the Taylors suggest that this was the length of the Saxon church, I would suggest that the N/E quoins meant a turning of the wall, hence a narrower chancel than at present. There is one round-headed double-splayed window of Saxon date, about the same dimensions as those in the tower, and about the centre of the nave north wall.

The tower arch is 7ft. wide and 12ft. 4" tall. It is round-headed, and the arch is set back on the jambs by about 2 inches in the Saxon fashion. The whole, with the exception of the imposts is plastered, being almost certainly of flints. The imposts are simple, and the stone does not appear to be limestone. Above this, and showing in both nave and tower, is a rectangular opening, that was the upper doorway, although the original shape of the head seems to have been altered. A west doorway in the tower is now blocked up, but the details show up clearly inside. It is 2ft.11" wide by 7ft. 9" tall, and follows the shape of the tower arch including the imposts. Here we see the Saxon tradition of using one piece of stone for each impost, and notice that they are of differing lengths, and neither are the full length of the wall.

The south doorway is early Norman; note the jambs and capitals, but it has a renewed pointed head of the Early English period. Both nave and chancel have windows of the Early English and Decorated periods, but none of the later periods. Most of course have been restored at varying times. The church roof was re-tiled in 1981.

N 52. INGWORTH. St. Lawrence.

I3. Sheet 133. Map Ref. T.G. 193 296

Tower, Chancel and North Nave Wall Early SAXON

Tower Grd. Floor only	
Internal Diameter Grd:	10ft. 5"
Tower Wall Thickness	2ft. 8"
Bells 1	
Chancel Width	14ft. 9"
Nave Width	21ft. 5"
Chancel Length	25ft. 3"
Nave Length	38ft. 4"

This small church still has its cottages nearby on the B class road 1 1/2 miles north of Aylsham. It consists of the remains of its round tower, now roofed with thatch, nave, chancel, and south porch.

There is primary evidence of this church being Saxon at all four corners, by reason of the quoins. The N/W and S/W can still be seen as large blocks of conglomerate with some early tiles as well. The N/E and S/E corners are of early dressed stone, and appear by their small size and method of laying to be Norman; but abutting them are large blocks of conglomerate. (plate 36). It is as if the early quoins of this stone had been cut back to allow the dressed stone to be inserted. Proving this to be the case, the bottom block in each case, is conglomerate. It was apparently thought wise not to disturb these foundation blocks, as they did not show above the ground.

The church and tower are roofed in Norfolk reed thatch, and the one bell is in a bell cote on the west end of the nave. The south side of the nave was widened from 14ft. 9" to its present width in 1390 to 1400 when the present porch was built, so records say. We can see this by the fact that the nave is off centre to the tower and chancel. Also the S/W nave quoins are in the west wall about six feet from the present corner. The thickness of the tower walls should be noted, as they are very thin indeed, and it is recorded that the tower fell in 1822. Note the tower arch, still with its Saxon jambs without dressed stone, but a Norman dressed stone head to the arch, while still retaining the characteristic of a set-back head from Saxon days.

The south porch has a room or parvise over, and the curious buttresses and arches mentioned by writers at the west nave wall, can be easily explained. Where most stair turrets added to a tower, served only the tower, with another staircase built to the room over the porch, if the church had one, here they utilised the one stair turret to the tower, for the upper room of the porch as well. A passage way connected the two.

The nave windows, north and south are Perpendicular, most probably dating from the time of the alterations to the south wall. Those in the chancel date from the Early English period.

The main building periods of this church are therefore:- Saxon tower, nave and chancel, built to the present length, with the nave 14ft. 9" wide. The Norman period saw the head of the tower arch refashioned and the N/E and S/E quoins altered to dressed stone. During Early English times new windows were put into the chancel. 1390 to 1400 was the time when the nave was widened, the south porch built, new windows inserted into the nave, and probably the tower may also have been raised at this time. The church remained substantially the same as this until the tower fell in 1822. The tower remained in ruins until the 1920s, when the ground floor was roofed with a cone of thatch by Canon Sapwell to be used as a vestry.

N53. INTWOOD. All Saints.

I6. Sheet 134. Map Ref. T.G. 196 042

Nave Early SAXON, Tower Middle SAXON.

Tower Height	60ft.	Chancel Width	15ft. 9"
Height of Circular Stage	40ft.	Nave Width	18ft.
Internal Diameter Grd:	10ft. 3"	Chancel Length	23ft. 1"
Tower Wall Thickness	3ft. 9"	Nave Length	26ft. 3"
Nave Ridge Height	35ft.	Nave Wall Thickness	3ft.
Bells 5			

Intwood is about 4 miles south of Norwich, and the church stands on a pronounced mound at a T junction. It consists of a round west tower with an octagonal top, nave, chancel, south porch and north vestry .

The nave gives us the first positive sign of a pre-Conquest dating with all four corners still surviving from its earliest days. They are as follows:- S/W, large blocks of conglomerate at the base with large selected flints between every few blocks to a height of about 12ft., then all large flints. The N/W corner is similar to the S/W, with the addition of two pieces of Roman tiles. The N/E is once again large blocks of conglomerate and some Roman tiles, but the flints here are not so large or so flat. The S/E nave is a distinctive corner, although it was recently repointed. Four horizontal blocks of conglomerate, with Roman tiles and flints between some, then a large block stood on end in the long-and-short style, followed by two more horizontal blocks and then six Roman tiles; two more blocks of conglomerate, then a mixture of tiles and large flints. The flints are cut to make a sharp corner. The north wall rests on a plinth of flints standing out about 4 inches. There is no plinth visible on the south side, although it may be here but covered by the risen churchyard.

The chancel looks later, although its width would deny this. The walls have many cut flints, and a lot of early bricks have been used in its building. So we possibly have here some extensive refacing, or at the worst rebuilding on the ruinous walls.

Turning now to the tower, five bells hang here plus the Sanctus bell in the base of the tower. The top is octagonal with battlements, and these appear to be 14th. century. The bell frame is inscribed "John Pearce Archt. Norwich. G, Day & Sons. Bell Hangers Eye 1885."

One of the five bells is inscribed "John Warner 1888." The octagonal stage is of small flints with dressed stone quoins, and four belfry windows of double-lights have rounded heads. They seem to be cemented, over the early dressed stones. The circular stage is constructed of whole and cut flints and some early brick. It has quite a good shape, so it seems to be nearer the 1,000 date, while inside we can plainly see the straight side of the nave west wall, especially on the first floor, that tells us this tower was added to the earlier Saxon church. On the ground floor to the west, we can see an alcove with a triangular head, and outside we can see that this is a blocked up west doorway, for below the Early English west window are the voussoirs of the west doorway.

All the church windows save one, are in the Perpendicular style, although they all seem to be Victorian in date.

N54. KESWICK. All Saints.

I6. Sheet 134. Map Ref. T.G. 214 047

Ruins of Chancel East Wall SAXON

Tower Height	41ft.
Internal Diameter Grd:	7ft.
Tower Wall Thickness	2ft. 10"
Bell 1	
Chancel Width	9ft.
Nave Width	18ft. 2"
Chancel Length	7ft. 3"
Nave Length	14ft.

This church is south of Norwich and not far from Intwood. It was built from the ruins of the old church which was Saxon. It was made considerably smaller. It consists of a round west tower, nave and apsidal chancel.

The tower with brick bell openings was restored in 1893, with much of the eastern side renewed. The church was rebuilt in 1898, and in this case certainly seems to be a rebuilding and not a restoration, for old photographs show only very small pieces of the west wall standing beside the relatively complete tower. The new church is certainly much shorter and with a completely new apsidal chancel .

Ten feet above the first floor of the tower is a ledge of about 3" to 4" to thin the walls. This is only on the western half, which suggests that this part of the tower is probably the original Saxon wall. The eastern half (inside) is of cut black flints, while the western half is of whole flints. The eastern side, at least up to the first floor, is flattened, and the flooring also shows this up. But this again, because of the repairs is inconclusive for calling it a tower that was added to an earlier church. There are some masonry blocks in the eastern half, but they are not wall ties, but rather random blocks used with the flints. There are four belfry windows and only one other; the ground floor west window. The one bell in the tower is inscribed:- " Josephus Carter Me Fecit 1609."

The tower arch is tall and has cut flints at the jambs, and a Victorian brick round-headed arch. The jambs do not appear to be original, but perhaps the width denotes the Saxon size of the original arch.

All the nave is restored and shortened, and the apsidal chancel is entirely new. The ruined east wall of the old chancel is still standing and shows the N/E and S/E quoins as large cut flints.

N55. KILVERSTONE. St. Andrew.

E9. Sheet 144. Map Ref. T.L. 894 840
Tower and Church Middle SAXON.

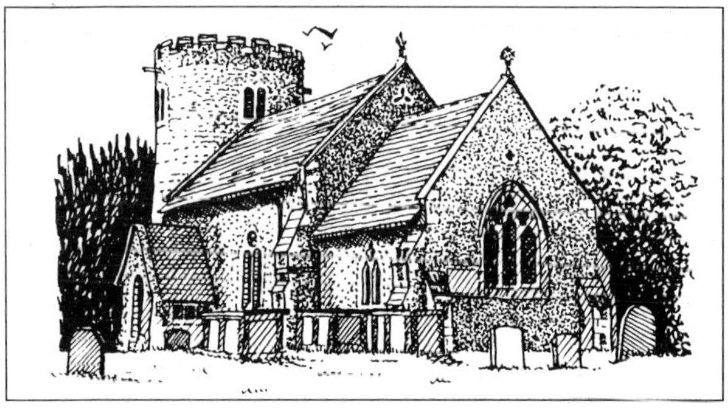

Tower Height	39ft.
Internal Diameter Grd:	11ft. 9"
Tower Wall Thickness	3ft.11 "
Bells 1	
Chancel Width	12ft. 2"
Nave Width	16ft. 6"
Chancel Length	16ft. 10"
Nave Length	30ft. 1"

This small church situated near the Hall is at the end of a grassy lane and cannot be seen from the road. It is on a very slight slope and consists of round west tower, nave, chancel and south porch.

Munro Cautley, although calling this tower Norman, says he believes it may be pre-Conquest, but gives no other reasons than that it is low and stratified. The wall thickness is a border line between Saxon and Norman, but having a large diameter does not prevent it belonging to the Saxon era. The four belfry windows are Norman with later battlements above. Below these on the first floor are three round-headed windows with dressed stone frames outside, almost certainly Norman, but inside the tower we see the first indications that this may indeed be a pre-Conquest tower. These three windows all have Saxon features. All have heads of flints and signs of the boards used to support the heads while the mortar set. In addition, the south window has its head set back 2 inches on the jambs, and most of the jambs are still of flints. All have some repairs to the jambs with dressed stone, but this is a very good indication that these windows were originally of flints and the repairs are of stone. For a stone faced window would not be repaired with flints. If money was not available for a proper repair, being in the tower, the window would have been blocked up. The ground floor west window is undoubtedly a Victorian pseudo Norman window, but on close study, one or two of the stones are seen to be early, that are easily overlooked at first sight, and so must indicate that this replaces a similar window. There are no fillets between tower and church that might have given us a more positive dating. The low pseudo Norman tower arch may possibly replace a similar arch, but one wonders why it needed replacing? There is no upper doorway to be seen from either nave or tower.

Both nave and chancel are narrow and follow the Saxon style of a narrow church, with the chancel being amongst the narrowest in the R/T group. All the windows were renewed in the restoration of 1906, but the south doorway is Norman. It has single engaged columns to each side, with volute capitals, and two rows of chevrons to the arch, with the outer row being Victorian. On the north wall outside, a piscina can be seen showing that this church could once boast a north aisle.

This is not much on which to date this building. Church and tower were obviously built together. The south doorway and belfry windows give us positive evidence that the church stood here in Norman times. But while the nave width, and tower walls give us good grounds for dating this church to pre-Norman times, the tower windows of flints, give us positive evidence of this.

N56. KIRBY CANE. All Saints.

K8. Sheet 134. Map Ref. T.M. 374 941
Tower and Church. Middle SAXON.

Tower Height	51ft
Internal Diameter Grd:	8ft.10"
Tower Wall Thickness	3ft. 9" to 4ft.
Nave Ridge Height	31ft.
Bells 5	
Chancel Width	17ft.
Nave Width	16ft. 6"
Nave & Aisle Width	35ft. 8"
Chancel Length	30ft. 5"
Nave Length	34ft. 7"

The church is now well away from the village to the north, and the ground slopes away towards the south, and rises only slightly to the north and west. The church consists of round west tower, nave, chancel, north aisle, south porch and north vestry.

All writers call this tower Saxon, mainly because of the pilasters at the base, and even the Taylors, with a more critical approach, still confirm the lower part of the tower as Saxo-Norman, and say the walls of the tower are 4ft. 6" thick. I have differed with the Taylors on wall measurements on a number of occasions, and this one is rather critical, as if it is under 4ft. it is a good sign that it is Saxon. But if over 4ft. there is a real possibility that it is Norman. The tower wall in this case, was very difficult to measure, but I am certain that it was not over 4ft.

The tower is constructed of uncoursed whole and cut flints with large mortar gaps; and has a series of nine short pilasters round the base, although two are now covered by triangular red brick buttresses. They are about 8 inches wide and 3 inches deep and about 2ft. 9" apart. They are built entirely of flints, as the tower. There were fillets between church and tower, which is a certain Saxon feature, but they are now partly obscured. The one to the south by a brick buttress and a thickened nave west wall, where the fillet shows at the bottom, and might be called another pilaster, but it also shows at the top, which confirms it as a fillet. On the north a similar thickening of the nave wall covers all but small traces of the fillet, which are not very conclusive as being the original. There are five bells, and the tower is circular for its full height with later battlements. The ground floor west window looks rather like a Victorian double-light Decorated style window, but outside, the cement rendering suggests that this may be a much earlier window. Above this are two rows of slit windows. The first row at roughly N, W, and S, is 21ft. from the ground, and the second at 31ft. They are mainly of flints outside, but inside the wide splays are of flints with many repairs in brick. The lintels are of oak boards still in place. The four belfry windows in the diagonals (unusual) are narrow lancets of Transition Norman/Early English date. The battlements are capped with early brick. No upper doorway could be seen, but there is a ledge to thin the tower walls, just below the three upper slit windows at 28ft. 9". This I have found is often seen in Saxon towers but not so far in Norman.

The tower arch is 4ft. 9" wide by 10ft. 8" tall, it is round-headed with no imposts and is constructed entirely of flints now plastered over and colour washed. The arch is now closed in with a modern oak screen and door .

The external roofs are in red-brown tiles. The nave has Early English, Decorated and one Perpendicular window, while the chancel has Decorated windows, and two small round-headed windows high up on the south side, that are most probably Norman. They are faced with dressed stone, but much of this has been renewed. The north aisle has been shortened, and now the east end has a door of Victorian age.

The tower is undoubtedly Saxon, with the uncoursed flintwork, the wall thickness, the ledge to thin the walls, the two rows of flint windows, and finally, the fillets and pilasters. The tower arch of flints, although now covered, will place this part also in pre-Conquest times. The narrow nave and chancel make this certainly the ground plan of the original Saxon church, and the Norman windows high up in the chancel walls imply that these walls were here in Norman times. If they have stood from Norman times against a Saxon tower, then we can be certain that they were built with that tower or they would have been moved to make a wider church. The wall texture is also of Saxon rather than Norman date.

Without the original belfry windows to give us the original height of the tower, it is difficult to date the tower closely, but I would think that it was the later part of the Middle Saxon period.

N57. LETHERINGSETT. St. Andrew.

G2. Sheet 133. Map Ref. T.G. 061 389

Tower Late SAXON.

Tower Height	50ft.
Internal Diameter Grd:	8ft. 11"
Tower Wall Thickness	3ft. 6"
Bells 3	
Chancel Width	15ft.11 "
Nave Width	16ft. 8"
Nave & Aisles Width	41ft. 11"
Chancel Length	25ft. 3"
Nave Length	36ft. 1 "

The church stands in a delightful setting close to the river Glaven. It consists of a round west tower, clerestoried nave, chancel, north and south aisles and south porch.

Nearly all writers call this tower Norman, but it was Rev. Linnell who first recorded in his *"Guide to Letheringsett Church"*, the blocked up circular windows outlined in brick above the present belfry windows. These would place all the tower except the very top in the late Saxon period, 1,000 to the Conquest. The flints of the tower are evenly selected and well coursed, while the four belfry windows are from the Decorated period. There are four other windows in the tower, all narrow round-headed and constructed of flints. The west one on the ground floor is about 10ft. up, and on the first floor 20ft. up, there is one in the south face, while the north window at this height is blocked. The last is on the second floor at 29ft. and is in the north face. An upper doorway is on the first floor 3ft. 6" wide by 4ft. 4" tall, but is most probably taller for it goes down below the present floor which is now at a different level. The largest of the three bells has no inscription, while the other two are inscribed the same:- "Charles Newman Made Mee 1700. R. Girdlestone. C.W. " . The bells and bell-frame were last overhauled in 1959. Many repairs and alterations have left us a difficult task if we try and put a date to the present church. We can say that when the tower was built a church was built with it, and so almost certainly the nave west wall is Saxon. The nave and chancel are virtually the same width and appear to be of Saxon dimensions, so there is a strong possibility that the ground plan is original even if nothing more.

The 13th. century saw the north and south aisles added as we can see by the quatrefoil piers, and the south doorway is also from this period. The chancel windows were put in during the next century while the 15th. century saw the insertion of the present clerestory windows and the windows of the aisles. Repairs and restorations appear to have gone on steadily throughout most of the life of this church for it does not appear to have suffered any neglect in the past.

N 58. EAST LEXHAM. St. Andrew.

D5. Sheet 132. Map Ref. T.F. 861 172

Tower and Church Early SAXON.

Tower Height	41ft. 6"	Nave Width	17ft. 8"
Internal Diameter Grd:	12ft. 4"	Chancel Length	23ft.
Tower Wall Thickness	3ft. 6"	Nave Length	32ft.
Nave Ridge Height	25ft. 6"	Nave Wall Thickness N.	2ft. 7"
Bells 1		Nave Wall Thickness S.	2ft. 4"
Chancel Width	17ft. 10"		

This church and tower stand on a small mound, and appears to be in a circular churchyard. One of the very few said to be on the site of a pagan temple. It is approached through a farmyard peculiar to a number of these village churches. It consists of a round west tower, nave

and chancel in one, and south porch.

This tower is recognised by all writers as pre-Conquest, but while some regard the evidence of the long-and- short quoins as proof of Saxon work, others disregard it. The Taylors accept the western quoins but suggest that the eastern are quite late restorations .

The tower must certainly be our first consideration (plate 1), for it appears to be one of the earliest round towers of the group. It is very roughly constructed with a great deal of mortar used to set the flints, and it rises with a taper that is by no means constant, and the shape looks a very crude circle. Though the Taylors say it is built entirely of flints, internal inspection shows that from the first floor the internal wall face is of hard chalk (clunch) like a number of other round towers. Besides the modern west window on the ground floor, there are only three belfry windows in place of the usual four. The Taylors describe these in detail but do not state if they regard them as original or contemporary with the tower. My opinion is that the S/W window (plate 25) is the only one that is contemporary with the tower, and the others have had the stone inserts placed in the early openings at some later, probably early Norman, date. The original S/W window is constructed entirely of flints under a large round-headed arch. Slightly recessed are two round-headed lights with their heads set back on the jambs, and supported in the centre by the usual Saxon baluster, made in this case from a column of flints bound together by mortar, and with a cushion capital, which appears to be an erratic found locally. This is now encased in a coating of cement. The main flint construction of the window however is plain for all to see. The N/W window has a single stone insert carved to represent a two-light window with round heads and a centre baluster that bulges in the centre. The last window is very unusual, depicting a Maltese Cross carved from a single block leaving a stone frame all round.

On the first floor is a triangular-headed upper doorway 2ft. 6" wide by 4ft. 9" tall, and below this, which was probably part of this upper doorway, is an opening into the roof timbers closed by a door. Internally, the tower is vertical, without steps or taper, all the thinning of the walls being done externally. Although not conclusive, there appears to be a ring of circular double-splayed windows about 2ft. above the belfry windows. They are blocked up with flints and plaster. The tower arch, 8ft. wide by 14ft. 9" tall is cruck shaped and is fully plastered and little can be learned from this at the moment, although it seems rather wide for an original Saxon arch.

The church must certainly be of the same date although all the windows are from the Perpendicular period. But the narrow nave and chancel in one, and with walls not parallel, giving different measurements at various points, and there is no chancel arch. All of which are early features, including the wall thickness as given at the head of this article. The main features of the church however, are the long-and-short quoins at all corners. They are much too consistent to my thinking for this early church, and the way this church has been restored gives cause for concern. The entire church has been cement faced and painted with white plastic paint. This is the appearance of over restoration. The Taylors pointed out that the N/E and S/E quoins appear to be restorations, but confirmed the western corners as Saxon. While I have noted that the N/W corner shows the use of differing types of stone as if found locally, the lowest stone at the S/W corner rests on flints, which suggests that this corner has been changed from its original state. This does not mean that the church had to be rebuilt, but I feel it means that the present quoins, although early, are not the original ones of the church. Only by careful work on the corners by skilled workmen can we learn more about these features.

N59. WEST LEXHAM. St. Nicholas.

D5. Sheet 132. Map Ref. T.F. 842 173

Tower and parts of Chancel SAXON.

Tower Height approx.	35ft.
Internal Diameter Grd:	10ft. 7"
Tower Wall Thickness	2ft. 6"
Nave Ridge Height approx.	28ft.
Bells 1	
Chancel Width	16ft. 10"
Nave Width	16ft. 7"
Chancel Length	24ft. 11"
Nave Length	32ft. 8"

The church stands on a very prominent mound and overlooks the small village and a farm. It consists of a round west tower, nave, chancel, south porch and north vestry.

We see here a small church much restored after falling into ruins. It is not clear what caused the decay or for how long it remained in this state, but a sketch in the church dated 1891 apparently shows the church at this time with the tower and chancel standing, but only the lower parts of the nave walls. However, it now appears, that this sketch has the wrong date, which should read, 1881, when the church history records, a major restoration was begun. The sketch shows that it was only the nave that had to be rebuilt, and it shows up clearly where this happened, for as well as flints, red bricks were used to stabilise the old walls and to use as piers. The nave windows on the north are Victorian copies of a re-set Y-tracery Early English window on the south, while the chancel retains its original Early English windows.

The tower is the most interesting part, although even here we cannot be too certain, or point to any definite features at present. It is encased in cement rendering although this is now flaking off in parts. In 1992, the centre core of chalk clunch was showing in many places, and some cracks were appearing giving cause for concern. It was hoped that repairs would soon be in progress to avert what had happened at Cockley Cley, not too far away. The tower is "D" shaped to the top, which must be the result of the restoration; but although leaving us with a restored east side, nevertheless the west side is still the original early tower. There is an unusual pitched roof inside the plain parapet, and just below this are the four belfry windows, once more in the diagonals. They are 14th. century Decorated windows with trefoil heads. The N/W and S/W are blocked with whole flints. The only other window in the tower is a tall narrow ground floor west window with a dressed stone frame and a trefoil head. Certainly not the usual type of Decorated window, and it clearly resembles the tall and narrow Saxon window at Runhall, opened slightly and faced with dressed stone .

I have been unable to ascend this tower, so there may be features waiting to be seen inside. The short tower and very thin walls on the west must surely indicate a positive Saxon dating, and although large parts of the church are rebuilt, the width, and the sketches before the rebuilding prove this to follow the original ground plan of the ancient building.

N60. MATLASKE. St. Peter.

H3 Sheet 133. Map Ref. T.G. 151 349

Tower and Nave Early SAXON.

Tower Height	45ft.
Height of Circular Stage	33ft.
Internal Diameter Grd:	9ft. 1"
Tower Wall Thickness	4ft.
Nave Ridge Height	30ft.
Bells 1	
Chancel NONE	
Nave Width	15ft. 9"
Nave & Aisle Width	28ft. 6"
Sanctuary Length	8ft. 6"
Nave Length	31ft. 6l'

This interesting church with its village still around it is called Norman by all writers, but there is ample evidence to the contrary. It consists of a round west tower with an octagonal top, nave, no chancel, south aisle and north porch.

We commence with the tower which is built of uncoursed flints including some very large ones (peculiar to the early Saxon builders), conglomerate and early brick; with large mortar gaps. 15ft. from the ground there is an offset of 4 to 6 inches where the tower steps in to thin the walls as at Burnham Deepdale and a number of other Saxon towers. Above this the tower rises straight up to the top of the circular section at about 33ft. There are only two windows of 14th. century date in the circular stage; a double-light at ground floor level, and a single-light on the first floor, and both are in the west face. Although the lower part of the tower measures 4ft. in thickness, this is reduced to 2ft. 10" by the first floor level. The 14th. century octagonal belfry stage has double-light windows at the cardinal points and bold battlements of flints and dressed stone. The one bell is inscribed:-"SUBUENIAT DIGNA DONANTIBUS HANC KATERINA".

The diameter measured on the first floor is 9ft. 6" N. to S. against 8ft. 6" E. to W. Therefore this tower is oval, giving us another positive sign of early work. There is a Sanctus Bell window on the first floor which was surely an altered upper doorway. The bands of tiles in the west face of the tower referred to by Pevsner as Roman, can be clearly defined as much later wall tiles to hold cracks in the tower, and used before the more modern steel rods were in use. These can be seen as masonry blocks in a number of towers, about the same size, 20" by 4', so the tiles are certainly not Roman, but contemporary with the date of the repair. There are six bands up the west face where most cracks occur, and a number more can be seen within the tower. The stair turret was added in the 15th. century, reaching to the top of the circular section, and like several others, has been built into the thickness of the tower wall, with only an enlarged fillet on the south to provide the extra room. These stair turrets have weakened many of these towers when built in this way.

Turning to the church, we know from the church records that the chancel fell in 1726 and has not been replaced. The N/W and S/W quoins are of very large flints and conglomerate, telling us quite plainly that this west wall is Saxon. There is no fillet on the north between tower and church, and on the south we can see an enlarged fillet that is part of the stair turret with a supporting arch at the bottom. The very narrow nave, as well as the construction of the north wall that is very similar to that of the tower, support the view that this is also of Saxon date, although the Perpendicular windows were inserted into the old walls. Some interesting corbel faces look down from the old nave roof. The north porch was built when the nave windows were put in, but the south aisle is from the Decorated period, some 100 years earlier.

The tower arch of Saxon dimensions 4ft. 6" wide by 14ft. 6" tall has been refaced with brick and whole flints in later days. This and all the ground floor stage of the tower, which is in the same style though not original, is very attractive. The tower was restored in 1982.

N61. MAUTBY. Sts. Peter & Paul

L5. Sheet 134. Map Ref. T.G. 481 124

Circular part of Tower and Nave North Wall Early SAXON.

Tower Height	46ft. 6"	Nave Width	19ft. 2"
Height of Circular Stage	30ft. 6"	Chancel Length	36ft. 6"
Internal Diameter Squared	8ft.x 8ft.	Nave Length	48ft.
Nave Ridge Height	32ft. 6"	Nave Wall Thickness N.	2ft. 7"
Bells 1		Nave Wall Thickness S.	1ft. 9"
Chancel Width	17ft. 9"		

This church with its round west tower having an octagonal belfry stage, nave and chancel under one roof, and south porch, is in open countryside. It is in a low spot, and has little sign of habitation nearby .

Although the tower is 46ft. 6" tall, the circular section is only 30ft. 6", and this from my studies, places it in the early Saxon period or 900 to 950. The construction confirms this as the lower parts contain many very large flints, followed by a band of very pale conglomerate. Then more flints that are laid in herringbone pattern, and once more, very large blocks of granite, sandstone, and other erratics. More flints, then two bands of dark conglomerate. Above these bands the flints are of average size mixed with smaller pieces of conglomerate. No conglomerate is seen above 15ft. All this rough walling points conclusively to the Saxon period, and to before 950 when the technique was becoming more regular and orderly. The Victorians, however, have made the base of the tower internally, square, so I could not get the original diameter or the wall thickness. Also, I could not tell from the alterations whether the tower was built with or after the church.

The top stage is octagonal with battlements, probably of the Perpendicular period. It has four single-light belfry windows and one inscribed bell. A 15th. century turret on the north leads to the first floor and is constructed of brick, flints and some conglomerate. Besides the belfry windows, there is only the ground floor west window and one blocked window on the first floor. The upper doorway is blocked but can still be seen from inside the tower. It is 29ft. above the ground and is 21 inches wide by 3ft. 1" tall. The height cannot be quite correct, as I could only measure from the filling of red bricks, but it must have been taller than this. The width seems fairly accurate as the jambs were of flattish flints, and can be seen clearly, and outside of these the flints are of a rounder nature. There are no fillets to the tower, but in the west nave wall are various blocks of dressed stone carved with initials and dates. One is 1883, probably a restoration?

As the nave quoins are of dressed stone most writers would ascribe a 15th. century date as from the nave windows, but the north wall is undoubtedly Saxon, as the large flints and large blocks of conglomerate prove. The flints laid in herringbone fashion and the large mortar joints all favour this dating. The chancel windows are Early English, but the walls also appear to be of the same date as the nave. However, there was once a south aisle, which has since been removed, so how much of the original south wall remains is debatable. The nave and chancel are now under one continuous roof of Norfolk reed thatch, although the chancel is one foot narrower.

N62. MERTON. St. Peter.

E7. Sheet 144. Map Ref. T.L. 912 981

Church Early SAXON. Tower Middle SAXON.

Tower Height	42ft.
Internal Diameter Grd:	10ft. 6"
Tower Wall Thickness	3ft.
Nave Ridge Height	33ft. 1"
Bells 3	
Chancel Width	17ft. 10"
Nave Width	17ft. 5"
Nave & Aisle Width	28ft. 10"
Chancel Length	33ft. 10"
Nave Length	45ft. 2"
Nave Wall Thickness	2ft. 9"
Nave South Arcade	2ft. 3"

This fascinating church stands in the grounds of Merton Hall and is close to the lake. It has a round west tower, nave, chancel, south aisle, and north and south porches.

This Saxon tower was built on to an existing church as Taylor and Taylor says, although they call it Norman. The straight east side confirms this, and it continues flat as far as the belfry windows. Also it is not bonded into the nave west wall, as gaps can be seen on the first floor. Next, the single-splayed window at first floor level confirms that there never was an upper doorway to this tower. One wonders if the open stairway following the curve of the tower and entering the first floor at the edge of the floor, is the successor to an original stairway of like shape. If so, then it was probably one of only a very few round towers to have such a staircase as most seem to have been entered by the more popular upper doorway into the nave.

The tower is circular for its full height of 42ft. And is most likely to be rather late in the Middle Saxon period close to 1,000. It has a diameter of 10ft. 6" and the walls are only 3ft. thick. These are good pointers to a Saxon dating. But more positive signs are to be seen in the windows. The tower can be seen to be built in three distinct sections, and appears to be mainly original with perhaps a foot or so added height above the belfry windows, and a few necessary repairs besides the ground floor west window which is of Perpendicular date. The four belfry windows:- The east window has been mainly closed by the raising of the nave roof, and now only a small part framed in red brick still shows. The three others at north, south and west are double-light with round-headed arches. They are, or were entirely of flints, and the jambs and sills are of flints except where some flints have fallen out to be replaced by bricks. The centre columns are circular with cushion capitals and bases of dressed stone. They are at the outer face of the tower walls, as at Snailwell, Gissing and Kilverstone, and not in the usual Norman fashion. The west column looks decidedly new, and the south one is the most weather worn. The south column on the other hand is composed of seven pieces of dressed stone, which is certainly not in the Norman tradition. Certainly all this dressed stone is later than Saxon, but the jambs and sills are still of flints, and that could never be under Norman supervision.

On the first floor there were three slit windows, all with frames of flints. The west window has been blocked with flints, but the jambs and sill can still be seen. The north and south, 17ft. from the ground, are 2ft. 6" tall by 8 inches wide at the face, with a flat stone lintel and some early brick for the sills inserted at a later date. Inside, they splay out to 3ft. wide and the splay and jambs are in flints. The flat heads have old wooden lintels of five stout planks each.

Inside the tower the flints are reasonably coursed. They are rather large and are from gravel beds. Two feet below these first floor windows at 15ft. the tower walls have a step of about 4 inches to thin them (outside) as at Matlaske and Burnham Deepdale. There is no other step inside or outside. The tower walls are reasonably coursed with large mortar joints. The flints outside appear to be from both gravel and chalk beds. This then places the tower firmly in the Saxon period and therefore, the church, unless rebuilt, must be at least 50 years earlier. There are no fillets between church and tower.

The tower arch, which is Saxon by its size and shape, is 11ft. 4" tall by 6ft. 6" wide, and now has dressed stone facings of Norman age with imposts both into the nave and returned into the tower. If this tower had been built in Norman days with this dressed stone available on site, the tower windows would never have been built of flints.

Moving now to the church, which I have said must, be at least 50 years older, we can see on close examination the N/W quoin of flints that Taylor & Taylor call inconclusive. But if this is the original quoin, and no builder after the Conquest used flints for quoins, or even to repair them, then this confirms that the west and north nave walls are at least of the early Saxon period. The north wall measures 2ft. 10" thick which is within the Saxon measurements, and the south arcade wall, which is the original nave wall is 2ft. 8". The north wall where measured may have a thicker plaster now and measurements of flint walls can never be expected to be the same all over. As nave and chancel are of similar width and the walling cannot be fully examined because they are cement rendered and pebble dashed, there are still reasonable grounds for assuming that the nave and chancel belong to this early Saxon period. As all the windows belong to the Decorated period, it is most likely that the south aisle was added at that time; quite a large reconstruction. The chancel has a simple hammer-beam roof and the nave roof is arch-braced.

No scratch dials were to be seen, but there are faint signs of one or two votive crosses on the north doorway.

N63. MORNINGTHORPE. St. John the Baptist.

I8. Sheet 134. Map Ref. T.M. 218 925

Tower and Church Middle SAXON.

Tower Height	56ft.
Internal Diameter Grd:	11ft. 5"
Tower Wall Thickness	4ft. 2"
Nave Ridge Height	28ft.
Bells 3	
Chancel Width	18ft. 4"
Nave Width	17ft. 9"
Chancel Length	31ft.
Nave Length	32ft. 11"
Nave Wall Thickness N. & S.	3ft. 3"

One of the Hempnall Group of churches, Morningthorpe stands beside the village street. It consists of a round west tower, nave, chancel and south porch.

Many questions can be asked about this church and tower, not the least of which is, are they Saxon? For although most writers place them both in the Norman period, the Taylors call attention to two features, a blocked up opening to the east of the south porch, probably an early window, they say, with flat stones marking the arch and laid non-radially, called *"Tredington fashion"* by Baldwin Brown, and classed as Saxon. Also the tower arch, a tall unmoulded round-headed opening with simple imposts of square section, and 6 inches in height; with slightly rounded edges and two shallow grooves along their faces.

One further fact to add to the written evidence, is what I was told by a parishioner when I did my survey, He said that graves could not be dug beyond four feet to the west of the tower because they came upon masses of large flints. As this area is not by nature of a flinty character, it seems certain that either there were two churches in this churchyard or the present church replaces a previous stone church.

The tower is circular for its entire height, and has a small step inwards just below the belfry stage. This part from the step to the top appears to be of a later date. There is however more to be learned from this tower. In 1987, the Round Tower Churches Society gave a small grant towards repairs to the tower, and I was called by the rector to see what the builders had found. The tower had been raised twice, similar to Barsham in Suffolk. Originally, the tower had been less than 40 ft. high. Then an octagonal stage was added of about 8ft. This is what had been found beneath the falling flintwork. Later the tower was raised again, this time returning it to a circular tower by adding flints to the octagonal section. After the repairs, there is now no sign of the octagonal stage. The flints are of mainly average size, but not uniform in shape or colour, and there is little sign of coursing. The tower walls are not good and straight but bulge in places, giving the impression of early work, and probably due to the additions. There are no fillets, which with a curved inside wall of the tower would imply that tower and church were built together. The belfry windows are Decorated from the 14th. century, probably when the tower was raised from about 44ft. with its octagonal top. The battlements however are of 1889. The ground floor west window is a restored Perpendicular of two lights, while on the first floor is probably another Saxon feature. In the west is a slit window of flints with a piece of dressed stone (probably later) at the head, while on the north and south the slit windows are entirely of flints. These three windows are most probably the original Saxon belfry windows.

The tall unmoulded tower arch is a very strong pointer to a pre-Conquest date for the building: at 6ft. 6" wide by 14ft. 3" tall, the simple imposts before mentioned being the only stone in the opening. The biggest obstacle to a pre-Conquest dating appears to be the thickness of the tower walls which I have measured at 4ft. 2". The Taylors however say they are 6ft. which means that this is another time that I disagree with them. Over the tower arch it measures 4ft. 1", while the return wall measures 5ft. 9", which is what the Taylors must have done.

The church has nothing by which we can date it save the blocked up opening referred to by the Taylors, and the narrow nave and chancel of almost the same width. The wall thickness at 3ft. 3" is once again more like Norman than Saxon work, but the blocked up opening appears to contradict this. First, Saxon circular windows are often found in this position, as at Framingham Earl in Norfolk, and Thorington in Suffolk. Next, the flint frame to this opening is in flints laid in Tredington fashion (non-radial), this sets the seal on it being Saxon. All the windows of the church were inserted in the 15th. century although the nave piscina is from a century earlier.

We therefore have three slit windows of flints in the tower, that were most probably the Saxon belfry windows, an unmoulded tower arch with only simple imposts, and the most positive feature, the blocked circular window beside the south porch roof, that is certainly Saxon. The proof that I needed after my last book, is certainly here in the features I have described.

N 64. MOULTON. St. Mary.

K6. Sheet 134. Map Ref. T.G. 402 066

Church and Tower Middle SAXON.

Tower Height approx.	35ft.
Internal Diameter Grd:	7ft.10"
Tower Wall Thickness	3ft. 9"
Bells 1	
Chancel Width	18ft. 9"
Nave Width	18ft. 6"
Chancel Length	34ft. 2"
Nave Length	49ft.11 "
Nave Wall Thickness N.	2ft. 6"
Nave Wall Thickness S.	2ft. 9"

This church is now closed. It is not on a hill, but on fairly high ground not far from the Acle marshes. It has a round west tower, nave and chancel in one and south porch.

I feel that the tower and church are Saxon, although there are few features to identify them as such. The tower is short and narrow, being only about 35ft. tall with an internal diameter of 7ft. 10" and a wall thickness of 3ft. 9" it is certainly of Saxon date, especially as the wall construction is in the Saxon style. The height and wall thickness place this tower in the middle period. I was not able to ascend the tower, where there may be more positive features to see. The ground floor west window is a double-light of the Perpendicular period, but it is now blocked. The only other windows in the tower are two belfry windows. A rectangular one with a wooden frame on the north and a slit window having a dressed stone frame facing south.

The tower, which is a plain cylinder with a red tiled cap, very similar to nearby Freethorpe, and is built of uncoursed flints. There are no fillets between tower and church, and the tower internally is curved on its eastern side, which confirms that tower and church were built together. The tower arch is tall, being 13ft. 9", and there is no sign from the nave of an upper doorway.

The south porch is of Tudor brick and has a fine large scratch dial on the S/W corner of the entrance, and one faint possibility on the eastern jamb below the hood-mould. This has been spoiled by scratching in our own time. The central hole still retains a piece of the original gnomon embedded in the central hole. There are two or three other faint scratch dials on the centre nave buttress close together. There is one votive cross on the R/H jamb of the south door.

The nave and chancel are continuous, without a chancel arch, which is an early sign, and the nave wall thicknesses give even further proof. The nave width of 18ft. 6" is another feature quite common in Saxon churches. The windows of both nave and chancel are mainly Early English with two Perpendicular in the nave. Most of the chancel windows have been fitted with wooden frames, although keeping the traditional tracery. The nave has a modern roof, while the chancel is plastered. Outside, all the roofs are in red-brown tiles. This is another round towered church that is in the care of the *"Redundant Churches Fund"*.

N 65 . NEEDHAM. St. Peter.

I9. Sheet 156. Map Ref. T.M. 231 819

Tower and Nave Middle SAXON.

Tower Height	53ft.	Bells 3	
Height of Circular Stage	40ft.	Chancel Width	13ft. 6"
Internal Diameter Grd:	8ft. 7"	Nave Width	18ft. 8"
Tower Wall at West Window	3ft. 7"	Chancel Length	16ft. 1"
Tower Wall over T/Arch	3ft. 4"	Nave Length	45ft. 4"
Nave Ridge Height	29ft.	Nave Wall Thickness at sills.	2ft. 8"

This church stands on the north side of the village street in quite flat countryside. The river Waveney winds its way not far away to the south. The church consists of a round west tower with an octagonal top, nave, chancel and south porch.

Although no writer to my knowledge has referred to this church as Saxon, there can be no doubt about it when all the features are seen and recorded. The tower is 53ft. high and the circular part just 40ft., which places it in the middle Saxon period. The octagonal belfry has Perpendicular windows and quoins of brick, which would seem to place it with the stair turret of knapped flints and brick in the Tudor period. The brick porch with stepped gables is also of this age.

Below the present belfry, which houses the three bells, can be seen the four original belfry windows at 32ft. from the ground. The west and north have been blocked, and the east and south have been made into smaller rectangular lights The closed north window is now an alcove with a wooden frame as if to take a door to make it a cupboard. The circular stair turret to the first floor is at the south of the tower. The tower arch, which adds more weight to our Saxon dating is 9ft. 4" tall and is cut straight through the flint wall with no dressed stone facings or imposts. It has a cruck shaped head and only a simple chamfer towards the nave and it is now plastered over. The internal diameter at the ground is 8ft. 7" and no steps could be seen in the tower walls to thin them, but the nave west wall has a ledge at a height of 10ft. 6" to thin this wall by about 4 inches. This has been noticed in many Saxon churches but not in Norman The flints of the tower are entirely uncoursed and there are no fillets between tower and church. Once more the nave is quite narrow being only 18ft. 8" wide with an even narrower chancel at 13ft. 6". The nave walls slope, i.e. thin towards the roof, and are only 2ft. 8" thick at the window sills. So although buttresses hide the early quoins, enough evidence remains to call the tower and nave Saxon. The chancel has been rebuilt on its old plan in red brick.

There is a scratch dial four feet up on a buttress to the east of the porch. The roof is arch-braced with a high collar and also braced longitudinally. The arch braces are moulded and the tie-beam near the chancel arch is well carved. The original belfry windows still show their triangular heads. The upper doorway, not seen from the nave, can still be seen inside the tower at 17ft. 3" from the ground. It now has a pointed head of modern bricks.

N66. NORTON SUBCOURSE. St. Mary

K7. Sheet 134. Map Ref. T.M. 407 986
Tower and North Wall SAXON.

Tower Height approx.	45ft.
Internal Diameter Grd:	9ft. 7"
Tower Wall Thickness	4ft. 2"
Bells 6	
Chancel Width	23ft. 3"
Nave Width	23ft. 3"
Chancel Length	39ft. 10"
Nave Length	62ft. 8"
Nave Wall Thickness N.	2ft. 8"
Nave Wall Thickness S.	2ft. 7"

This church is in the cluster of R/T Churches near Haddiscoe in the Waveney Valley. It consists of a round west tower, nave and chancel in one, and has no porch.

The roofs are of slate, and the church is interesting because we can see the one major change over the centuries. The tower, entirely circular and without battlements has a parapet of red bricks, and these extend down to the very tall Y-traceried belfry windows with dressed stone frames. They are of Early English date. There are nine windows in all below the belfry, mostly of the narrow lancet type, which makes this tower quite unique. It is constructed of whole and cut flints, average to small in size, with little other materials mixed in. The tower is curved internally on its eastern side, and is off centre to the church, so after being built together, the church was widened towards the south to its present width of 23ft. 3". As all the windows and piscinas date from the Decorated period (14th. century) it seems most likely that this was when the church was widened. This appears to be the last major change as all the important features are of this date. The narrowness of the church before this, points strongly to a Saxon dating, in spite of a thick tower wall of 4ft. 2". There are no other surviving features except an unmoulded tower arch that must always have been low because of the low level of the upper doorway. The width of the nave before the widening was only 14ft. 11". The upper doorway is round-headed and only 12ft. from the ground, but there is nothing to establish its age. There is, however, a 6 inch ledge to thin the tower walls at 9ft. from the ground which would reduce them to 3ft. 8".

The bells were rehung in 1883 when the treble was presented by the Vicar, Arthur T. J. Thackeray M.A., to complete the peal of six. The fifth bell was recast in memory of the above Vicar in 1951.

The bells were again restored by Public Subscription, and aided by the Baron Bell Trust; and re-dedicated on 12th. December 1964.

N67. NORWICH. St. Benedict. TOWER

I6. CITY
Middle SAXON

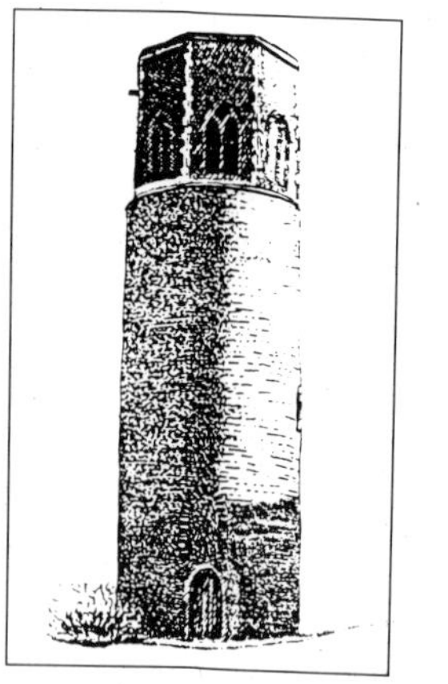

Only the tower remains, preserved by the city, after the church was destroyed by the raid on Norwich in April 1942. It is circular with an octagonal belfry and has a parapet without battlements. Y-traceried windows are in alternate faces with flushwork copies in the others.

The flintwork is uncoursed and the ground floor west doorway shows that they were not as unusual as is generally supposed. An upper doorway can be seen in the east face, but the interior has not been seen and no features survive to point to for a date.

We are left with a Norman dating by most writers, who cannot give us any positive dateable feature, and Mr. Whittingham, who calls it 13th. century, based on the flintwork, and some masonry used in a put-log hole. My dating is based on the narrow nave of the original church, and the wall thickness, which I feel certain is under 4ft. thick.

N68. NORWICH. St. Etheldreda

I6. King Street

Tower and Church SAXON.

Tower Height	38ft. 6"
Height of Circular Part	25ft.
Internal Diameter Grd:	10ft. 4"
Tower Wall Thickness	3ft. 8"
Bells removed	
Chancel Width	19ft. 7"
Navc Width	19ft. 3"
Chancel Length	25ft. 2"
Nave Length	46ft. 1"
Nave Wall Thickness N. & S.	2ft. 4"

This is one of the redundant churches of Norwich, and although few Saxon features have survived, it must nevertheless be placed in this class. It is in thc city in King Street, and is on quite a steep slope west to east, but not at the top of the hill. It has a short round tower with an octagonal top, nave, chancel and south porch.

The circular part of the tower is only 25ft. high, and it is quite probable that this was once taller. The total height at present with its octagonal belfry is 38ft. 6", while the diameter internally is 10ft. 4". The wall thickness is 3ft. 8", so the measurements fall into the Saxon pattern. The octagonal section has been very much restored in Victorian and recent times, but appears to be of Tudor form. The bells have been removed. There are fillets between church and tower, and although they seem to have been restored are fairly certain to be Saxon. The tower and nave walls are of whole flints, but the chancel, which must have been refaced is of cut flints. The tower and church were certainly built together and the walls have every indication of Saxon workmanship. The nave walls which measure only 2ft. 4" are very thin even for Saxon builders, but the Norman doorway to the south prevents the mistake of thinking that they are post-Norman. To the south of the nave is a shallow buttress, 32 inches wide and 6 inches deep, which although it now has its edges of dressed stone, is no doubt a Saxon pilaster dressed up with later adornments.

The church windows are a mixture of Early English, Decorated and Perpendicular, and show how, being amongst the wealth of the city, the older and historical features rapidly disappear as the latest thing in fashion is introduced.

No votive crosses were seen but there is one scratch dial on the R/H jamb of the south doorway at the springing of the arch.

N69. NORWICH. St. Julian

I6. CITY

Base of Tower, North Nave and South Chancel SAXON

Height of Tower Base Approx	20ft.
Internal Diameter Grd:	12ft.11"
Tower Wall Thickness	3ft. 5"
Bells 2	
Chancel Width	15ft.
Nave Width	17ft. 2"
Chancel Length	20ft. 9"
Nave Length	33ft. 2"

This church and tower were partly destroyed by bombs in the last war, but the bombing showed up some of the blocked Saxon windows in the nave and chancel that had long been forgotten. Thankfully these remain to tell us its age although those we knew in the tower have been lost.

The stump of the tower has been recased in cut flints and is now only about eaves height. Its internal diameter is 12ft. 11" with a wall thickness of 3ft. 5". The tower stump is roofed and there are fillets which are hardly original since they are recased with cut flints the same as the tower, but they certainly enclose the original Saxon fillets beneath the newer casing.

J.H. Parker's *"Architectural Notes of churches in the city and neighbourhood of Norwich"* 1847, shows the tower with a double-splayed window. Rev. Messent, in *"The City Churches of Norwich"* in 1932 also shows this window. So there is good evidence that the tower was Saxon although only about half the present stump, which reaches the eaves, is original.

The two bells which were in a frame to the south of the tower, in the churchyard, have been overhauled and re-hung in the thickness of the wall on the west side of the tower. The medium bell is inscribed "AVE GRACIA PLENA DOMINUS TECUM". The small bell is inscribed: "J. Warner & sons London. 1904. "

Of the church, most of the north nave wall, but little of the north chancel wall remains from the pre-Conquest period. These details are from drawings by the architects in Taylor and Taylor's book *"Anglo-Saxon Architecture"*. In the old nave north wall is the main doorway, and near the east end of the nave is a restored Y-traceried window, while above and slightly west is the circular Saxon double-splayed window. Further west and about the centre of the nave is a round-headed double-splayed window, while above the north doorway is a pointed window.

West of this is the feature of two windows cutting into each other. The nave is 17ft. 2" wide and the chancel 15ft. In the south chancel wall that remained standing, the Taylors told us that internally we could see the other Saxon circular window, but in 1976 this was not visible, and had been plastered over. However, careful searching outside, has resulted in finding the blocked up window outlined in flints, but it is not easy to see.

N70. St. Mary-at-Coslany

I6. CITY

TOWER Late SAXON

Tower Height	48ft.
Height of Belfry sills	33ft.
Internal Diameter Grd:	10ft. 1"
Tower Wall Thickness	3ft. 6"
Bells removed	
Chancel Width	19ft. 6"
Nave Width	26ft. 1 "
Chancel Length	36ft. 4"
Nave Length	66ft.10"

Another redundant city church that stands on flat ground. It has a round west tower, nave, chancel, north and south transepts and south porch .

This is just one more R/T church that was not recognised as Saxon until repairs on the neglected tower revealed the Saxon belfry windows in late Victorian times. It may, therefore be well to examine these first and then to see what other Saxon features remain.

The four double-light Saxon windows with triangular heads are 33ft. from the ground. They are constructed entirely of flints at the jambs and heads, but the balusters and through stones are not Saxon, although the Taylors make much of these stones and their shapes, even stating the stone is from Caen. Although some may be early, I believe that most of this stone is from the date of the repairs, as one report at that time stated that four or five different types of stone were in these windows. This implies that they had been repaired more than once. It also implies that although we can rely on the flintwork of these windows; whatever date or style the stonework is, does not alter the date of the windows. The balusters are of several pieces, and even half cylinders; and the projecting annulus at the middle of each baluster does not conform to any Saxon or Norman tradition.

The tower, which is now 48ft. tall was lowered at the time the Saxon belfry was discovered, for before then an octagonal belfry was above this section. The ground floor diameter of 10ft. 1 " and wall of 3ft. 6" thick is what one would expect in a Saxon tower and I would place it in the late Saxon period. It is constructed of large flints, whole and cut, and not coursed in any way. It is circular for its full height and has no battlements. Besides the belfry windows, the only other window is in the west face on the ground floor. Between the church and tower on the south side we can see part of a fillet over the porch, and the north side shows one clearly for its full height. This one must have been covered at some time by a north stair turret, as the two blocked up doorways at the N/E of the tower show internally. One at ground level, and the other on the first floor at 20ft. 6". Outside, at the N/E of the tower is a base of flints that confirms the existence of the stair turret mentioned above. The fillet was covered by this and survived the demolition.

Internally, the tower is straight on its eastern side, which denotes it was added to an earlier church, which would have been in the late Saxon period, but as we shall see, little if any of this has survived. There is no upper doorway, and this was most probably completely blocked up when the later church was built.

All the windows in the nave, chancel and transepts are Perpendicular, so there was a massive reconstruction during that period, but can we place any part in an earlier period? With a nave width of 26ft. 1", it seems impossible that this has survived from the original Saxon church, and the chancel width of 19ft. 6" is still rather wide. Here, however, there is a blocked up Decorated window which places the chancel at least in the 14th. century. So once more the wealth of the city, while producing these fine churches, does at the same time destroy the history of these buildings.

N71. SOUTH PICKENHAM. All Saints

D6. Sheet 144. Map Ref. T.F. 857 041

Middle SAXON

Tower Height approx.	40ft.
Height of Circular Section approx.	30ft.
Internal Diameter Grd:	11ft. 7"
Tower Wall Thickness	3ft.
Bells 1	
Chancel Width	18ft. 8"
Nave Width	18ft. 8"
Chancel Length	24ft. 3"
Nave Length	42ft.
Nave Wall Thickness N. & S.	2ft.10"

The church of All Saints stands on quite a mound in the centre of its small village. The ideal spot for those who want to call these Watch Towers. It has a round west tower with an octagonal top, nave and chancel in one and north porch .

The tower is short and stubby and constructed of whole and cut flints with quite a lot that are cut and heavily cemented. I believe that it has been extensively resurfaced, but not an added layer, as the walls are only 3ft. thick, and the nave west wall over the tower arch is only 2ft. 8". The continuous nave and chancel without a chancel arch, of only 18ft. 8" wide and 66ft. long fits ideally into Saxon measurements, so I got the feeling that this tower and church could well be pre-Conquest. I have so far been unable to climb the tower to gather more evidence, but there is enough to justify a Saxon dating.

The octagonal belfry has four double-light windows of the 14th. century, but the battlements of brick are not shown on Ladbrooke 's print, so they are probably of the 1870 restoration. The circular stage is only about 30ft. tall which gives it an indication of being very early. There are steel ties through the circular and octagonal sections. There are only two windows below the belfry. In the west face, on the first floor is a rectangular window faced in brick, and about 10ft. from the ground is a slit window, the only feature that is possibly Norman. It has a dressed stone frame of evenly sized stones, and the lintel is a single stone with its lower edge shaped into a semi-circle. Inside, this window is well splayed and could well be from the Norman period. This window and the narrow church should be enough to agree with other writers that here is a tower at least Norman, but the walls are far too thin for a post-Conquest dating. Over the tower arch the measurement is only 2ft. 8", so although the interior is curved, there is the possibility that the Saxon church is earlier than the tower. There are no fillets and no signs of an upper doorway from the nave.

The church has 13th. century north and south doorways without hood-moulds, and windows of all periods. The remarkable feature is the number of blocked up windows between the present ones, that has destroyed most of the original walls. Why was each new window cut through afresh, and the old one blocked up? It seems so unnecessary. To the north of the chancel is what appears to be a semi-circular buttress of cut flints of recent date, but it is referred to by earlier writers as *"a peculiar chimney"*. It must therefore be the flue of a Victorian slow combustion stove for heating the church.

The east window is rather special, being a four-light Reticulated window, but the lights have ogee heads, which is very rare in these windows. At one time the chancel roof was lower, leaving much of the tracery of this window above it. The Victorian restoration thankfully altered the roof line to bring it back once more within the church. The organ with a very fine case, came from West Tofts in the Thetford Battle Area.

N72. LITTLE PLUMSTEAD. Sts. Protase & Gervase

J5. Sheet 133. Map Ref. T.G. 307 109

Tower and Church Middle SAXON.

Tower Height	44ft. 7"
Internal Diameter Grd:	7ft. 6"
Tower Wall Thickness	3ft. 4"
Bells 1	
Chancel Width	17ft. 3"
Nave Width	17ft. 3"
Chancel Length	21ft.10"
Nave Length	52ft. 7"

This tiny church, hidden away behind the trees, stands next to Little Plumstead Hospital. It has a round west tower, nave and chancel in one, and south porch.

The church is interesting, if only for no other reason than the dedication is unique in Britain. Since my first book, I have been able to ascend the tower and to confirm Ladbrooke's print, and even add more to what I believed. The tower is 44ft. 7" tall and 7ft. 6" diameter at ground level; it is horse-shoe shaped indicating it was added to a towerless church. The small battlements and single-light Early English style belfry windows are of Victorian date, and the tower has been raised from what must have been very short originally. The battering tower walls with large mortar points indicate Saxon rather than Norman workmanship and the wall thickness at 3ft. 4" adds more weight to this belief. This can be finally established within the tower where three Saxon circular double-splayed windows can be clearly seen, although they are now blocked, confirming Ladbrooke's print. There are no fillets to the tower, but a small circular aperture at eye level in the west face, is a squint to enable latecomers to see how far the Mass had progressed before entering.

The plan of the church is undoubtedly Saxon by virtue of its narrowness and length. The walls however, clearly show that if not rebuilt, they have been altered and refaced several times over the years. All the windows are Perpendicular, and all have been more or less restored. But one wonders, with all the repairs and patchwork of the flints, just how much of the original walls remain. The south doorway is Norman with its hood-mould of billet ornament, and the north doorway has its inner Norman frame, but while these features place these walls to this period at least, they make too easy the real task of finding the age of when these churches were built.

N73 . PORINGLAND. All Saints.

J7. Sheet 134. Map Ref. T.G. 271 017

UNCERTAIN

Tower Height	47ft.
Height of Circular Stage	33ft. 6"
Internal Diameter Grd:	8ft.10"
Tower Wall Thickness	3ft. 6"
Nave Ridge Height	30ft. 6"
Bells 1	
Chancel Width	17ft. 5"
Nave Width	23ft. 6"
Chancel Length	31ft. 3"
Nave Length	42ft. 6"
Nave Wall Thickness N.	3ft. 3"
Nave Wall Thickness S.	3ft. 2"

This is another church that still stands on a slight rise in its village. It consists of a round west tower with octagonal top, nave, chancel, south porch and north vestry. Since 1976 an octagonal church hall has been built on the north and connected to the church via the north vestry by a glass-sided passage-way .

Although I have been to the top of this tower, there is no sign of Saxon work here, or for that matter Norman. In the church there are no features earlier than the 14th. century, Although I am certain that the walls were here well before that. All the early writers call this tower Norman, but there is nothing to prove this except the circular shape of the tower, and this is as much Saxon as Norman, and the wall thickness of the tower in my opinion excludes a Norman dating.

The tower is constructed of whole flints with some small pieces of conglomerate here and there. The octagonal top is 14th. century with four double-light belfry windows in alternate faces and flushwork tracery in the others. There are no battlements. Below the belfry windows, the tower is a perfect cylinder with no other features except one round-headed window in the west face with a brick frame . There is no upper doorway and no signs of any blocked up windows. The tower arch has a pointed head and dressed stone facings to the nave only.

All the chancel windows are from the Decorated period, while those of the nave are Perpendicular. The unusual feature here is the six clerestory windows of the 15th. century to the north and south with no aisles beneath them. Probably it was intended for aisles to be built, but perhaps the finance could not be found. The church walls are of whole flints, and one piece of conglomerate was seen in the chancel. The nave walls slope slightly to thin them, so this early trend has continued.

N74. POTTER HEIGHAM. St. Nicholas

K4. Sheet 134. Map Ref. T.G. 419 199

Tower Middle SAXON

Tower Height approx.	48ft.
Height of Circular Stage approx.	35ft.
Internal Diameter Grd:	9ft. 9"
Tower Wall Thickness	3ft. 9"
Nave Ridge Height approx.	35ft.
Bells 3	
Chancel Width	16ft. 4"
Nave Width	16ft.10"
Nave & Aisles Width	39ft.
Chancel Length	33ft. 3"
Nave Length	59ft. 6"
Arcade Wall Thickness	2ft. 1"

This round towered church is on a slight rise overlooking flat countryside and near the river Bure. It has a round west tower with an octagonal top, nave, chancel, north and south aisles and south porch.

Once more, the credence of church writers is called to question, as one after another calls this tower Norman with no features they can point at to substantiate their claim. The round tower with its octagonal belfry stage and battlements, has only four belfry windows and a ground floor window, all Decorated and of 14th. century. Neither the tower arch nor the south doorway is earlier, and yet they insist that features such as windows and doorways must determine the age of a building.

Let us now examine the tower in the light of the new evidence I have found. Although I was not able to ascend the tower, there was sufficient evidence to call it Saxon. The circular stage is about 35ft. tall, which would place it in the Middle Saxon period. The total height is about 48ft. There are large fillets between tower and church, which I have found to be a reliable guide to a Saxon dating, and it is these that gives the first positive dating. With a diameter of 9ft. 9" and a wall thickness at 3ft. 9" the measurements also coincide. Then the construction of the tower walls, with whole flints from chalk beds, and some very large ones that are uncoursed, can override the evidence of later windows. No upper doorway can be seen from the nave, and the tall tower arch has been altered in later years. The curved east wall inside the tower, confirms that tower and church were built together. Of the three bells in the tower, two are pre-Reformation.

The chancel is only 16ft. 4" wide, and so must almost certainly be the original building and the ground plan of the nave whose width is 16ft.10" must also belong to the original church, although how much of those walls remain is very uncertain. The 14th. century aisles are seemingly of the same date as the alterations to the tower, and possibly also the chancel windows. The nave roof is a single-hammerbeam of modern construction and the church is roofed in Norfolk reed thatch. The clerestory windows, six to the north and six to the south are exceptional for their size in such a village church, and the moulded brickwork of the south porch is also very fine.

N75. QUIDENHAM. St. Andrew

F9. Sheet 144. Map Ref. T.L. 028 877

Tower Middle SAXON

Tower Height including Spire approx.	80ft.	Chancel Width	18ft. 9"
Tower Height to Battlements approx.	58ft.	Nave Width	19ft. 2"
Height of Circular Stage	38ft. 6"	Nave & Aisle Width	32ft. 1"
Internal Diameter Grd:	11ft. 1"	Chancel Length	31ft. 2"
Tower Wall Thickness	4ft.	Nave Length	52ft. 3"
Nave Ridge Height	34ft. 6"		

This beautiful church at the edge of Quidenham Park, is within sight, says the legend, of the resting place of Boudica. The church consists of a round west tower, with octagonal top and spire, nave, chancel, south aisle, south porch and north transept.

This tower is classed as Saxon by some writers, but Norman by others, most probably on their interpretation of the four blocked circular windows only. These are at north, south, N/W and S/W, and about 23ft. from the ground. They were shown up by facing the circular openings with cut black flints. It is these that swayed the Taylors to accept the tower as Saxon, although these windows do not show inside the tower. However, when I visited this church in 1992, the tower had been restored, and these windows had been restored with new facings of conglomerate in long blocks. A very sad restoration I thought of these early windows. There are other features however, that add further confirmation for a Saxon dating, for there are two quarter-round fillets between tower and church, that taper off where they reach the roof. They are fairly large and about 23ft. high . The tower is constructed of whole flints of average size with slightly larger ones at the base. They are not coursed, and are set in mortar with large joints. The only window in the circular stage is the ground floor west window, a single-light of the Perpendicular period with a squared head, and this is filled with stained glass. Near the top of the circular stage is a clock, but it is not working although the mechanism is still in the tower.

About four feet above the nave ridge the circular stage ends, and this was probably the original height of the tower. Above here the tower is octagonal with four double-light belfry windows of the Decorated period, and on alternate sides are four dummy windows with similar tracery in flushwork of dressed stone and cut black flints. The octagonal stage is finished with deep battlements of dressed stone and whole flints, and at each corner there is a fine pinnacle (one was replaced in 1925). The tower is crowned with an octagonal spire that reaches to 75ft. or 80ft., recorded by Charles Cox, as added about the time of Richard II i.e. late 14th. century. However, if we are to believe the sketch in the church, the present spire is much taller than the one drawn when there were no pinnacles to the battlements.

Inside the church we see a Norman tower arch that is quite tall, and is most probably a Saxon arch faced with dressed stone during the Norman period. At 18ft. above the floor, and only to be seen inside the tower, is the upper doorway, 1ft. 8" wide by 6ft. tall. There are eight bells to the peal of this tower which has a wall thickness of 4ft., which is once more within the Saxon measurements.

The nave and chancel roofs are in red tiles, while the south aisle is leaded. The south aisle is built of knapped black flints and dressed stone facings, while the simple 13th. century doorway has a half-round hood-mould with a large carved face as the R/H stop and a ladies face at the L/H. At the north of the nave is an early Norman doorway with one engaged column on either side and cushion capitals with scroll work at the top. The imposts have a simple chamfer, and the head is a simple arch of plain dressed stone, and a three-quarter moulding, and a hollow chamfer to the outer order. A north transept projects from the east end of the nave, and the walls are of knapped black flints. The north and east chancel walls seem to be the oldest still standing, as all the rest are faced with knapped black flints. So even if the cores are ancient, no features remain to identify them. Almost all the windows have been renewed from the 14th. and 15th. centuries when they were inserted, but a few still have a little of the early stonework.

N76. RAVENINGHAM. St. Andrew

K7. Sheet 134. Map Ref. T.M. 398 963

Tower and Church Middle SAXON

Tower Height	49ft. 3"
Height of Circular Stage	35ft.
Internal Diameter Grd:	8ft. 4"
Tower Wall Thickness	3ft. 9"
Nave Ridge Height	35ft.
Bells 5	
Chancel Width	20ft. 1"
Nave Width	20ft. 4"
Nave & Aisle Width	32ft. 5"
Chancel Length	37ft. 8"
Nave Length	51ft. 8"
Aisle Wall Thickness N.	2ft. 2"
Nave Wall Thickness S.	2ft.10"

This church is situated in the grounds of, and close by the Hall. It is on flat ground and is in a circular churchyard..

Although this place goes back to pagan times as a site for worship, we have to search for the Saxon features that remain. It consists of a round west tower with octagonal top, nave, chancel, north aisle, north vestry and south porch.

The church and tower appear to have been built together, and the only Saxon indications are the three round-headed windows on the first floor of the tower. They have their heads set back on their jambs, and are of flints inside the tower. These show their Saxon origins, although dressed stone on the outside has altered their flint facings. Likewise, the tower arch, inside the tower it is of rough flints, but in the nave it is faced with cement. There are five bells in the tower and they were rehung in 1885 by George Day and Son, Bell Hangers of Eye. The north and south round-headed windows on the first floor of the tower are blocked with flints, and there is a square opening on the second floor on the east side at 24ft. 6" from the ground that gives access to the roof timbers, but this cannot be said to be an upper doorway .

The top stage is octagonal and is finished with stepped battlements. There is no stair turret and the four belfry windows are Early English lancets. Below these are only three round-headed windows, all in the west face, on the second, first and ground floors. The tower arch, is round-headed and appears to have only the imposts of dressed stone, but we cannot be certain of this, as it is cement rendered. There are no fillets between church and tower.

The nave and chancel are only just over 20ft. wide and the south nave wall is 2ft.10" thick, so both the width and the wall thickness come within the Saxon measurements that I have found by recording.

The four arcades of the north aisle have octagonal piers and wide pointed arches with double chamfers. They are cut through the wall, and there does not appear to be much dressed stone used in the arcade. The external roofs are of slate, and most of the windows are from the Perpendicular period with one lancet in the south of the chancel, and the east window being a three-light from the 14th. century. Most appear to be original with slight restorations.

Two lancets, one Y-traceried window and the south priest 's door have bcen blocked up in order to install the large and significant Bacon Memorials. All the walls are cement rendered so nothing can be learned from these.

N77. REPPS-WITH-BASTWICK. St. Peter

K5. Sheet 134. Map Ref. T.G. 422 169

Tower Middle SAXON

Tower Height	46ft. 9"
Height of Circular Stage	31ft. 9"
Internal Diameter Grd:	9ft.10"
Tower Wall Thickness	3ft. 9"
Nave Ridge Height	31ft. 9"
Bells 3	
Chancel Width	17ft. 8"
Nave Width	22ft. 1"
Chancel Length	34ft. 5"
Nave Length	36ft.10"
Nave Wall Thickness N & S.	3ft.

Round tower with octagonal top, nave, chancel, and south porch. The roofs are of slate and the walls are of flints containing many cut flints.

The tower contains the only positive Saxon features, but it was built against an earlier stone church, of which at least the west wall remains standing. This we can tell by the flat wall inside the tower, and the measurement over the tower arch which is only 2ft. 8" against the 3ft. 9" measured at the west window. The Saxon tower, or circular part is 31ft 9" tall and has a diameter of 9ft. 10" and the walls measure 3ft. 9". With its octagonal belfry stage it measures 46ft. 9" and there are three bells to summon the faithful. The four belfry windows are double-light with triform lights under a round-headed arch. There are four dummy windows in the alternate faces. Only one other window is still open, which is on the ground floor in the west face. The tower is not sectionised and there are no fillets, but its eastern side is flat internally, and it is clearly not in bond.

There are a number of features to fix this tower in the middle Saxon period, with this or an earlier stone church. The height of the circular stage gives us the period, and the tower arch is tall and round-headed; it has simple chamfered imposts and the head is set back on the jambs by about 3 inches. The entire arch and jambs are cement rendered, so I cannot be certain if the walls and facings are flints or dressed stone, but suspect it is flints. The ground floor west window is about 10ft. from the ground, is round-headed and has no dressed stone inside, so may well be Saxon with a later frame of dressed stone on the outside. Internally, 16ft. above the floor there is a 6 inch step to thin the walls of the tower and this is quite usual in Saxon towers, but not so in Norman. On the first floor, 18ft. 6" up, to north and south are single-splayed round-headed windows, that are now blocked up. These look very much like Saxon windows with flint frames and they have their heads of flints laid in non radial fashion. Ridges of the boards can be seen in the heads where they were put until the mortar set. The outside frames however, cannot be seen now. On the east is a repair in red bricks that seems to be Victorian, and the signs are that this was an upper doorway, as the flints around this are selected for flatness and they appear to frame a round-headed arch.

As stated before, I have seen nothing to confirm a Saxon dating for the present church, and the nave windows are Perpendicular with restorations. The chancel presents us with a slight problem for while Charles Cox tells us it is late Decorated, Pevsner calls it 18th. century. It is built in red brick and has all its windows of Victorian age. So, was this done after the visit by Charles Cox, i.e. early this century, or did Cox make an error?

N78. ROCKLAND. St. Peter

F7. Sheet 144. Map Ref. T.L. 990 971

UNCERTAIN

Tower Height	56ft.
Height of Circular Stage	42ft.
Internal Diameter Grd:	11ft. 9"
Tower Wall Thickness	3ft. 8"
Nave Ridge Height	38ft.
Bells 2	
Chancel Width	16ft. 2"
Nave Width	22ft. 6"
Chancel Length	32ft. 1"
Nave Length	43ft. 9"

Situated on flat ground well away from its scattered village, the church consists of a round west tower in two stages, separated by a stone string course and an octagonal belfry without battlements, nave, chancel, north and south transepts, north porch and south vestry.

This is another church having a thatched roof that was damaged by fire when burning rubbish in the churchyard in 1948. The tower, in 1974 was in rather poor shape as the repairs done in 1909 were not considered to be very satisfactory. On the roof are two lead castings, one says:- "Lacey and Upcher Architects. J. T. Gibson Plumber Norwich. Waters and Sons Builders Watton. 1908." The other one is inscribed:-"J.A.B. Fleming Rector. C. H. Colman, A.S. Sayer. Ch. Wardens. 1908. " The four belfry windows have double-lights with ogee heads of the Decorated period. The alternate faces have dummy windows. There are two bells, a medium sized made by John Warner and Sons Ltd. London 1902 and one small bell, probably a Sanctus bell. Below the belfry, in the upper circular stage, are three rectangular windows which are 1ft.11" wide by 3ft. 9" tall. They have stone lintels and sills inside and full stone frames outside. There is another large opening to the east, this must be the old upper doorway, although the original shape and frame cannot now be defined. At the N/E, between the splays of two windows, can be seen an old fireplace with a flue at the back. Flints and early bricks are in the jambs. Opposite, at the S/W, a similar alcove, with an ash-pit, was probably an oven for baking the wafers. The flue seems to have been filled in. We see also the familiar masonry ties, one above the other on the south, west and north, three at each point.

There are no steps to thin the walls of this tower and no fillets. The stair turret at the S/E corner carries up to the top of the circular stage. The tower is curved on the east, so tower and church were built together. The tower is constructed of whole flints of average size with no coursing, and there are some curious blocks of stone at the base, which I believe are erratics and not dressed stone. This adds more weight for a Saxon dating of the tower which is 11ft. 9" in diameter and has a wall thickness of 3ft . 8". The tower arch is tall and pointed but little can be learned of its date,

The north porch, which is dated 1624, is built of cut black flints and dressed stone, with brick window frames, hood moulds and decorations on the buttresses. Massive pillars guard the entrance, while a simple pointed arch encloses the south door. There are no votive crosses, but on a south buttress are two scratch dials, one being very faint .

The nave still retains its thatch in spite of the fire but the chancel and north and south transepts are tiled. The church walls are of whole flints with the corners of dressed stone. The south vestry was built in 1908 at the same time as the church was restored after sadly falling into disrepair. As the London Graphic stated at the time :-"Queen Alexandra contributed £5 towards the restoration of the quaint old thatched roofed church of Rockland St. Peter. The architecture of the church is mostly Early English and the roof is one of the few remaining in England that are thatched. "

This church has suffered much from neglect, fire and also from drastic restoration, but the loving care shown for it now gives one hope for the future.

N 79. ROLLESBY. St. George.

L5. Sheet 134. Map Ref. T.G. 446 158

Tower Late SAXON

Tower Height	66ft.
Circular Stage Outside	28ft.
Diameter Grd: N. to S.	10ft.11"
Tower Wall Thickness	3ft. 6"
Nave Ridge Height	31ft.
Bells 3	
Chancel Width	17ft. 2"
Nave Width	12ft. 5"
Nave & Aisles Width	42ft. 2"
Chancel Length	31ft. 3"
Nave Length	47ft.
Arcades Thickness	2ft. 6"

This church has few houses nearby, and has the tallest of all the Norfolk round towers. It has a round lower stage of its west tower, and two octagonal stages, a tall nave, chancel, north and south aisles and north porch .

The dedication of St. George, is generally regarded as being late, but the tower here at least is Saxon. This is the tallest of the Norfolk round towers, being 66ft. tall, with only Mutford in Suffolk being six inches higher. This tower looks even taller by reason of its two narrow octagonal stages. Internally, however, we can see that it is not all it appears to be, for like the octagonal section of Ashby in Suffolk, the lower octagonal section here was circular in the first place. When built, the round tower was 46ft. high, but in the 14th. century they cut the outer face of the top half, to make it octagonal, which is confirmed by the circular internal shape up to 46ft. Then a further octagonal stage was added, octagonal inside as well as out. The belfry has four windows of the Decorated period, which gives us the date of these changes. The height of the circular part gives us the late Saxon period for its building, although its oval shape would imply that it was earlier. It is oval to the extent of being 10ft.11" north to south and only 9ft.11" east to west.

There are three bells in t he tower, and apart from the belfry windows, there is one small window in the lower stage of the octagonal section, and the wall thickness here is only 2ft. 4", further proof of the wall being thinned. A ground floor window was inserted in the 15th. century.

The tower arch is very tall with a pointed head, but it is faced with dressed stone. At its head it measures 3ft.

Most of the church is in the Decorated style, with a particularly narrow nave, and wider aisles. The two west piers of the arcades are circular, and the others octagonal. The small cubicle at the S/E corner with an opening to the altar and the west has still not been explained. Outside, the chancel has some fine carved pinnacles.

There are four scratch dials on the south doorway; three are on the west jamb and one on the east.

N80. ROUGHTON. St. Mary

I2. Sheet 133. Map Ref. T.G. 220 365

Tower, Parts of Nave and Chancel Late SAXON.

Tower Height	50ft.
Internal Diameter Grd:	8ft.
Tower Wall Thickness	3ft. 8"
Nave Ridge Height	34ft.
Bells 3	
Chancel Width	16ft. 7"
Nave Width	16ft. 9"
Nave & Aisles Width	37ft. 4"
Chancel Length	32ft. 2"
Nave Length	50ft. 5"
North Aisle Wall Thickness	2ft. 2"
South Aisle Wall Thickness	2ft. 5"

This church is situated just outside the village on rising ground, and almost at the top of a hill. It has a round west tower, nave, chancel, north and south aisles, and north and south porches. The nave, chancel and north porch are slated, and the two aisles and south porch have lead roofs.

This is a very fine Saxon tower built mainly of conglomerate and flints. It is circular inside towards the east, so we can say it was built with the church. This tower and church have been placed in the late Saxon period because the Saxon part of the tower is well over35 ft. common to the early towers, and the technical ability of the builders is superior.

The base of the tower for about 3ft. is large flints, then there is a section of conglomerate in herringbone pattern, and then one row of flints followed by one row of conglomerate. Another single row of flints is once more followed by a further section of conglomerate in herringbone fashion and then more flints. We have now reached the height of the double-played circular windows, at north, south, and a round-headed window at the west. These circular windows are reliable Saxon features, and these are built of conglomerate. For about 10ft. above these windows there is a section of much smaller flints, followed by another section of larger flints with no coursing. We then reach the three slit windows at north, south and west. Above these we reach the belfry stage which is almost all conglomerate. The four double-light Saxon windows are constructed almost entirely of conglomerate, even the balusters and through stones, although some of the balusters now have bricks at the back to give support. Above the belfry stage is mainly flints, but with some conglomerate and brick mixed in. Then at roof level is a course of early brick, and the battlements are a panelling, of early brick and cut white flints. The height of the tower is 50ft. with an internal diameter of 8ft. and a wall thickness at the west of 3ft. 8" . There are fillets between tower and church, once more mainly of conglomerate with the occasional flint.

The three bells are inscribed as follows :-

East bell:- Tho. Newman Made Me. 1713.
Middle bell:- ANNO DOMINI 1612.
West bell:- ANNO DOMINI 1612.
The east bell is still bright inside as though it had recently been tuned.

The inside of the tower is lined mainly with large flints up to belfry level, and conglomerate above this. At 16ft. up, on the first floor, is an upper doorway 2ft. 6" wide by 4ft. 10" tall. It has been altered in shape and is hidden from the nave by the organ. The tower arch is tall and has been opened out to the full width of the tower, so although the Taylors refer to its head as Cruck-shaped, I feel sure that its shape cannot be called original.

Turning now to the church, the old S/W quoins are plainly seen to be large blocks of conglomerate and while the N/W are not so plain, one or two blocks can be made out. This then, proves that the church was also Saxon before the addition of the two aisles, and the width of the nave and chancel confirm this. The old church would not have been pulled down, but merely enlarged and so the Saxon parts can possibly be identified. The chancel would still be the original with later windows inserted, but the east end may have been shortened or lengthened.

Just to the east of the chancel arch is a south priest 's door, and at the east jamb, the plaster has been cut away to show the conglomerate jambs at several points. These jambs then are from the original Saxon doorway, although the head has been altered. While the chancel has retained its windows from the Decorated period, the nave windows were altered about 100 years later .

It is strange to find so little old furniture inside such an ancient exterior. This must no doubt be due to the extensive restoration of 1865. In 1926-28, there was a major restoration of the tower when the circular windows were discovered. In 1959 to 66, the bells were rehung and the tower floors were restored. At this time the tower was tested before the organ was placed over the tower arch and it was declared to be in extremely good shape.

N81. ROYDON St. Remigius

G9.Sheet. 144. Map Ref. T.M. 096 804
Tower and Church Late SAXON

Tower Height	62ft. 6"
Height of Circular Stage	45ft.
Internal Diameter Grd:	10ft. 6"
Tower Wall Thickness	4ft.
Nave Ridge Height	35ft. 6"
Bells 1	
Chancel Width	18ft. 7"
Nave Width	17ft. 8"
Nave & Aisle Width	32ft. 9"
Chancel Length	34ft. 5"
Nave Length	55ft. 7"
Nave North Wall Thickness	3ft.
South Aisle Wall Thickness	2ft. 9"

Roydon church, with its unusual dedication has little left to show its age. It consists of round west tower with an octagonal top, nave, chancel, south aisle, north and south porches. Its site is not elevated at all and few houses were close by, but new development means that new homes are being built to give, we hope, new life to this delightful church.

It is truly Saxon in shape, and before the aisle was added in the 13th. century was tall, long and narrow, having a chancel width of 18ft. 7" and the nave only 17ft. 8" The west wall of the nave thins by about 6" at the springing of the tower arch, as do a number of Saxon churches. The church is entered by the north porch, which is a fine example of Perpendicular work, with five niches for statues round the entrance. It has such strong connections with the one at Gissing that most probably both were designed or built by the same person.

The north wall of the church, which must be the oldest, is built of whole flints of various sizes and no coursing is apparent. All the windows on the north are Perpendicular in style although many have been heavily restored, but two in the north of the chancel have particularly fine cusps in the heads. The east window, and all those on the south are Victorian in the Decorated style. A south priest's doorway in the chancel seems to be from the 13th. century and is without a hood-mould. This was when the south aisle was built. The arcades were cut straight through the wall, and the old wall still serves as the piers for the four arcades with simple chamfers to the piers and arches. This south aisle was heavily restored in 1864, and the south porch which had been built in 1840 was then removed and rebuilt at the east end of the south aisle to house the organ.

The tower is 62ft. tall and its diameter is 10ft. 6" with a wall thickness at the west window of 4ft., while over the tower arch it is only 3ft. 7". The impression this gives, is that the tower was recased in the Victorian restoration. It is curved inside which indicates that church and tower were built together, but little can be learned , as both church and tower underwent such drastic restoration in 1864. The tower till then, had a shallow lead cap to a short circular tower, but then, the octagonal stage and battlements were added. The belfry, which used to contain three bells, now only has one small bell, for the three original bells were sold in 1975 to pay for repairs needed to the tower. This is now cement rendered up to the first string course, and from there to the base of the belfry stage is the Victorian casing of knapped black flints. The belfry stage is of knapped flints with dressed stone facings ;and the battlements with pinnacles have flushwork and cut flints, and shields in quatrefoils round the parapet. The small slit windows below the belfry have dressed stone frames outside and the inner splays are of Victorian red bricks.

Here is another church and tower, where a quick visit will surely say it is Norman or later. The arcading of the south aisle proves that this work was done in the 13th. century. The church must have, been standing then, but it cannot be Norman, as the walls are too thin and the plan of the church too narrow.

N82.RUNHALL. All Saints

G6. Sheet . 144. Map Ref. T.G. 058 069
Tower and West Wall Middle SAXON

Tower Height approx.	40ft.
Internal Diameter Grd:	11ft.11"
Tower Wall Thickness	3ft. 3"
Nave Ridge Height Approx.	25ft.
Chancel None	
Nave Width	26ft. 9"
Width of Chancel Arch	13ft.10"
Sanctuary Length(part of Nave)	7ft. 4"
Nave Length remainder	30ft. 5"
Nave Wall Thickness N. & S.	3ft.

Another very small church in a very small community. It has lost its chancel and is in grave danger of closing its doors. So far I have not been able to ascend the tower, where I feel certain more evidence of a Saxon dating is to be found, but from the ground there is still enough.

Internally, the tower is straight on its eastern side, and there is no bonding to the nave west wall. Therefore it was added to this wall of a church that was here before the tower. It is about 40ft. tall, and is almost 12ft. in diameter with a wall thickness of only 3ft. 3", thin even for Saxon builders, and surely too thin for Norman work. The ground floor west window is a narrow slit window and quite tall, with a flint frame. On the first floor is another flint framed window that is now blocked up. Both these windows must be Saxon, for we have no evidence of the Normans building such windows without dressed stone. There are no fillets; and the flintwork of the tower is roughly coursed of flints of many sizes which show through the cement rendering. They are well coursed above the nave roof, and there is more brick and tile near the top. The parapet is of well coursed flints and contains a lot of brick and tile.

The tower arch has a 13th. century door under a pointed roof of dressed stone, and a fine original door with much original and fine ironwork. It is hard to tell whether this was the west entrance of the towerless church or if a tall tower arch was closed in and this door fitted in the Early English period, for although a great deal of dressed stone covers the wall behind this door, there is no frame of a tower arch to be seen. The large amount of carved dressed stone with chevrons and other mouldings however, are clear indications that some important Norman feature has been removed. The probability is, it was the south doorway. The north doorway is now the most elaborate and is from the 14th century. Why I wonder was this more impressive than the south? Was it the main entrance at this time? The window to the east of the north door has billet moulding round the head, and shows how old Norman stone from some other part was re-used to build this window.

The windows of the church are a mixture of Early English and Perpendicular; and we have seen the evidence of the Norman work, although not now in the features they once occupied. The nave width at present is too wide for the church that must have been here in the middle Saxon period, and we can see cracks in the nave west wall that may represent the extent of the original nave of this early church. The present arrangement of the nave roof suggests this, with its brackets and wooden columns as of a cheap version of side aisles.

The chancel was burnt down about the middle of the 16th. century, and the foundations can still be traced outside. So parts of the nave west wall are the oldest in this building, with the Saxon tower built against this. The tower was raised in the Early English period when the present belfry windows were built.

N83. RUSHALL. St. Mary the Virgin

H9. Sheet. 156. Map Ref. T.M. 198 826

Tower and Church Middle SAXON

Tower Height	51ft. 6"
Height of Circular Stage	35ft.
Internal Diameter Grd:	7ft. 5"
Tower Wall Thickness	4ft.
Nave Ridge Height	33ft.
Bells 1	
Chancel Width	20ft. 6"
Nave Width	19ft. 4"
Chancel Length	26ft. 2"
Nave Length	47ft. 7"
Nave Wall Thickness N & S	3ft. 2"

Rushall's church stands beside the green with a few houses nearby. It has a round west tower with octagonal top, nave, chancel, and south porch.

The tower is 51ft. 6" tall with the circular stage 35ft. This places the tower in the middle Saxon period, of about 950 to 1,000. The octagonal stage was added in the 13th. century with Y-traceried windows and dressed stone quoins. No parapet or battlements were added. The diameter of the tower is only 7ft. 5", which is very narrow, and the wall is 4ft. thick. On the first floor, and 22ft. from the ground, is a blocked circular window. It was this feature that made Pevsner say, this might be a Saxon tower. It has a circular frame of early bricks in the outer face, and has been blocked up with flints. It has obviously been deliberately left in situ, and in spite of the considerable splay and decay on the inside, I would confidently call this a circular Saxon window. Other Saxon features in the tower are a ledge at 20ft. 6" that thins the wall by 4" to 6" which is common in Saxon towers. On the first floor is an upper doorway now showing a fairly large pointed head of the 13th. century. It is blocked on the nave side, and in the tower gives no idea of its true size and shape. The tower arch is 12ft. tall, with a shallow pointed head, called by the Taylors cruck-shaped. It is cut straight through the wall and has no dressed stone in its frame.

The one bell in the tower is inscribed:-
John Goldsmith Fecit (made me) 1712.
To the Glory of God and in memory of Mary Eliza Gape.
Recast by her daughter Mary Elizabeth Campbell 1912.
J.E. Player. Vicar.
E. Pymar) Churchwardens
E. Algar)

The construction of the tower is of small to average whole flints of many hues and not coursed. It is sectionised, Showing where work finished for each season. There is no conglomerate in the walls. To the S/E corner of the tower is a stair turret, with a door inside the tower, but the stairway is in ruins. Like the previous tower of Runhall, this was added to an earlier church, and the tower shows clearly inside by not being circular, but a little over a D plan. With a narrow nave of 19ft. 4" and the chancel walls sloping to thin them, there are good indications that this is the church against which the Saxon tower was built .

In the north nave wall is the blocked up arch of an old chapel. The nave windows are Perpendicular with the chancel being Early English, although most of these have been renewed. The east windows are most unusual, being two, and not the usual three lancets of the Early English period. Scratch dials:- one on the east jamb of the south priest's door 4ft. up, and another 5ft. up on the S/E quoins.

N84. GREAT RYBURGH. St. Andrew

F4. Sheet 132. Map Ref. T.F. 962 272

Tower and Church Late SAXON

Tower Height	52ft. 6"
Height of Circular Stage	40ft. 6"
Internal Diameter Grd:	13ft. 3"
Tower Wall Thickness	4ft.
Nave Ridge Height	32ft.
Bells 6	
Chancel Width	18ft. 9"
Nave Width	22ft.
Chancel Length	38ft. 11"
Nave Length	46ft. 11"
Nave Wall Thickness N. & S	2ft. 7"

Great Ryburgh church, on the west bank of the river Wensum, appears to lie in a hollow, for the ground rises on all sides. It consists of a round west tower with an octagonal top, nave, chancel, north and south transepts and south porch. The roofs are red-brown tiles and the church walls are mainly of whole flints .

The tower is 52ft. 6" in height, with the circular part 40ft. 6". It has a diameter of 13ft. 3" and a wall thickness of 4ft. On the first floor there is an upper doorway with a triangular head. The jambs and head are of flints but the head is not set back on the jambs in the usual Saxon fashion. This however may well be due to later plastering filling in this rebate. It is 2ft. 4" wide by 7ft. 1" tall. To the west, on this floor is a round-headed window with jambs and head of flints and odd stones laid *non radially*, i.e. in Saxon fashion. Outside, this window still has some of its original frame of conglomerate. Much conglomerate in large blocks are in the lower parts of this tower. About 12ft. up, the tower walls change from conglomeratc to a band of quite small flints for about 4ft. then they become average in size to the top of the circular section. The octagonal top has four double-light Decorated windows and dressed stone quoins. The parapet, without battlements is of cut flints and dressed stone. There is no stair turret, but a wooden staircase leads to the first floor. No fillets are between tower and church. The tower arch was modified in Norman times and the inner face of the tower is curved, implying that tower and church were built together. There is a peal of six bells. The west tower doorway was probably the main entrance in early days, although many of these have now been lost, but the church guide tells us that there used to be a porch to shelter this west doorway until 1891 when the present south porch was built, and the west porch was demolished.

Nearly all the church windows are Perpendicular, from when the transepts were added, but the east window appears to be a Victorian copy or a Perpendicular restoration. The corners show that the same walls are here from Saxon days. At the S/W, the quoin has been replaced with dressed stone in small blocks, but the lowest stone is a megalithic block stood on end in the long-and-short style from Saxon times. The N/W corner has remained undisturbed behind the buttress (plate 37) and is still visible as large blocks of conglomerate. These large blocks can be seen in the boiler room at this point going down 3ft. below the present ground level.

The east and north walls of the chancel look distinctly Saxon with the large amount of conglomerate in them, and proof of their age can be seen on close examination of the buttresses at the N/E and S/E. Large blocks of conglomerate can be seen behind these that are clearly corner stones of the wall before the buttresses were added. Thus we can see clear signs in all the walls except the transepts and porch to date them to the late Saxon period.

One further point noticed on my visit in 1979, there are certain signs in the tower, just above the nave ridge of at least four circular windows, as seen outside. There may possibly be eight . These have not at present been checked inside, but I am certain that they are there and are Saxon. An overwhelming amount of pre-Conquest evidence, yet the Taylors said "The indications of pre-Conquest workmanship are far from conclusive."

N85. SEDGEFORD. St. Mary

C2. Sheet 132.Map Ref. T.F. 707 365

Tower and Parts of Church Middle SAXON

Tower Height	56ft. 6'
Height of Circular Stage	40ft.
Internal Diameter Grd:	10ft. 5"
Tower Wall Thickness	3ft. 7"
Nave Ridge Height	40ft.
Bells 3	
Chancel Width	18ft. 1"
Nave Width	17ft. 7"
Nave & Aisles Width	54ft.
Chancel Length	22ft.10"
Nave Length	73ft. 11
North Arcade Thickness	3ft. 7"
South Arcade Thickness	3ft. 9"

St. Mary's Sedgeford is in a valley and very low. It is below the level of the village which is unusual, and I have found nothing to explain it. The church has a round west tower with an octagonal top, nave, chancel, north and south aisles, south transept and north and south porches. The aisle roofs are leaded, nave and porches slate and the chancel felt.

The main walls of the church are whole flints, with carstone, which came from nearby quarries, used for repairs. The clerestory is cut white flints.

St. Mary 's Sedgeford is the largest church in the R/T group, being almost a cathedral in its size and complexity among these small village churches, and having a total width of 54ft. and length of nave and chancel being 96ft. 9". All the windows except two in the north of the chancel are Perpendicular, and these odd ones out are an Early English lancet that is original and a two-light window of Victorian age. But in spite of its size, there are still only three bells in the tower.

Let us examine this church and try to see how and when the new parts were added. First the tower: the tower arch has been widened out, and so we cannot see whether the church was here before the tower or not, so we will say they were built together. The tower is 56ft. high and the circular part 40ft . with a diameter of 10ft. 5" and wall thickness of 3ft. 9". So the circular section has indications of a Saxon date; the top, or belfry stage is octagonal with no battlements or spire, and the belfry windows are double-light Y-tracery and have centre columns, so I feel that they are late in the Early English period. There are three other windows and one blocked window in this tower, and we need to look closely at these. The ground floor has a double-light Perpendicular window, but on the first floor at the west, the outside shows a triangular-headed window which is round-headed inside the tower. But another blocked up window is triangular-headed. To the south on this floor there is a triangular-headed opening that was a window, but which now looks into the gap between the tower and vestry. A chimney breast in the north vestry would have covered or blocked any opening on this side. Towards the east, repairs or blocking of the tower wall may well be the upper doorway but no distinct shape can be made out to confirm this. The tower is 3ft. thick at this height.

On the second floor a quatrefoil window of dressed stone is later, and inside it is round-headed, not circular . The tower shows no sign of carstone, although in the later west wall, built out to the western face of the tower, there is a pattern of carstone blocks and large flints laid alternately. Carstone has also been used in the church walls, but it appears, for repairs only. It would appear that the tower, narrow nave of 17ft. 7" and chancel were built first, then the octagonal belfry and the two aisles added in the Early English period, followed by the south transept a century later, and the two porches built in the 15th. century. Later still the aisles were extended to the west of the tower to make two vestries, most probably in Victorian times. I would think that the circular part of the tower, nave and chancel were built in the middle Saxon period, of 900 to 1,000 based on the tower wall thickness and the two triangular-headed windows. The church was repaired in 1842 and again restored in 1882 .

N86. SEETHING. St. Margaret

J7.Sheet 134. Map Ref. T.M. 320 979

Tower Late SAXON. Possibly Chancel also

Tower Height to top of Spire	66ft.
Height to top of parapet	56ft. 9"
Height to ridge of flints.	37ft. 3"
Internal Diameter Grd:	11ft. 3"
Tower Wall Thickness at W. window	4ft. 6"
Tower Wall Thickness at T/Arch	3ft. 9"
Nave Ridge Height	38ft.
Bells 3	
Chancel Width	16ft. 6"
Nave Width	26ft. 7"
Chancel Length	30ft. 5"
Nave Length	50ft.10"
Nave Wall Thickness N. & S.	2ft.10"

This church is well supported and is kept in quite good shape . This was the cleanest tower that I had so far been up and it was in very good condition. The windows below the belfry are all glazed and the belfry windows have wooden frames and behind this is strong wire netting, which really keeps the birds out. The church has a thatched nave, slated chancel and north vestry and round west tower with a small spirelet and a south porch that is slated.

The tower is 56ft. 9" tall but it is 66ft. to the top of the spire, and it has a diameter of 11ft. 3" and a wall thickness of 4ft. 6" at the west window. There are three bells and at 33ft. from the ground there is a ledge of about 4 inches to thin the tower walls internally.

There are fillets between tower and church of the type that is well known on Saxon towers. A patch of medieval brick below the west window, is I believe the blocking of a west doorway, as the tower is flattened inside at this point . The upper part of the tower from nave ridge level has also been extensively repaired and there is a ridge here on the outside that reduces its diameter, and which could well be the original height of the tower.

The tower was raised and the belfry windows inserted in the 15th. century. A small Norman window can be seen on the first floor, and the ground floor west window is from the 14th. century. The tower is fully circular internally, so the tower and church were built together. The difference between the wall thickness on the west, and over the tower arch, I believe is due to a recasing of the tower. There is an upper doorway on the first floor that is round-headed, but alterations make this untrustworthy for dating purposes .

Although the chancel could well be Saxon, the nave at 26ft wide is too wide for this period. Close examination of the nave west wall however, gives reason to believe that the nave has been widened, for there appears to be the old flint quoins about four feet in from north and south corners. The north side of the church has two windows from the Early English period. The south of the nave has two examples from the 15th . century.

Not much evidence of Saxon date, but the quarter-round fillets are a very positive feature, and the ledge to thin the tower walls has not been seen in any Norman tower. The evidence of the nave west wall is very strong by reason of the flint quoins that can be seen; and the chancel width is based on the large number of narrow chancels seen in Saxon churches . When naves were widened, the chancels were generally left, or the whole church would have been rebuilt on a larger scale .

The south porch is Perpendicular and is in whole and cut flints, but now has no niche or windows. Inside the nave, the flooring of at least two earlier levels have been uncovered and preserved and can be seen by lifting; wooden covers . This church was re-thatched in 1992 thus keeping its tradition in spite of the great expense of this form of roofing.

N 87. SHEREFORD. St. Nicholas

E3. Sheet 132. Map Ref. T.F. 887 296

Tower and Church Middle SAXON

Tower Height approx.	40ft.
Internal Diameter Grd:	11ft. 4"
Tower Wall Thickness	4ft. 4"
Bells 1	
Chancel Width	16ft. 9"
Nave Width	17ft.11"
Chancel Length	23ft. 6"
Nave Length	43ft. 9"

St. Nicholas Church Shereford, is not far from Fakenham and quite close to the river Wensum. It has a round west tower with a lead cap, nave and chancel roofed in red-brown tiles, a shallow open south porch and signs of a 13th. century north aisle that has since been removed and the Norman doorway reset, probably for the second time in the north nave wall.

The most positive Saxon signs are in the nave, so we will start there. The Saxon round-headed double-splayed window in the south of the nave (plate 27) is only one of the features that date this church as Saxon. The whole nave, except for the altered windows, Norman doorways and filling in of the north arcades is of Saxon date. The herringbone work below, and the large amount of conglomerate, (not carstone as per Taylor) above this double-splayed window, all speak of Saxon workmanship. The N/W and S/W quoins are of early brick below, probably repairs, but above these are large flints, and above these again for the top eight feet are large blocks of conglomerate. The N/E quoins are still visible and are also of large flints and conglomerate. The S/E quoins are the only original quoins that are missing.

The north and south doorways were altered in Norman times when dressed stone became available, and inside the low nave doorway can be seen the taller opening in use before the newer doorway was inserted. In the Early English period a north aisle was added, and the north wall cut through for the arcades. The Norman doorway was moved and reset . Later, when the aisle was removed, the old Norman doorway was moved back into the original north wall. This doorway is now blocked up, but is still in the wall.

The walling of the chancel appears later than the nave, but this may be due to refacing of the surface. The nave west wall is thinned by a six inch ledge at 20ft. from the floor, and there is also a slight thinning at 12ft. over the tower arch. This is quite common in Saxon churches, but I have never seen it in Norman walls.

The tower diameter at 11ft. 4" is wide, but by no means unusual in Saxon towers. The wall thickness at 4ft. 4" is very unusual, but I believe that the other features will outweigh this. At 16ft. up on the inside a ledge narrows the tower by 6 inches, and behind the Norman tower arch is a taller arch of undressed stone with a round head, which must be before the early Norman arch and so must be pre-Conquest. The walling of the tower is very roughly constructed of whole flints with bands of conglomerate at various levels. The west face has been flattened with conglomerate, probably when the window was made smaller. The tower roof was a wooden cone inside battlements, but had deteriorated to such an extent that by 1976 repairs were undertaken that have radically altered the shape of the top. The battlements have been filled in, and a shallow lead cone covers the top completely.

There are only two belfry windows, of Y-tracery of the 13th. century at north and south, while the ground floor window of early brick is the only other window in the tower. The first floor window appears to be inside the conglomerate frame of a larger blocked triangular-headed window and above this is another blocked up window showing parts of its jambs as conglomerate. Inside, the tower is curved at the east, which implies that tower and church were built together. There is a great deal of evidence here to place this tower and church beyond dispute in the Saxon period .

N88. SHIMPLING. St. George

H9. Sheet 156. Map Ref. T.M. 156 826

Tower and Church Middle SAXON

Tower Height	53ft.
Circular Stage	38ft.
Internal Diameter Grd:	7ft. 7"
Tower Wall Thickness Grd:	4ft. 8"
Tower Wall Thickness 1st. floor.	3ft. 5"
Nave Ridge Height	30ft.
Bells 3	
Chancel Width	17ft. 3"
Nave Width	17ft. 3"
Chancel Length	29ft. 3"
Nave Length	42ft. 8"

Shimpling is another church with the dedication of St. George, and it stands at the end of a grassy lane surrounded by green fields. It has a round west tower with an octagonal belfry and a shingled spire. The nave and chancel are the same width, and there is a north porch. Although the walls of nave and chancel are the same height, the chancel roof, with its steeper pitch raises it above the nave. The porch has a base of red brick and a timber top.

Although the tower is regarded as Norman and the church later, there is ample evidence of

Saxon workmanship that I hope to show. The tower is 53ft. tall and the spire adds another 25ft. The circular stage is 38ft. tall, and if we can prove a Saxon dating, this would probably place it in the middle Saxon period, or 900 to 1,000. It has an internal diameter of 7ft. 7" and the wall is 4ft. 8" thick. This is very thick for a Saxon tower, but I believe that it has been recased. Its internal east wall is curved, so tower and church were built together. There are three bells in the tower that were checked about 1980 and are now rung by clappers. The spire is covered with shingles and not lead as recorded by Cautley, and there are no fillets between tower and church. The octagonal belfry stage has four double-light Decorated windows of the 14th. century, and on alternate sides are four dummy windows in flushwork of dressed stone and knapped flints. The construction of the tower is of whole flints of all colours and of average size with no coursing. There is some early brick mixed with the flints and the ground floor window is a large Perpendicular window of two lights. There is no upper doorway, and a stair turret of Tudor date is on the south side and opens into the return wall of the tower arch. It is built of brick and flints with a brick staircase.

The tower arch is 20ft tall and 5ft. wide; it is cement faced and has only a simple chamfer on the nave side. The head is Cruck shaped, and there is every reason to suppose it is built of flints. Although the tower walls are 4ft. 8" thick on the ground floor, at first floor level this has reduced to 3ft. 5". therefore, although the tower arch may be the only positive feature, the wall thickness is now seen as much more like Saxon work.

Moving on now to the church, we examine the quoins. The N/W are Megalithic for about 10ft. and are somewhat like long-and-short work, and face alternate above. The S/W corner has similar quoins, Megalithic for the first 10ft . The narrow nave and chancel of 17ft. 3" and being without a chancel arch, must be regarded as early. Towards the end of the Saxon era the naves were getting wider, and near to or over 20ft. wide. With the quoins to support our thinking, we can now regard this nave and chancel as pre-Conquest. In the south wall of the nave is a blocked Norman window, so we have positive evidence that this wall is at least Norman in date, and our other evidence pushes this back to Saxon times .

The nave has four Perpendicular windows and the chancel windows are all Early English, but this does not mean that the nave and chancel have been rebuilt, see the N/W and S/W quoins. These windows all appear to be original with some restoration work in most. Some interesting early glass can be seen in a number of windows . On the west buttress of the south wall about 5ft. up is a scratch dial, it is in fine condition. No votive crosses were seen. This church is now cared for by the *"Redundant Churches Fund"*.

N 89. SIDESTRAND. St. Michael

J2. Sheet. 133. Map Ref. T.G. 260 397

Built in 1881. Replacing an Early Church

Tower Height	49ft. 6"
Height of Circular Stage	22ft. 6"
Internal Diameter Grd:	8ft. 9"
Tower Wall Thickness	3ft. 5"
Nave Ridge Height	32ft. 9"
Bells 3	
Chancel Width	15ft. 8"
Nave Width	27ft. 1"
Chancel Length	23ft. 6"
Nave Length	39ft. 7"
Nave Wall Thickness N. & S.	2ft. 9"

This church, situated in a very small village on the main Cromer road, was reconstructed from the materials of the Norman round tower church that stood on the cliffs about one third of a mile to the east. It was built as near as possible to the style of the original church, with a round west tower with an octagonal top, nave, chancel, south porch and north vestry. All the roofs are of lead except the vestry which is of slate. The construction is of whole flints that are fairly large and dressed stone facings.

The tower is 49ft. 6" in height with an octagonal top and battlements, and an internal diameter of 8ft. 9". It was rebuilt in the style of the earlier tower. When the church was demolished and the materials used to build the new church, the old tower was left standing on the cliffs until the sea finally claimed it in 1916. Around the tower on the cliff top a garden was created with poppies and called "The Garden of Sleep". Many poems were written and countless picture cards published concerning this tower and garden and its connection with Flanders and the Great War. The differing shape of the cliff top tower and the present tower causes some confusion when saying the church was rebuilt in the same style, until it is pointed out that the tower of the cliff-top church had fallen in 1841 and had been replaced by a smaller tower. This, it was felt, was not worth moving, so it was left on the cliffs, and the tower on the new church copied as far as possible the tower that had fallen in 1841.

There are three bells all cast in 1881. The first is inscribed: "I am the Tenor of three Bells Purchased with money collected by Elma Katie Hoare. F.G. Simpson-Rector. J. Warner & Sons LONDON. 1881."

On the first floor of the tower there are three circular windows with dressed stone frames. I wonder if these are copies of Saxon windows known to have been in the original tower, but I don't suppose we shall ever know. There are signs of cemented vertical cracks on the first floor at the S/W and the N/W. This, within 100 years of its building is a fine tribute to the strength and workmanship in these early towers and churches. The tower is straight on its eastern side as are those towers which were built on to existing churches. I wonder why this tower was built this way and not circular inside? Was it copied like this from the old tower?

N90. LITTLE SNORING. St. Andrew.

F3. Sheet. 132. Map Ref. T.F. 953 326

Tower Middle SAXON Church Early NORMAN.

Height of Tower to top of cap	44ft. 6"
Height to top of Tower Walls	37ft. 6"
Internal Diameter Grd:	10ft. 4"
Tower Wall Thickness	3ft. 6"
Bells 1	
Chancel Width	22ft. 7"
Nave Width	21ft.10"
Chancel Length	25ft. 5"
Nave Length	59ft. 9"
Nave Wall Thickness	3ft. 4"

The only detached round tower in Norfolk. It stands on a hill away from the village, and has a conical cap. The tower stands to the S/W of the church, which consists of nave, chancel and south porch.

All writers appear perplexed that this tower, which they variously call Norman or Saxon, should have had its church demolished so soon and a new one built. Pevsner even suggests it was never completed, because, he claims the two buildings are of a very similar date. On close inspection, we can see that the tower belonged to a completed church, for we can see the roof line. I would place the two buildings at least 150 years apart, and I agree with a local man who gave the reason for the rebuilding as the stream that runs past the church to the east. Although now only the merest trickle, no doubt in Saxon times it was both wider and deeper, and may have flooded the nearby land at certain times. He thinks, and I agree, that when thinking of enlarging the church in early Norman days, they decided against extending towards the stream (or river) and preferred to build another church where they would not be so restricted. The fact that the present church extends past the tower to the west supports this view. The size of the present church, which is wider and longer than most early Saxon village churches also points to an early Norman date .

Let us now examine the tower, which is the oldest part, and see what we can discover. It has a conical cap of red-brown tiles containing four dormer windows. There were no fillets between this tower and the old church. The walls contain a very large amount of conglomerate mixed with the whole flints, and this gives a decided sectioning effect to the tower. There are also signs that the conglomerate has been laid in a herringbone fashion. Much of the conglomerate is in the lower parts, in quite large blocks. It is 37ft. 6" to the top of the tower walls, which gives us the period of Middle Saxon. The one bell is dated 1770. The internal diameter at ground level is 10ft. 4" with a wall thickness of 3ft. 6". The tower arch is 6ft. 9" wide by 11ft. tall and is round-headed and built entirely of conglomerate. The jambs are of very large blocks, and some sizes are as follows:- 23" x 16" x 11"; 20" x 17" x 13"; and 17" x 11" x 15". The material and also the size are far different from Norman practice, but I believe that the arch from the imposts has been altered, albeit with the same material, whether in Norman times or perhaps later, in order preserve the tower after the demolition of the church. The four original belfry windows are much lower than the height of the tower at present . These windows inside the tower are built of flints, and the north one is completely blocked, while the south and west are closed down to slit windows. There is one other blocked up window in the tower. There was an upper doorway which is now blocked, and it had a triangular head as can be seen from inside the tower. The weather strip of the nave roof, on the east side of the tower, refutes Pevsner's suggestion that this church was never completed.

The walls of the church are of whole flints, early bricks and conglomerate, and the roofs of dark grey-black tiles. The north nave and chancel doors are now blocked up. The two west quoins are of conglomerate, while buttresses at the east, hide whatever quoins are there. This appears to put a Saxon date on this church, which could well make 100 years difference to its age. More likely, these quoins were reused from the old church in early Norman days before dressed stone was readily available . From my studies I have found that while the Normans liked to use dressed stone for their corners, they were not against reusing the old blocks of conglomerate in the early days. Although late Saxon churches were getting wider, and some were as wide as Little Snoring, the wall thickness of 3ft. 4" helps us to give this church a positive Norman dating.

To the east of the south doorway there is a panel of walling bordered by neatly cut dressed stones laid in the long-and-short manner. This however is far too new and neat to be Saxon work, and appears to be more like Victorian, but it was here in Ladbrooke 's day. So far I have heard no explanation of why this work was done .

Having settled the question that the present church was not built until at least Norman times, there is no shortage of evidence to place it in the Norman era. The north nave doorway is early Norman and there are two Norman round-headed windows in the nave, one north and the other south. The south doorway is very curious, and something of a mystery. It has three arches, the inner, round-headed; the middle pointed; and the outer, stilted or horseshoe. While some writers see this as a Transitional doorway, others believe that it has been altered from an earlier doorway; and we have seen this done in many churches. It is certainly quite pleasing.

The church windows show all the periods, Norman, Early English, Decorated and Perpendicular, and the three large lancets of the east window are Early English and are shafted inside .

No votive crosses were seen, but there is one scratch dial on the S/E window in the chancel.

N91. WEST SOMERTON. St. Mary

L4. Sheet. 134. Map Ref. T.G. 475 195
Tower and Church Middle SAXON

Tower Height approx.	55ft.
Height of Circular Stage approx.	40ft.
Internal Diameter Grd:	9ft.
Tower Wall Thickness	4ft.
Bells 1	
Chancel Width	17ft. 7"
Nave Width	19ft. 2"
Chancel Length	34ft.
Nave Length	60ft. 2"
Nave Wall Thickness N.	3ft.
Nave Wall Thickness S.	2ft.11"

Here we have a round west tower with an octagonal top, nave, chancel, and north porch. It stands on a hill, well above the village and one entry is through a farmyard, although there is also a narrow lane that leads to the church. In the churchyard lies Robert Hales, the Norfolk Giant, who was 7ft. 6" tall and weighed 33 stone. This is inscribed on the casket tomb on the north side of the church. The tower's one bell is inscribed:- *"Johanne de Lenne me Fecit"*. It is a good example of the Lynn foundry and was cast before 1300. So says the history of the church. The tower, which I was unable to ascend as it requires a very long ladder to reach the first floor, is about 55ft. tall to the top of the octagonal section which has no battlements, and about 40ft. to the top of the circular stage . It is constructed of whole flints of medium size, and besides the double-light Decorated window on the ground floor, there is only a very narrow slit window in the west face near the top of the circular section. This has a frame of early brick, and may well prove to be Saxon. Above this, the very tall octagonal stage of the 14th. century is of flint with dressed stone quoins. The belfry windows are wide lancets on four sides, and dummy lancets on alternate faces. The top and parapet is of early brick and appears to be later. Many put-log holes are to be seen outside and three are left open. Inside, the tower is curved towards the east, which means the church was built with the tower. The tower arch is tall and narrow, and is almost certainly of Saxon age, for no dressed stone is returned into the tower.

The church walls are cement rendered, but much of this is now peeling off, so we may soon be able to assess these walls much better. The nave has windows from Early English times to the 15th. century, while the chancel windows are all Perpendicular, with embattled transoms and ogee-headed lights . The east window is very large of five lights . The north wall leans outward and is supported by a brick buttress, and the north porch was built in the 14th. century.

The nave and north porch are thatched in the Norfolk tradition while the chancel is slated. There is one small scratch dial that has been re-set below the S/W nave window, it is only 3 1/2 inches across. The fine series of wall paintings were restored between 1976 and 1979. There are signs that there may have been a west doorway in the tower before the west window was inserted.

N92. STANFORD. All Saints

D8. Sheet 144. Map Ref. T.L. 858 947
NORMAN at least.

Tower Height approx.	40ft.
Height of Circular Stage approx.	30ft.
Chancel Width	20ft.
Nave Width with Aisles	50ft.
Chancel Length	20ft.
Nave Length	34ft.

Stanford church is in the Thetford Battle Area, and my visit was at the courtesy of the Army authorities. It is very difficult to gain access at the present time. I took no measurements, and the tower height is an estimate, and the other measurements were taken from *"Blomefield's Norfolk History"*. It is remote from any village and consists of a round tower with an octagonal top, nave, chancel, north and south aisles and south porch. The roofs are of red-brown tiles, and the walls of well coursed whole flints . The tower is circular up to nave ridge height, about 30ft. and with the octagonal top containing four Perpendicular belfry windows and four flushwork dummy windows, it is about 40ft. tall. Its pre war conical lead cap has now gone. The only other windows in the tower are a ground floor Perpendicular window to the west, and a slit window with a dressed stone frame on the first floor. There is still a clock face, only one, showing westwards near the top of the circular stage. There are no fillets, and no features are visible to give any idea of a Saxon dating. But at least it is Norman, for a fine Norman arch in dressed stone leads from the nave into the tower. Circular columns are at the jambs, made up of small stones of even size, with cushion capitals and simple chamfered imposts. The round-headed arch is again in even sized small stones carved to a three quarter-round moulding of a similar size as the columns at the jambs.

The north aisle has five Perpendicular windows, three in the north wall, one west and one east. The south aisle would seem to have one less where the south porch is situated. The chancel windows I cannot recall or have any record. Little else can be said, as this was only a short visit, but some odd masonry had been inserted into the south wall. These include a carved face, probably a corbel, some chevron moulding, two crosses and part of a quatrefoil that appears to have been part of a border. No votive crosses or scratch dials were seen.

N93. STOCKTON. St. Michael

K8. Sheet. 134. Map Ref. T.M. 388 941
Tower and Nave Middle SAXON

Tower Height	43ft. 6"
Height including Spire	70ft.
Internal Diameter Grd:	8ft. 9"
Tower Wall Thickness	4ft.
Nave Ridge Height	31ft. 6"
Bells 1	
Chancel Width	15ft.11"
Nave Width	15ft.11"
Chancel Length	22ft.10"
Nave Length	52ft. 9"
Nave Wall Thickness N.	2ft.11"
Nave Wall Thickness S .	2ft. 7"

The church consists of a round west tower with a lead spire, nave and chancel in one, south porch and north vestry. Only a few houses are in this narrow lane off the main Beccles to Norwich road.

The tower is 43ft. 6" tall with circular battlements, and a lead spire adds a further 25ft. making a total of about 70ft. There are a great many scratchings round the base of the spire including "Robert Bernard of Stockton 1816 and E. Godard of Hardley 1816". The internal diameter of the tower is 8ft. 9" with a wall thickness of 4ft. The tower, being curved on the eastern side, seems to prove that tower and church were built together, so if we can prove one to be Saxon, the other most probably would be also. The church gives us the first clue, being long and narrow, 75ft. long, and nave and chancel the same width at 15ft. 11". The nave wall thickness also implies Saxon work, while the windows include every period from the Early English to Perpendicular. While no major reconstruction appears to have altered its size in any way, the parishioners seem to have kept in the fashion by inserting one or more windows at each major period of church building. as can be seen by these walls.

The tower and church were once completely cement rendered, but most of this has come off the chancel, which seems mainly of red brick and flint mixture . One wonders just how much of this part has been repaired. Much of the rendering is now peeling off the nave and tower, which should give us a better idea of the wall construction. The nave and chancel in one are roofed in Norfolk thatch, and the south porch and chancel door are of the 15th. century and built with medieval bricks that blend well with our native flints. There are no fillets between tower and church, but the tower arch does not appear to have any dressed stone; it has a pointed arch and a simple chamfer towards the nave and rough flints inside the tower. The four belfry windows are Early English lancets, and on the ground floor is a double-light Decorated window. On the first floor at a height of 22ft. are two circular windows . They now have an inside diameter of 2ft. 6" and are single splay, but they might well prove to be Saxon, and altered, especially if the west face could be opened up and another window found.

No Norman features are to be seen, but there are many pointers to a Saxon dating. The tower height and wall thickness are closer to Saxon work than to any later period.

N94. STODY. St. Mary

G2. Sheet. 133. Map Ref. T.G. 056 351
Tower and West Nave Wall Middle SAXON.

Tower Height	51ft.
Internal Diameter Grd:	9ft.10"
Tower Wall Thickness	3ft. 7"
Nave Ridge Height	28ft.
Bells 1	
Chancel & Nave Width	17ft. 6"
Chancel Length	30ft. 2"
Nave Length	49ft.
Nave Wall Thickness	2ft. 4"

St. Mary's church consists of a round west tower, nave, chancel, north and south transepts and south porch. It is situated on a hill but there are few houses near by. Messent and Cautley suggest the possibility of a pre-Conquest date because of the stratification of the tower walls.

The tower is 51f't. tall with an internal diameter of 9ft.10" and a wall thickness of 3ft. 7". There is one bell in the tower. The tower is constructed of' whole flints and the varying sizes used make sections that undoubtedly correspond to each seasons building. The wall thickness is clearly much too thin for Norman work, while over t he tower arch it measures one foot less at 2f't. 7", which gives every indication of being added to a towerless church, despite being circular inside. There is one fillet on the north but the one on the south is covered by a stair turret built of flints and early brick. The one remaining gives good grounds for a Saxon dating.

There are four Decorated belfry windows below the flushwork panelled battlements and one more 14th. century window to the west on the ground floor. On the first floor facing south is a small window that has been reduced from a much larger window. The one on the north is completely blocked. These were probably the original belfry windows of the early tower. Internally, there is a ledge of about 3 inches at a height of 32ft., another Saxon feature, but there is no upper doorway. The tall and narrow tower arch has a cruck-shaped head, believed by Taylor to be a Saxon feature, and there appears to be no dressed stone in the jambs or the head.

Turning to the church, the N/W and S/W quoins are a mixture of flints and bricks. These appear to have survived from the Saxon flint quoins, but it is sad that these smart corners are not the original stones or the corners as they were. The width of nave and chancel at under 18ft. gives us positive evidence of a Saxon plan and the wall thickness at under 3ft. adds credence to this. There is some conglomerate mixed with the flints as far as the first nave window in the north wall.

The transepts and south porch are from the 15th. century, and the roofs are leaded. Internally, there is a continuous roof from east to west, with cross vaulting where the transepts intersect the main roof. The roofs are arch-braced and the wall-plates have alternate angels and shields. The 13th. century octagonal font is of Purbeck marble. The east window has intersecting tracery of four lights, while the remainder of the chancel windows are Decorated with various forms of tracery in the heads. The nave and transepts are lighted by Perpendicular windows, of which two have early stained glass in their heads. There is no chancel arch, an indication of an early church. Although all the measurements and a number of other features indicate a Saxon date for tower and church, heavy restoration has obliterated the usual signs by which we recognise a Saxon church.

N95. LONG STRATTON. St. Mary

I8. Sheet 134. Map Ref. T.M. 197 923

Tower and Church Possibly Late SAXON

Tower Height	53ft. 6"
Internal Diam. Grd;	9ft.
Bells 6	
Chancel Width	19ft. 2"
Nave Width	18ft. 1"
Nave & Aisles Width	47ft. 9"
Chancel Length	35ft.11"
Nave Length	50ft. 6"

The church is situated in the centre of the village to the east of the main Norwich road It has a round west tower with a small lead spire, nave, chancel, north and south aisles and south porch.

The tower is 53ft. 6" tall and the small spire and weather vane adds a few more feet to its height. It has an internal diameter of 9ft. There is a peal of six bells and one is inscribed:- "To the Glory of God." The peal was rehung and this bell was added A.D. 1904. G.D. Barry, Rector.
D. Alexander)
J.M. Wellor) Churchwardens

The church clock which faces west was made and fitted into the tower between 1675 and 1700. It is on the first floor and faces west from what seems to have been an old west window.

The construction of the tower is a mixture of all sizes and colours of flints, but mainly medium and whole. Below the battlements the four belfry windows are single-light Decorated and there are only two windows below these, both in the west face. On the floor below the belfry is single light of the 14th. century, and to light the ground floor stage is a double-light window. there are no fillets between tower and church, but on the south side is a stair turret to the first floor added in the 15th. century. On this floor, opposite the clock is an upper doorway opening into the nave. The tower arch appears to have a Norman head, but it is much taller than usual and it only has simple imposts. there does not seem to be any dressed stone in this opening, but it is not possible to be certain as the entire arch has been cement rendered and painted with plastic paint .

A nave width of 18t. 1" adds more weight to the so far weak evidence of a Saxon date. All the windows of the church are Perpendicular, which shows the extent of the restoration at this time. There are seven clerestory windows to the north and south and even the tower has lost any early signs it may have had. There is one very worn scratch dial on the west jamb of the south priest's door but no votive crosses.

The basic plan follows the Saxon measurements so well that this must surely be pre-Conquest in origin although the added aisles and restorations have hidden all the early features.

N96 SURLINGHAM. St. Mary

J6. Sheet 134. Map Ref. T.G. 306 065

Tower and Nave Middle SAXON.

Tower Height	56ft. 3"
Height of Circular Stage.	44ft.
Internal Diameter Grd:	10ft.10"
Tower Wall Thickness	3ft.10"
Nave Ridge Height	26ft. 3"
Bells 4	
Nave & Chancel Width	18ft. 2"
Nave & A isle Width	30ft. 2"
Chancel Length	16ft. 4"
Nave Length	38ft.11"

The church stands on raised ground overlooking the river Yare which would have provided easy transport for any dressed stone if it was available. The village is rather scattered at the present day.

The church consists of a round west tower with an octagonal top and a plain parapet, nave, chancel, north aisle and vestry and south porch. A turret staircase of the 15th. century has been built on the north side of the tower, and there is a balcony across the west end of the nave. The stairs for this lead up from the north aisle.

The chancel was rebuilt in red brick probably in the 18th. century. The vestry added to the east of the north aisle is built of masonry blocks of many sizes and looks quite out of character on this ancient church. All the windows in the south and east of the church have been renewed. Four buttresses of red brick support the north wall outside and at the N/W corner there is also one inside, so this wall has really given trouble.

The first Saxon feature is the S/W nave quoin of large flints and close by, between church and tower is a fillet. Rather flat, and it tapers off where it meets the nave roof. These are two positive features and place the tower and this corner firmly in the pre-Conquest period. The north fillet has been covered by the stair turret and the north wall was replaced by the north aisle. The tower wall has every sign of Saxon workmanship, although the flints have at least been repointed. The large flints have wide mortar joints and they are of all sizes and colours. No carstone or conglomerate was seen but a number of early tiles had been used in repairs, or to block up unwanted windows. There is one pointed west window on the ground floor and two small rectangular windows have frames of early brick. One of these is the original west belfry window which is otherwise blocked up. The other three old belfry windows are completely blocked, and are about 30ft . from the ground. There is also an upper doorway at 23ft. from the ground.

The tower has four bells but there is provision for five. Was one removed or was another expected? The tower is curved on its eastern side that implies the tower and church were built together. There is possibly a blocked up circular window in the west face of the tower, which if opened out would give us still more proof of its Saxon age. All the roofs are of slate, and the north doorway in Norman style is built of Victorian bricks.

N97. SUSTEAD. Sts. Peter & Paul

H2. Sheet 133. Map Ref. T.G. 182 370

Tower and Church Middle SAXON.

Tower Height	48ft.
Internal Diameter Grd:	7ft.
Tower Wall Thickness	3ft. 4"
Nave Ridge Height	27ft. 6"
Bells 1	
Chancel & Nave Width	19ft.
Chancel Length	25ft.10"
Nave Length	44ft. 4"
North Nave Wall Thickness	2ft. 8"
South Nave Wall Thickness	2ft. 6"

Sustead is in the Cromer area and quite near Gresham and Roughton. It has a round west tower, nave and chancel of the same width, but the nave roof is about a foot higher than the chancel. There is also a south porch.

The tower is 48ft. high with circular battlements built mainly of early bricks, and below these are four Y-traceried belfry windows apparently of the 13th. century, but Ladbrooke's print shows belfry windows of the Decorated period, and Charles Cox calls them 14th. century, seen apparently before they were changed. So these windows are late Victorian. There is only one other window in the tower and that is a slit window in the west face on the first floor. It now has a dressed stone frame outside, but inside the tower it is constructed entirely of flints with a triangular head. I am not too certain if this was its original shape, but I am confident that it started life as a Saxon window. There is no sign on this floor of an upper doorway. On the ground floor there is no window or tower arch, but a south doorway of the 13th. century and inside to the east is an alcove that undoubtedly held the Holy Water Stoup. This is made even more certain by no signs of one in either the porch or the nave. This doorway then, like the one at Aylmerton, was the main entrance to the church from its earliest days, and the tower arch to the church was undoubtedly blocked up when the new south doorway was inserted in the Decorated period. There is no sign now of this opening or any indications of its size. The tower wall thickness is only 3ft. 4" which is quite thin even for a Saxon tower.

There is one bell rung by the clapper and inscribed:-"AVI: MARIA: ORA: PLENA: NRS: OC: CUM :" but no makers name. The bell frame is dated 1884

The Saxon features by which we can date this church and tower are the wall construction and the nave west quoins . The N/W and S/W quoins are large blocks of conglomerate and not carstone as described by Taylor & Taylor. The material and size of the blocks both indicate a Saxon origin. The walls of both tower and church contain conglomerate mixed with the flints of many sizes and confirm its pre-Norman construction. The height of the tower, which was almost certainly raised when the Decorated belfry windows were inserted would place it in the middle Saxon period. The width of nave and chancel has remained the same, but whether the chancel has been altered in length we cannot say without further research outside the east end.

The north and south doorways are from the Decorated period as can be seen from the ogee shape of their arches . The nave has one and the chancel two windows of the Decorated period with slender columns at the sides, while the remainder of the nave windows are a century later. We are reminded that a Decorated transept on the north has been lost by the blocked arch remaining and the 14th. century mouldings still visible. There is a scratch dial on the west jamb of the porch entrance.

N98. SWAINSTHORPE. St. Peter

I7. Sheet 134. Map Ref. T.G. 219 009
Tower and Church Middle SAXON.

Tower Height approx:	46ft.
Height of Circular Stage approx:	35ft.
Internal Diameter Grd:	9ft. 7"
Tower Wall Thickness	3ft.10"
Bells 4	
Nave Ridge Height	35ft.
Chancel Width	13ft.11"
Nave Width	18ft. 6"
Nave & Aisle Width	31ft. 9"
Chancel Length	23ft. 6"
Nave Length	33ft. 6"
North Arcade Wall Thickness	2ft. 9"
South Nave Wall Thickness	2ft. 9"

The church is situated on high ground to the west of the village and the building is in good condition after a series of restorations and redecorations during the past years. It has a round west tower with an octagonal top, nave, chancel, north aisle and south porch.

I was unable to ascend the tower as my ladder would not reach the first floor, so whatever features show inside remain to be discovered. The diameter at ground level is 9ft. 7" with a wall thickness of 3ft.10". There are no fillets and no upper doorway can be seen from the nave. While the Taylors say the nave is the earliest, and they would not date the tower, it is my belief they were built together, and the tower measurements confirm a Saxon dating. T he octagonal battlements and belfry stage of four double-light windows are from the 15th. century. The tower below this must surely be contemporary with the nave. The slit window on the first floor has a flint frame on the outside and this should be sufficient to place it in the Saxon period. The height of the circular part of the tower being below 40ft. puts it in the early tower period from 900 to 1,000, and the nave corresponds with this. The two western quoins confirm the Saxon dating and the original width of the church. The N/W corner starts at the base with a medium block of conglomerate and is followed by large flints, mostly cut to give a sharp corner. There is one odd block of stone 5ft. up, with some early bricks and tiles thereabouts. Then all flints almost up to the eaves where new dressed stone has been fitted to support the roof. The S/W corner:-(plate 39) except for the base which is flints, there is a 5ft . 6" section of repairs with red bricks. Then one early brick and the reminder is very large flints cut to give a sharp corner, and only three early tiles at odd points. The modern dressed stone takes over at about the same height as in the N/W quoin.

Over the south porch to the east of the sloping roof, the roof appears to cut into a circular window which is now blocked, and would be Saxon.

This is mentioned in the Taylors' *"Anglo-Saxon Architecture"*. It has an upper arch marked in tiles that are not laid radially. The N/E quoin which is not mentioned by the Taylors, is also of large flints and one piece of conglomerate. We can therefore be fairly confident that the tower, nave and chancel is of middle Saxon age. The north aisle has two large and two small arcades from the nave with octagonal piers and double-chamfered arches . The tower arch has been much altered so nothing can be learned from this. There are four bells:- one is dated 1629, and one is damaged and so cannot be rung. There is one scratch dial on the west jamb of the south door but no votive crosses.

N99. SYDERSTONE St. Mary.

D3. Sheet 132. Map Ref. T.F. 833 327
Church SAXON

Tower Height approx.	46ft.
Internal Diameter Grd:	10ft. 9"
Tower Wall Thickness	3ft.
Nave Ridge Height approx.	28ft.
Bells 1	
Chancel Width	17ft.
Nave Width	17ft. 4"
Chancel Length	32ft. 1"
Nave Length	54ft. 2"

Syderstone is at the N/W of Norfolk quite near Docking. Barmer, another R/T church is close by. The small church of St. Mary consists of a round west tower, nave, chancel and north vestry.

The round tower, if not Saxon, must surely be 13th century, for its wall is only 3ft. thick, much too thin for Norman builders. Its flat east side, indicates it was built after the church which is definitely Saxon. The tower, of which I have only glimpsed the interior is about 46ft. tall and the church history suggests that it was built about 1220. However there are many very large flints in the lower part of the tower which is against an Early English date.

Moving on to the church where the dating is more definite, the S/W quoins are large flints and conglomerate. This nave west wall therefore, is original Saxon, and the remaining parts of the nave north and south walls are also. The south aisle was Norman, and there were Norman transepts, while the north aisle was added in the 14th. century. A fine church this must have been, but by 1784 the condition of the aisles and transepts had deteriorated to such an extent that they were pulled down leaving a church of a similar size to when it began. The south doorway was removed from the south aisle, and was inserted in the west of the tower, where it is now the main entrance.

There is one bell. A scratch dial on the west doorway proves that it was once facing south.

N100. TASBURGH. St. Mary the Virgin

I7. Sheet 134. Map Ref. T.M. 201 959

Tower and Part of Nave West Wall Late SAXON

Tower Height	49ft.
Internal Diameter Grd:	10ft. 1"
Tower Wall Thickness	3ft. 9"
Nave Ridge Height	32ft. 6"
Bells 5	
Chancel Width	16ft. 2"
Nave Width	25ft. 9"
Chancel Length	31ft. 9"
Nave Length	39ft.
Nave Wall Thickness N. & S.	2ft. 9"

This church is situated in a growing village and consists of a round west tower, nave, chancel and north and south porches.

Munro Cautley lists a south and west porch, which is obviously a printer's error as there has never been a west porch.

The most interesting and striking feature is the round tower which is definitely Saxon. It has two stages of arcading and the upper one has been broken into when the present belfry stage was added in the late 13th. century. This arcading is peculiar to only three round towers, the others are at Thorington near Halesworth and Thorpe-next-Haddiscoe. Both these towers however, have only one row, so this tower is surely later, being in the late Saxon period. Like the others, the round-headed arches are recessed two or three inches below the general surface of the tower wall, and it is all done in the same flint rubble as the rest of the wall.

The belfry windows are single-light with pointed arches and framed in early brick. T hey have hood-moulds in dressed stone and the belfry holds a peal of five balls. The tower is circular to the top with a plain parapet of early brick. Four gargoyles are below this to carry off the rainwater.

In the lower stage of the arcading there are three round-headed windows, placed at north, south and west. They have flint frames and so are of the same age as the tower. Lower down in the west face, lighting the ground floor, is yet another round-headed window framed in flints, larger than the others, but still smaller than most west windows. It is also higher than usual, and poses a question, "Was there once a west doorway below this?"

There are no fillets between tower and church, but what looks like large rectangular fillets, we can see on close examination, are really the lower parts of the old nave west wall. They do show us however, the original width of the old church, as the old flint quoins are still here. They also strengthen our conviction that very few village churches were pulled down and rebuilt in Norman days, if so, some sign would usually show, as it does here. We can see plainly here how the later church was built with a wider nave against the old tower and nave wall.

The tower arch is obscured on the nave side by a later medieval door, but inside the tower the true Saxon arch can be seen almost 17ft. tall and 4ft. 7" wide. The jambs are flints only slightly plastered over, and rough stone imposts are below the round-headed arch of roughly shaped blocks of stone. The upper part has now been filled in. Above this archway, at 19ft. 9" above the ground is a round-headed upper doorway 6ft. tall by 1ft.11" wide. It is closed by a wood frame and glass, but its details cannot be seen under the heavy plaster covering.

The nave windows were all inserted in the 15th. century, while the chancel windows were here 100 years before. On my visit in 1979 I saw that a new church hall had been built to the south of the church and joined on to the south porch by a glass passage-way.

N101. TAVERHAM. St. Edmund

H5. Sheet 133. Map Ref. T.G. 161 138

Nave Early SAXON, Tower Middle SAXON

Tower Height	51ft. 6"
Height of Circular Stage	37ft.
Internal Diameter Grd:	11ft. 5"
Tower Wall Thickness West	3ft.10"
Wall Thickness over T/Arch	2ft.10"
Nave Ridge Height	32ft. 6"
Bells 1	
Chancel Width	15ft.11"
Nave Width	18ft.
Nave & Aisle Width	29ft.11"
Chancel Length	38ft. 9"
Nave Length	51ft.10"
North Nave Wall Thickness	2ft. 6"
South Nave Wall Thickness	2ft. 3"

The church stands among new houses in the village, and the nave and chancel roofs are thatched. It consists of a round west tower with an octagonal top, nave, chancel, south aisle and south porch. Contrary to all writers, this tower is middle Saxon and the nave is earlier, with the chancel probably of the same date as the nave.

The tower is 51ft. 6" tall and 37ft. to the top of the circular stage, which is the Saxon part. This places it in the middle Saxon period, or 900 to 1,000. The tower is constructed of whole flints with large mortar gaps and the flints are uncoursed. It is a good circular shape. A stone string course separates this from the Perpendicular octagonal stage. This belfry section has stone corners and flint rubble walls, and the four Perpendicular windows have double-lights, but t he south window has lost its tracery. The flushwork of the battlements has cut white flints, and there are stone crosses on each of the corners. In the south face just below the nave ridge, is a single light pointed window with a stone frame,(it could be any age). But the ground floor west window 10ft. up, is round-headed with a frame of flints and conglomerate . This is certainly a Saxon window, and helps to confirm the dating of the tower. There are no fillets, but the N/W quoins are proof that the north wall is also pre-Conquest, for they are constructed of flints and conglomerate. About 10ft. to the east is the north nave doorway, one of only four such door-ways, mainly unaltered in the R/T group. It has flint and conglomerate jambs and rough imposts with a simple chamfer to the underside. The round head is set back on the jambs by about 2 inches and the head is in flint rubble . This is another Saxon doorway discovered mainly unaltered. Since writing these notes in 1975 this doorway and the N/W corner have been cement rendered completely covering the flints and conglomerate of these features, but my notes are clear, and I have been assured that the features beneath have not been disturbed.

The tower arch, 3ft. 3" wide by 8ft. 1" tall is a round-headed door-way and is built entirely of flints, one more Saxon feature to confirm our dating. There is no feature in the chancel on which we can base a Saxon date, but the width will suggest that this is quite probable. The chancel was certainly very much restored in the 14th. century, when windows and priest 's doors were inserted. 100 years later the nave windows were changed. The south aisle is Victorian of 1863.

Charles Cox records that the nave was destroyed by lightning in 1459, but the north wall certainly is standing still from pre-Conquest times. The single bell in the tower is dated 1635.

In January 1981 I was called to the church to inspect a window found in the nave west wall while a west gallery was being constructed. Two feet over the tower arch, or actually, the tower doorway, for it is only 8ft . tall, where a doorway was being cut through, a round-headed window was found only 10 inches wide within the tower, and splaying out within the nave. It was built of flints and two pieces of dressed clunch (hard chalk) were used for the sill, one in situ and the other loose. Although in the position of the usual upper doorways, this was certainly not one, for the 10 inch opening was very definite. This window established the fact that the church was here before the tower, although the usual signs we looked for in these cases were absent. The tower internal east wall was curved, although it only measured 2ft.10" over the tower doorway compared with 3ft.10" at the west window. An examination of the opening however gave the answer, and also provided us with a new feature. The usual straight nave west wall was overlaid with an extra layer of flints to give the tower interior a circular shape.

We now see after checking our measurements of towers that many more towers with curved east walls may well prove to have been added to towerless churches. We will only know for certain that this was the case where the wall surface is disturbed.

N102. THORPE ABBOTTS. All Saints.

I9. Sheet 156. Map Ref. T.M. 188 789
North Wall SAXON. Tower NORMAN

Tower Height	55ft
Height of Circular Stage .	37ft
Internal Diameter Grd:	9ft
Tower Wall Thickness	5ft. 1"
Bells 2	
Chancel Width	15ft. 7"
Nave Width	18ft. 6"
Chancel Length	20ft. 5"
Nave Length	52ft. 8"
North Nave Wall Thickness	2ft.10"
South Nave Wall Thickness	3ft.

The church stands beside the Diss to Bungay road and well to the south of the present village . It has a round west tower with an octagonal top, nave, chancel and south porch. The Taylors, I believe are correct in their assessment, but although I was able to go inside the church which they did not manage, I still was not able to ascend the tower until 1991. The only pre-Conquest work to be seen is in the north and west walls. The N/E. nave quoin is of selected flints, while all the others are in dressed stone. Most of the north chancel wall appears to be the same age, but towards the east end a vertical joint may well be the end of the Saxon chancel. but was it square ended and extended, or apsidal and the end squared off? About the centre of the north nave wall is a blocked up Saxon doorway with a round-headed arch and jambs of flints. The Taylors believed that nave doorways were always at the west end of the nave, and so here was a very short nave, with the west end being later. Chapter 10. explains how I found the error of concluding that church doorways were always at the west end of the nave.

The construction of the tower is of average sized flints, many whole and with very little signs of coursing. A string course of dressed stone is at the top of the circular section, followed by a plain octagonal stage of the 15th. century, with early bricks at the corners while the sides slope out to fit the circular tower. Another string course is at the base of the belfry which contains two bells. There are four double-light windows at the cardinal points and flush-work dummies in dressed stone and cut black flints on alternate sides. The top is finished with a plain brick parapet .

The circular section of the tower is 37ft . tall, which one expects to be middle Saxon, but with a wall thickness of 5ft. 1", this part of the tower appears to be decidedly Norman. The tower arch has a pointed head with a simple chamfer facing the nave. It has the appearance of being built of rubble without dressed stone facings, but the plaster renders this still a question to be answered.

The nave west wall has two rebates to thin the wall. One at 12ft. 6" is about 4 inches deep, and at 22ft. there is another, this time it is sloped rather than a step, but again of 4 inches. This would still be a Saxon feature, although the tower arch still poses a problem. No upper doorway was visible, from the nave or within the tower, although there is a rough patch of plaster over the tower arch that might be the filling of such an opening.

The church has no buttresses which of itself usually signifies early work, and the chancel shows a blocked lancet window, with the other Victorian restorations. The nave has one window from Early English times and four Perpendicular double-light windows.

N103. THORPE-NEXT-HADDISCOE. St. Mathias.

L7. Sheet 134. Map Ref. T.M. 436 981

Nave Early SAXON, Tower Middle SAXON.

Tower Height	45ft.
Height of Saxon Stage	30ft.
Internal Diameter Grd:	10ft.
Tower Wall Thickness	3ft. 9"
Nave Ridge Height	26ft. 9"
Bells 2	
Chancel Width	17ft.11"
Nave Width	15ft. 4"
Chancel Length	24ft. 6"
Nave Length	26ft. 2"
Nave Wall Thickness N. & S.	2ft. 8"

This interesting church, south of the Haddiscoe marshes, is less than two miles from the fine Saxo-Norman tower of Haddiscoe. It has a round west tower, nave, chancel and south porch.

I accept the reasoning of the Taylors, except for their dating into period C3, which is 1050 to 1100, although they definitely state that the nave was built before the Conquest.

The tower (plate 8) is 45ft . in height with the Saxon part only 30ft. tall. The internal diameter of 10ft. with walls 3ft. 9" thick is very common in these Saxon round towers. The chequered top with its battlement are rather similar, though not as fine as those at Haddiscoe, and are 15th. century. Below these are four double-light Norman belfry windows which could date around 1100 or a little later. T hey are flush with the tower wall and not recessed as is the general nature of Norman belfries. Within the belfry are two bells, the smaller one is dated 1632 while the larger is undated and probably about 1450. It bears a prayer to the Virgin Mary as follows :- "Ara mente pia pro nobis Virgo Maria".

Below the Norman belfry is the Saxon tower, which was originally somewhat higher than its present 30ft. for we can see how the Norman top has cut into the arches of the arcading, and there would have been some walling above this for the belfry windows . This arcading is a series of sunken arches round the tower of about 2 inches in depth, and constructed of the same flint rubble as the tower itself. The same technique has been used at Thorington and Tasburgh. A little strange that the only three examples of this work in round towers all begin with a T, but I do not believe it has any significance. Four round-headed windows with dressed stone frames are at N/E, N/W, S/E and S/W in the sunken arches of the arcading. These frames are undoubtedly Norman, and would have replaced the earlier Saxon flint frames .

Below the arcading are a further three windows of similar size and style and on the ground floor is a modern round-headed window of a larger size. Between tower and church are Saxon quarter-round fillets of flints that terminate above the nave wall with tapering blocks of stone. Within the tower it can be clearly seen that it was built a against an earlier nave. Firstly because on the ground and first floor we can see the flat face of the nave west wall, and secondly there are distinct gaps between the tower and the nave west wall at various points showing they are not bonded together. One further feature is the circular double-splayed window in the nave west wall about 22ft. from the ground which confirms that this was a towerless church, and also that these windows are much earlier than was formerly accepted; and must have been in use as far back as 850 to 900.

On this evidence of the tower we must place this in the middle Saxon period, and so the church which includes the nave west, north and south walls that are only 2ft. 8" thick is early Saxon or 800 to 900. The chancel was rebuilt, Charles Cox tells us in 1838, in red brick and is slated but the nave retains its thatched roof.

A number of scratch dials and votive crosses are to be seen on both north and south doorways. The Taylors noted that the south doorway appears to have been rebuilt, but also, there must have been a rebuilding or at least a re-use of stone in the north doorway, because there is one definite and one possible scratch dial in the stonework.

N104. THREXTON. All Saints.

D7. Sheet 144. Map Ref. T.F. 885 002

Tower and Church SAXON.

Tower Height approx.	40ft.	Nave Width	15ft.11"
Internal Diameter Grd:	8ft. 4"	Nave & Aisle Width	22ft.10"
Tower Wall Thickness	4ft.	Chancel Length	22ft. 3"
Nave Ridge Height approx.	30ft.	Nave Length	42ft.
Bells 1		North Aisle Wall Thickness	2ft. 3"
Chancel Width	16ft. 7"	South Nave Wall Thickness	2ft.10"

This small church stands on a small mound in a valley and next to a farm. The church history records that it was probably built on the site of a Roman villa because of the number of Roman finds nearby and also in the churchyard, one being a small gold cross. The mound on which the church stands may therefore be man made, and the cross would indicate Christian teaching or belief on this site before the present church.

It consists of a round west tower, nave, chancel, north aisle, north vestry and south porch.

This is another church where it was not possible to ascend the tower, which was a great pity, because with the feeling of antiquity but so few definite features, it might have given us a much more positive dating. The church history however, tells us that when the porch was built in 1865/8, the south doorway was removed, and it was seen to have been turned, the worn inner mouldings were Norman. We have therefore, fairly strong evidence that this building goes back to at least Norman times, and our measurements would place it earlier .

The tower and church are constructed of whole and cut flints of all sizes and odd stones with large mortar joints, and it has a pre-Conquest appearance. The tower has a thin covering of cement rendering that hides most of the flints. Inside, the tower appears to be oval in shape, which would indicate an early date.

There are no fillets and no sign from the nave of an upper doorway. The three Early English belfry windows are at west, S/E and N/E, and the ground floor west window is of a similar date .

Charles Cox tells us that evidence of a Saxon nave 11ft. wide was found during the restoration in 1865. The north aisle, which had until then been used as a mausoleum for the families of Knopwood and Burton, was then brought into general use. The north aisle was built in the late 13th. century and the north vestry at the Victorian restoration. If an earlier Saxon nave was here, it certainly means that this church is Saxon, for the width of the present church and the wall thickness can point to no other period.

N105. THWAITE. All Saints.

I3. Sheet 133. Map Ref. T.G. 193 334
Tower and Church Middle SAXON

Tower Height approx.	45ft.
Internal Diameter Grd:	8ft. 6"
Tower Wall Thickness	3ft.10"
Bells 1	
Chancel Width	16ft. 2"
Nave Width	16ft. 2"
Nave & Aisle Width	26ft.10"
Chancel Length	25ft.11"
Nave Length	41ft. 2"

Round west tower, nave, chancel, south aisle, south porch and north chapel. This church was extensively restored in Victorian times, probably when the north chapel or Sunday School was added, and it appears that much of the church and tower walls were refaced then with whole flints. The tower has a plinth of whole flints at the base, most probably from this restoration.

The circular shape of the tower internally indicates that tower and church were built together . There is no sign of an upper doorway and no ground floor west window. There is, however, the signs of a ground floor doorway to the south of the tower. It shows within the tower as a blocked up archway, and outside it has a frame of medieval brick, and outside this, an arch of cut white flints. This church is not far from Aylmerton and Sustead that still have their tower doorways. The one bell in the tower I could not reach to examine, but the belfry windows are Y-traceried of Early English style, but they may well be of the Victorian restoration.

The tower wall thickness at 3ft. 10" would seem to be pre-Conquest, while the tower arch at 4ft. 8" wide by 12ft.10" tall and round-headed would support this view as it appears to have no dressed stone in either jambs or head.

The most interesting and positive Saxon features are the N/W and S/W quoins, which are large blocks of conglomerate, some blocks of which seem to be laid in the long-and-short style. My studies of this material in these churches would date this nave along with the narrow chancel firmly in the Saxon era from the evidence of the west corners. We must however bear in mind that repairs may have renewed the face of the walls in some cases. It is a great pity that the refacing has covered so much of the early work.

N106. TITCHWELL. St. Mary

C1. Sheet 132. Map Ref. T.F. 762 438
Tower and Nave West Wall Middle SAXON.

Tower Height	40ft. 6"	Chancel Width	17ft.
Height to top of spire approx.	58ft.	Nave Width	24ft. 7"
Internal Diameter Grd:	9ft. 4"	Chancel Length	25ft. 8"
Tower Wall Thickness	4ft.	Nave Length	36ft.11"
Nave Ridge Height	34ft.	Nave North Wall Thickness	2ft.10"
Bells 1		Nave South Wall Thickness	2ft. 9"

This church is situated on slightly raised ground above the salt marshes of the north Norfolk coast. It consists of round west tower with spire, nave, chancel and south porch.

It is not far from Burnham Deepdale, and is in many respects a sister church. The tower is almost the same height, and many features are similar. There appears to be at first sight no positive proof of a Saxon dating here, but like a number of these towers, one feels instinctively that there may be hidden features. There are no fillets between tower and church, but the tower itself is not straight but bulges, especially at the base, and has all the appearance of early workmanship. Many very large flints are in this tower, another early sign, with large mortar gaps. There is also no real attempt at coursing. The belfry windows which are above a stone string course, seem to be early Norman, but once again, like those at Snailwell, there is no recessing of these double-arched windows. The centre column is in line with the face of the tower wall. The centre column looks almost square, with quite simple chamfers to capitals and base. The north one looks as though it has been rounded. The ground floor west window is a Victorian copy of a Norman window, and is the only other window in this tower besides the belfry and one small window on the first floor. Looking at this small window from outside, it has a flint frame, with two large flints making a triangular head, and looking Saxon. Inside, on the first floor, this window is seen to have been much altered, and looks as if it has been cut down in size, so it is difficult to be positive about this window at all. Besides flints in this tower, there are some pieces of brick, a few pieces of carstone, and some blocks of stone that appear to be erratics. The tower is capped with a lead spire about 20ft. tall.

There was once a north aisle, but this has long since been pulled down; the north doorway remains but is blocked up with dressed stones. The east wall of the chancel cannot be later than Early English as the three lancets prove. They have been shown up by cutting back the plaster to show they were here before the present window. In the south chancel wall is the preserved remains of half a Norman window. So the chancel can be positively dated from at least Norman times.

The nave width we can see is wide for a Saxon church, and so we examine the nave west wall outside. Here we can see where the nave has been widened at the S/W by about 4ft. The N/W flint Saxon quoin is not so clear, but can be found on close inspection. The tower arch has a cruck-shaped head, and appears to have no dressed stone in its construction. There is a ledge to thin the tower walls at 17ft. 6" from the ground and also an upper doorway, but this has been altered.

Therefore, by the west flint quoins, we know that the west nave wall is pre-Conquest, although the north and south nave walls are later. The chancel walls, which line up with the original nave, and show Norman features, must consequently also be from the original church, for the walls are much too thin for Norman builders. Finally we come back to the tower. Clearly being built with this Saxon wall, it must be pre-Conquest unless rebuilt. But there are too many features that would not be repeated in later years, notably the bulging walls, its height, and the later Norman belfry. Its height gives us its age as the middle Saxon period of 900 to 1,000.

N107. TOPCROFT. St. Margaret

I8. Sheet 134. Map Ref. T.M. 266 929

Possibly SAXON

Tower Height	59ft.
Circular section Externally	19ft. 6"
Internal Diameter Grd:	9ft. 8"
Tower Wall Thickness	4ft. 9"
Nave Ridge Height	29ft. 6"
Bells 3	
Chancel Width	18ft. 4"
Nave Width	18ft.11"
Nave & Aisle Width	31ft.10"
Chancel Length	32ft. 7"
Nave Length	53ft. 4"
Nave Wall Thickness	2ft.10"

The church guide tells us that this village is at one of the highest points in Norfolk. The site on which the church is built is moated, or at least there is a ditch all round the churchyard. The church has a round west tower with three octagonal stages, nave, chancel, south aisle and south porch. A number of modern dwellings are close at hand.

Either neglect or disaster must have dogged this church, for a great many repairs have been executed in red brick. The chancel was rebuilt in this material in 1712, and the tower appears to have suffered collapse early in its life, for the first two octagonal stages contain Early English windows. Within the tower however, we see a different picture . Like Rollesby and Ashby, we find that the two lower octagonal stages have been cut back, for the tower is circular internally at this height. At 1ft. 9" above the second floor are eight narrow lancet windows, four of which are now blocked. They are framed with early brick and are cut through without any splay, indicating that they were the original belfry windows. The similarity of this ring to those at Bexwell, Holton St. Peter and Rushmere St. Michael, suggests these may be Saxon round-headed belfry windows, altered in the Early English period. The tower wall thickness however, points strongly to a Norman date as at present there is nothing to show the tower has been recased. In the upper octagonal stage, four single light Tudor windows are at the cardinal points, but possibly the tracery has been lost from probable double-light windows, as on alternate sides, flush-work, traces double-light dummy windows. A large Tudor window is on the ground floor to the west, while above this are two Early English lancets. There is also another of these narrow windows in the east face above the nave ridge.

This was the first tower I had measured where the east wall was thicker than the west, and it exceeded this by 1 foot. The height of the circular stage externally is only 19ft. so the appearance of a tower collapse seems remote, and more probable is that like Rollesby, and Ashby, the first octagonal stage has been cut back from the round tower for about 10ft. and a further octagonal stage added.

No early features appear to have survived so we cannot give a positive dating to the tower or church. The nave and chancel widths, the nave wall thickness, and the original belfry windows, as well as their height, give good grounds for a Saxon dating. Against this, the tower wall thickness favours a Norman date. The tower was restored in 1983, when the eight lancets (original belfry windows) were restored, and the tower re-pointed and cracks repaired.

The south aisle dates from the 14th. century and the arcade has a decided lean towards the south. Many knapped flints are in the south wall, but this is of course 14th. century also. However, the north wall appears to be of the same age as the tower, but so far no signs are seen before the Early English period.

N108. TUTTINGTON. Sts. Peter & Paul

14. Sheet. 133. Map Ref. T.G. 227 272

Tower Late SAXON.

Tower Height	44ft. 6"
Internal Diameter Grd:	10ft. 1"
Tower Wall Thickness	3ft. 7"
Nave Ridge Height	34ft.
Bells 1	
Chancel Width	19ft.10"
Nave Width	28ft. 6"
Chancel Length	35ft. 8"
Nave Length	51ft. 3"

This church is situated in the small village and is on flat ground. It has a round west tower, nave, chancel and south porch.

Few Saxon signs were seen, but enough to place the tower in the late Saxon period. The belfry windows are Early English with Y-tracery but the east and west have lost their tracery and have been blocked up with red bricks. The other windows of the tower are now rectangular and have their outer frames of cement, while the inner splays are broken and give no clues whatever. Some of these windows have lintels of wood or stone, but even this is of little help. The small spire on the roof I am told replaces a taller one that used to dominate the village.

The tower now contains only one bell which is inscribed:-

Edward Blake Esqr) Church
Benjamin Brettingham Bomarks Gent.n) Wardens.
Robert Wiffen Blake Esq. J.P. Sherrif of Norwich acting for his brother 1852

One bell was sold for £20, and two more were sold later to pay for repairs. This was around 1800.

There is a small fillet to the north of the tower, but this appears to be modern repairs, although it may well prove to be original and refaced like much of the tower. The surface of the tower is of whole and cut black flints, but mainly cut, suggesting refacing. There are two distinct bands of these cut flints, one at 5ft. and the other about 20ft. up. They are each about four flints deep, and on close examination it is seen that not only are the faces cut but also the sides of many to fit them into the existing flintwork. This is very strong evidence of fitting small flints into the large mortar gaps of Saxon flint-work.

I saw the tower again in 1985, after it had been re-pointed, and this galleting had been removed, but the true Saxon surface could not now be positively identified.

The south porch was built in the 14th. century and had an upper room. The floor of this has now been removed and the windows blocked up, but the stairway is still visible although in ruins. These and many more signs show how these fine buildings are slowly losing their splendour for lack of sufficient funds for their proper upkeep. There is no upper doorway, but a ledge in the west wall of the nave that thins the wall by 6 inches at a height of 24ft. A ledge like this has been seen in many Saxon naves, so it is a good indication of a possible Saxon date .

The chancel walls show distinct Saxon signs with quite a lot of conglomerate, but no other features to prove it. The remainder of the church is of cut flints which appear to be refacing. There are three Decorated windows in the chancel, but all the remaining windows are from the Perpendicular period .

The width of the nave appears too wide for a pre-Conquest church, although the chancel is within the measurements we have come to expect. The ledge on the nave west wall may well imply that the Saxon nave was widened at some later date. There are no Norman features although most writers call the tower Norman.

N109. WACTON. All Saints

H8. Sheet 134. Map Ref. T.M. 179 917

Tower Late SAXON

Tower Height	56ft.	Chancel Width	25ft. 5"
Internal Diameter Grd:	9ft. 4"	Nave Width	25ft. 5"
Tower Wall Thickness	3ft. 9"	Chancel Length	28ft. 7"
Nave Ridge Height	46ft. 6"	Nave Length	53ft. 6"
Bells 3			

This church stands on a slightly raised site in a scattered village. It consists of a round west tower, nave, and chancel.

The church appears to be almost entirely of the Decorated period, with ogee arched doorways and windows, and the windows are of an

extremely large size for this period. The piscina and sedilia are also of the 14th. century. The width of nave and chancel at 25ft. 5" seems too wide for a Saxon church, and yet if it has been widened, why was it built without a chancel arch. Also one might ask, why was one not put in when all the fine windows were inserted? The doorways are very wide, but where is the porch? This is very unusual, especially with the size and apparent wealth of this church at the time of this building.

The appearance of the tower is certainly one of age, but there are few features to prove this point. The height would place it later than 1,000 unless it was raised, but inside, the flints and workmanship appear to be the same for its entire height. The only feature which might identify this tower closer, is the triangular-headed window in the lower part of the upper stage, where the tower takes a step inwards. The outside of this window is of early brick or flints, but it is now mostly covered with cement. Inside, the head is not set back on the jambs, and there is no evidence to support a Saxon dating. While this window may still prove to be early, closer examination will be necessary when the cement rendering has fallen off.

Pevsner says, "The upper half recessed and as thin and tapering as a windmill." While there is a recess, the taper is more apparent than real, as a line dropped from the top has shown. What then is the reason for this rough upper stage of the tower? It seems quite inconceivable that in Norman or later times such a rough additional stage would be put on an early tower. Also, by the time the Saxons were building to this height, their technique was superb, as witness Forncett St. Peter close by, and others. The most likely possibility appears to be that the facing flints of the top section fell away, perhaps due to frost getting at the mortar before it was properly set. The core was then rendered with mortar but without another facing of flints, giving the rough appearance.

Although the tower is circular inside, implying it was built with the church, the outside is horseshoe shaped like some that have been built on to the earlier churches. This does not appear to have happened here, but the shaping may be later facing.

The church must be a rebuilding in the 14th. century, but the tower has enough features of the Saxon period to call it late. The small window mentioned before would make it much more certain if it was carefully examined.

N110. EAST WALTON. St. Mary

C5. Sheet. 132. Map Ref. T.F. 743 161

Tower and Nave West Wall Middle SAXON.

Tower Height approx.	56ft.
Internal Diameter Grd:	9ft. 2"
Tower Wall Thickness	3ft. 9"
Nave Ridge Height approx.	35ft.
Bells 1	
Chancel Width	22ft. 9"
Nave Width	23ft. 3"
Chancel Length	28ft. 5"
Nave Length	52ft. 8"
Nave Wall Thickness N.	3ft. 1"
Nave Wall Thickness S.	3ft. 3"

Hidden among the trees, down a short lane, this church still has its small village clustered round it. It has a round west tower, nave, chancel and south porch.

All the windows of nave and chancel are large ones from the Perpendicular period, when a great deal must have been spent on restoration, as the battlements of the tower probably date from this period. The south porch was built a century earlier, and the four belfry windows were put in when the tower was raised in the 14th. century. The original height was 38ft., which would place it in the middle Saxon period. The present height is 56ft This is another tower that could not be climbed, but even so it was interesting even at ground level. Many put-log holes are to be seen both inside and outside framed in brick and masonry. There are no fillets, but the tower is clearly seen to have been built against the earlier nave west wall. The tower does not bond into the nave wall, and the flat face of the wall can be clearly seen inside the tower. Also, the tower inside is horseshoe shaped which clearly shows it was an addition. There is only one window below the belfry, and that is the ground floor west window, which is 13th. century, so I hope for more information when I can ascend the tower.

The one feature that was seen, if only in part, beside the S/W buttress, was the S/W quoin. This appears to have been of conglomerate, rough sandstone blocks and flints. Some large blocks of rough stone, probably sandstone or carstone can also be seen in the base of the tower and in the nave west wall. The N/W corner is similar, but no quoins can be seen.

The north wall, above the window sills is of cut flints, and is 13th. century or later, but below, is probably earlier for the walling is entirely different. The chancel is cement rendered so nothing can be learned here.

Internally, the west nave wall has a step to thin it by 4 to 6 inches at a height of 13ft. Therefore, this nave west wall, by reason of the rebate, and the S/W quoin is almost certainly pre-Conquest in date. The north wall appears to have fallen into ruin quite early and to have been rebuilt from the height of the window sills about 1300, for above these the wall is of cut flints and uncoursed. This therefore is the sum of our knowledge to date; and we trust that more will be found later. As I have shown, there are very good indications of pre-Conquest work.

N111. WATTON. St. Mary

E7. Sheet. 144. Map Ref. T.F. 921 009
Tower and Nave Middle SAXON.

Tower Height	48ft. 6"
Height of Circular Stage	33ft.
Internal Diameter Grd:	10ft. 6"
Tower Wall Thickness	3ft.11"
Nave Ridge Height	32ft.
Bells 6	
Chancel Width	13ft. 9"
Nave Width	17ft. 7"
Nave & Aisles Width	64ft.11"
Chancel Length	22ft.10"
Nave Length	37ft. 7"
Original Nave Wall	2ft. 2"

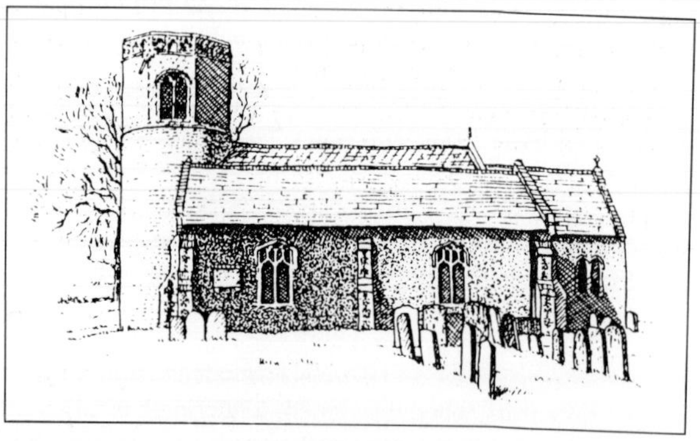

The church is on flat ground at the edge of this country town. The plan is of a west round tower with an octagonal top, nave, with north and south aisles, all three of which have individual pitched roofs that are of slate; chancel and north transept.

So drastic were the restorations of 1852 and 1892 that hardly anything is left by which to date this building. There are however, a number of Saxon features that have escaped the restorers. The early writers are also a long way out in their interpretation. Charles Cox tells us that the church has a north and west porch, and Munro Cautley follows him. But there is no north porch only a north transept at the east end of Victorian date, and a vestibule inside the door of the south aisle which can hardly be called a porch. Charles Cox also refers to a two-light Early English window in the north wall of the chancel, which is in fact in the south wall. Pevsner tells us the south arcade is Early English and the north is Perpendicular. He does not explain how the Perpendicular windows came to be in the south and the Early English in the north. I do not wish to be unduly critical, as some of these errors may be due to the printers, but it is as well to sort out any errors at the beginning.

Most of the church and tower seems to have been refaced in the Victorian restorations . The tower is in whole flints and the church in cut flints . The north aisle windows are Early English, with some Victorian restoration, while those in the south aisle are original Perpendicular. Inside, however the arcades to north and south seem to belong to the Decorated period, with four engaged columns. Could these be part of the restorations, but I have not given them enough study to be certain?

The chancel is the earliest part we can date with any certainty, for there are three stepped lancets in the east wall and a double-lancet in the south wall of Early English date, although both have received some restoration. The chancel walls have been cement rendered, so there may be something interesting beneath this. A low-side window at the S/W of the chancel is rare, and the width at 13ft. 9" gives grounds for believing that this might go back to pre-Conquest days.

The tower has a ground floor west doorway, but the door frame is Victorian, so we cannot gain any help from this. The whole flint facing of the circular section, I would think belongs to the 19th. century restoration. The belfry stage was certainly restored then, including the entire belfry windows of double-lights. Also altered at this time was the parapet surrounded by quatrefoils and trefoils in dressed stone.

The tops of two fillets are to be seen to north and south of the tower, but these are probably Victorian when the aisle roofs were altered as they are necessary to run off the rain water from these roofs.

Inside the tower on the first floor is an upper doorway, which is round-headed, but it is in an unusual place; at the N/E corner. Inside the tower on the ground floor and first floor, the east side is flat, that implies it was built on to a towerless church. Therefore, the narrow nave and chancel would suggest an early Saxon church without a tower. The tower arch is round-headed and constructed of dressed stone, but there are no imposts. Parts of the tower walls show flints of average size, whole and cut with large mortar gaps. These and the wall thickness give grounds for a Saxon dating.

N112. WEETING. St. Mary

C8. Sheet 144. Map Ref. T.L. 777 892
Chancel Decorated. Tower Rebuilt in 19th. Century

Tower Height	55ft. 6"
Internal Diameter Grd:	10ft. 1"
Tower Wall Thickness West	3ft. 8"
Tower Wall Thickness East	5f't. 6"
Nave Ridge Height	39ft. 6"
Bells 2	
Chancel Width	17ft. 8"
Nave Width	21ft. 8'
Nave & Aisle Width	34ft.10"
Chancel Length	30ft. 2"
Nave Length	42ft. 2"
South Nave Wall Thickness	3ft. 1"
North Nave Wall Thickness	2ft. 5"

This church is on slightly raised ground, and a new estate has sprung up around it. There is a round west tower, nave, chancel, north aisle and south porch.

The tower we are told fell down and was rebuilt in Victorian times, and the workmanship inside and outside confirm this. I wonder if the three circular windows on the first floor copy three Saxon windows, or are just the architect's fancy. The tower is constructed of whole flints of uniform size and not coursed, and it is circular for its full height . There are four double-light Y-traceried windows in the belfry stage, and above these is a battlemented parapet. Below the belfry stage at sill height there is a stone string course and the walls thicken by 4 to 6 inches. Lower still on the second floor there are three rectangular windows with stone frames at N, W, and S; and below these on the first floor are three circular windows with quatrefoil inserts . Lower down there is another 4 to 6 inch ledge with a stone string course against weathering and on the ground floor, are three lancet windows. At the base of the tower are two more stone string courses where the tower walls increase in thickness in both cases. The large difference in wall thickness between east and west, is no doubt due to the rebuilding. There are no fillets and no stair turret . One of the bells here is inscribed:- *"Given by Francis Hobman Rector of Weeting. Robert Made Mc. 1668".*

The earliest chancel windows are Decorated, and appear to be original, and in the north wall. Where the priest's door is now, there used to be another tall Decorated window, seen inside and outside by the dressed stone frame still in place. A number of the chancel and nave windows however are completely Victorian.

The only early feature that I found in the church was the N/E nave quoin that is of quite large blocks of stone, and a pointer to possible Saxon influence.

N113. WELBORNE. All Saints

G6. Sheet 133. Map Ref. T.G. 067 101

Tower and Church SAXON.

Tower Height approx.	40ft.
Height to top of Cap approx.	46ft.
Internal Diameter Grd:	10ft. 6"
Tower Wall Thickness	3ft. 9"
Nave Ridge Height approx.	34ft
Bells 1	
Chancel Width	18ft.
Nave Width	25ft. 1"
Chancel Length	29ft.10"
Nave Length	45ft. 5"
Nave Wall Thickness N.	2ft. 6"
Nave Wall Thickness S.	2ft. 4"

All Saints is situated close to the Hall and with a mixture of old and new property close by and still retains its truly rural setting. It is a very unusual church and tower which I do not believe have been fully appreciated. It consists of a round west tower, nave, chancel and south porch. The one bell has no inscription.

Here, and at near by Wramplingham, are I believe, the only cases where towers and churches, although attached, are a separate entity. In all other cases, either tower and church were built together with the east of the tower bonding into the nave west wall, or the tower was built on to the flat side of the nave west wall, and this east side of the tower would be thinner than the west. In these two cases, the tower east wall is as thick as the tower west wall plus the nave west wall. Here it is 5ft.11". The implication therefore is that either *could* have been added to the other .

At first sight, there is nothing to suggest an early date, and no Norman features remain although the tower is called Norman by most writers. The nave at 25ft. 1" appears too wide for pre-Conquest work, and the interior has all the appearance of over restoration. All the windows are Victorian, and we do not know how far they copy what was here before. The west nave wall displays on the inside, a large blocked up lancet window over the tower arch, which has led some writers to call the tower 12th. century, but Charles Cox states that this is unreasonable.

The tower is constructed of flints of all sizes, whole and cut, many quite large and also some odd stones, especially below the west window. It is here that we get our first Saxon feature, for the west window is a round-headed double-splayed window constructed entirely of flints, but it is too refined to be original. But can we really expect anyone to construct such a window without many more Saxon features to influence the decision? Surely it is a restored Saxon window. There is no other window in this circular tower. Between the tower and church are two fillets, and because of the deeper gap, they are different to the usual quarter-round fillets we usually see. The one on the south is a very large three-quarter-round fillet that tapers off just below the nave roof and is finished at the top with slates, which are of course modern. The one on the north, is a small flat pilaster that stops at nave roof level. It is here that we find our next feature, for behind the N/W buttress, we can see that these N/W quoins are in flints. They are quite clear, and prove what we would not care to guess at with a nave width of 25ft that the nave is also Saxon. The S/W quoin has been replaced by bricks, Victorian at the base, but some early bricks remaining at the top. Stone quoins would hardly have needed replacing, or if so dressed stone would have been used. Here the flints either fell out, or they were replaced for their looks. The chancel was mainly rebuilt in Victorian times, and the nave walls slope to thin them, which is usually an early sign. Although the tower walls are fairly straight, there is a slight bulge about t he middle which would suggest with its shortness, an early date. I therefore believe it is from the middle Saxon period or 900 to 1,000. The nave, with its extra width, may well be a later addition, replacing an earlier building.

N114. WICKMERE. St. Andrew.

H3. Sheet 133. Map Ref. T.G. 166 337

Tower, Nave and Chancel Middle or Late SAXON.

Tower Height	47ft. 6"
Height of Saxon part approx.	42ft.
Internal Diameter Grd:	7ft.10"
Tower Wall Thickness	3ft. 9"
Nave Ridge Height	31ft. 9"
Bells 1	
Chancel Width	17ft. 8"
Nave Width	17ft. 5"
Nave & Aisle Width	42ft. 9"
Chancel Length	36ft.10"
Nave Length	42ft.10"
Nave Wall Thickness	2ft. 5"

Situated in open fields about one mile west of the village, St. Andrew Wickmere, has a round west tower, clerestoried nave, chancel, north and south aisles and south porch. Taylor and Taylor note most of its early features and get closer to its building date than most by calling it Saxo-Norman. Their description of the blocks of brown building stone as carstone however is wrong as usual, for it is conglomerate.

The tower rises straight internally without apparent taper or steps to a height of 47ft. 6", while outside it tapers slowly to the top. The internal diameter is 7ft.10" and the wall is 3ft. 9" thick. There is much conglomerate in the lower parts of the tower, and about three feet up is a band of conglomerate laid in herringbone fashion and another just below the west window. Above the west window there are only odd pieces of this stone among the whole flints, and the taper from here is more pronounced. T he ground floor west window was inserted in the 14th. century, and apart from a rectangular window at first floor level facing south, the only other windows are the four Decorated belfry windows. Above these, the flush-work battlemented parapet in dressed stone and cut flints appears to be 15th. century although it was heavily restored in 1901 and again in 1938. The tower has only one bell, inscribed:- "Sheffield 1868 Patent Castel 4963". The tower is circular inside indicating it was built with the church, and yet outside it has the appearance of being added, as it does not keep its circular form, but is horseshoe shaped. The south fillet however is a genuine Saxon feature and is entirely of conglomerate that tapers off to finish at eaves level. It does not appear to be in bond with either tower or nave. There is no upper doorway or features inside the tower to date it more precisely. The tower arch is plastered, with only a chamfer towards the nave, and the head, as the Taylors note, is not a true pointed arch, but cruck-shaped, and as the construction is almost certainly of flint rubble, we can confidently class it as pre-Conquest. As we can see no blocked up windows in this tower, or distinct signs of it being raised, we must conclude that it is either towards the end of the middle Saxon period or the beginning of the late period, judging from the height of the tower and the style of the workmanship.

We can see that in the first place the church was quite narrow, as the west wall has much conglomerate, and the old west quoins can still be seen as large blocks of conglomerate, giving a nave internal width of 17ft. 5". The chancel measures 17ft . 8" which is near enough the same, for these f lint walls, as no two measurements ever fully agree. As the external walls show large amounts of conglomerate, we conclude that the walls are original to a long narrow church. The two aisles, each have three bays with a good section of the original wall to east and west. This being only 2ft. 5" thick is on its own a good indication of pre-Conquest work. The aisle walls, though being of the Decorated period, contain large quantities of conglomerate, which is primarily a Saxon building material. It seems to have been the practice however, throughout the medieval period, to reuse the materials from the old walls into the new, when aisles were added.

The chancel has retained all its Decorated windows, while only one has been preserved in the nave, the rest having been replaced with the Perpendicular style about a century later.

I saw no votive crosses, but one scratch dial on the S/E buttress of the south aisle. The gnomon hole can be seen and small holes in an arc over this centre hole, but none underneath. I wonder if this stone has been reused upside down?

N115. WITTON. St. Margaret

J3. Sheet 133. Map Ref. T.G. 331 316

Tower and Nave Middle SAXON

Tower Height	59ft.
Original Height approx.	40ft.
Internal Diameter Grd:	12ft.
Tower Wall at East	3ft. 4"
Nave Ridge Height	35ft.
Bells 1	
Chancel Width	17ft. 5"
Nave Width	17ft. 7"
Nave & Aisle Width	30ft. 5"
Chancel Length	30ft.
Nave Length	60ft. 2"
Nave Wall Thickness N.	2ft. 8"
Nave South Wall (arcade)	2ft. 8"

St. Margaret's Witton, is on high ground in open rolling countryside, less than two miles from the sea, and three miles from North Walsham. It has a round west tower, nave, chancel, south aisle, south porch and north vestry. All writers accept the nave as Saxon, and most will also include the tower.

Looking first at the church. In the north wall of the nave are two Saxon circular double-splayed windows, near the top of the wall before it was raised. They are built of flint rubble and are about 2ft. in diameter at the face of the wall and with mid-wall openings of about 9". The east end of the nave is marked externally by a vertical band of conglomerate quoins against which the north wall of the chancel is built. This implies that originally the chancel was narrower than the nave, and in later years widened to the same width as it is now.

The N/W and S/W quoins are entirely in large blocks of conglomerate that date this west end clearly as Saxon, and inside the church to the south, is a small section of the original nave wall which is 2ft . 8" thick. Further east are the five bays into the 14th. century south aisle, and in the south wall are the flints and conglomerate reused from the old nave wall. These features give us a firm dating for the nave as pre-Conquest, a 14th. century south aisle, and a chancel that was widened, but when? The windows here are all Victorian, but the piscina and sedilia are Early English, witness the dog-tooth moulding. Therefore, almost certainly, the chancel was widened during the Early English period.

We turn now to the tower, of which the Taylors are doubtful. While we must admit that the Saxon signs are few, we have positive evidence of the nave west wall being pre-Conquest, and of the tower being in bond with the nave wall. Then the pilasters joining tower to church give the final proof, for none of these have been seen on Norman towers, while a goodly number of Saxon towers have them.

The tower is constructed of whole flints, quite a lot of early bricks, and a few pieces of conglomerate. At belfry level the flints and bricks are about equal in quantity. Many iron ties show that at some time this tower was in a poor state. The pilasters to north and south are 16 inches wide by about 3 inches deep. The battlements and belfry windows are probably 15th. century, if they were not restored when the ties were put through the tower. There is only one small slit window below the belfry and no ground floor west window. Charles Cox tells us, "The lofty arch into the chancel is of the same date, and also the small archway into the tower. "The present tower arch could under no circumstances be called small, and so I wonder if this was opened out in this century for the organ which stands below. The arch is almost 12ft. wide, and very tall, and one wonders if the ties were put through the tower at the time the arch was opened up, or if they were needed before.

N116. WOODTON . All Saints.

J8. Sheet 134. Map Ref. T.M. 285 946

Tower and Church Middle SAXON.

Tower Height approx.	63ft.
Height of Circular Stage	37ft.
Internal Diameter Grd:	9ft. 6"
Tower Wall Thickness	3ft. 1"
Bells 6	
Chancel Width	16ft. 2"
Nave Width	15ft. 8"
Nave & Aisle Width	30ft.
Chancel Length	25ft. 9"
Nave Length	50ft. 3"
Nave North Wall Thickness	2ft.10"
South Arcade (Orig. S. Wall)	2ft.10"
South Aisle Wall Thickness	2ft. 4"

This is one of the six round towers in the Hempnall Group, all of which are quite close. It has a round west tower with two octagonal stages, nave, chancel, south aisle, south porch and north vestry.

The tower is circular for the first 37ft. built in whole and cut flints and above this are two octagonal stages surmounted by battlements. The octagonal sections are of knapped flints with dressed stone quoins, and in the battlements there are odd pieces of red brick. They appear to be capped with early brick. There are no fillets between tower and church.

This is one of the towers that I was not able to ascend to the roof because of the dangerous ladders, but I was able to examine most of the internal walls below the roof. The survey showed that the tower here is certainly Saxon of the middle period, 900 to 1,000, as the original belfry windows showed at 30ft. 9" from the ground. They were 52" by 29" with round heads and flint frames . T he upper doorway is still here 24ft. above the floor, and the head is set back on the jambs, but only by 1 inch. There is a blocked up window in the west face with a flint frame inside and out, and inside it has very wide splays. Let into the old belfry window on the south is a square wooden frame with glass, and on the north a similar square blocked with flints. These were the faces for the church clock, one facing the village, the other facing the Hall. There is now no sign of the clock mechanism.

The present belfry windows are double-light with pointed arches, but actually they are quite large single-light windows that have been divided into two by wooden frames and louvres.

This was the second tower that I had measured that has a thicker east wall, and it is quite close to Topcroft, the other tower with a similar wall. The wall thickness at the west window is 3ft. 1" while over the tower arch it is 3ft. 5". This difference can just as well be explained by the tower not being a true circle, as by the nave being added on at some later date. I feel certain that the tower and church were built together.

There are six bells in the tower, and like the congregation at Aslacton did some years earlier, they had them restored, and did the labouring work themselves. Also in 1988 they had the south slopes of nave and chancel roofs re-tiled.

So much for the positive signs of the Saxon tower. When we come to the church, there does not at first appear to be any positive Saxon features. The shape is certainly Saxon, being long and narrow, and there being no chancel arch, points strongly to a church with a continuous nave and chancel before the south aisle was added in the 13th. century. Further evidence of Saxon dating is the original north wall that is only 2ft.10" thick. The return wall of the original south wall can also be seen at the end of tile south aisle. It measures the same as the north wall. The north wall has now been repointed, and it has covered most of the original Saxon signs that assist us in the dating. However, at the N/W corner, above the vestry roof, are large flints which are part of the N/W quoin that has escaped the restorations of the other corners. No doubt the building of the north porch in the 14th. century was the reason this corner escaped. It is this old porch that is now the vestry. There is a curious chimney stack of knapped flints from the fireplace in this vestry at the N/W corner.

N117. WORTHING. St. Margaret.

F4. Sheet 132. Map Ref. T.F. 995 194
Church Early, Tower Middle SAXON.

Tower Height	25ft.
Internal Diameter Grd:	8ft. 3"
Tower Wall Thickness at T/Arch	3ft. 2"
Nave Ridge Height	25ft.
Bells 1	
Chancel NONE	
Nave Width	17ft.10"
Sanctuary part of Nave	5ft. 9"
Nave Length	30ft.
Height. of Nave Walls	20ft.
Nave Wall Thickness	2ft.10"

This small but very interesting church with the shortest tower of all, stands well outside the present village. It has a round west tower nave and south porch. The most inexplicable fact about this church are the words of Charles Cox who wrote "The fabric has fortunately never required severe restoration, as several acres of land were bequeathed for its maintenance and repair." Yet the church shows many signs of great poverty. It has lost its chancel and there is no east window. Part of the nave is now used as the sanctuary. The tower was obviously taller than at present, with its mean looking windows, and lastly the font appears to be a crude hollowing out of what may have been a churchyard cross.

Our study shows this to be an early tower built on to an even earlier church, as the straight east side of the tower shows. The construction of the tower as well as its height, which is not very reliable, would place it in the middle Saxon period or 900 to 1,000, and the church would therefore be 800 to 900.

The S/W and N/W quoins are of large flints cut to give a sharp corner, which is a certain Saxon feature, and the walling has no coursing which again denotes early work. While the N/E and S/E corners are now in dressed stone, closer examination shows that like Ingworth, we have *primary evidence* of Saxon dating, for below the dressed stones at ground level are the original quoins of flints as at the west end. As these were corners, the old chancel was evidently narrower than the nave, but when was it demolished? So far we have no idea . It seems probable that with the reset Perpendicular niche in the east wall, that it was after the 15th. century. There is no east window and only one window to north and south of the nave.

The south porch shelters a simple Norman doorway with single columns, having cushion capitals at the jambs, and zigzag moulding round the arch. The tower contains one bell, dated 1744. and it is constructed mainly of large flints with some early brick mixed in above the halfway mark. There is no real coursing of the flintwork, and no fillets between tower and church, but there is a chimney at the north angle. There are only three belfry windows near the top, with early brick frames and wooden frames inside these, with louvres. Inside the tower, on the north, is a small alcove with three-quarter-round moulding at the sides. Was this a Holy Water Stoup? If so, then there was a doorway in the tower which could have been the main entrance to the church, but now there is no sign of a doorway.

There are two votive crosses on the R/H jamb of the south door near the handle. Two scratch dials can be seen on the L/H jamb, the lower one is the best and the faint signs of a third is lower still. There is also one dial on the R/H jamb .

One wonders why, with the reserve, as stated by Cox, that the chancel was not replaced, and that such a poor font and furnishings were allowed to prevail, as well as the condition of the tower, which also shows signs of poverty in the belfry windows, these being only wooden rectangles.

N118. WRAMPLINGHAM. Sts. Peter & Paul

H6. Sheet. 144. Map Ref. T.G. 114 060.
Tower and Church Middle SAXON.

Tower Height	46ft. 6"
Height of Circular Stage	31ft. 6"
Internal Diameter Grd:	9ft. 2"
Tower Wall Thickness	3ft. 7"
Tower West Wall	5ft. 7"
Nave Ridge Height	29ft. 6"
Bells 3	

Chancel Width	16ft. 9"
Nave Width	17ft. 3"
Nave & Aisle Width	28ft. 3"
Chancel Length	32ft. 9"
Nave Length	42ft. 1"
South Nave Wall Thickness	2ft. 6"

This church, standing on raised ground about a quarter of a mile to the south of the river Yare, poses some interesting questions. It has a round west tower with an octagonal top, nave, chancel, north aisle and south porch.

From chapter 8 we see the usual method of joining tower to church, and a thicker east wall should denote a tower built before the church. But then it is only 4 to 6 inches thicker. In this case, the east wall of the tower is more or less the tower wall plus the nave wall, i.e. tower wall 3ft. 7" nave wall 2ft. From the height and construction of the tower we can say it is middle Saxon, 900 to 1,000. Looking first at the tower, there are quite straight fillets to north and south that reach almost to roof level. The five windows below the belfry have almost no splay at all. The three on the second floor, are almost certainly the original belfry windows. They have outer frames of early brick, and inside, flints with wooden lintels that could be original. Two other lancet windows, both with little splays, one of early brick is on the first floor, but on the ground floor, the window with the dressed stone frame is Victorian. The octagonal top was added in the 14th. century, and the resurgence of the brick industry in this area supplied the quoins without the necessity of bringing in expensive limestone.

There is a remarkable set of put-log holes in this tower that are surely original. Quite a number can be seen from outside, but even more inside, where on the upper floors almost all have been preserved. They are formed of early brick and go well into the wall; some even go right through as light can be seen in a few cases. The height of the circular part is 31ft. 6" which relates to the middle Saxon period. The second floor windows appear to be the *original Saxon belfry windows*, which would fix this as the probable original height of the tower. It is constructed of uncoursed average sized flints mainly from gravel beds. The construction is smooth, so it could well be towards the end of the middle Saxon period. The octagonal belfry stage is early Decorated and includes the battlements.

The nave is firmly in the Saxon period, not only because it is narrow and tall, but the N/W and S/W corners are built of average sized flints, that have not required cutting to shape the corner. The north aisle was not added until 1872, but the simple Norman doorway and Decorated windows have been reset into the modern wall. Since Ladbrooke's time the thatched nave roof has been replaced by slates, and the two windows in the south of the nave are quite different in shape from the three shown in his sketch. However, the fine Early English windows of the chancel, well documented in many church guides and text books, are well preserved. This does not mean however that the whole chancel was rebuilt, but it was most probably lengthened.

N119. YAXHAM. St . Peter.

F6 Sheet 133. Map Ref. T.G. 007 107

Tower and Church Late SAXON.

Tower Height	52ft.
Belfry Window Sills	38ft.
Internal Diameter Grd:	13ft. 1"
Tower Wall Thickness	4ft. 2"
Nave Ridge Height	35ft. 6"
Bells 6	
Chancel Width	16ft. 9"
Nave Width	20ft. 6"
Nave & Aisle Width	35ft. 2"
Chancel Length	33ft. 4"
Nave Length	55ft. 6"
North Nave Wall Thickness	2ft.11"

Called Norman, Saxo-Norman, and also Saxon, by various writers, this church has a round west tower, nave, chancel, south aisle, south porch and north vestry. It is situated near the centre of the village at the end of a short lane.

The tower is 52ft. tall and has four Decorated belfry windows at 38ft. from the ground. There are no signs of any other blocked belfry windows at a lower level so the windows may possibly replace the original Saxon windows at this level. This would place the tower in the late Saxon period. The tower is constructed of conglomerate and whole flints, with the major part of the conglomerate being in the lower half. There are five distinct bands of this stone up to eaves height. The tower is quite oval, as can be seen on the inside from the ground floor, and this is a good indication of early work.

If we accept that the 14th. century belfry windows were added to later stage above a shorter tower, then we must date the tower as middle Saxon or 900 to 1,000. The oval tower points to this dating as later work was more precise. But if, because we cannot see any blocked up belfry windows, we believe that this was the original height, then the date is late Saxon or 1,000 to the Conquest, as I have dated it. The internal east wall of the tower is curved over the tower arch, and although the east side is 4 inches thinner, I do not believe that this is enough to say it was added to a towerless church. The N/E and N/W quoins are large blocks of conglomerate that confirm a Saxon date. The length and width of the original nave implies a late Saxon, or late in the middle Saxon period.

Returning inside the church we find the tower arch is rather wide for a Saxon archway, but it is built of conglomerate in traditional Saxon style with narrow rectangular voussoirs. The jambs are of large blocks. The upper doorway, some 20ft. above the ground and over the tower arch, is in the same style and material. The tower is circular to the top and has battlements with small crenellations constructed of medieval bricks at the same time as the belfry windows. One more interesting feature before we leave the tower, the turret staircase on the south side has very worn stairs that turn anti-clockwise. This is very unusual, as the early defensive practice of circular stairways going clockwise still persists. Also, there is an odd arrangement of two old doors at the head of these stairs within two feet of each other. There are large quarter-round fillets of flints and conglomerate to north and south of the tower to supply us with yet another Saxon feature. There is a peal of six bells. These were rehung in a steel frame by John Taylor & Co. Loughborough in 1957. *"In memory of our parents John & Anna Cole"*. One bell is dated 1625 and on another is the following:- *"Charles & Sarah Featherstone B.G. D.G 1957"*.

An old carved stone coffin lid stands between the 14th. century arcades, whose piers still stand on the flint rubble of the old Saxon nave wall. The south porch was built at the same time as the aisle, and the corners were built of the conglomerate from the south wall, probably the S/W quoins .

N120. MORTON-on-the-HILL. St. Margaret

G5. Sheet 133. Map Ref. T.G. 127 159

Church Early, Tower Middle SAXON

Tower Ruins	
Tower Diameter	9ft. 1"
Tower Wall Thickness	3ft. 4"
Nave & Chancel Width	16ft.
Nave & Aisle Width	28ft. 5"
Sanctuary Length	7ft. 6"
Nave Length	45ft. 7"
Nave Wall Thickness South	2ft. 2"

This small and ancient church stands near the Hall on the Morton Hall Estate. It is in a commanding position above the surrounding countryside, but is hidden by the trees and its lack of a tower. Domesday only mentions the church as the second church of Helmingham parish, but the other church has long since disappeared. It consists of the ruinous remains of a round tower, nave, chancel, north aisle and south porch.

Charles Cox tells us it was restored in 1865 when it had a 14th. century octagonal belfry above a second circular stage which made it a very tall tower, this may have contributed to its downfall. A sketch of the tower appeared in Messent 's book *"Round Towers to English Parish Churches"* in 1958, but in April 1958, thankfully after the Easter service, the tower fell. The church was desolate for twenty years, but in 1979 it was leased to the *"Norfolk Churches Trust"* and with the co-operation of Lady Prince Smith and voluntary labour it was restored. Now a number of services are held each year.

Pevsner says "The Saxon circular window in the tower has disappeared. But as this was written before the restoration, the error can be understood. The window referred to is the round-headed double-spayed window over the tower arch, but it is still complete and visible. This is probably the first Saxon feature noticed, and with the flat east side of the tower internally it proves the church was Saxon and stood here before the tower was added later. The tower arch below this window is round-headed and built entirely of flints and conglomerate, another Saxon sign. The N/W and S/W quoins are of large blocks of conglomerate, more evidence of pre-Conquest work, and the north nave doorway is one of only five remaining unaltered Saxon doorways still open in the round tower churches. It is round-headed and constructed of conglomerate and flints without any imposts .

The nave wall thickness is only 2ft. 2", thin even for Saxon flint walls. The width of nave and chancel at 16ft. also indicates an early church. The 15th. century south porch is ruinous as well as the western half of the nave, caused by the collapse of the tower. The restoration was completed in 1982. The west end of the remaining nave was filled in with a wooden frame which was glazed, and the remaining walls and porch have been stabilised and capped with tiles. The north aisle is 14th. century of two bays with double chamfered arches and a north door. The east aisle window is a Victorian insertion of 1865 in the Decorated style. The chancel has an east window of 1300c. with intersecting tracery.

Turning to the tower, which is also Saxon although later than the church, I have no information of the height, other than Cox, but it was indeed very tall. The remains vary in height from about nave ridge height on the north to about 8ft. on the south. The wall measures 3ft. 4" thick and the core is of solid flints, and not just filled with small rubble. The walls are now capped with tiles as is the church. The three bells from the tower are now in the peal at Attlebridge. There is a small bell here in a frame at the western end of the nave. It is dated 1793 and was found in the coach house at Morton Hall. The 15th. century font has been cleaned and moved from the west of the nave into the covered part. The Jacobean pulpit from Morton, was moved after the disaster to Mutford in Suffolk, which is also a round tower church.

VISIBLE RUINS

N121. APPLETON. St. Mary
C3. Sheet 132. Map Ref. T.F. 706 273

These ruins on the Sandringham Estate consist of a wide round tower, and church that is roofless. I have seen these ruins, but so far have not measured or studied them, so I make no comment.

N122. BURGH St. Mary
L5. Sheet 134. Map Ref. T.G. 455 144

The latest maps have omitted marking this prominent ruin, which was on the old (126) map so visitors will have to rely on the map ref. It lies near Filby Broad, a few hundred yards up the by-road to the north of the A1064, and one mile west of Filby. It can be seen clearly across the fields to the north of the road.

These are the ruins of a Saxon church and tower. Charles Cox tells us it was in ruins in the fields in his day. He gives its measurements as tower outer diameter 18ft, church internal 42ft. by 16ft. Nave and chancel in one, and he classes it as a Norman church and tower, with a Perpendicular octagonal top and tower arch.

My survey has shown this to be a Saxon church and tower. The narrowness of the nave is the first pointer, while the fillets between tower and church, and the flint west quoins confirm this belief. The N/W corner shows where the actual flints have fallen out, but the shapes of the flints and rough stones can be seen left in the mortar. The S/W corner is more ruinous. The south fillet is of large flints and Roman tiles, and some large blocks of chalk clunch, and erratics.

Some very large flints have been knapped to give large thin slices, almost like tiles in shape and thickness. The north fillet is like the south but none of the flints are flaked in thin slices. Both fillets are rectangular and reach to about eaves height.

At the top of the circular section are three round-headed openings. There is no sign of a west opening . The north and south appear to have been the Saxon belfry windows, and the east was the upper doorway. The upper doorway is framed with conglomerate.

N123. BURLINGHAM St. Peter.
J6. Sheet. 134. Map Ref. T.G. 368 101

Tower Height before 1906	about 46ft.
Internal Diameter	7ft.11"
Tower Wall Thickness	3ft.
Chancel Width	15ft. 5"
Nave Width	18ft.11"
Chancel Length	22ft. 2"
Nave Length	38ft. 6"
Nave Wall Thickness	2ft. 9"

St. Peter's had a round west tower, nave, chancel, south porch, north porch and north vestry.

The nave and chancel are still roofed in slate although they are not safe. There is a Victorian arch-braced roof to nave and chancel. The tower arch is in early brick, probably by a previous restoration. The S/W corner is in dressed stone, but the N/W corner is large flints, cut to give a sharp corner, but now only the lower two are in situ. There were no fillets between tower and church. The tower is, or was, built of flints of varying hues, and not coursed; with some very large ones near the base. The nave walls appear contemporary with the tower, but the chancel has been rebuilt or refaced as the surface is of cut flints. There is enough evidence here to say the church was pre-Conquest.

N124. KIRBY BEDON. St. Mary
J6. Sheet 134. Map Ref. T.G. 281 054

Charles Cox tells us that drawings made in 1814 showed that this church had already been ruinous for a long time. Most of the tower and nave however, still stands today in spite of being ivy covered.

The tower is uncoursed and of whole flints. It is about 45ft. high. There are a number of put-log holes to be seen. The four belfry windows that are still partly there, were probably double-light with brick frames. The nave roof had a steep pitch so was probably thatched. The tower arch has a flattened Tudor style head. There is a smoother texture to the walling from the belfry to the battlements, which were of cut black and white flints, mixed with no patterning. Three small windows with brick frames are below the belfry windows, and these are set in much larger blocked up windows that were undoubtedly the original belfry windows.

The N/W quoins that are still standing are of very large whole and cut flints. So this corner at least is SAXON, and the tower which was at first only just above nave height means that this also was pre-Conquest .

N125. GREAT RINGSTEAD. St. Peter.
C2. Sheet 132. Map Ref. T.F. 702 403

Ringstead St. Peter's Church was partly demolished in 1771 and the materials used to repair St. Andrew's in the same parish.

Only the tower remains standing in the grounds of "Bury House" which was the Rectory. Much repair work has been done at the base to preserve this landmark, but no Saxon features can be identified.

N126. THORPE PARVA. Near Scole
H9. Sheet 56. Map Ref. T.M. 161 791

Only two pieces of this tower remain in the middle of a cornfield, and no signs whatever remain of its age. See back cover.

N127. WHITLINGHAM. St. Andrew
J6. Sheet 134. Map Ref. T.G. 273 078

This is another ruin on private ground, and in the Colman Estate. The round tower was completely circular and was standing until 9th.

February 1940. It had been out of' use for about 200 years. The *"Gentleman's Magazine of 1795"* says, "The round tower was repaired in 1620 when an additional stage was added and crowned with four statues." These were four angels .

Only a few inches of the tower remains, and not even a complete base. The rest of the tower has fallen over the cliff which is a sheer drop at this point. There are not sufficient remains to give any measurements of the tower. The nave and chancel are 17ft. wide; chancel length 17ft. 6" and nave length 27ft. The width of nave and chancel would indicate a Saxon church.

N128. WOLTERTON. St. Margaret
H3. Sheet 133. Map Ref. T.G. 165 323

The tower stands in the park of Wolterton Hall, home of Lord Walpole. Only the round tower remains, circular for about 32ft. with an octagonal stage that raises it to about 46ft. The top stage has dressed stone quoins, and the whole tower is faced with cut white flints. There is no sign of an upper doorway, but the tower arch appears to be still intact. It is 4ft. 4" wide by 15ft. tall, and the jambs are of large blocks of conglomerate. The internal diameter is 8ft. 9" and the wall thickness is 3ft. 9". There is a stair turret to the south.

Notes from 1807:- "Wolterton St. Margaret, nave and chancel same length, and thatched. South aisle and north chancel vestry are down (demolished). Tower round at bottom and octagonal at top. Two bells inscribed "Robertus Plummer me fecit, in Honore Sancte Margarete."

The tower is mainly complete and was recently restored.

RECORDS OF ROUND TOWERS NO LONGER VISIBLE

N130. ALDBOROUGH. St Mary
Sheet 133. Map Ref. T.G. 183 344

B. Harmer, writing in *"Round Tower Churches Society Magazine"* Vol. 4. page 19. tells us that Bryant recorded that the foundations of a round tower could be traced..

N131. ASHBY. St. Mary. Nr. Thurne.
Sheet. 134. Map Ref. T.G. 422 152

This round tower and church were shown up by aerial photography in 1976 and recorded in *"East Anglian Archaeology 51"* in 1991.

N132. WEST BECKHAM. All Saints.
Sheet 133. Map Ref. T.G. 146 391

The tower fell in 1783. Blomefield says, "Round at the bottom, above octangular." The church walls can still be traced in the churchyard.

N133. BOWTHORPE. St. Michael.
Sheet 134. Map Ref. T.G. 177 091

Excavations in 1985 uncovered a nave and round west tower of pre-Conquest date. The tower had been deliberately felled by fire, and the N/W and S/W quoins of the nave were of large blocks of conglomerate .

N134. BRINTON. St. Andrew.
Sheet. 133. Map Ref. T.G. 038 357

The present square tower is 14th. century, but there is some indication of Saxon features in the south wall. Messent says there is slight evidence on the floor inside that a round tower once existed. If this is correct, it must have been covered at the 1873 restoration.

N135. BURSTON. St. Mary.
Sheet 156. Map Ref. T.G. 137 833

This village is near Diss. Messent says "There is documentary evidence that the round tower fell in 1757."' While Munro Cautley and Pevsner say it collapsed in 1753, but they do not state its shape. Hugh Bryant, however, records that the tower was round.

N136. NORTH CREAKE. St. Michael
Sheet 132. Map Ref. T.F. 854 378

Recorded by "East Anglian Archaeology 51" 1991. This church was abandoned in the first half of the 16th. century. Fragments of the round tower remain, quite close to St. Mary's, the parish church.

N137. ECCLES-by-the- SEA. St. Mary
Sheet. 133. Map Ref. T.G. 416 288

Much has been written about this round tower that was buried in the sand dunes and later stood for 30 years on the beach pounded by sea and wind. It was round with an octagonal top, but only two small pieces still remain on the beach.

N138. FLORDON. St. Michael
Sheet. 134. Map Ref. T.M. 189 973

There is Saxon work in this church. The tower fell in 1775 and Mackerell, in his "Church Notes" says that the tower was round.

N139. HOLVERSTON. St. Mary
Sheet. 134. Map Ref. T.G. 304 030

This church was recorded by Messent. but he gave no indication of where his information came. *"East Anglian Archaeology 51"* 1991, gives a full report on this church and prints an aerial photograph. It shows a narrow church with a round west tower and apsidal east end. This was later extended to make a square east end, as at Framingham Earl. A south porch was also added as the crop marks show up. Bryant (1910,VII,38) records it as a round tower, although he does not give his source. He also says it had circular windows with wide splays as seen at Hales. The publication "EAA 51" gives a very full report on this find.

N140. KIRBY BEDON. St. Andrew
K7 Sheet. 134. Map Ref. T.G. 278 054

The church guide by Leslie Fenn records:- "Most of the original round western tower of flint had been pulled down and the remains were surrounded by a kind of wooden dovecot for the 3 bells. The church and tower were rebuilt in 1876-85. The tower now is square."

N141. GREAT MOULTON. St. Michael.
Sheet 144. Map Ref. T.M. 166 908

Blomefield records that there was a round tower here until 1700.

N142. MUNDFORD. St. Leonard
Sheet 144. Map Ref. T.L. 801 938

The church guide informs us that the foundations of a round tower were found within the church during restorations.

N143. NORWICH. St. Mary in the Marsh
Cathedral Area. NORWICH

A round tower church replaced a chapel of that name about 1100. In 1564 the parish of St. Mary was consolidated with the parishes of St. Peter Parmountergate and St. Vedast.

N144. NORWICH. St. Paul's
Barrack Street

This round tower church was destroyed by bombs in the last war. A new estate his been built over the site. The tower was Saxon, as witness old photographs showing Saxon circular windows.

N145. ORMESBY. St. Peter
Sheet 134. Map Ref. T.G. 491 146

This is another church that had C. Farrow researching into Blomefield's M.S.S., and giving the *"Round Tower Churches Society Magazine"* a rough idea of where it once stood. In 1986, aerial photographs by *"Cambridge University Collection BYJ 29"*, pinpointed the site as given above. *"East Anglian Archaeology Survey EAA51"* 1991 published a full report on their findings. The crop marks show a narrow church with a round west tower, and an apsidal east end. This church also had its east end extended and made square. It had been turned into a barn by the turned into a barn by the time Blomefield saw it.

N146. REDENHALL. St. Mary
Sheet. 156. Map Ref. T.M. 264 844

An old church guide tells us that the foundations of a round tower were found within the church during restorations in 1858.

N147. SAXLINGHAM NETHERGATE. St. Mary
Sheet. 134. Map Ref. T.M. 232 972

Messent tells us that early this century during the incumbency of the Rev. R. W Pitt, the foundations of a round tower were discovered just below ground level.

N148. SIDESTRAND. St. Michael.

This old round tower stood on the cliff edge until 1916, but the church was taken down and rebuilt further inland mainly from these materials in 1881.

N149. THURGARTON. All Saints
H3. Sheet 133. Map Ref. T.G. 182 358

The round tower was taken down as it was unsafe in 1882. The rough west wall still shows where the tower was attached. The church is now redundant and in the care of the *"Redundant Churches Fund"*.

N150. WROXHAM. St. Mary.
Sheet . 134. Map Ref. T.G. 296 175

C.W. Farrow, in *"Round Tower Churches Society Magazine"* Vol. 5. p.32 draws our attention to Dawson Turner's Notes. He made a note under Wroxham, taken from a communication from J.A. Repton in 1842. It reads as follows :- "Are you aware that within the tower of Wroxham Church the foundations of the original round tower may be found."

N151. GREAT WALSINGHAM. All Saints.
Sheet . 132. Map Ref. T.F. 939 378

Situated to the north of Great Walsingham St. Peter's Church in a field about 200 yards away. None of the stone walls are above ground, but they show as mounds and are plainly visible. The church was also known as St. Mary and All Saints. An aerial photograph shows this as a square tower, but a 16 inches to the mile map shows it as a round tower, and that is what appears from a ground view.

UNRELIABLE RECORDS OF ROUND TOWER CHURCHES

There are a number of reasons for the claims of round towers that cannot be substantiated. Some researchers have collected the various lists of round towers and compiled their own from the many sources, to include the greatest number possible. There are certain dangers in this. For example, Gasthorpe was wrongly called round by Messent, and included in other lists, when a visit would have shown up the error.

"Peeps at the Past" 1892 prints a list of Norfolk and Suffolk round towers that was taken from *"East Anglian Vol. I."* Starting with the many errors in this list:- BRISTON near Melton Constable. *"Norfolk Record Society Vol. I"* records Briston had a square tower. Blomefield writing much nearer the date of its demolition also records it as square. It seems this village was once spelled Burston.

HILLINGTON. St. John. This is clearly a printer's error for Hellington, whose dedication is St. John the Baptist, which does have a round tower. Hillington's dedication is St. Mary and it has a square tower.

SCOULTON. Mistaken for a round. It has a square tower with an octagonal top stage, which is the finish of a number of round towers.

SHELFORD. Another printer's error for Shereford.

SOUTH WALSHAM St. Lawrence. Although not on the list of round towers, this church was, nevertheless, called a round towered church in the text. However, the fine tower still stands of a much later date with no records of an earlier tower being here.

Charles Cox, in *"County Churches Norfolk"* 1910 lists the following:-

BURLINGTON St. Peter. A mis-print for BURLINGHAM.

HELHOUGHTON. This is a 14th. century square tower, and must have been so when Charles Cox saw it.

SAXLINGHAM THORPE. Cox says "The church has been long abandoned, the ruins show a round Norman tower, with 14th. century belfry." Visited by myself in 1983, the ruined tower was clearly square and had been so since medieval days.

WITTON. Near Norwich. This church has an octagonal belfry set on the nave roof at the west end. But there is no tower as such, certainly not a round tower or even a round belfry.

FRAMINGHAM PIGOT. Revd. C. Messent in *"Round Towers to English Parish Churches"* 1958 says :- "The old church was demolished in the last century, and a completely new church erected." Although the old church was certainly Saxon, it never had a tower. It was replaced with a Victorian church still without a round tower. The mistake arose from one of Ladbrooke 's prints of *'Framingham Earl'*, mistakenly captioned *'Framingham Pigot'*. Several writers have carried on this error.

GASTHORPE. Revd. Messent was the first writer to make this error. He said he had been prevented from making a sketch because of the ivy. The tower is in ruins. However, it stands for most of its height and is clearly square.

WEETING All Saints. These ruins are to the south of the village, while the old church of St. Mary still stands. Messent and local tradition call this ruin a round tower church. This was probably caused by Blomefield calling the ruins on the south side of Weeting, 'St. Mary' and the north church still standing, 'All Saints.' In Blomefield we read in Vol. 2. "T his church stood in the south part of the town, and is now in ruins, by the fall of the tower on it about 40 years past..... At the west end of the nave stood a handsome square tower."

MUNDESLEY All Saints. This church was in ruins for many years, and a small square tower stood at the west end as at present. Although local tradition says that it had a round tower, and local Directories and Town Guides for many years as well supported this view, there appears to be no reliable records to say that there ever was a round tower here. All the modern writings seem to come from local tradition with no reliable backing. However, there are a number of stones with Norman mouldings preserved in the building, so it must date back to the Norman period.

CHEDGRAVE. Doubtful:- I have taken this church off my list, because there is at present insufficient proof. Ref. C.W. Farrow who supplied the following information in July 1980; from a short history of Chedgrave recently issued. "In 1951, in the course of digging the grave nearest the west wall, the workmen came across a mass of buried flint masonry. The Rev. Wynter Blathwayt, who was rector at that date suggests, here were the foundations of a round tower standing in the customary place. After the tower collapsed, it was found easier to demolish its remains and raise the north chapel into a belfry instead."

SPROWSTON All Saints. *"Round Tower Churches Society Magazine" Vol. 4* p.9. "The base of the tower is flints, with further work in brick." It was perhaps the flint base that gave Revd. Caddy the impression of an earlier round tower, but the size of the base would be wrong, as well as the shape. Checked on site.

CHURCH NOTES - SUFFOLK

S1. ALDHAM. St Mary

G9 Sheet. 155. Map Ref. T.M. 041 445
Church Early, Tower Middle SAXON

Tower Height approx.	40ft.
Height of Spire approx.	55ft.
Internal Diameter Grd:	10ft. 2"
Tower Wall Thickness	3ft
Bells 1	
Width at Chancel Arch	16ft. 7"
Reducing to	14ft. 8"
Nave Width	19ft. 10"
Chancel Length	24ft. 4"
Nave Length	37ft. 10"
Nave Wall Thickness	2ft. 9"

This small church with its only access through a farmyard stands on a well raised knoll away from the village. It consists of a round west tower, surmounted by a slender spirelet, nave, chancel, south porch and north vestry.

This church stood as a Saxon towerless church before 900. The N/W and S/W quoins of flints and Roman bricks confirm this, although the N/W corner has been cement rendered since I made my notes in 1973. The thin nave walls also speak of Saxon builders. The east side of the tower internally is flat, showing that the tower was built later against the nave west wall. Still further proof is seen in the tower walls being only 3ft. thick at the west window. Very thin, even for Saxon tower walls; also, these walls are quite crudely built, not being by any means circular or truly perpendicular. The present height, and its build would date it in the early tower period of 900 to 1,000.

The tower may have more early features hidden, for I have been unable to ascend this tower so far. It is circular to the top with a plain parapet and is surmounted by a slender spirelet. For the first 4ft.6" the tower is cement rendered, then the whole uncoursed flints can be seen, and many put-log holes, framed with early brick and masonry. There are no fillets between church and tower. The Early English ground floor west window is fairly high up, and on the first floor, there are similar windows at west and south. The north window at this level has been blocked up. These I believe to be the original belfry windows, but until I can see inside, I cannot be sure. In the next or belfry stage, are four Early English windows, framed in brick, and the wall surface here is of cut flints, a sign that the tower was refaced here or raised, with the latter being the most probable. The tower arch, which is only a normal sized doorway, is also Early English and faced with brick in a similar manner which I would think was done at the same time as the belfry windows. No upper doorway is visible, but who knows what will be found above the first floor.

The first and most positive proof of Saxon work are the N/W and S/W quoins. These are built of flints, Roman bricks and pieces of masonry, although now only the S/W corner still shows its Saxon workmanship as the N/W corner has been cement rendered since my first visit. In the S/W corner is a piece of a broken churchyard cross, carved with a cable design, that matches another piece in the sill of a south nave window. It is said to be Saxon, and is almost certainly from the present churchyard. We have seen that the nave and chancel walls are under 3ft. thick, so with the corners for confirmation, we can be sure that the church was always at this width, and of the early period, 800 to 900. The unusual taper of the chancel from 16ft. 7" to 14ft. 8" is very rare but not unique. It may be due to changing the east end from apsidal to square. In two places the nave walls have been repaired with modern bricks, which is due we are told to a renewal of this part. The chancel has been cement rendered, all of which spoils the charm of this tiny village church. Early English and Decorated windows light this church, with only the east window being entirely restored in Victorian times. Dare we think that it copies the one before?

The chancel arch is Victorian, and a simple 13th. century piscina to the south of the chancel with engaged columns and a pointed head has a circular basin. Next to this, in a lowered window sill is a stone sedilia. The church is roofed in tiles while internally, the nave has embattled tie-beams and collars with arched braces, while the earlier chancel roof has tie-beams and king-posts. Internally it was heavily restored in Victorian times, but the main structure has escaped. Raven's *"Suffolk Church Bells"* states:- One bell inscribed "Sancta Maria Ora Pro Nobis."

S2. ASHBY. St Mary

L2 Sheet. 134. Map Ref. T.M. 489 991
Tower and Church Middle SAXON

Tower Height	50ft.	
Height of Circular Section	15ft.	6"
Internal Diameter Grd:	9ft.	2"
Bells 1		
Chancel Width	16ft.	
Nave Width	14ft.	2"
Chancel Length	29ft.	3"
Nave Length	54ft.	5"
Nave Wall Thickness	2ft.	6"

This is another church reached through a farmyard and it stands on level ground. It consists of a base of a round west tower with an octagonal top, and nave and chancel in one. This is another church and tower where I must differ from earlier writers, for although the main features are plainly 13th century, the pre-Conquest signs are here for all to see, especially when compared with other churches of this group.

We look first at the church which is a long narrow building in the Saxon style and with no chancel arch. The chancel walls appear to differ from the nave, which may mean, either a lengthening or a squaring off of an apsidal east end. All the windows of the church are Early English in style, with three having been altered outside in the 15th century. We know therefore when the last major alterations were made, but it is the wall thickness of 2ft. 6" and the western quoins that tell us we have here a pre-Conquest Church. The N/W quoin is composed of modern red brick for about 4ft. and above this is dressed stone laid side alternate but not regular. The S/W corner is as follows:- base one piece of erratic, then early brick, followed by one large flint, topped with a large piece of sandstone to a height of 3ft., while above this is dressed stone. We have here, therefore, all the signs of the last remnants of the pre-Conquest quoining using odd pieces of local stone and flints.

The thatched all in one roof, is a very ancient single-framed roof with collar, showing at the west end of the nave, some very roughly fashioned poles as rafters.

The tower (plate 11) does not appear to have had sufficient time devoted to it to learn its secrets. The first main point we notice from the inside, is that the tower did not suffer a disaster, and fall as the upper part must have done at Heckingham. For although the round section is only 15ft. 6" tall, the interior is circular right up to the base of the belfry windows at 26ft. from the ground. Proving that up to this point it was a circular tower and was cut back on the outside to conform to the new fashion in the 13th. century. Above here it was raised in the usual manner with eight straight walls, and the eight lancets, one on each side. The corners of the octagonal section are brick, but it is only in recent years that archaeologists have realised that brickmaking had restarted in East Anglia by the 13th. Century. The heavy battlements at each corner hide the vaulted roof of groined brickwork that covers the tower. It is the only example, with the exception of the Victorian tower at Higham, to have such a roof. The only other window in the tower is the west window on the ground floor also of Early English date. The upper doorway was also refashioned probably one hundred years later, giving the west end a very dignified appearance.

The tower contains one bell inscribed:- "J. Warner & Sons London. 1859." But in Raven's book *"Church Bells of Suffolk"* it states the bell has no inscription.

S3. BARSHAM. Holy Trinity

K3 Sheet. 156. Map Ref. T.M. 397 896
Church Early, Tower Middle SAXON

Tower Height	54ft.	6"
Original Tower Height	33ft.	
Internal Diameter Grd:	10ft.	4"
Tower Wall Thickness	3ft.	9"
Nave Ridge Height	31ft.	
Bells 5		
Chancel Width	19ft.	9"
Nave Width	19ft.	9"
North Aisle Width	14ft.	9"
Chancel Length	37ft.	9"
Nave Length	52ft.	9"

This beautiful example of a thatched village church stands well back from the Beccles to Bungay road on flat ground. It consists of a round west tower, nave, chancel, north aisle and south porch.

This is one of those churches where writers give us differing dates, for while Bryant says the lower part of the tower is pre-Conquest, as is the narrow window in the north of the nave, Pevsner calls both Norman. But neither have recorded the basic evidence here.

The tower and church were built together, or so we thought, by the interior of the tower being curved on its eastern side. The N/W and S/W quoins are certainly pre-Conquest by reason of their construction. The S/W corner has three large erratics at the base, followed by flints and other odd stones. The N/W corner, again with some large erratics at the bottom uses larger flints that have been cut to give a square corner. We know for certain then that this was the original width of the church, and the wall should be the same unless we can see some alterations. The entire south wall is original, and we can see signs of herringbone work in the flints. The north wall is original as far as the aisle, with part of the Norman window, which had its lower part cut away when the north doorway was inserted. The north aisle, Bryant tells us, was built in 1527, pulled down in 1785, and was rebuilt in 1908. The chancel was mainly rebuilt in the 17th. century, which was most probably the date of the unique east wall and east window which have a continuing diamond or lozenge pattern over the entire surface. There is also a low-side window in the chancel.

The tower is circular to the top, with the top section containing a lot of early brick, probably Tudor. The parapet which is eighteen inches thick is of Tudor brick which contains many pebbles in their structure. Until early 1988 the tower was crowned with a spire of tinplate that was tarred, but during the storm of 1987 it was damaged and leaned awkwardly at an acute angle for many months before being removed. The tower walls are constructed of mainly whole flints of average to small size and there are no fillets between church and tower. A ridge can be seen just below the height of the nave ridge, and above this, the flints are a little larger. From the belfry windows to the parapet there is a great deal of Medieval brick, and I believe this section is Tudor. The large single-light belfry windows appear to have had tracery at some time, and were perhaps double-lights from which the worn tracery has been removed. There are six other windows in this tower. Two are on the second floor at north and south, with frames of Medieval brick, three round-headed windows on the first floor, which we can see were the original belfry windows, below the octagonal stage. The ground floor west window is a Victorian double-light.

The five bells are hung in a square wooden bell frame and the tenor weighs 6 cwt. 2 qtrs. 7lbs. The tower upper doorway has been altered to a pointed window which is now glazed. The great interest of this tower is being able to see what great alterations have been made. It started as a round tower only about 33ft. to 35ft. in height. 3ft. 6" above the second floor or (33ft. from the ground) are eight jambs of dressed stone, that makes it certain that from here it was raised with an octagonal stage that was 7ft. tall, the height of these quoins, raising the height of the tower to 40ft, or a little more. The next alteration was to further raise the tower to 54ft., and it seems they were not too happy to put 14ft. on to the thin octagonal stage. This was therefore filled out to make the whole tower circular once more. Whether the spire was added then or later I am not certain,as the one that has recently been lost was not of that age. The tower arch has a pointed head and has certainly been altered. It now has a splay both into the tower and the nave, but it remains without any dressed stone.

In September 1979, a disastrous fire destroyed the thatched roof of the nave, and there were fears that the church would close, or at any rate if restored would not be in thatch. The parish however decided that this church must be restored in its traditional way, and since my last book was published this has been done. The fire slightly damaged the Trafalgar window, installed in 1906 the centenary of the battle. As often happens, falling plaster after the fire exposed another window in the west wall of the nave. It was double-splayed and round-headed, which now looked into the tower. Here then, we have the same situation as we found at Taverham in Norfolk, where a tower, curved on its eastern side, was still a tower that was built on to the earlier church. Fig. 8 explains this.

S4. BELTON. All Saints

L2 Sheet. 134. Map Ref. T.G. 485 029
Tower 1849, Church 14th Century

Tower Height	59ft. 9"
Internal Diameter Grd:	12ft.
Tower Wall Thickness	3ft. 3"
Nave Ridge Height	40ft. 9"
Bells 1	
Chancel Width	16ft. 10"
Nave Width	26ft. 8"
Chancel Length	32ft.
Nave Length	70ft. 10"
Nave North Wall Thickness	2ft. 7"
Nave South Wall Thickness	2ft. 10"

The church is on flat ground, well outside the old village which must have moved, but new estates are being built round the church, so once more it should be the centre of the village. It has a round west tower, nave, chancel and south porch.

The tower was in ruins in 1822, (Clemence), and was rebuilt in 1849. It is circular for its full height, and has no traces now of an upper doorway. There is nothing to tell us how old the original tower was. The four belfry windows are single-light and pointed, and all the features are faced with dressed stone. The one bell is inscribed "John Darbie Made Me 1664."

The church has nothing to show us before the 14th. century, which may possibly have been a rebuilding, for the nave width is from Norman or later times, and no Norman features are present. All the main features are 14th century except where they have been restored in the same style. The church is still interesting, and has fine north and south doorways with ogee heads. The south, has a floriated carving at the head, and a hood-mould with carved faces as stops.

S5. BEYTON. All Saints

E7 Sheet. 155. Map Ref. T.L. 934 628
Tower Middle SAXON, Church Uncertain

Tower Height	43ft. 6"
Height to Belfry sills	38ft.
Internal Diameter Grd:	10ft. 6"
Tower Wall Thickness	3ft. 9"
Bells 1	
Chancel Width	16ft. 3"
Nave Width	17ft. 5"
Nave & Aisle Width	30ft.
Chancel Length	32ft.
Nave Length	33ft, 1"
North Aisle Wall Thickness	2ft. 1"
South Nave Wall Thickness	2ft. 7"

All Saints Beyton, which in earlier times was spelled Beighton, stands within its village in beautiful countryside. The church consists of a round west tower with two massive buttresses towards the west, nave, chancel, north aisle, south porch and a vestry to the south of the chancel that is entered by a covered way from the priest's door on the south.

Bryant, in *"County Churches Suffolk"* (2 vols), tells us there is nothing early except the Norman tower and the Norman north doorway. But although the doorway is plainly Norman, with one or two stones renewed, the north aisle in which it stands is clearly later. Also by what features can the tower be dated Norman? There are no Norman windows or tower arch, and the wall thickness appears too thin for this period.

As the tower seems to be the oldest part of the church, we will try to find its age from what we can see. First, it is oval, often a feature of the early Saxon towers, but not of late Saxon or Norman towers. The height as given above, would also not correspond with any period after 1,000 and the wall thickness of 3ft. 9" at the west window also implies a Saxon date. As the east side measures 3ft. 3", this suggests a re-casing of the tower at the time the two buttresses were added. and strengthens the case for a Saxon dating. The ground floor west window is Victorian in the Perpendicular style, and the only other noteworthy feature below the belfry stage is a blocked window to the south on the first floor. It is still visible within and without, but it is inside that provides us with most clues. Here, although the frame left in situ is dressed stone, the head is triangular, and one wonders if this has been preserved from its original shape. No upper doorway is visible, but the inner wall surface has been plastered from the first floor level of 18ft. to a height of 25ft. 6" which would cover any blocked openings up to this height. There is nothing that could possibly indicate a Norman dating, but many indications of Saxon work.

The tower is constructed of uncoursed flints mainly whole, of medium size, seeming to be of a later date than either Saxon or Norman. There is a thickening of the base by four inches to a height of about eighteen inches with dressed stone as a weather course. There is a string course of dressed stone two feet above eaves level, and another one at the base of the belfry 38ft up. The belfry stage is very narrow, and a very low plain parapet of large yellow bricks is only about six inches in height. The two buttresses are at N/W and S/W, with two offsets, and they finish at the base of the belfry stage. The three rather nondescript belfry windows have pointed heads and are at north west and south. They are framed with early brick, and apparently do not fit into any architectural period. But to the left of the north belfry window is a block of dressed stone with the date 1780 cut by a mason. This then is probably the date of the belfry, which appears to be an addition. But was this done at the same time as the two buttresses and the re-casing of the tower which has effectively covered all original openings except the before mentioned blocked window on the first floor.

The tower arch faced with dressed stone towards the nave and tower is entirely Victorian in the same style as the chancel arch. Just about everything visible in the structure of the church is Victorian. Most probably the restorations of the nave, (called a rebuilding) in 1854, when the north aisle was probably built and the Norman doorway re-set. The chancel was restored and lengthened by ten feet in 1885. Every window and doorway except the Norman doorway is Victorian in the Perpendicular style except two windows in the chancel that are in the Decorated fashion. The walls are faced with whole uncoursed flints that stand well proud of the mortar, that is a feature of 19th century flintwork. It would thus be very easy to say the entire church had been rebuilt in the 19th. century, but from the experience of other churches and the 14th century piscina, which although much restored still stands in the chancel, this does not seem to have happened. So here again, the obvious Victorian features everywhere are apparently covering a much earlier church, but of what age we can only guess. The vestry to the south of the chancel in flint and brick was built in 1973.

S6. BLUNDESTON. St Mary

M2 Sheet. 134. Map Ref. T.M. 514 972
Tower, West & North Nave wall, Middle SAXON

Tower Height	56ft.
Internal Diameter Grd:	8ft. 7"
Tower Wall Thickness	3ft. 8"
Nave Ridge Height	40ft.
Bells 2	
Chancel Width	21ft.
Nave Width	29ft
Chancel Length	43ft. 8"
Nave Length	76ft. 8"

Two miles from the sea and about the same from the river Waveney, St. Mary's stands on flat ground, and is in the village which is large enough to support a church of this size. It is within 2 1/2 miles of four other R/T churches. Plan: - round west tower, nave, chancel and south porch.

The *"Church History"* tells us Blundeston is mentioned in the Anglo-Saxon Chronicles of 666, and also in Domesday. The History also says that the tower was built in 988, although it does not say where this record was found. It is however, one of the very few dates given to these round towers that fits in with the evidence of the stones. The tower, which is tall and slender, tapers gently towards the top (plate 9). It is constructed of very large to very small flints, whole and cut. Bricks whole and broken, are mostly used in repairs to the lower part, but more have been used in blocking windows, in the battlements, and also above the nave ridge. The fillets between tower and church are constructed of very large flints at the base, changing to smaller ones higher up. They taper off at the top of the nave west wall. The south fillet appears to have been disturbed, perhaps when the nave was widened, and now is a little lower. The flints of the tower are well coursed from about half way, but lower down they are rather ragged. Above the four Early English lancet belfry windows, the top is battlemented, still in the circular shape. There are ten other windows, and at least four blocked windows in the tower. These four blocked round-headed windows are 24ft. from the ground, and were the original Saxon belfry windows. There are also small round-headed windows between each that may well indicate here, a ring of belfry windows, as at Bexwell, Holton and South Elmham All Saints. That they are Saxon there can be no doubt, for their construction internally is entirely of flints. This ring of Saxon windows indicates a raising of the tower from this level in the 13th. century.

Inside the tower, the upper doorway can be seen on the first floor with a round head and faced with dressed stone. It is 2ft. 7" wide by 5ft. 9" tall and 15ft. above the ground. The tower is curved internally on its eastern side so it appears that tower and church were built together. The tower arch is faced with flints inside the tower, as it was in Saxon times, but towards the nave dressed stone has been used to improve its looks. The tower contains two bells, and the smaller one came from the ruined church of Flixton close by. Raven in *"Church Bells of Suffolk"* gives us their inscriptions:- 1. T.B. 1661; 2. E.T 1675.

The church we can see, is off centre to the tower, but this is not as rare as one might expect. We find the reason in the early Saxon tradition of narrow churches, and later, a bigger population, or more room wanted for processionals or both, so that the nave needed to be larger. It could not expand west for the tower, or east without swallowing the chancel, so it grew to north and south usually by means of adding aisles. Some times however, the nave was widened by moving one or both walls. Perhaps this was done if the roof needed replacing, but at any rate it has happened in a number of churches.

At Blundeston the south wall was rebuilt almost doubling the width of the old nave, but the original north wall still stands. We can see the results of the rebuilding, for the Norman south doorway was re-set in the new wall and the shafts were replaced upside down. The north wall still retains its simpler Norman doorway, giving us ample evidence of improvements to church and tower in Norman times.

The chancel we can see was rebuilt to centre it on the new nave. Pevsner tells us the chancel was rebuilt in 1851 but the church history makes no mention of it. One votive cross can be seen on the R/H column of the south doorway. Two scratch dials, one above the other are on the buttress to the east of the south porch. A small stone font stands in the churchyard to the south of the chancel. It came from the ruined church of Flixton, where the smaller bell also used to belong.

S7. LITTLE BRADLEY. All Saints

B8 Sheet. 154. Map Ref. T.L. 682 521
Nave & Western Chancel Early SAXON, Tower Middle SAXON

Tower Height approx.	45ft.
Height of Circular Stage approx.	30ft.
Tower Wall Thickness	3ft. 10"
Internal Diameter Grd:	10ft. 9"
Bells 1	
Chancel Width	12ft. 2"
Nave Width	16ft. 10"
Chancel Length	28ft. 2"
Nave Length	31ft. 1"
Nave Wall Thickness	2ft. 6"

The tiny church of Bradley Parva is well away from the few cottages that make up the village. It consists of a round west tower with an octagonal top, nave, chancel and south porch.

Writers in the past have given us every conceivable interpretation on the age and sequence of building this village church, including the statement that the tower was built first as a defence tower and the church added later. Both Munro Cautley and H.M. Taylor destroyed this assertion by showing that the tower was not a complete circular building as it stopped at the straight nave west wall and was not in bond with this wall. Therefore, it could never have stood as a solitary structure, and the church must have been here first.

H.M. Taylor, I am certain gives the correct sequence of events, viz. nave and chancel built first, then the tower, then the extension and squaring the east end, and finally the octagonal top to the tower and the late windows. What I hope to do is to date more precisely when the church was erected and when the alterations took place.

Taylor, in his *"Anglo-Saxon Archaeology"* vol. 1. dates the original nave and chancel C3 (1050 to 1100) but later quotes that it must be very early Norman or Anglo-Saxon by reason of the long-and-short quoins, (plate 33). This overlooks Haddiscoe and Herringfleet agreed by Taylor to be C3, (after the Conquest), and Dunham Magna, also C3, and using dressed stone in the Saxon manner. These quoins could well be Saxo-Norman insertions in an Anglo-Saxon building, as has been done on countless occasions. The small size and relative evenness of the stones convinces me that they are post-Conquest. The short circular stage of the tower suggests a date between 900 and 1,000, while the narrow nave and chancel belong to the early Saxon period of 800 to 900. I feel certain that it was apsidal because it measures 12ft. 2" near the chancel arch, and only 10ft. 4" at the east end (similar to Framingham Earl). This is very unusual unless the wall was being turned for the apse. I believe that dates, or periods given for the alterations by other writers are far too close to be a practical proposition and would favour around 50 - 100 years between each of these major alterations. Therefore, the tower was built on to the earlier church between 900 and 1,000. The chancel was lengthened and made square in the Saxo-Norman period, Conquest to 1100, when the quoins would have been inserted, replacing flint corners. All the Norman features i.e. tower arch, chancel arch, and windows in chancel and tower, and south doorway would have been inserted then or soon after. Although the evidence for the date brackets in this church may be small, they fit in with the pattern over the entire group, and they make sense when viewed from almost every angle.

The late 14th. century saw the half-timbered porch built, while the present church windows were inserted in the Perpendicular period when the tower was raised and the present belfry windows inserted. There is a low-side window to the south of the chancel which is now blocked up. The tower has one bell which is inscribed "R.G. 1652" as per Raven's *"Church Bells of Suffolk"*.

S8. BRADWELL. St Nicholas

L1 Sheet. 134. Map Ref. T.G. 503 038
Tower Middle SAXON, Church Plan SAXON

Tower Height	55ft.
Internal Diameter Grd:	10ft. 10"
Tower Wall Thickness	3ft.
Nave Ridge Height	37ft.
Bells 3	
Chancel Width	16ft. 9"
Nave Width	17ft. 8"
Nave & Aisles Width	38ft. 4"
Chancel Length	38ft. 7"
Nave Length	52ft. 3"

This is a fairly large church for the tiny village that was Bradwell, but now, with large new estates built near the church, it is the centre of a large community. It has a round west tower, nave with north and south aisles, chancel, south porch and north vestry.

My first impression after seeing this church, was that there was nothing to show before the Decorated period, but there were a number of pre-Conquest indications, that Saxon features might lie hidden beneath the later restorations. Hugh Bryant's notes confirm this belief, but throws doubt on any definite features coming to light in the future. Bryant says, "A low tower", (at 55ft.?) also, "A Decorated church standing on the site of a Norman structure, of which the tower, with circular windows formed part." These windows are no longer to be seen. Bryant can be relied upon to give a true picture of what he saw, and it is only with the help of later knowledge, that we can now date some of these churches and towers earlier than he would dare to presume.

The low tower quoted must mean an addition to the height at the turn of the century, while the circular windows must mean that the tower is at least Saxon, as the wall thickness would also indicate. However, all the early features are now hidden beneath the Victorian restorations.

The flat internal wall on the east of the tower, shows clearly that the tower was added to an earlier towerless church, and this nave west wall still stands. The two lower windows on the ground and first floors have Victorian facings outside. On the second floor, which is just below the nave ridge are three windows at N.,S., and west. These are the original Saxon belfry windows. They are narrow, round-headed, and faced with medieval brick, and show their origins by only having a very shallow splay. The four present belfry windows are also framed with medieval bricks and have a pointed head outside, but internally they are round-headed. From the belfry sills to the top of the tower there is quite a lot of medieval brick mixed with the flints in facing this tower. At 17ft. from the ground the flat east wall of the tower finishes sharply with a crescent ledge which is eight inches deep at its widest point, and at 24ft. there is another ledge of three inches. This is a feature noticed only in pre-Conquest towers. The tower wall thickncss of 3ft. at ground level just cannot be Norman. The tower contains three bells all inscribed as in Raven's *"Church Bells of Suffolk"*.

The width of nave and chancel, being well under 20ft. has strong indications of being well before the Conquest, for even Saxon naves were getting wider by the year 1,000. Rebuilding after the fire in the 17th century (Church History), would in most cases be a re-roofing and furnishing, as the stonework was rarely affected. The enlarging of the church in the late 14th. century seems to have followed the general pattern of adding two aisles and almost certainly lengthening the chancel. The nave windows were inserted in the Perpendicular period, while all the chancel windows were renewed during the Victorian restorations that are recorded as in 1850, 1875 and 1897, while the south porch is said to have been built in 1889.

It will be seen from the above and also from a visit, that although the tower is certainly pre-Conquest, the many restorations and the additions of the aisles, have left little if anything of the original church. We can, however, be reasonably certain that the original central plan has remained of nave and chancel.

S9. BRAMFIELD. St Andrew

K5 Sheet. 156. Map Ref. T.M. 399 738
Tower NORMAN, Church Decorated

Tower Height	43ft. 6"
Internal Diameter Grd:	10ft. 7"
Tower Wall Thickness	4ft. 6"
Bells 5	
Chancel Width	18ft. 2"
Nave Width	20ft. 1"
Chancel Length	38ft. 9"
Nave Length	63ft. 2"

This church is still in its village, which itself is on a well raised site. It has a detached round tower at S/W. nave, chancel, south porch and north vestry.

This is the only round tower in Suffolk that is detached, and the only other round tower to be separated from its church is at Little Snoring in Norfolk. The roof is reached through a circular trap-door, which I believe is the only one of this shape in a round tower. The cap is lead covered, and follows the pattern of so many of these towers that now have battlements, in that they still keep a conical cap inside their parapet which is now seldom seen, but which reminds us that these towers were all at one time roofed with a cone of thatch. The woodwork of this cap is radial rafters, taken from a cross-beam with two supporting struts. The cross-beams are 8 inches by 8 3/4 inches.

The tower is constructed of average sized whole flints, and there are medieval bricks here and there, also some put-log holes framed in medieval bricks both inside and out. The tower must surely be Norman, although there are no Norman features to be seen. The wall thickness is our only guide. The flints are not coursed. The four belfry windows are single-light with four-centred heads and inside they speak of the Tudor period when the battlements were built. The capping, at least now, appears to be Victorian. On the first floor are four pointed windows in medieval brick. No upper doorway to this tower, and an altered window at the west on the ground floor. The east doorway is Decorated with three recessed chamfers and no hoodmould.

The church is entirely thatched and the ridge was being restored when I visited the church in June 1976. Munro Cautley dates the old tie-beam and king-post roof as 14th century, which would make it the original roof when this church was built. A simple chancel arch, but the most beautiful screen in Suffolk says Cautley. The windows remain as they were, so here we have a 14th.century church almost unaltered, and a round tower with little alteration except the belfry windows.

There are five bells. Rehung 17th. April 1890 says Raven's Bells.

S10. BROME. St Mary

H5 Sheet. 156. Map Ref. T.M. 145 765
Tower and Church SAXON

Tower Height	50ft. 9"
Height of Circular Stage	31ft. 9"
Internal Diameter Grd:	10ft. 9"
Tower Wall Thickness	4ft.
Nave Ridge Height	29ft. 9"
Bells 5	
Chancel Width	19ft.
Nave Width	17ft. 9"
Nave & Aisle Width	32ft. 8"
Chancel Length	31ft. 3"
Nave Length	42ft. 10"
Nave Wall Thickness S.	3ft. 4"
Aisle Wall Thickness N.	2ft. 2"

Just over half a mile from the main Norwich to Ipswich road, this church stands on flat ground. It has no claim to a strategic position, and consists of a round west tower with an octagonal top, nave, chancel, north aisle, north transept and south porch.

This church was reputed to have been almost entirely rebuilt during the Victorian restoration of 1863, see Pevsner. But this is far from the true situation. In my last book I explained that I considered the old Saxon church and tower to have been completely refaced with an extra layer of knapped flints. Since then during the late 1980s, this outer Victorian layer became detached from the main walls, and a decision had to be made, whether to strip the entire facing and repoint the walls underneath, or to restore the Victorian facing to keep the church looking as it has been for the past 100 years. The latter idea was employed, and Hogg & Son, of Coney Weston were entrusted with the work. I am informed that when examined, there was a two inch gap between the old walls and the Victorian facing flints, and much of the trouble was due to poor mortar. The facing has split vertically in several places and had been tied (unsuccessfully) to the inner core by large iron nails driven in at intervals. The restoration began by stripping the facing flints and cleaning them. Then they were rebuilt tight up against the ancient core, and tied to it with stainless steel ties. It now looks as it did in 1976, but is now a really sound structure that should stand the test of time. These repairs were undertaken in 1990 and 1992.

The surface of the church walls are of knapped black flints interspersed with rectangular blocks of dressed stone. The windows, although all are of Victorian date, appear to be copies of what was here prior to 1863, as both Decorated and Perpendicular styles are to be seen. The south porch was the main entrance in bygone days, but now it is the vestry, and the north door has become the main entrance.

The south porch is faced with cut flints and at the entrance has flushwork arcading. Two plain shields are in the spandrels and a larger shield is in a shallow niche over the porch entrance. The hood-mould has two carved faces as stops. The diagonal buttresses have pinnacles with crockets and carved heads at the four corners. Carved beasts heads drain the water from the porch roof, which is battlemented with flushwork surrounds. The nave and chancel also have their roof battlemented, again with flushwork which is also found in several fine buttresses.

The arcading of the north aisle and north transept have semi-circular arches with pseudo Norman capitals ornately floriated and pseudo dog-tooth moulding. The most interesting features of this church are the many tombs and monuments, the most noteworthy being the Cornwallis tombs.

The tower received the same treatment as the church, and it now looks far different to what it did in early Victorian times. The north stair turret and octagonal belfry stage are additions of 1875. Before then, the shorter tower was roofed with a shallow lead cap. Any fillets between tower and church are now covered by the stair turret and flint facings. The present wall thickness of 4ft. although it appears to be Norman, is in fact of normal Saxon thickness, without the extra layer of Victorian flints. The octagonal belfry stage is faced with whole flints and the top is battlemented. The quoins are of bricks and there is a lancet window in each of the eight faces. At the base of the belfry stage is a stone string course. The rainwater spout from the roof is a gargoyle that has worn a great deal over the years. Below the belfry there are only two windows, both in the west face. A lancet is on the first floor and a massive double-light Tudor style window on the ground floor. The first floor of the tower is reached via the stair turret at the N/E corner.

The tower holds five bells. All were made by Thomas Newman in 1737. Four are inscribed "Thomas Newman of Norwich made me 1737". The other one says "Thomas Newman FECIT S. NEWSTEAD & P. RODWELL C.W." as Raven's Bells.

S11. BRUISYARD. St Peter

J6 Sheet. 156. Map Ref. T.M. 325 663
UNCERTAIN

Tower Height	44ft.	3"
Internal Diameter Grd:	10ft.	4"
Tower Wall Thickness	4ft.	3"
Bells 1		
Chancel Width	15ft.	
Nave Width	19ft.	4"
Chancel Length	24ft.	
Nave Length	40ft.	7"

Rather isolated except for a farm and four modern houses, it has a round west tower, nave, chancel south transept and south porch.

The tower is constructed of whole flints of all sizes and no coursing. There are no fillets, but some quite large flints are in the lower parts. At eaves level on the south is a large section of brick repairs. There is a considerable bulge all round at this point, but whether it is the result of early building or later repairs it is hard to say, although this does not preclude an early date. Inside the tower, from 28ft. up, the flints change from average and large uncoursed, to average coursed. There is a step or ledge to thin the walls by nine inches at 32ft. from the ground. The four double-light belfry windows of the 15th century have been restored between 1966 and 1976, when the bell was removed from the belfry and placed in the base of the tower. There is only one large single-light window in the west face on the ground floor, and one small pointed-arched window on the first floor which is now blocked with bricks. There are no put-log holes and no upper doorway. About 40 years ago, the lead cap was renewed, and as soon as the scaffolding was removed a storm tore it off. It was not repaired as they were short of money, and so the woodwork and stonework deteriorated. It is now weatherproof. The tower arch has a pointed head with a large chamfer and a quirk towards the nave, and three half-rolls to the arch. It looks as if it might have been built without dressed stone. The one bell standing in the base of the tower is inscribed "Cast by John Warner 1867." This is as seen by Raven in 1890 and recorded in *"Church Bells of Suffolk"*. Davy had earlier noted three bells. The tower is circular for its full height and there are no battlements. It now has a lead cap within its parapet.

The church walls are of whole flints and there is much brick in the south transept. The windows are 15th. century with brick frames. There is a Norman arch leading to the transept, so there are features of this date. Whether any parts are earlier we cannot say as there is nothing to which we can point.

S12. BUNGAY. Holy Trinity

J3 Sheet. 156. Map Ref. T.M. 338 897
Tower, West & North Walls Late SAXON

Tower Height	55ft.	9"
Height of Circular Stage	49ft.	4"
Internal Diameter Grd:	12ft.	6"
Tower Wall Thickness	3ft.	9"
Nave Ridge Height	35ft.	5"
Bells 1		
Chancel Width	20ft.	3"
Nave Width	21ft.	5"
Nave & Aisle Width	40ft.	8"
Chancel Length	19ft.	2"
Nave Length	56ft.	3"
Nave North Wall Thickness	2ft.	5"
S. Aisle Wall Thickness	2ft.	6"

In this small market town, three churches once stood close together. St. Thomas's has long since been lost, and now St. Mary's has closed for worship, but the oldest, Holy Trinity, still stands with its ancient tower. It consists of a round west tower with short octagonal battlements, nave, chancel, south aisle and south porch.

The south aisle and porch with its upper room, are from the 14th century. The aisle having three bays of quatrefoil piers and wave-moulded arches and the fourth bay to the east is of the Perpendicular period. The nave has the unusual feature of a dormer window at the S/W corner, and the chancel was extended in 1755 after being in ruins for many years. The east end was rebuilt in 1926, with a flying buttress at the N/E corner to enable a pathway to continue round the church, which is only a few feet from the boundary wall at this point. Thus only the nave west and north walls, apart from the tower, can be from the original church, and it is here we begin our search.

The S/W quoin can be seen on close inspection of the nave west wall, and this was certainly of flints, while at the N/W corner, four of the stone blocks appear to be erratics, as they are not cut as dressed stones, while the remainder of the quoin is of flint and early brick. Near the top, these bricks may well be repairs during the Middle Ages. In the north wall, which is original, is a blocked up round-headed window, now blocked on the inside, but looking more Saxon than Norman which it is generally called. The wall thickness is certainly Saxon, for no Norman walls were ever so thin.

The tower, which can be dated quite clearly from its many pre-Conquest features, and the technical skill of its builders combined with its height, is seen to be from 1,000 to the Conquest, and was built with the original church as can be seen from inside the tower where the east face is curved. Although few writers say anything about the Saxon features of this tower, just about all those noted by me and quoted here were mentioned by Dr. J. J. Raven in *"Proceedings of the Suffolk Institute of Archaeology Vol. IV."*

I was privileged to ascend the scaffolding when the tower was repaired in 1972, and it shows far more of its ancient features than is at first suspected. The locals say you can see the blocked up circular windows in certain conditions. This is just after it has been raining, but I was able to see them clearly close up from the scaffolding, and found eight near the top, two between each of the belfry windows. Lower down there are four more, one at each of the cardinal points. Inside the tower, all these can be clearly seen blocked in red bricks, so they are certainly Saxon circular double-splayed windows, and they conform to the usual positions as at Forncett St. Peter.

The tower is constructed for the first 6ft. of whole and cut flints of all sizes and uncoursed. Then there is a double herringbone of small sized sandstone blocks. This is the only round tower with sandstone in any quantity, (plate 16). Then a small band of rough flints, followed by a second band of sandstone blocks in herringbone fashion. This pattern repeats itself, although at higher levels it is not so noticeable as repairs and alterations have disturbed the surface. On the first floor internally are three large alcoves with round heads and only very slight splays. They appear to be blocked up windows, yet they are very large. There were deep cracks extending deep into the wall from the heads of these alcoves up to the four circular windows and in one case beyond when I inspected the tower. The entrance to the first floor is through a modern four-centred archway, that is set within a round-headed flint archway, which is again within a large triangular-headed blocked opening constructed entirely of flints, and the gable end is set back on the jambs. This is on the east, where the upper doorway is situated, and is at the same level as the three large alcoves, There is some evidence inside the tower of herringbone work although not so much as outside.

The belfry windows, Dr. Raven tells us were blocked up until 1852, when J.B. Scott discovered them, opened them out and put in the ground floor west window to the same design. The west belfry window is more or less intact, while the north and south windows, although opened, have lost their tracery and now have wooden frames and lattice panels to close the openings. The east window has been left closed. Above this circular section, which is all pre-Conquest, is a short octagonal battlemented section 6ft. 5" tall with carved shields on each side which were placed there in 1757, having been moved from lower down. Inside the battlements is another conical cap roofed in red tiles. The single bell is from the 15th century and was bought from another church. It is inscribed:- "Fac Margareta Hec Munera Leta".

S13. BURGH CASTLE. Sts. Peter & Paul

L1 Sheet. 134. Map Ref. T.G. 477 049
Church Early SAXON, Tower Middle SAXON

Tower Height	50ft.
Internal Diameter Grd:	13ft. 3"
Tower Wall Thickness	2ft. 7"
Nave Ridge Height	30ft
Bells 3	
Chancel Width	13ft. 3"
Nave Width	15ft. 4"
Nave & Aisle Width	27ft. 6"
Chancel Length	31ft. 9"
Nave Length	45ft. 1"
Nave Wall South	3ft.

The church stands alone above Breydon Water and quite close to the Roman Fort of Burgh Castle, from where no doubt many of the bricks used in this church and tower came. It consists of a round west tower, nave, chancel, north aisle, north vestry and south porch.

The tower is straight inside to the east, which implies that the church was here first. The very narrow nave and chancel as well as the south nave wall thickness is enough to establish these walls as original pre-Conquest, while the north aisle was built in 1847.

The tower is circular to the top and battlemented. A great deal of early brick has been used with the flints in its construction, and most probably they came from the Roman Fort near by. The very thin walls of the tower are thin even for Saxon builders. The first 18ft. is of whole and cut flints with the addition of Roman bricks; and they are uncoursed. The next 22ft. which takes it to the top of the belfry windows is of cut flints with early brick, probably refaced. Then the last 10ft. to the battlemented parapet is all early brick which I am certain is later than Roman. The four belfry windows are Early English lancets, with frames of early brick. There is no upper doorway to be seen, and the tower over-rides the nave west wall as at only two other R/T churches, Fritton and Holton St. Peter, all in Suffolk. While a number of nave west walls have ledges to thin the wall higher up where there is less weight to be carried, the wall here has been undercut, or thinned below the 19ft, mark, within the nave. There is at first no explanation for this, until one has studied a very large number of these churches. A few have had the side walls cut away into arches to give the nave more room, probably at less cost than building an aisle when seating was installed. This nave is very narrow, and the aisle was not built until the middle of the last century, so it is reasonable to assume that this wall was cut away to give more room, for it would never have been built like this. The tower arch is pointed at the head and has been opened out to almost the full width of the tower. When one examines these towers and sees what the later builders have done, (taking liberties), by cutting away the walls, opening out the tower arches, and putting stair turrets in the thickness of the tower walls, with the tremendous weight that is carried above, it is a wonder that any of them have survived.

Before 1847, the chancel had only one window is the south wall, but now there are two. Are both of these Victorian? the north aisle was added in 1847, and yet does not appear on the plan of J.L. Clemence, of 1858. He only shows two windows in the south of the nave, where now there are four, including one that is partly blocked by the south porch. The diameter of the tower north to south is nearly 2ft. longer at 13ft. 3" than from east to west, giving the tower a definite oval shape. This is to be seen in a number of early Saxon towers, but not as far as I have seen in any Norman tower.

There are three bells in the tower as in Raven's day (1890). He records:-

1. Thomas Newman cast me new in 1732. John Pitcearn Rector.
2. Thomas Killett. Churchwarden, George Harris Over Seer. 1732.
3. John Darbie Made Me. 1663.

S14. SOUTH ELMHAM. All Saints

J4 Sheet. 156. Map Ref. T.M. 329 828
Tower and Church Middle SAXON

Tower Height	39ft. 6"
Height of String Course	24ft. 6"
Internal Diameter Grd:	7ft. 4"
Tower Wall Thickness	3ft. 4"
Nave Ridge Height.	24ft. 6"
Bells 1	
Chancel Width	15ft. 1"
Nave Width	15ft. 1"
Nave & Aisle Width	26ft. 7"
Chancel Length	21ft. 10"
Nave Length	26ft. 3"
North Nave Wall Thickness	2ft. 7"
South Aisle Wall Thickness	2ft 5"

This church is very remote, in flat and open countryside and is approached through a farmyard. It is now in the care of the *"Redundant Churches Fund"*. It has a round west tower, nave and chancel in one, south aisle and south porch.

This church was heavily restored in 1870 and at first sight has little to show even of Norman date. The walls appear to have been refaced with whole flints at the restoration. The tower is curved inside, which tells us that the tower and church were built at the same time as one unit.

The tower is circular for its full height and is battlemented. The stair turret is Victorian and there are fillets between tower and church. The walls are faced with selected whole flints of average size, and the workmanship is such as we expect from Victorian builders. But this must be a refacing of the walls, although they are still thin at 3ft. 4", for inside we can see its age in the features and workmanship.

The tower arch is 6ft. 5" wide by 8ft. 3" tall, Norman in style with dressed stone and simple chamfered imposts, but the head is set back on the jambs by three inches. This is a Saxon feature although the stone is later. Most probably this is a later facing of a Saxon arch, and the builders have copied the shape faithfully. There are four belfry windows and seven other windows in the tower. The four single-light belfry windows are Victorian, as the tower from the base of the belfry stage is entirely a new construction from the 1870 restoration. The one bell in the belfry is inscribed:- "Anno Domini 1603", as in 1890.

Just below the base of the belfry stage are six windows. All are round-headed with their heads at the same height, but the sills vary alternately as there are two sizes of windows. The taller are at N,W, and S, while the shorter ones are at N/W, S/W, and S/E. There is a circular repair over the stair turret at the N/E, which might have been another small window at this point. All these windows are constructed of flints and mortar inside, and have ridges where boards were used to shutter the heads while the mortar set. Their heads are set slightly back on the jambs. They do not have very wide splays, and have almost level sills, which are the usual features of belfry windows. Their width is about 20" to 25"; the tall windows are 3ft 9" and the short ones 2ft. 6". This ring of windows has the appearance of the belfry windows at Bexwell and Holton St. Peter, plates 4 and 12. There is also a small west window on the ground floor. The stair turret is of brick and flints and the stairway is dressed stone from 1870. At 18ft. 9" from the ground, there is a three inch ledge inside the tower to thin the walls, and above here the walls are only 2ft. 6" thick. At first floor level 14ft. 6", there is a round-headed upper doorway with no dressed stone within the tower, although dressed stone of Victorian age faces the nave.

Within the church there is a ledge to thin the nave west wall by three inches just fourteen inches above the tower arch, or 9ft. 5" from the floor. These ledges have been found to be Saxon features used by the builders to conserve materials. The plan of the church shows a nave and chancel of the same width, or a simple rectangle when it was first built, and it is still of the same narrow dimensions. It seems fairly certain that the old walls still remain. Further proof of this is to be found in the two round-headed slit windows, one in the north nave and the other in the north chancel wall. While these may be Saxon windows faced with dressed stone in Norman times, they at least are not later than Norman, and so set an early date to the entire north wall, while the south wall was pierced for the south aisle in the 15th. century. The octagonal piers and double chamfered arches are from this period, but the windows are all Victorian from the restoration and appear to reflect the Decorated period. The south porch was rebuilt in 1871, Bryant tells us.

The Saxon features are as follows;-

1. Thin tower wall.
2. Low tower (base to belfry 24ft. 6")
3. Fillets between tower and church.

4. Upper Doorway without dressed stone within tower.
5. Tower Arch with set-back head 3".
6. Six windows in tower without dressed stone, and heads set slightly back on jambs.
7. Ledge to thin tower wall 18ft. 9" from ground.
8. Ledge to thin nave west wall.

S15. FRITTON. St Edmund

L2 Sheet. 134. Map Ref. T.G. 473 002
Tower, North Wall & Apse Early SAXON

Tower Height	43ft.
Internal Diameter Grd:	9ft. 3"
Tower Wall Thickness	3ft.5"
Nave Ridge Height	31ft.
Bells 1	
Chancel Width	11ft.4"
Nave Width	21ft.
Original Nave Width	12ft.
Chancel Length	21ft. 2"
Nave Length	51ft. 9:
North Nave Wall Thickness	2ft. 7"

St. Edmund's is quite close to Fritton Lake, which, we are told, in early times opened into the Waveney Estuary. The countryside is quite flat and the village has only a scattering of houses. The church stands on rising ground but not at the top of the hill. It consists of a round west tower, nave, apsidal chancel, south porch and north vestry. The village is mentioned in Domesday, so in all probability there was a church here then.

This church has many interesting features, many legends, and many questions still unanswered. Although the *"Church History"* lists a number of Saxon features, I cannot give them my full support, as in a number of cases they do not fulfil the requirements of proof. The history tells us that the apse was built first as a Wayside chapel, and the chancel later, when the tower stood separate. These complex explanations are quite unnecessary, and the simple building plan was surely, tower, with a narrow nave of 12ft. wide, and apsidal chancel, all built as one unit. This would have been in the Early Saxon period of 850 to 950.

The tower has been completely refaced and so the walls can give us no positive dating. At the base there is a plinth of bricks, now cemented over, and up to 10ft there are a lot of bricks and masonry of varying sizes mixed with the flints. From 10 to 18ft. on the south side, there is a section that contains about 50% brick with the remainder flints and masonry. From the belfry sills to the top, the tower is faced with cut white flints well coursed and is clearly a raised section, while the coping is medieval bricks without battlements. In the west of the tower are seven rectangular blocks of masonry 14" by 4", one above the other and about 4ft. apart. While they were a puzzle to understand at first, I am now satisfied that these are wall ties, used to bind cracks in tower and church walls before the introduction of modern steel rods. Internally on the first floor are four more of these masonry blocks.

To the east on the first floor there are faint traces of blocking, that may be the old upper doorway. The core and inner skin of this tower is of clunch (chalk lumps). This has also been noted at Feltwell St. Nicholas. The belfry windows have single lights to north and south and double lights to east and west. These and the other windows of the tower are framed with dark grey bricks that look Victorian or early this century. The clunch seen inside the tower, does not extend above the first floor windows, which suggests that this was the original height, and the tower has been raised at some later date, most probably in Victorian times. There are no fillets between tower and church, but even these could have been covered when the refacing was done. The one bell in the tower is inscribed:- "Sydnor Escvier 1598. M & S LONDON." As in Raven's *"Suffolk Church bells"*.

In 1350 we are told the nave was widened from 11ft. 4" to 21ft. on the south side. This gives the tower and chancel their offset appearance; unusual, but by no means rare in round tower churches. On the other hand, the tower projecting into the church as this does, I only know of two other cases, at Burgh Castle and Holton St. Peter; both quite close. We can therefore be fairly certain that the tower, nave west and north walls, and chancel are all original to the first building, but the south wall is 1350 as the windows indicate. The Norman window at the east of the chancel, only confirms that it was standing when this window was inserted, but it tells us nothing of how long the wall stood before it was inserted. No other windows of Saxon or Norman date have survived, but there are wall ledges so often seen in Saxon churches, where the walls were thinned to save materials, that help to support a Saxon dating. The wall thickness of both tower and church are much too thin for Norman builders, that a Saxon date is the only one possible.

The nave and chancel are still roofed in reed thatch, and a trap door to the south of the chancel, just below the thatch is known locally as the *"Smuggler's Loft"*. Other treasures include two lenten rings, Jacobean Holy Table, Jacobean three decker pulpit, early wall paintings, a pillar font, and outside, a scratch dial.

S16. FROSTENDEN. All Saints

L4 Sheet. 156. Map Ref. T.M. 479 818
Tower, Nave West & North Wall Middle or Late SAXON

Tower Height	54ft.
Internal Diameter Grd:	9ft.
Tower Wall Thickness	4ft. 2"
Nave Ridge Height	30ft.
Bells 3	
Chancel Width	19ft.
Nave Width	19ft.
Nave & Aisle Width	32ft. 6'
Chancel Length	32ft.
Nave Length	44ft. 5"
North Nave Wall Thickness	2ft. 10"

Frostenden, we are told, was a port at the time of the Conquest, so it could qualify as a defence tower by some writers. It is next to a farm, but well away from the present village, and it is on raised ground. The church has a round west tower, nave, chancel, south aisle and south porch.

A church here was mentioned in Domesday, and there are good indications of Saxon origins in the tower at least. The tall tower arch, altered in later years, and the fillets of quarter-round section between tower and church built mainly of flints, are never seen against Norman towers.

The construction of the tower is of well coursed whole flints, and there are a few medieval bricks framing put-log holes. Just below the circular battlements are five slit windows with modern looking frames, Then there are four single-light belfry windows with pointed heads. At the sills of these windows there is a string course of dressed stone. Below these are small windows in the north and south face, and the west ground floor window is similar to the belfry windows and probably dates from that time. Inside the tower, all the windows except the one on the ground floor, have been framed in Tudor brick with four-centred heads, but some of the jambs have since been repaired with dressed stone. This implies that some special care has been taken with this tower, as it is rather unusual to have such well cared for window frames on the inside of a tower. The tower arch is tall and narrow in the Saxon tradition, but the nave side is in dressed stone and has a pointed head. Inside the tower the jambs are in dressed stone as far as the springing, but there are no imposts, and the head of flints is cruck shaped which Taylor classed as Saxon. This unmoulded head would seem to indicate an unmoulded arch that was later faced with stone, and if so, is a strong pointer to a pre-Conquest date.

Outside once more, we must pause to look at the dressed stone alcove inserted in the tower a few feet to the south of the west window. This is the only one I have seen in a round tower, and was to hold a statue as is usual over the porch. About three feet from the base of the tower, and set into the flintwork are two querns. One below the west window, and one a few feet to the south. Why, we do not know. Were they just odd stones used for repairs? or did they have any other significance? Whatever caused them to be placed in this tower, their presence will always provoke a question.

The north wall of the nave, which no doubt is original with the tower, thins internally before the chancel. Outside it is constructed of medium and small flints with much mortar and uncoursed in the Saxon style. The east window, although Perpendicular in style with modern tracery, has an internal frame of the 13th century showing dog-tooth moulding. This can also be seen on the chancel piscina showing that these walls cannot be later than this. The south aisle and south porch which are in one, are late Decorated, at 1380. The porch is particularly fine with the centre boss carved as a pelican. All but one of the windows of the church are Perpendicular in style, but they have all been heavily or completely restored in the Victorian restoration.

Of the three bells:- the treble dates from 1450 or earlier; the middle says:- John Brend made me 1639; and the tenor, with an inscription in Latin is undated although it is suggested that the date is about 1430. On a beam of the tower roof, written in black paint is the following "H. PLANT 21 MARCH 1894". Carved into the bell cage beam is this:- "KINDRED Ch. WARDEN."

There is one scratch dial on the base of the buttress to the west of the centre of the south aisle, and three votive crosses can be seen at the entrance to the south porch.

S17. GISLEHAM. Holy Trinity

L3 Sheet. 156. Map Ref. T.M. 514 885
Tower and Church Middle SAXON

Tower Height	55ft. 6"
Height of Circular Stage	39ft. 6"
Internal Diameter Grd.	7ft. 10"
Tower Wall Thickness	4ft.
Nave Ridge Height	32ft.
Bells 2	
Chancel Width	16ft. 7"
Nave Width	17ft. 7"
Chancel Length	35ft. 1"
Nave Length	42ft. 9"
Nave Wall Thickness	2ft. 10"

Rather strangely, only Arthur Mee refers to this tower as Saxon. Others, including Munro Cautley, dismiss it as Norman. This church stands on a slight hillock at a road junction less than one and a half miles from the sea. Only a few houses are close by. It consists of a round tower with an octagonal top, nave, chancel, and south porch.

The circular section of the tower was cement rendered, although parts were flaking off when I saw it in 1976. By 1991, this was removed and the flintwork repointed. Between the tower and church are quarter-round fillets, so well known on many Saxon towers, as at Mutford and Rushmere close by. These taper off at a little above eaves height. The octagonal belfry stage with battlements is in knapped black flints and dressed stone facings with four Y -traceried bell openings and not later than the 14th. century.

When we examine the inside of the tower, we first see a Norman style tower arch with dressed stone facings and chamfered imposts towards the nave, but the head is set back on the jambs by about three to four inches, probably following the original Saxon arch. A rebate like this can also be seen at Gunton and Ingworth, and is never used in normal dressed stone arches. The west nave wall, has a ledge or step to thin it by about six inches at eaves height in the way the Saxons used to build. Going up to the first floor of the tower, we find towards the east, a triangular-headed upper doorway, (plate 19) in the same fashion as at Hales and Mutford, built entirely of flints, with selected flat flints for the jambs and head, and the head is set back two inches on the jambs, which was the practice of the Saxon builders. On the second floor are the original Saxon belfry windows. The north and south are completely blocked, but the flint frames remain. The west window has been closed in leaving a small inserted window to light this floor. The east window, although blocked, still has its splays as the west one, and it can be seen as blocked from the outside over the nave ridge. 30ft. from the ground, inside the tower, there is a ledge to thin the tower walls by about 3", another Saxon feature. The present belfry holds two inscribed bells.

The church does not hold as many features to prove its age, but the ground plan is enough to prove the foundations were laid in the middle Saxon period, (900 to 1,000). The north nave wall has a plinth of flints, and the wall thickness is additional proof that this is pre-Conquest. The flintwork, well coursed and stratified, follows the style one would expect to see in a wall of this period. The simple Norman north doorway is now blocked up, and Suckling tells us that a fine north porch was pulled down early in the 19th century.

Apart from the Victorian copy over the north doorway, all the nave windows are 15th. century, but the chancel windows are by no means easy to classify. Now, there is an east three-light window, and four double light Victorian copies of Decorated windows, two on the north and two on the south. Internally however, these appear to be original 14th century windows. Further complications arise however, since Suckling in 1846 quotes "Some good windows lighted the chancel ....but now built up with masonry. The east window alone remains." Then L.G. Clemence, 1858, shows no windows in the north or south walls in his plan, but yet he shows the two south windows in his elevation sketch. The conclusion must surely be that both Suckling and Clemence were correct, and the windows that were blocked up when Suckling saw them were still blocked up when seen by Clemence, although the window tracery was still in place and able to be drawn in 1858. After his studies, all the windows were opened and Victorian copies, all identical were inserted, leaving untouched the internal 14th. century work. Clemence also shows the church was thatched to an least 1858. Bryant tells us that restorations were made to this church in 1861, 1887 and 1907. The south porch is a fine example of Perpendicular work.

S18. GUNTON. St. Peter

M3 Sheet. 134. Map Ref. T.M. 543 958
Church Early SAXON Tower Middle SAXON

Tower Height	42ft. 3"
Saxon Stage approx:	33ft.
Tower Wall Thickness W. Window	5ft.
Tower Wall over T/Arch	3ft. 2"
Bells None	
Chancel Width	15ft. 4"
Nave Width East	14ft. 9"
Nave Width West	13ft.11"
Chancel Length	21ft.
Nave Length	34ft. 9"
Nave Wall Thickness	2ft. 8"

This small church to the north of Lowestoft was in a lane with hardly a house near by. Since the Sixties, modern housing estates have grown up around it and tarmac roads and street lighting have brought new life to this once almost forgotten church. It has a round west tower, nave and chancel in one, south porch, north vestry and annex.

This is another church where the Saxon signs are apparently few, but where a search will reveal convincing evidence of its early age. It is a very narrow church as a single rectangle, without a chancel arch, thin church and tower walls, a short tower with fillets between tower and church and positive signs that the tower was built on to an even earlier church. There are undoubted signs that the church has been here from at least Norman times, by reason of the two Norman doorways, the Norman window in the north wall and part of a blocked Norman window in the south wall. When coupled with the Saxon features I have mentioned, we must finish with a pre-Conquest building.

The tower, which had been ruinous for many years, once had a small spire we are told, and the belfry windows are from the 15th. century. In 1982 the tower was restored and a new lead roof put on. The parapet was renewed with modern hard bricks, and the belfry windows repaired. The whole tower was repointed at the same time. It was while the scaffolding was up that I was able to measure he tower and to see inside. The inner shape was a definite "D" as with other towers built on to towerless churches. The fillets between tower and church are a positive Saxon sign, and the wall thickness is another sign of Saxon builders. The wall thickness must be 3ft. 2" which is very thin even for Saxon workmen. but the 5ft. thickness at the west window is due to the base of the tower being altered to a square internally. I am not certain whether this alteration was done to increase the seating capacity or to strengthen the tower, for the alteration was done prior to 1858 when J.L. Clemence who surveyed all the Lothingland Churches drew a plan of St. Peter's showing the squared off base. The congregation then, must have been very few. The construction of the tower walls follows the style of the early towers, with many very large flints and some conglomerate near the base, and masses of mortar between the flints. The flat eastern side noted within the tower is continued above the nave roof to the top of the tower seen also at Gayton Thorpe in Norfolk.

Turning to the church, the tower arch is Norman, as are the two nave doorways. The north doorway is the richer of the two, with three orders, so this was probably the main entrance in Norman times. Looking closer at the tower arch, we can see that above the imposts, the arch is set back on the jambs by about three inches, a feature seen in Saxon openings built of flints. This means then, that this Norman arch merely frames a Saxon flint opening. Norman arches like this are very few indeed, but face similar openings at Gisleham close by and Ingworth in Norfolk.

The nave south doorway, although the poorer, was probably more ornate than at present, for it seems to have lost two or four columns from its jambs, perhaps when the 16th century porch was built. The evidence for this, is the base of the L/H jamb is a carved capital complete with a scratch dial facing the R/H jamb. There are also vacant spaces where the missing columns should be.

The church walls are similar to the tower, with uncoursed flintwork of all sizes and a fair amount of conglomerate to be seen at many points. The simple rectangular plan which is quite narrow and also narrows the church from east to west, all point to the early period when details were not as important, but the strength of the wall was paramount. Restorations must have taken place in the Norman period; north and south nave doorways, tower arch, one north nave window and in the south wall, part of the frame of another Norman window. The 13th century saw the insertion of two chancel windows and the angle piscina. The next major restoration that we know of was in 1700 when Charles Boyce restored the church, as recorded on a tablet over the south door. Then it seems the tower was raised, see the change in the flints, the new belfry windows inserted, probably also the south porch. The roof was also repaired. No doubt in honour of this, he was buried in the nave.

The church was in a very poor state towards the end of the 19th century, when the tower was without a roof, and obviously the church roof was little better. In 1901 to 1903, the children of Georgiana and Robert Cook Fowler, owners of the old Gunton Hall, restored the church as a memorial to their parents. A completely new roof was put on the church, including the timbers and tiles, all the windows were either repaired or renewed, the interior walls were re-plastered and a new organ installed. To commemorate Queen Victoria's Diamond Jubilee, a new vestry was built against the north of the chancel..

In 1990 an annex was built to the north of the nave with kitchen facilities but separate from the church to accommodate small meetings. There is no bell in the tower and no record of one. Raven's *"Church Bells of Suffolk"* states, "No bell, no return in 1553 and no bell in Robert Reeve's time." However, St. Benedict's, the modern sister church to St. Peter's built 1956, does have a bell. it came from St. Benedict's in Norwich, also a round tower church, that was bombed in the last war.

S19. HASKETON. St Andrew

I8 Sheet. 156. Map Ref. T.M. 250 504
Tower and Church NORMAN

Tower Height	60ft.
Height of Circular Stage	38ft.
Internal Diameter Grd:	9ft.
Tower Wall Thickness	5ft.
Nave Ridge Height	30ft.
Bells 6	
Chancel Width	14ft.
Nave Width	19ft. 2"
Chancel Length	24ft. 9"
Nave Length	58ft. 1"
Nave Wall Thickness	3ft. 5"

The church is on the south slope of a low hill, and not at the top. It is still in its small village. It has a round west tower with octagonal top, nave, chancel, south porch and north vestry.

St. Andrew's church Hasketon, appears to be quite a straight forward church, and yet it poses some questions that must be almost unanswerable. The sole Saxon feature is part of a round-headed window of dressed stone preserved in the south wall of the nave (plate 28). Undoubtedly of Saxon origin, as it follows the pattern of similar windows found at Avebury in Wiltshire and Wainsford in Northants. But with no dressed stone in East Anglia, except a few pieces of broken churchyard crosses being all the pre-Conquest dressed stone so far identified in these round tower churches, one wonders just where it came from? Or why it should be the sole survivor? Next, the tower wall thickness of five feet as measured at the west window and the tower arch, places it firmly as Norman, for both the Saxons and later in Early English times, the walls of churches and towers were built thinner. And yet, not a single Norman feature remains, in spite of their skill at carving. As these questions cannot at present be answered, I will therefore give the details of this interesting church with no further comments.

The tower, which is the tallest round tower in Suffolk next to Mutford, is built of flints of all colours and is uncoursed. There is a plinth at the base of flints with a stone string course at the top. The octagonal belfry stage has four Decorated windows, which was probably when this stage was added to the circular tower. On the first floor are three windows with pointed heads, and they have dressed stone frames within and without the tower. The upper doorway at first floor level, 22ft. 9" has a pointed head also, and dressed stone facings. It measures 2ft. 8" wide by 6ft. 4" tall. There are no fillets between tower and church.

The church walling is similar to the tower, and the preserved Saxon window has been set in the south nave wall near the centre about 9ft. up. There is one lancet window at the N/W of the nave, while the 14th. century saw the south doorway renewed as well as the tower raised. Two windows remain from the next century, while the rest were heavily restored in Victorian times.

There is one scratch dial on the N/W window sill, but from its position on the north of the church, it has been moved.

Today there are six bells in the belfry, but in Raven's *"Church Bells of Suffolk"* he tells us, there were five as follows:-

1, 3, 4 and 5. Miles Graye Made Me. 1628

2. T. Mears of London Fecit 1832. Samuel Randale Churchwarden.

S20. HENGRAVE. St. John Lateran

D6 Sheet. 155. Map Ref. T.L. 824 686
Tower and Church Middle SAXON

Tower Height	38ft. 6"
Internal Diameter Grd:	12ft. 8"
Tower Wall Thickness	3ft. 3"
Bells 1	
Chancel Width	14ft. 8"
Nave Width	14ft. 8"
Nave & Aisle Width	28ft. 10"
Chancel Length	17ft. 9"
Nave Length	25ft
Nave Wall Thickness	3ft.

This small church is now a retreat, used for the unification of the churches. It is in the grounds, and close to the Hall. It stands on flat ground and is hemmed in by trees. It has a round west tower, nave, chancel, north aisle and south porch.

The circular tower is clearly Saxon, and the nave width and wall thickness are surely of the same age. Rigold dates the chancel before 1300, saying only the windows were inserted at this date. This is further evidence for a Saxon dating, for Norman walls were never as thin as these. The tower is constructed of small to average sized whole flints with no real coursing, and there are no fillets between church and tower. The top is circular and battlemented, and there is a later stair turret on the north. There are two belfry windows close together on the south and on the north is a fully blocked window. At the S/E, the belfry window has been blocked at the wall face, but an alcove has been left internally. These are all round-headed windows with stone frames outside. However, inside the tower their frames are of flints, and in one of the south windows, the flints of the head have been laid in a non radial fashion. There is no step to thin the tower walls and no put-log holes. The upper doorway on the east does not show inside the nave, but it has a triangular head in flints, although the jambs have been repaired and are mostly in dressed stone. There is a chimney stack inside the tower as in a number of others, which makes one wonder if they were for a bread oven for the baking of the holy wafers. The one bell is inscribed 1796, but as the church was out of use except as a mausoleum from 1589 to 1900, the bell must surely have come from another church. On the ground floor to west and south are circular windows. They are now plastered and made into single-splayed windows, but I was told that previously they had been the usual Saxon double-splayed type.

The over restored nave and south porch, that are now battlemented, lead into a narrow nave with three bays of the Decorated period separating the north aisle, which now runs the length of nave and chancel. The piers are four engaged columns with spurs between (Pevsner, semi-polygonal shafts and spurs in the diagonals) and a carving of a demi-angel at the apex of each arch. The south doorway, is also from this period with fleurons and other carvings. The north aisle was extended to its present length, making the north chapel in 1540. Over the arcades are six clerestory windows.

The many large and elaborate tombs in the aisle and chancel tell us of when the church was in use only as a mausoleum.

S21. HERRINGFLEET. St. Margaret

L2 Sheet. 134. Map Ref. T.M. 477 978
Tower Late SAXON Church Early or Middle SAXON

Tower Height	47ft
Internal Diameter Grd:	10ft. 10"
Tower Wall Thickness	4ft.
Nave Ridge Height	29ft. 6"
Bells 2	
Chancel Width	14ft. 7"
Nave Width	17ft. 9"
Chancel Length	31ft. 8"
Nave Length	35ft. 10"
Nave Wall N. & S.	2ft. 9"

This small church is in open countryside with few houses, and about two miles from Haddiscoe church which has a number of similarities. It has a round west tower, nave, chancel and south porch.

Here we can see the narrow Saxon church, and from inside the tower the flat west wall of the nave is visible, giving clear evidence that the church was here before the tower. So what can we see in the church. The quoins are of dressed stone, and there is only one buttress at the N/E corner of brick, so this was built for support and not for show. Although the absence of buttresses points to early work, it will not separate Norman from Saxon. We are left therefore with only the narrow church and thin walls. The tower however, can be dated more precisely as late Saxon, with the belfry stage refashioned in the Saxo-Norman period, either copying the near by tower of Haddiscoe, or restoring what was already here but with crude materials. Note the east belfry window that has none of the Norman features, and a much lower standard of work in the stones. An earlier church must be pre-Conquest. The only query therefore is if the church has been rebuilt. There does not appear to be any records of neglect, or ruinous condition, or even of a so called rebuilding, which is generally a restoration. Unfortunately we cannot see the flintwork for more positive identification as it is all cement rendered, but the balance is greatly in favour of a pre-Conquest building.

Turning to the tower, which is circular to the parapet, and has no battlements or stair turret, we find that the flints are selected for average size and laid in well coursed rows, while two bands of larger selected flints have been used for decoration. It is this care in selection and laying that enables us to place this tower in the late Saxon period. There are four belfry windows, the north, west and south are in the Saxon style of double triangular-headed windows, with a cylindrical centre column having a cushion capital. Two slabs of dressed stone make each inverted V head, and there are three-quarter-round engaged columns at each side. Outside this there is billet moulding on the jambs, and this is carried on the round-headed arch that is over each pair of windows, whereas at Haddiscoe it is on the double-triangular headed windows themselves. The steeply sloping sills are protected with early tiles. These are the Norman restorations. The East window however, has none of these Norman features except the presence of dressed stone, which we do not know whether it is Norman or even later. Two pieces of squared dressed stone are at the jambs of the centre column, which is much rougher in its carving, and is set further back in the wall. The inverted heads are double rows of stones, the inner consists of about six blocks to each side, with a single stone for each side on the outer face. There is no billet moulding on this window, leading us to believe that it could be the original Saxon window with later repairs. Between the belfry windows at N/W and S/W there are small round-headed windows in early, probably Roman, bricks for the heads and flint rubble for the jambs. These do not follow any Norman pattern, but examples can be seen in a few Saxon towers, such as Blundeston not far away.

On the first floor to the east is an upper doorway 2ft. 5" wide by 7ft. tall, which cannot now be seen from the nave. The tower arch appears Norman, but it is now plastered over completely and does not show the billet ornament recorded by Cautley. There are fillets between tower and church, which are Saxon features, and only continued into the Saxo-Norman period on the few examples we can now recognise. In 1991 the tower was restored, and it was rather sad to see that instead of it being repointed between the flints, it was encased in plaster, which I had thought we had now ceased to support.

This is one more of these village churches to be still roofed in thatch. There is an early Norman south doorway, but this merely proves that the wall here was not later than the doorway itself. The very narrow chancel is striking when we look from the nave, and the east window displays a variety of early stained glass said to have come from Cologne.

Both bells in the tower are dated. One is inscribed 1837; the other is Anno Domini 1611.

S22. HIGHAM. St. Stephen

C6 Sheet. 155. Map Ref. T.L. 747 656
Tower and Church built 1861

Tower Height	56ft. 8"
Height to Conical Top approx:	76ft. 8"
Internal Diameter Grd:	12ft.
Tower Wall Thickness	4ft. 2"
Bells 1	
Chancel Width	15ft. 10"
Nave Width	19ft.
Nave & Aisle Width	30ft. 10"
Chancel Length	29ft. 2"
Nave Length	48ft. 10"

Half a mile south of the Newmarket Bury Road, this church stands in a sparsely populated area, on flat ground with a round west tower, nave, chancel, north aisle and south porch. This parish was formed from the parish of Gazeley in 1861, and was formerly called Higham Green. Sir Gilbert Scott R.A. designed the church, and Messent tells us that it cost £6,000.

The walls are constructed of whole and cut flints with dressed stone facings, and the roofs are tiled. The tower is circular to the top with a conical cap of slates. The first floor of the tower is vaulted with a rib vault, and the font is beneath this as a Baptistery. This is only the second Round Tower with a vaulted roof. There is a tall tower arch and on the first floor at the east is an upper opening taking the form of a circular window with a quatrefoil insert. The single bell is inscribed :- "Cast by Warner and Sons 1861". There is a large fillet on the north and a stair turret to the south, thus including all the main early features.

The tower wall thickness given above was measured at the ground floor west window. But measured at the east side of the tower, it was 4ft. 9" or seven inches thicker, and we know for certain that in this case the tower and church were built together. This rather goes against Munro Cautley's assertion that this proves that the tower was built first as a free standing structure.

The tower and church are built in the Early English Geometrical style.

S23. HOLTON. St. Peter

K5 Sheet. 156. Map Ref. T.M. 403 779
Tower and Church Middle SAXON

Tower Height	52ft.
Height of String Course	31ft. 6"
Internal Diameter Grd:	8ft. 3"
Tower Wall Thickness	3ft. 4"
Nave Ridge Height	24ft. 3"
Bells 3	
Chancel Width	12ft. 3"
Nave Width	16ft. 8'
Nave & Aisle Width	31ft 2"
Chancel Length	28ft. 6"
Nave Length	33ft. 10"
Wall Thickness N. Aisle	2ft. 6"
Wall thickness S. Nave	2ft. 10"

This church is at the edge of its village and there are no prominent hills around. There are several round towers near by. It has a round west tower, nave, chancel, north aisle and south porch.

The Norman south doorway tells us at once that the building here is at least of Norman age, and the tower is circular inside on the east, which implies that tower and church were built together.

The tower (plate 12) is of the same construction up to the string course at 31ft. 6". One is tempted to think that the string course, and a ring of slit windows above, date the tower as Norman, until we examine the inside of the tower. It is constructed of whole flints, fairly well coursed, and of the same construction up to the string course. It is circular to the top and battlemented, and the 15th century belfry stage contains a lot of red brick. Inside the tower, we find that four of the ring of eight round-headed windows, those in the diagonals, have been blocked, and the other four, at the cardinal points are built of flints. Not only do we see that these windows are of Saxon construction, but they also show a very strong resemblance to the ring of Saxon belfry windows at Bexwell in Norfolk. This is not the only pre-Conquest feature, for there are quarter-round fillets between tower and church that finish just above the eaves, and these are built of flints. There is an upper doorway, also of flints, at 17ft. 3" from the ground, although the head is now almost flat. It is 2ft. wide by 4ft. tall, although it has been shortened by reason of altering floor levels, but it does not show into the nave. The circular tower projects into the nave as at Fritton and Burgh Castle, but I could see no reason for this. The tower arch is 5ft. 11" wide by 14ft. 7" tall and the head is cruck shaped and has a simple chamfer. It has dressed stones at the jambs, but only to a height of five feet, which suggests that these are repairs. So there is plenty of evidence for a Saxon dating.

The church on the other hand, like so many more, relies mainly on the fact that it is in bond with the tower, and there is no evidence of complete rebuilding. The Norman south doorway is proof that this wall has been here from this age, and the wall thickness and nave width confirms my belief in a pre-Norman building. The S/W quoins, although of dressed stone are very mixed and rough but I could not date them with accuracy.

The Norman doorway has engaged columns at the jambs, with cushion capitals and bases. The arch has an outer order of double scallops and inside is a three-quarter-round moulding. The inner order is a hollow chamfer and a three-quarter-round moulding. There are simple chamfered imposts at the base of the arch, while at the apex is what appears to be a Griffin. The doorway is sheltered by a 15th. century porch. The north aisle was built in 1897, and is of cut black flints, built on a base of whole flints. The windows are mainly Victorian, with two Perpendicular windows on the south side, and the chancel east window is intersecting, from the Early English period.

There are three bells in the belfry today, but in 1890, Raven recorded only one inscribed:- M.H.M. 1881. (by Moore, Holmes & Mackenzie).

S24. ILKETSHALL. St. Andrew

K4 Sheet. 156. Map Ref. T.M. 379 872
Tower and Church Middle SAXON

Tower Height	64ft. 9"
Height of Circular Stage	35ft. 9"
Internal Diameter Grd.:	11ft.
Tower Wall Thicknes	4ft. 4"
Bells 3	
Chancel Width	18ft. 1"
Nave Width	17ft.
Chancel Length	28ft. 7"
Nave Length	63ft.
Nave Wall Thickness	2ft. 11"

St Andrew's church is in very open countryside, and is one of a group of hamlets, the Ilketshalls and Elmhams distinguished by their dedications. The church consists of a round west tower with an octagonal top, nave, chancel and south porch.

This fine lofty tower, which is circular for 36ft. of its height suggests an early Saxon tower. The octagonal belfry stage blends into the circular tower without the usual stone string course. The lower part has flints of all hues and sizes and no attempt has been made at coursing, while all the flints have been set in large amounts of mortar. Inside the early battlements is an octagonal lead cap, not seen from the ground. It is not as tall as the usual conical cap, but is just another reminder of the days when all these towers were capped in this way. The four belfry windows are single-light, while the diagonals have flush-work tracery of double-light windows. One pointed window in the south face near the top of the circular section is framed in early brick, and the only other window in this tower is the ground floor west window which is a restored Perpendicular. To the north of the tower is a later stair turret that leads to the first floor, but there is no sign here of an upper doorway. The tall pointed tower arch is cement rendered as is the entire ground floor of the tower, which prevents any attempt at further dating.

The three bells in the tower were recast in 1890 by John Warner & Sons of London. This was the restoration of the bells after a fire in the tower some years previously. The church still holds three small pieces of the old bells. One piece is dated 1598, another 1623, and the other shows clear signs of melting. With the intense heat required for this, and the tower still standing strong, a fire is not likely to be the cause of a tower or church collapsing.

There are no fillets to convince us of its pre-Conquest age, and the western quoins are to all intents dressed stone of an early date as they are not symmetrical in size or shape. But the N/W corner rests on a block of rough masonry, probably an erratic, and the S/W has a base of flints. This then is a good basis for believing that the Saxon flint corners have been replaced as we have seen in other churches. The Norman south and (north blocked) doorways give us the latest date for this church and tower, but there are other features that help us to place them before the doorways, into the Saxon era.

The narrow church, and thin walls, and also the way the walls run, giving different measurements at almost every point, suggest early work; and the walls taper towards the top. They also lean outwards, calling for restoration in the not too distant future. A church therefore where there is much more to be learned.

S25. ILKETSHALL. St. Margaret

J4 Sheet. 156. Map Ref. T.M. 350 852
Tower and Church Middle SAXON

Tower Height	49ft. 6"
Internal Diameter Grd:	11ft. 9"
Tower Wall Thickness	3ft. 7"
Bells 3	
Chancel Width	18ft. 9"
Nave Width	17ft. 4"
Chancel Length	25ft. 6"
Nave Length	39ft. 11"
Nave Wall Thickness	2ft. 10"

This church stands on flat ground within its small hamlet, and is known as one of the *"Saints"*. It consists of a round west tower, nave, chancel and south porch.

The tower, as high as the base of the belfry stage, about 40ft., and most of the church must be Saxon, probably before 1,000.

Flints of all sizes are in the tower walls, uncoursed and set in much mortar. I was able to see this, as although the tower had been rendered, when I saw it in 1976, much of the rendering had fallen off, enabling me to see what was underneath. In August 1993 the tower was restored, but instead of the usual repointing, English Heritage decided the whole tower should be rendered. The reason given was that this was the way these towers were built. I cannot accept this, for there are too many towers with decorative bands of flints to have been constructed only to be covered up. During this restoration, two Saxon circular double-splayed windows were discovered about ten feet from the ground, one in the north face and one in the south.

When I measured the tower in 1976, I noted the Saxon belfry windows inside the tower. The west one was open, although reduced in size. This remains unaltered. The east one showed as an alcove, and the south one was blocked, but they still showed their shape framed with flints. Now however, probably minor repairs internally, have lost these features for the alcove has gone, and the flint frames cannot be seen.

To the south of the tower is a quarter-round fillet of flints, that fixes the tower in the pre-Conquest era, while on the north is a later stair turret to the first floor which covers the fillet at this point. The tower is a full circle internally indicating that it was built at the same time as the church. It is circular to the top with a ring of small battlements that blend well with the church, and the four Decorated belfry windows are at the cardinal points, and three bells hang within. Below the bell-cage, once there could have been seen, the Saxon belfry windows, all round-headed and built of flints., but only the west one, and that reduced in size can be seen at present. The ground floor west window is of the Decorated period, and similar to the belfry, and the tower arch has probably been altered more than once, so little can be learned here.

The Saxon indications in the church begin at the west quoins. The S/W corner is built of whole and cut large flints and rough blocks of stone (erratics), while at the N/W corner the stair turret has covered both the fillet and the quoin. But we have good evidence on the south, and the nave width and wall thickness favour a middle Saxon period. The nave windows were inserted in the 15th. century, but all have been heavily restored, while the chancel has retained its Early English windows, although these too have much new stone in them. The north wall of the church has been cement rendered, but this is now flaking off, revealing that masses of mortar shows between the flints in true Saxon fashion of the early to middle period. Where once there was a north door, this has now been blocked up and a circular window with a trefoil insert takes its place. Not a great deal of visible evidence, but what there is, is very strong, and rebuilding these village churches was not undertaken as often as we have been led to believe.

S26. LOUND. John the Baptist

L2 Sheet. 134. Map Ref. T.M. 506 990
Tower probably SAXON

Tower Height	57ft.
Internal Diameter Grd:	11ft. 3"
Tower Wall Thickness	3ft. 9"
Nave Ridge Height	43ft. 6"
Bells 3	
Chancel Width	17ft. 10"
Nave Width	24ft. 11"
Chancel Length	35ft. 11"
Nave Length	62ft. 4"
Nave Wall Thickness	2ft. 11"

This church is in the village on flat ground, and is well known by visitors as the *"Golden Church"*, for the rood screen, font cover and organ case were designed by Comper who lavishly painted and gilded the entire church in 1914. The painting and gilding were restored in 1976. It has a round west tower, nave, chancel, south porch and north vestry.

The tower is circular to the top and has no battlements. There are two triangular buttresses at the base, and five tie-rods used to hold the tower together, but in 1986 the tower was repointed and cracks repaired. While this work was carried out, the tie-rods were removed and the latest form of wall ties inserted, namely stainless steel rods with knobs on the ends, buried below the surface is of the flints. This weakness of the tower walls, is probably not a weakness of the construction, but of later alterations. On the south side a stair turret has been built within the thickness of the tower wall, and not far from the large opening of the tower arch. The tower wall is only 3ft. 9" thick, and the resulting instability has come from this. There are two fillets of flints and early brick, running right up to nave roof height, with straight sides, (not rounded as usual), and this, together with the facing of the tower, places doubt on the tower being pre-Conquest. The lower 15ft. of the tower is of knapped flints, some quite large, with only an occasional piece of early brick. Next comes a band of about three feet where some pieces of masonry are also in with the flints. Above this for the remainder of the tower, early brick and flints are about half and half. The four belfry windows are double-light Decorated, and the only other window in the tower is at the west on the first floor. It is of early brick and is round-headed. No upper doorway and no features of distinction were seen.

The church walls as well as the tower must have been refaced, note the amount of knapped flints, while the nave width at 25ft., must be after the Conquest. No Norman features remain, so the earliest dateable features are the Early English windows of the nave, followed by the chancel windows that are all Decorated from the following century when the south porch was built. Much has been renewed however in the Victorian restorations of 1856, 1875 and 1893. In the west wall of the nave, at the north corner, is a small circular squint, much the same as at Blundeston not far away. This we believe was so that latecomers could see how far the service had progressed (before the days of clocks) before they entered the church.

There are three bells as recorded by Raven in 1890:-

1 and 2. Tho., Newman of Norwich Made Mee. 1730.

3 Tho. Newman of Norwich Made Mee. 1730.

John Kett & William Ellis C.W.

S27. METTINGHAM. All Saints

K3 Sheet. 156. Map Ref. T.M. 363 900
Church Early SAXON Tower Middle SAXON

Tower Height	51ft.	Nave Width	17ft. 7"
Height to Belfry Sills	34ft. 6"	Nave & Aisle Width	32ft. 9"
Internal Diameter Grd:	8ft. 2"	Chancel Length	28ft. 10"
Tower Wall Thickness	4ft.	Nave Length	36ft. 9"
Nave Ridge Height	28ft.	Nave N. Wall Thickness	2ft. 9"
Bells 3		Nave S. Arcade Thickness	2ft. 4"
Chancel Width	18ft. 7"		

This small church is near the top of a pronounced slope in rolling countryside. The ground slopes away to the north where the Waveney flows less than a mile away. It has a round west tower, nave, chancel, south aisle and south porch.

Domesday informs us that a church was here in 1086, although all writers consider that this tower and church are Norman. The Taylors dismissed it from their list of Saxon churches, but nevertheless there are more than sufficient grounds for placing the tower and church firmly in the pre-Conquest period.

The tower is decidedly oval, which at once suggests early work, and above the first floor it is more square with rounded corners. Very similar in fact to the shape of Howe tower in Norfolk. The east side is straight, and this continues well above the first floor. Chapter 8 explains how this proves the tower was added to an earlier church. The present belfry windows are Early English, but below them on the first floor are two of the original belfry windows. They are round-headed with frames of selected flat flints, and the heads with these flints are laid in *non-radial fashion.* On the same floor and facing east is the upper doorway with jambs of selected flints. A thick board has been placed across the head to support it, as above this the mortar has crumbled away, so no true height can be obtained. At 22ft. 6" from the ground is a ledge to thin the walls by three to four inches which I consider is a fairly certain Saxon feature, and the tower arch which is cement rendered, with only a simple chamfer towards the nave, is most probably also of flints. The top of the tower which is entirely circular is finished with later battlements. There are fillets between tower and church, not seen on any post Conquest tower.

As we have seen, the tower was built against an earlier towerless church, we must now seek to prove if this early church still stands. The north doorway, being Norman, places this wall firmly in or before the 12th. century. The N/W quoin is constructed of flints and erratics and the S/W quoin is the same, but shows signs of disturbance when the church was widened by the south aisle and south porch. This, with the evidence of the north wall thickness of 2ft. 9" and the arcade wall of 2ft. 4", added to which the north nave wall is resting on a plinth of flints, and the wall is of uncoursed flintwork, and it is perfectly clear that this nave and chancel were here before the tower. We must therefore date the church as Early Saxon, 800 to 900 with a low tower of under 40ft. added between 900 and 1,000. The Normans added or altered the north doorway, and the tower was raised in the 13th . century. The south aisle is from the Decorated period and further windows were inserted in these old walls from the Decorated to late Perpendicular days. The tower holds three bells, but there were four here early this century Hugh Bryant tells us.

S28. MUTFORD. St. Andrew

L3 Sheet. 156. Map Ref. T.M. 486 886

Tower, Nave and Chancel Middle SAXON

Tower Height	66ft. 6"
Height of Circular Stage	47ft. 6"
Internal Diameter Grd:	10ft 4"
Tower Wall Thickness	4ft.
Nave Ridge Height	33ft.
Bells 3	
Chancel Width	16ft. 11"
Nave Width	17ft.
Nave & Aisle Width	33ft. 9"
Chancel Length	31ft. 3"
Nave Length	43ft. 3"
North Nave Wall Thickness	2ft. 8"

Standing on raised ground to the north of the present village, this church was saved from redundancy in 1973 by the efforts of the village. Great efforts were made to put the church and tower into a safe state of repair. It has a round west tower with octagonal top and west porch, nave, chancel, south aisle and south porch.

The tower, the tallest of all the round towers, is a fine example of this ancient group of churches and is the only one with a west, or 'Galilee porch'. Although classified as Norman, it must certainly be regarded as Saxon in the light of our present knowledge. It is constructed of average sized flints, fairly well coursed. There are fillets to north and south of the tower, of quarter-round section and built of flints, and these are the first Saxon features we notice. The tower is curved internally to the east, so telling us that the church was built with it. The Galilee porch has been variously dated as Norman by Suckling, and Decorated by modern writers, but I prefer the Norman dating as the entrance is round-headed, and the blending into the tower is all in flints which would hardly be the case in later years. Also, my studies show that although many churches had an entrance through the tower or nave west wall in early times, this soon changed to the north or south doorway. Over this porch is an Early English lancet window, and above this again on the first floor is a slit window framed in flints, which the inside will confirm is Saxon. Sadly, a small repair done by a local builder, has inserted a wooden frame with a lancet head into this opening, although at present, the original flint frame can still be seen.

On the south side of the tower we can see two blocked up slit windows framed with flints, which study has shown to be Saxon in date. The circular stage is 47ft. 6" tall, which is higher than when it was first built, as we can see from the inside. The octagonal stage was added in the Decorated period or 14th. century, so it is probable that it was raised the first time in the 12th. or 13th. century. The four wide belfry windows, with dummy windows of flushwork in the diagonals, are below a fine flushwork battlemented parapet.

This parapet has holes at the eight corners that suggests there were crosses or other ornaments to grace the corners of the battlements.
Going inside the tower, the ground floor is cement rendered, but on the first floor at 25ft. is our next major Saxon feature, for on the east is a perfect example of a pre-Conquest doorway with a triangular head (plate 18) and this is also visible from the nave. Except for its size it follows precisely the one detailed by Taylor and Taylor at Hales in Norfolk. It is 2ft. 3" wide by 4ft. 9" tall, although the new flooring of the 1975 restoration has left one foot of its height below the present floor. It is constructed of selected flat flints, and the head is set back about two inches on the jambs. It is quite high at 25ft. but then the tower arch is 19ft. 9" tall, and this doorway just shows inside the nave ridge, so the nave was always at this height, and it was not raised as some might suggest.
Only one foot higher than the upper doorway at N,S, and W, were three windows, the north and south of which are completely blocked and the west has been closed down to a slit window, seen above the lancet window externally. These three windows are seen to be the original Saxon belfry windows from when the tower was first built. They were large round-headed windows constructed entirely of selected flat flints, and their heads are arched in a *non-radial* manner that Baldwin Brown called *"Tredington fashion"*. These, with the upper doorway, not only place the tower firmly in the pre-Conquest period, but they give us the tower height within small limits, and so we can date it around 950 to 1,000 or Middle Saxon.
The three bells, now of course in the octagonal belfry, are inscribed
Large Bell:- "John Brend Made Mee 1638"
Medium Bell:- "John Brend Made Me 1636"
Small Bell:- "ANNO DOMINI W.B. 1615"
These were restored by the "Whitechapel Bell Foundry" in 1975 at the time of the tower restoration. They are now rung by their clappers and not swung.
Here we can see that the original church was a nave and chancel in one, and of the same width. At least the west and north walls are original. Most probably the south chancel is also, but the east end may well have been extended or changed from an apsidal shape. The so called "Founder's Arch" set in the north wall is the only Norman carving left in the church, and Pevsner suggests that this may have come from the entrance of the Galilee porch. The south aisle is referred to as from the Decorated period, yet the windows indicate the Early English on the south side while the west is Decorated. Yet the piscina and the piers which are octagonal reflect the 15th. century. I would think that an early date in the Decorated period with perhaps the Early English windows being reset, and a later restoration in the 15th. century is most likely for this part of the church. The chancel arch appears to be from the same time as the south arcades, and at this time it must have been a magnificent church, for as well as the south aisle, there were north and south transepts. The one on the north we can see by the blocked up arch both within and without the church, and the south was demolished and walls rebuilt with red brick in Victorian times, and is sadly out of character for this lovely church.
So although few features remain in the church to date it, the tall walls always here, (see the upper doorway), the narrow chancel and nave, and the north wall only 2ft. 8" thick, is a sound basis for a Saxon date when joined to the undoubted Saxon features of the tower. The N/W quoin should also be examined, as the stones are very rough and not stepped or laid side alternate as usual, but appear to be replacements for the original flint corner. The windows are mainly Decorated and Perpendicular with three Victorian on the south. The east chancel wall below the window also contains some fine flushwork contemporary with the battlements.

S29. ONEHOUSE. St. John the Baptist

F7 Sheet. 156. Map Ref. T.M. 514 885
Tower and Church Middle SAXON

Tower Height	44ft. 3"
Internal Diameter	7ft. 8"
Tower Wall Thickness	3ft.
Nave Ridge Height	30ft.
Bells 2	
Chancel Width	15ft. 10"
Nave Width	15ft. 10"
Chancel Length	22ft. 5"
Nave Length	39ft. 6"
North Wall Thickness	2ft. 8"
South Wall Thickness	2ft. 10"

This church is on a slight rise in open countryside. It stands in a field next to a farm through which one must pass when approaching from the south. From the north, where most of the present village is situated, there is a trackway across the fields from the distant road. Onehouse is mentioned in Domesday, and there are a number of points that could link this present building with the one here in Saxon times. The plan is of a round west tower, nave and chancel in one and a south porch.
This is possibly the only round tower that has taken a lean to the west. It has a quaint look as one approaches, and it is this repair that makes the fillets doubtful. The thin tower and church walls, the cruck-shaped tower arch that may well be built of flints, and the fillets between tower and church, are all Saxon indications, but little of positive evidence as the fillets are suspect.
I was able to ascend the tower during repairs in November 1980, but little new evidence was found. The tower is built of whole and cut flints with small amounts of early brick and Roman tiles. The flints are uncoursed and there are a few blocked up put-log holes low down. The tower some years ago settled on its west side, giving it a permanent lean which opened up a gap between tower and church. This had been filled with a straight fillet, which must not be confused with the quarter-round fillets of pre-Conquest times. The fact of the tower subsiding in this way gives grounds for believing that it was built on to a church that was already here; but internally there are no features to corroborate this.

It was in 1980 that the tower was restored and repointed after cracks had been found, and it seemed to be a fine restoration. However, within eighteen months many more cracks had appeared, and the tower had to be shored up to prevent a collapse. It stayed like this while investigations were made into the cause. It soon became apparent that after the original subsidence, it had been underpinned with mortar that was now disintegrating, and it was feared that the internal core of the wall had collapsed. In 1986 the repairs were declared urgent, but many problems delayed the work until 1990, when a new method of bonding the core was tried. It proved a disaster, as the resins injected to stabilise the core, ran down the walls causing runs and staining. To save a complete collapse, the top of the tower was demolished as far as the nave ridge. A sad fate for another of this dwindling group.

The four belfry windows are, or were Early English, and faced with dressed stone, and inside, the edges of the splays were of early brick, with splays of flints. Only two other windows were in this tower, both Early English, that followed the belfry windows in shape though not in size. The tower was circular for its full height, with battlements that appeared to date from the time of its windows. Messent's sketch of 1958 shows a small spirelet which had disappeared by 1976. The tower was unusual in having a solid concrete roof supported by a concrete beam N. to S of nine inch by twelve inch dimensions, and a concrete tabernacle for a flag post was built into this construction. There was no sign of an upper doorway within the tower or nave, and no blocked up windows were seen.

The tower arch is cruck-shaped, which indicates Saxon work, and it appears to be built of flints, but as it is cement rendered, we cannot be certain. So this feature is still not conclusive until we can be certain if the construction is of flints or other material. The tower is curved on its eastern side, which denotes being built with the church, in spite of this side being ten inches thicker than at the west window. The nave west wall thins by about six inches at the top of the side walls or 15ft. up, and the fillets between tower and church usually a strong feature, are suspect because they were almost certainly added when the tower took a lean to the west.

The church has a narrow nave and chancel in one, and this is always early, and this width appears to be pre-Conquest, or early to middle Saxon. The nave walls are rendered, and the chancel walls very much restored, with the walls of whole flints uncoursed and blocks of masonry. There is only one Early English lancet window at the N/W, but the other north windows are 14th century. All the chancel windows and those of the south nave are Victorian in the Decorated and Perpendicular styles. The south porch does little to enhance this church and is built of Tudor brick.

The two bells are recorded by Raven in 1890:
1. R.G. 1673; 2. 1604 James Edbury.

S30. RAMSHOLT. All Saints

J9 Sheet. 169. Map Ref. T.M. 307 421
Tower and Church Late SAXON

Tower Height	56ft.
Internal Diameter Grd: N to S	10ft. 11"
Internal Diameter Grd: E to W	10ft. 4"
Tower Wall Thickness	3ft. 9"
Nave Ridge Height	28ft.
Bells 1	
Chancel Width	16ft. 10"
Nave Width	16ft. 10"
Chancel Length	26ft. 6"
Nave Length	34ft. 6"
Nave Wall Thickness	2ft. 10"

This church stands on a high point on the north bank of the river Deben. It has always been a landmark for the local fishermen and yachtsmen. It is three-quarters of a mile from the nearest road and has only a farm near by. The church consists of a round west tower, nave, chancel and south porch. (plate 10).

All the writers call this tower oval, although it is no more so than others that have not been quoted as such. But it does keep its shape all the way up. It is tapered on the outside to thin the walls, and I measured the tower walls at the S/W window on the ground floor. The three buttresses also enhance the oval shape, and must be noted as only Beyton, also in Suffolk, has buttresses for the full height of its round tower. These buttresses at Ramsholt are far more elegant than Beyton's and appear to have been built with the tower. Certainly they are also in the local septaria, which is found along the banks of the Deben and Orwell. The rest of the tower and church are also in this material.

In trying to date this church we must first look at the tower arch, as this is the only point where we can see any reliable early work. Inside the tower, the arch is very much like the one at Stody in Norfolk, except that it is lower. It is rough cut within the tower and entirely of flints. But on the nave side the arch has been closed in with an early Norman doorway of dressed stone and a door. This must place the tower at some time earlier than the door for if the church was here first, and the tower built later, (a) the wall would be flat within the tower as the nave west wall: (b) the dressed stone would be finer on the west side as this would have been the church entrance: (c) there would only be a low doorway, and not the tall tower arch that has been closed in to fit the smaller doorway. There is therefore undeniable proof that this tower is pre-Conquest, and about its present height, which is why I have classed it in the late Saxon period.

The construction of the tower is a mixture of septaria and flints, but mainly septaria. This is a local stone consisting of compressed clay. The fine tapering tower with its three tapering buttresses looks quite elegant standing in its commanding position above the Deben (plate 10). The buttresses are placed north, south, and west. The usual west window, in this case a lancet, is in the S/W face of the tower, and has deep splays to the jambs and sill. The three belfry windows are also lancets, which is why the early writers often call the tower Early English. The jambs are in dressed stone, but the heads are arched with two inch bricks. They are the only other windows in this tower.

The church has been cement rendered, and so little can be learned about whether these walls have been rebuilt. But from the early piscina in the chancel, one would say that the church has been standing with its tower from late Saxon days. The nave and chancel are paved with early brick, and the chancel is unusually lower than the nave. Still remaining in the nave are two double round-headed windows that at the latest must be Norman. They are unlike anything that we have been taught is Norman tradition.

The 19th. century two decker pulpit, and the unusual arrangement of the box pews, in which those east of the pulpit face west, all add to the character and sense of antiquity in this church. The single bell in the tower is inscribed: - "John Darbie Made Me 1679".

S31. RICKINGHALL INFERIOR. St. Mary

G5 Sheet. 144. Map Ref. T.M. 039 751
Tower, Nave and Chancel Middle SAXON

Tower Height	54ft. 6"
Height of Circular Stage	41ft.
Internal Diameter Grd:	10ft. 2"
Tower Wall Thickness	3ft. 4"
Nave Ridge Height	30ft. 6"
Bells 3	
Chancel Width	16ft. 8"
Nave Width	18ft. 6"
Nave & Aisle Width	38ft. 3"
Chancel Length	26ft. 11"
Nave Length	38ft.

The church stands at the end of a very long village street and in a hollow. It has a round west tower with an octagonal top, nave, chancel, south aisle and south porch.

The flints of the tower are whole and well coursed, and the octagonal belfry is surmounted by fine ornamented battlements. There are four double-light belfry windows of the 14th century, when the tower was raised, and internally the tower is curved on the east, telling us that tower and church were built together. The three bells are as follows:- large bell, no inscription; middle bell, dated 1636; small bell, has a Latin inscription.

The tower arch is Norman, with dressed stone towards the nave and also within the tower. It is this apparent lavishness with dressed stone, in sharp contrast to its absence in the work of Saxon times, that tends to make us forget any Saxon features. On the first floor, the west window, faced with dressed stone outside, has jambs of flints inside, while the head appears to have been repaired with rough blocks of masonry. Opposite, is an upper doorway, blocked on the nave side, but like the window has jambs of flints and a repaired head of rough masonry. We find our most positive pre-Conquest feature on the second floor, for 6ft. 3" above this floor, or 32ft. 6" from the ground, near the top of the circular stage, are four original belfry windows. They are round-headed and 2ft. wide by 4ft. 6" tall. The one on the west is open with a reduced opening but the others are blocked, leaving alcoves that allow them to be studied. They have jambs and heads of Roman tiles. The largest tile is six inches in length, and many are broken pieces as if rescued from another building. They are laid horizontally for the jambs, and for the round heads seem to take only one change of angle, or in the case of the north window, two angles, that finishes with a 'V' into which several small pieces are fitted. This is the *"Tredington fashion"* named by Baldwin Brown. The tower, therefore, is unmistakably Saxon.

The gabled south aisle of the 14th. century hides the early character of the church, for nothing of the Norman era has survived except the tower arch. The fine carving of the south arcades and the tracery of these windows is delightful. The original south porch was added then, but later an upper room was added, see where the walls were raised. The staircase to this room has now fallen into ruins, and the flooring has been removed. The nave roof is a 16th. century hammer-beam, (Cautley). The window tracery is very fine and mostly of the 14th. century, when the aisle was first built.

The only Saxon features left in the church are the nave width and the wall thickness, which is reasonably positive, for they do not in any way relate to the Norman tower arch, and there are no signs of a rebuilding.

S32. RISBY. St. Giles

C6 Sheet. 155. Map Ref. T.L. 802 664
Church and Tower Late SAXON

Tower Height	47ft. 6"	Nave Width	18ft. 6"
Internal Diameter Grd:	11ft. 7"	Chancel Length	37ft. 4"
Tower Wall Thickness	3ft. 5"	Nave Length	63ft. 4"
Nave Ridge Height	33ft. 6"	Nave Wall Thickness N & S	2ft. 8"
Bells 3			
Chancel Width	18ft. 2"		

St. Giles, Risby lies to the west of Bury St. Edmunds and less than two miles from that other round tower church of Little Saxham. It stands in its well kept village, but is well away from the village green. It consists of a round west tower, nave, chancel, and south porch.

The tower, circular for its full height is the average height for these late Saxon towers, and is surmounted by 15th. century

battlements. The flints are nearly all of medium size and fairly well coursed, with a nicely proportioned tower and no batter. These features seem to suggest a Norman tower, but this dispelled however, when one examines the double row of belfry windows (plate 23). These are all framed with selected flat flints to the jambs and heads. They are very interesting because there appears to be nothing quite like them elsewhere; and certainly not in a round tower. They are not a heightening of the tower with another set of windows over the first set, as they are still in the same style, i.e. single light round-headed, and with flint frames. They are placed neatly over each other, and are certainly not Norman in character. The Saxons appear to be the only builders that experimented in this way with one off examples, or of course the other examples may have been lost.

On the south side, there are two rows of belfry windows, built entirely of flints, with heads laid in Tredington fashion, and most flints are selected for flatness. On the west are two belfry windows one above the other, the same as on the south. To the north, two rows of two belfry windows again like the south, and on the east one window over the nave ridge, wider than the others, but it appears to have been either collapsing, as the semi-circular head has gone, or it may have been altered from two windows. Below the belfry are three single-light round-headed windows, with flint jambs but the heads have been renewed with single dressed stones, and the south and west have been blocked. Some of the belfry windows have been repaired with odd pieces of dressed stone, and it is this that proclaims them as pre-Conquest, for it seems that flints were not used to repair these Saxon features after the Conquest. The internal diameter of the tower at 11ft. 7" while large, is still within Saxon measurements, and the wall thickness at 3ft. 5" is well within them. The height of the tower helps us to date it as late Saxon.

There is an upper doorway 16ft. 3" above the ground, and these being present, usually denote that the tower has not been too drastically altered. This doorway is 2ft. 7" wide by 5ft. 8" tall. That the Normans improved or altered what was already here is apparent by the tower arch, which has engaged columns facing the nave, and squared stones on the return face. The chancel arch was also put in by the Normans, and was evidently a fine structure. The later builders, who demanded a pointed arch, could do no better than rearrange the earlier Norman stones to the newer shape. This can be seen clearly from the chancel side of the arch. The three bells were overhauled and re-hung by Alfred Bowell of Ipswich in 1909.

There are no fillets between tower and church, and the curved eastern wall of the tower confirms that the tower and church were built together. The nave and chancel width of under 19ft. ensures the ground plan as Saxon, and there is no reason to believe that the walls have been rebuilt for they appear to be similar to the tower. The nave windows are Early English with traces of a blocked Norman window in the north wall, giving us a latest date for the church. The wall thickness however, is against this, as they are too thin for Norman builders. The chancel windows of the Decorated period are insertions, perhaps when the chancel was lengthened. There was once a chapel to the north of the chancel, witness the drip course and one of the corbels here to remind us. A low-side window is in the south chancel wall, and a scratch dial can be found on a south buttress.

What can easily be missed, is the Saxon circular double- splayed window in the nave north wall. It is within a mas of scroll and picture wall paintings, and is not complete window, but only part of the inner splay. Quite probably some of the flints blocking this window fell out after the wall had been painted, for the splay is now plastered and painted like the wall on either side. This gives a positive Saxon feature for calling the nave pre-Conquest.

S33. RUSHMERE. St. Michael

L4 Sheet. 156. Map Ref. T.M. 495 880
Tower and Church Middle SAXON

Tower Height	47ft. 6"
Internal Diameter Grd:	8ft. 1"
Tower Wall Thickness	3ft. 6"
Nave Ridge Height	26ft. 6"
Bells 2	
Chancel Width	17ft.
Nave Width	14ft. 6"
Chancel Length	32ft. 10"
Nave Length	39ft. 5"
Nave Wall Thickness	2ft. 5"

Quite close to two other Saxon round tower churches and only two and a half miles from the coast, this church is situated in quite flat countryside, but very little of the village remains. The church consists of a round west tower, nave, chancel and south porch. Domesday mentions a church here.

The tower is constructed of whole and cut flints that are uncoursed and set in large amounts of mortar, but the top ten feet, from just below the belfry stage, the flints are coursed, and this appears to have been a raising of the tower, still in its circular shape. It has a plain parapet with billet moulding just below the brick coping. This suggests that the Normans raised the height of the tower, although the present belfry has four double-light windows of the Early English period. Below the present belfry, in what was the original Saxon stage of the tower, are the six blocked Saxon belfry windows, seen clearly within the tower, and to a lesser extent outside. They are round-headed, and not lancets as recorded by Bryant. Inside the tower they are clearly built of flints. Being six in number, they follow Bexwell and Holton in their layout. The tower was therefore about 35ft. tall in Saxon times, and this enables us to date it as middle Saxon. The fillets between tower and church are further features to convince us of its age, which is near the date of nearby Mutford and Gisleham. Two inscribed bells of the 15th. century hang in the tower, but there is no sign of an upper doorway. The ground floor and the tower arch are cement rendered, with no sign of dressed stone, but whether the arch is constructed of flints or not, I was unable to tell.

The walls of nave and chancel appear to be the same date as the tower, with most of the windows belonging to the 13th. century. Cement rendering of the walls internally, has hidden all the early features until this is removed. The only Norman feature to be seen is a piscina in the north wall of the chancel, often called an Easter Sepulchre, but as it has a drain, this cannot be so, but why is there another piscina in the south wall in the usual place? The wall structure and width of nave and chancel make it certain that this was the original church built between 900 and 1,000. The south porch of red brick seems to be a Victorian building.

There are two scratch dials; one on the S/E nave quoin at 4ft. 6" from the ground and another on the S/E chancel quoin facing east about the same height. This one therefore, must be a reused stone.

The church is completely thatched, and has been unused since the early 1960s, as it was considered too costly to restore. In 1992, efforts were made to restore the church, and the roof timbers were repaired, and the nave prepared for rethatching. This has now started, August 1993, and the north slope of the church is being rethatched, with the possibility of a reopening before Christmas.

S34. LITTLE SAXHAM. St. Nicholas

D6 Sheet. 155. Map Ref. T.L. 799 637
Tower and Church Late SAXON

Tower Height	55ft. 6"
Internal Diameter Grd:	10ft. 10"
Tower Wall Thickness	4ft. 1"
Bells 3	
Chancel Width	18ft. 6"
Nave Width	16ft. 3"
Nave and Aisle Width	28ft. 10
Chancel Length	33ft. 7"
Nave Length	33ft. 3"
Nave South Wall Thickness	3ft. 2"

Standing on slightly raised ground with only a few houses nearby, this church like so many more of this group, supplies the spiritual needs of very few people. There was a church here at the time of Domesday, but although I have dated it as late Saxon, there is still an element of doubt, by the few Saxon features we can see, and the wall thicknesses. It consists of a round west tower, nave, chancel, north aisle, north chapel and south porch.

The tower has been acclaimed the finest example of a round tower in Suffolk, and all writers refer to it as Norman. But while both Bryant and Cautley record the tower arch as being very tall, neither have noticed the striking similarity with the one at Haddiscoe. I believe that from this feature, and the tall nave doorways, we can reasonably call this church and tower Saxon, with Norman embellishments.

With the tower wall thickness of 4ft. 1", and an original south nave wall thickness at 3ft. 2", a Saxo-Norman date seems the most probable, and the tower arch and doorways could well follow the Saxon pattern, as they have done at Haddiscoe in Norfolk. It was only in 1982 that I was able to ascend the tower internally, and the only dressed stone there was the upper doorway. Unlike Haddiscoe, where all the windows were finished completely inside as well as out with dressed stone, here, the interior followed the Saxon fashion of flint construction.

The four belfry windows are each enclosed within a Saxon style round-headed opening 3ft. 7" wide by 6ft. 11" tall and the heads are arched in flints. This would hardly be likely if dressed stone was available at the time of building. It seems that the Norman windows and arcading was an embellishment to the top of this late Saxon tower. The twin openings of the Norman windows are each just ten inches wide. There are four of these double-light round-headed and recessed windows, with cushion capitals and circular columns of two orders outside, and the double window itself, with roll mouldings on the two outer orders. Double arched arcading between each belfry window, encircles the round tower with this round-headed decoration, and very shallow battlements crown the top.

The first floor windows at N., S., and W., are the same width internally as the belfry, but shorter, being only 4ft. 9" tall. But while the belfry openings have no splay, the lower windows are very deeply splayed. The outer face has three stones to each jamb; and while the single stone heads at Haddiscoe and most other towers are rectangular at the top, these are semi-circular at the top and below for the window opening. Another feature noticed in no other round tower either Saxon or Norman, is the unique construction that measures exactly the same diameter on each floor, with no steps inside or out to thin the walls and no tapering as they rise; for measured at the belfry openings, the wall was still 4ft. 1". This feature is so unique that I originally called it Saxon-Norman. However, later reflection weighs too much for a Saxon dating, bearing in mind the uncoursed flintwork and the many very large flints to be seen.

The tower arch (plate 30) is 4ft. 9" wide by 16ft. 3" tall and is faced with dressed stone towards both nave and tower. The imposts have a simple chamfer and a quirk above, while the round-headed arch has a half-round moulding and a hollow chamfer towards the nave and plain squared stones inside the tower. Above this arch is the typical upper doorway, again round-headed, and faced towards the nave and within the tower with dressed stone. The three bells here were recorded by Raven in 1890, but now only number three remains in the tower to be rung; this is dated 1603 and was cast by Thomas Cheese. The two inscribed pre-Reformation bells now stand in the nave.

Turning to the church, the nave south doorway is a relatively simple Norman example with a plain tympanum, but is narrower and taller than usual. The north doorway is Decorated, but a round-headed recess to the south of the tower arch may well have been formed from the stones of the original Norman doorway. There is an arcade of three bays to the 14th. century north aisle, when the south porch was also built, and the north chapel was built in the early 16th. century, by Thomas Fitz Lucas, solicitor general to Henry V11. All the windows are in the Perpendicular style, although most have been completely restored. The fine communion rails came from Little Livermere.

S35. SPEXHALL. St. Peter

K4 Sheet. 156. Map Ref. T.M. 378 802
Tower 1910 Church Middle SAXON

Tower Height	50ft.	
Internal Diameter Grd:	9ft.	5"
Tower Wall Thickness	3ft.	
Bells 1		
Chancel Width	18ft.	
Nave Width	17ft.	6"
Chancel Length	27ft.	2"
Nave Length	46ft.	3"
Nave Wall Thickness North	2ft.	9"
Nave Wall Thickness South	2ft.	6"

The church stands in flat open countryside in a rather scattered village. It has a round west tower, nave, chancel and south porch.

The tower which fell in 1720 was rebuilt in 1910. There is the distinct possibility that the present tower was built on a Saxon base or foundation. Inside, it is circular, and of brick, while the outside is faced with the traditional cut flints, and built at the beginning of this century. There is a string course and thinning ledge of three inches about eight feet up, while the next string course is at the base of the belfry about 34ft. The circular top is finished with battlements. The belfry windows are four single-light lancets, and on the first floor at the west, is a double-light window having the appearance of plate tracery, (although 20th. century). To the south of the tower is a stair turret, and on the north, a splay, rather than a fillet, to nave roof height; while the nave west wall is finished in cut flints in the same style, and almost certainly at the same time as the tower. These are most probably just facing the old wall. An upper doorway remains from the old tower, and now has a pointed head, and below this, the tall tower arch is in a similar style. The one large bell in the tower is inscribed:- ".....Meritus Dulcis Sutto".

The church walls are of whole and cut flints and the facings are of dressed stone. A flying buttress over the priest's door on the south is one of only three on the R/T churches, but its function of allowing the use of the priest's door is no longer required as the doorway is now blocked with flints. The north nave doorway, also blocked with flints is early Norman, and the south doorway is Early English. We can thus date the building as at the latest, Norman, and the nave width and wall thickness puts it earlier, so it must be pre-Conquest`. One interesting feature is the east wall, finished in a trellis pattern in brick and flints. It follows the lines of Barsham east wall. This wall is dated 1713 by Pevsner, but whether Barsham or this wall was the earlier is still debated.

S36. STUSTON. All Saints

H5 Sheet. 156. Map Ref. T.M. 135 779
Tower and Church Middle SAXON

Tower Height.	51ft.	
Height of Circular Stage	33ft.	
Internal Diameter Grd:	7ft.	10"
Tower Wall Thickness	3ft.	7"
Bells 4		
Chancel Width	17ft.	4"
Nave Width	16ft.	9"
Chancel Length	25ft.	2"
Nave Length	34ft.	9"
Nave & Chancel Wall Thickness	2ft.	10"

This little church is tucked away behind the old rectory and almost hidden from the road by trees. It is one and a half miles S/E of Diss. It has a round west tower with octagonal top, nave, chancel, north transept, north vestry and south porch.

Called uninteresting by Cautley, and terrible by Pevsner, this little church nevertheless, is well worth a visit, and there is much to be seen and learned here. Although there are few features by which we can positively date the church or tower Saxon, there are many pointers which when added together give us good grounds for our dating.

The tower is circular for 33ft. and its octagonal top of the 14th century and 15th. century battlements have raised it to 51ft. It is built of whole and cut flints, uncoursed, and pieces of early brick. The wall thickness is only 3ft. 7" so this follows the Saxon pattern, while the short circular stage adds more weight to a pre-Conquest date. This tower was very damp, so it was undercut and supported on concrete blocks, which has cured the fungus, but then cracks developed which were no doubt caused by movement after the alterations. The tower appears to have stabilised now, as no further trouble has shown. The earliest window in the tower is the Early English west window on the ground floor, while on the first floor is a quatrefoil window which one would like to think was a Saxon circular window. However, it is of dressed stone outside, and the inside has been altered too much to give proof of this. There are just slight traces of fillets at the top of a thickening of the nave west wall, but whether these are contemporary with the tower, or added at the time the nave west wall was altered, is purely conjecture. One other point that has been noticed in Saxon churches but not in later buildings is the practice of a step to thin the nave west wall internally. It can be seen here, but much higher than usual.

The nave and chancel are quite narrow, with the chancel being wider than the nave by seven inches. This is quite rare, but not unique. All the church walls are under 3ft. thick, so this church just cannot be of Norman date.

The chancel is dated 1861, when there was a major restoration, although this does not mean the walls were rebuilt. The north transept is new, and is dated 1862. This is not seen on a N/W view of the church on show inside, so we can be certain of the date. The old north porch has been turned into a vestry and a south porch added in Victorian times. In 1861 the church was thatched, but now it is roofed entirely in dark brown tiles.

There are four bells in the tower as recorded by Raven in 1890:-

1. No inscription
2. John Draper Made Me. 1627
3. C. & G. Mears, Founders London. Walter Chenery Rector. Osborn Tippell, Churchwarden. 1853.
4. C. & G. Mears, Founders, London. 1857.

S37. SYLEHAM. St. Margaret

I5 Sheet. 156. Map Ref. T.M. 205 789
Church SAXON with Norman Tower

Tower Height to top of Battlements approx.	48ft.
Measured Height to top of main wall.	44ft. 10"
Internal Diameter Grd:	7ft. 7"
Tower Wall Thickness W. Window	5ft. 3"
Wall Thickness at T/Arch	3ft. 6"
Bells 3	
Chancel Width	18ft. 2"
Nave Width	18ft. 5"
Chancel Length	27ft. 6"
Nave Length	47ft. 1"
Nave & Chancel Wall	2ft. 6"

This church is on very low ground on the south bank of the Waveney. It is reached by a lane that is actually a causeway over the marshes. It is four miles east of Scole, and consists of a round west tower, nave, chancel and south porch.

A church is mentioned in Domesday for this parish and the first recorded rector was about 1086. This is very early for any church to have its own rector. The tower is circular for its full height, and it is another tower that still has its conical roof inside the 15th. century battlements. Below these, the single-light belfry windows are at the cardinal points, while the base of this stage is ringed with chequer-work, which also outlines the belfry windows. Below this there are only two more windows. A slit window faces south on the first floor, and a west window on the ground floor. The tower is constructed of well coursed whole flints of medium size, and also some bricks. There are no fillets between tower and church to help us date the tower Saxon, indeed the wall thickness at the west window of 5ft. 3" would indicate a definite Norman date unless the tower has been recased. The measurement over the tower arch of 3ft. 6" would seem to imply that this may have been done, but 1ft. 9" seems too much, so I regard the tower as Norman, added to a towerless church, or replacing an earlier tower.

The tower arch however, which is plastered over, and does not appear to contain any dressed stone, has a pointed head of the shape the Taylors call *"cruck shaped"*, and so has Saxon implications. On the first floor towards the east is a small opening with a large internal beam. Was this a small Sanctus Bell window? Or more probably, this was the wooden step for the upper doorway. But there are no jambs or anything to point clearly to any definite opening. The main beam supporting the conical cap is carved with the following: "R.W. 1765".

The church is certainly Saxon, for the walls are in the Saxon fashion with large mortar gaps, and they are only 2ft. 6" thick, and appear to be of one date. The final point to clinch the dating is the N/W corner, (plate 34) where the lower three stones are erratics and laid in long-and-short fashion. Above these are smaller and later dressed stones where the corner has been renewed. Taken as a whole, we can be certain that the church is pre-Conquest but the tower is Norman.

S38. THEBERTON. St. Peter

K6 Sheet. 156. Map Ref. T.M. 438 659
Tower and Church Middle to Late SAXON

Tower Height	57ft.	Nave Width	24ft. 5"
Height of Circular Stage	38ft. 6"	Nave & Aisle Width	39ft. 3"
Internal Diameter Grd:	11ft. 6"	Chancel Length	44ft. 4"
Tower Wall Thickness	3ft. 8"	Nave Length	54ft. 9"
Nave Ridge Height	38ft. 6"	North Nave Wall Thickness	3ft.
Bells 6		South Aisle Wall Thickness	2ft. 5"
Chancel Width	20ft. 2"		

St. Peter's church stands on a mound beside the village street in this peaceful Suffolk village, four miles N/E of Saxmundham. It consists of a round west tower with an octagonal top, nave, chancel, south aisle, south porch and north vestry.

It is clear to see that much of this church was here in Norman times, although many parts have been altered or added since those days. The Saxon features are not easy to find, but as it is plain most of the walls were here in the 12th. century, both church and tower walls are much too thin to have been built by Normans. We must therefore look for evidence of pre-Conquest work. We are not helped by Bryant who said "The lower walls of the Norman tower are about 6ft thick." Most writers have just copied his remarks, and it has been believed. I don't know how he arrived at this figure, unless he took the tower arch return wall, but this, as I have explained in chapter 7, is often a long way out, see above, the measurement at the west window. The tower wall thickness, its original height, and being constructed of uncoursed flints, speaks loudly of a pre-Conquest date. Bryant said there were five bells here, but another has been added by Mears & Stainbank dated 1875 and now in a steel frame by John Taylor & Co. London. The octagonal belfry stage is Decorated with its four double-light windows and four flushwork copies in the diagonals. No upper doorway could be seen. Below the belfry in the west face, is a round-headed window and on the ground floor is a double-light window of Tudor date. The tower is curved internally on the east indicating tower and church were built together.

The nave and chancel are still roofed in the traditional reed thatch of East Anglia. The north nave doorway, now inside the vestry, is a fine Norman example with squared stones and two circular columns with cushion capitals at the jambs, and three orders of chevrons on the arch. Between the two north nave windows is a blocked up round-headed Norman window faced with dressed stone and Norman mouldings. But at 3ft. 9" wide by 5ft. 8" tall, it seems widely out of place in a village church. It is as if an unwanted doorway has been preserved in the wall, but why a complete doorway it is hard to understand.

1300 is given by Bryant as the time the chancel was lengthened, and we can accept this, even though we do not know the reason for this very long chancel, and a south priest's door of this period confirms the date. The south aisle is probably late Decorated, as the arcades would imply, but it was rebuilt we are told in 1848. The walls over the arcades are painted as they may have been in medieval days. The south porch however, is from the late 15th. century and has some fine flushwork panelling. Most of the windows were changed in the 15th century, although some were renewed in Victorian times. Munro Cautley also points out the corbel table on the south (Norman) and the chancel string course also 12th. century.

As we have seen the main walls were here in Norman times, although they are too thin to be Norman. We are forced therefore to believe that they are pre-Conquest, even though the nave is wider than we expect for a village church. The church was built on a slope and the floor is higher at the east than at the west giving us an insight into how they built in the early days. It also narrows towards the east, a feature that only measuring shows up.

S39. THORINGTON. St. Peter

K5 Sheet. 156. Map Ref. T.M. 423 742
Tower and Church Middle SAXON

Tower Height approx:	40ft.
Original Height approx:	30ft.
Internal Diameter Grd:	9ft. 8"
Tower Wall Thickness	4ft. 3"
Bells 1	
Chancel Width	16ft. 6"
Nave Width	15ft. 2"
Nave Width at Bench Height	16ft. 6"
Chancel Length	19ft. 5"
Nave Length	32ft.
Nave Wall Thickness	3ft.

Two miles south of Blythburgh and one mile to the west of the A12, is the interesting church of Thorington St. Peter. It is easily missed in the narrow road, as the trees surrounding it hide its beauty. It has a round west tower with octagonal battlements, nave and chancel in one, north porch and south vestry.

The Saxon features are few but definite. A short circular tower of flints of all sizes, mainly uncoursed, with some near the base laid in herringbone fashion. Near the top, shallow round-headed arcading round the tower, about two inches deep, and built entirely of flints, as at Tasburgh and Thorpe-next-Haddiscoe. The round-headed windows within this arcading have dressed stone frames and single-stone heads, and so can be dated as Norman, unless the Norman stones merely face a Saxon opening. In Norman times the tower was raised still in the circular shape, and has four double-light Norman belfry windows, very much repaired. They have round centre columns with cushion capitals and half-round columns at the jambs, and are recessed behind the wall face. The ground floor west window and also the tower arch are pseudo Norman from Victorian times, but one wonders just what they replaced. The tower is curved towards the east internally, indicating that tower and church were built together, about the same time as the tower of Thorpe-next-Haddiscoe. The top is finished with steeply stepped octagonal battlements of early brick which appear to be from the Tudor period.

In 1982 the tower was restored after cracks were discovered on the interior of the nave west wall. During this work, it was found that the west end had been strengthened, and at the same time straightened with a facing of bricks, and it was this work that had showed the cracks. Behind this brickwork, they found a round-headed upper doorway of Saxon age. This has now been restored and is visible from the nave. Raven records that the single bell is inscribed : "Samuel Owen Made Me for Wanstead. 1596." So this bell must have been bought second hand..

The very narrow middle-Saxon church was widened in later years in a rather unusual way, probably when the parishioners wanted to fit seats. Instead of the usual aisle, they cut back the walls to a height of 7ft. leaving piers to give sufficient strength, like the outside buttresses. This gives the appearance of arches or alcoves in the nave, and gives nine inches each side or one foot six inches additional width. The Norman period, besides the belfry, and Victorian copies, is represented in the south nave wall by a round-headed window, cut into by the Victorian vestry, and showing at the ridge of this building. The Norman star moulding confirms its date. The north porch is Perpendicular, with the nave windows also of the 15th. century but the chancel windows remain from the Decorated period. One on the north showing some nice flowing tracery, while some were completely restored in Victorian times.

S40. WEYBREAD. St Andrew

I4 Sheet. 156. Map Ref. T.M. 241 801
Tower and Church Middle SAXON

Tower Height	53ft. 3"
Height to base of Belfry	36ft. 3"
Internal diameter Grd:	9ft. 2"
Wall Thickness at West Window	4ft.
Wall Thickness at T/Arch	4ft. 5"
Nave Ridge Height	36ft. 3"
Bells 6	
Chancel Width	18ft. 1"
Nave Width	18ft. 11"
Nave & Aisle Width	42ft
Chancel Length	32ft. 9"
Nave Length	41ft. 1"
Chancel South Wall Thickness	2ft. 10"

Weybread St. Andrew is two miles south of Harleston, over the Norfolk border, and one and a half miles east of Needham in open and flat countryside. It is next to a farm and a cluster of cottages, and consists of a round west tower, nave, chancel, north and south aisles and south porch.

Although all writers call this a Norman tower and a Perpendicular church, I class it as middle Saxon. There are no Norman features in either the tower or church, or for that matter any Saxon, save the measurements. It has been heavily over restored, so only the basic walls remain of the original church, with new windows, and even the walls refaced. But the Normans would never build with walls as thin, and the later builders would use wider naves.

This is one of the few towers where the wall thickness over the tower arch is greater than at the west window. The tower contains six uninscribed bells in an iron bell frame. While the well formed tower appears Norman for its full height of 53ft., its wall thickness denies this. The later plain parapet is of knapped black flints, and below this is a string course of dressed stone. In the belfry stage are four single-light Decorated windows at the cardinal points, while between them are dummy windows outlined with stone arches and brick jambs, and filled as flushwork with knapped black flints. At the base of the belfry is another string course. Below this, are three rectangular windows of early brick, and in the ground floor stage, a single-light west window that is again rectangular, but it seems certain that the head has been altered from the pointed style. There are no fillets to this tower which is constructed of whole and cut flints of average size and many hues. A few pieces of masonry were seen as repairs, and about four pieces of conglomerate. From the base of the tower for about a foot high was a mixture of flints and early bricks. We can also see the slope of an earlier roof, much steeper and four to five feet lower.

The Perpendicular south porch has a fine flushwork panelled entrance, and angle buttresses surmounted by crowns. The pointed arch has a square hood-mould with carved animals, probably crowned lions as stops. In the spandrels are shields held by angels, while in the niche over the entrance is a modern statue of St. Andrew, the patron saint of the church.

Both aisles are Decorated with four arcades having octagonal piers on either side. Over the arcades the early Perpendicular clerestory windows are double-lights. All the windows of nave and chancel are Perpendicular, but the chancel arch and chancel piscina are from the 14th century and prove that the windows are insertions into earlier walls.

The roofs are modern arch-braced with floriated bosses at the intersections, and in the nave, fine large heads are at the bases of the wall-posts. The north and south aisles also have carved figures at the roofs, but these are in a different style to those of the nave. The entire seating in this church is Victorian, but nearly all of them still retain their plaques saying 'FREE' giving us a glimpse of when many pews were reserved for a regular payment. The bench ends are decorated round their edges with squared roses, and crowned with poppy-heads.

S41. WISSETT. St Andrew

K5 Sheet. 156. Map Ref. T.M. 366 793
Tower and Church Middle SAXON

Tower Height	50ft
Internal Diameter Grd:	9ft. 9"
Tower Wall Thickness	3ft. 9"
Nave Ridge Height	31ft. 3"
Bells 6	
Chancel Width	17ft. 11"
Nave Width	16ft. 10"
Chancel Length	35ft. 1"
Nave Length	61ft. 2"
Nave Wall Thickness N & S	2ft. 10"

This very interesting church stands in the village on flat ground just two miles N/W of Halesworth. It has a round west tower, nave, chancel, south porch and north vestry.

Listed in Domesday, this is another tower and church that have been missed by the earlier writers, although at least one of the Saxon circular double-splayed windows was open in Victorian times. Domesday says:- "In this church are 12 monks and under it a chapel."

This battlemented tower is circular for its full height and is well proportioned. The four 15th.. century windows in the belfry were restored in the general tower restoration of 1977 when the walls were repointed. On the first floor are three round-headed slit windows, and on the east side at this height, 15ft. 6" is a Saxon round-headed upper doorway, 1ft. 11" wide by 6ft. 11" tall. It is open to a depth of 2ft. and is constructed of selected large flints at the jambs, and the head is set back slightly on the jambs. The head, built of flint rubble, was boarded up until the mortar set with the boards going east to west into the wall. The opening is now blocked up with flints on the nave side and plastered. On the second floor, when I studied the tower in 1976, I noted two blocked up circles in red brick, that had all the signs (I thought) of Saxon circular windows, and outside could be seen the signs of a third blocked up window in the west face below the belfry window. As the churchwarden told me the tower was soon to be repaired, I requested that these patches of red brick should not be disturbed as I felt they could be Saxon windows. The architect decided that they should check the north one, and in the words of the builder who did the work, "I was told to remove the bricks and any loose material only. I found some loose flints a crow's nest, and in the centre of the wall a circular piece of glass. " This was identified by the architect as Victorian, proving the window was open at this time. The only work done to this window was to remove the loose debris, change the glass to a pane of clear glass, and spread a light coat of mortar over the surface. The other two windows, plus a third I had not seen on the east, were then shown up by recessing the flints, so they can be easily seen from the ground, but without opening the tower walls. These features prove to all students that the tower is pre-Conquest. Further Saxon features are the fillets to north and south of the tower, while the stair turret on the south was built in the 15th. century when many of these towers were so altered. This is one more tower that is thicker by four inches on its eastern side ie. 4ft. 1". Bryant tells us that the tower was raised about 1470, which confirms my view that here was a short tower at the beginning to a Saxon church of the middle Saxon period.

The nave roof is slates, and the chancel has tiles. The Village History records "In 1799 the chancel was thatched and there was a north porch of timber and tiles." The narrow nave and chancel show us once again the Saxon style; as well as being a long church, while the wall thickness and the laying of the flints with masses of mortar also points to this period. No Saxon windows remain in the church, but there is ample evidence from the Norman period. Starting with the Norman tower arch, 7ft. 5" wide by 13ft. tall, we find the return wall is 5ft. 6" against the wall thickness of 4ft. 1" quoted above, (showing the error of quoting this as the tower wall thickness). The south and north doorways are fine examples of Norman carving, with the north being the finer. This therefore was the main entrance, and the timber and tiled north porch referred to in 1799 confirms this. The present south porch dating from the 15th. century was probably when the main entrance was changed. The south doorway is interesting as the outer order of the arch consists of carved heads as ornament, eleven beasts heads and a beak.

All the nave windows are from the Perpendicular period, but all those in the chancel are Early English. But Bryant states, "The chancel was rebuilt in the 14th. century in place of a Norman one. " The Village History states "The chancel was ruinous for some years until four farmers restored it, but the south chancel windows appear to be original except for the stones in their heads." The stone with the date 1837, ' when this restoration was done', and which was originally at the head of the east window, is now in the sill of a south chancel window. The hurricane of 1987 brought further damage to this east end, for the wall became so dangerous that it had to be almost entirely rebuilt. Therefore, within two hundred years, this east end required rebuilding twice although previously it had stood for many hundreds of years.

S42. WORTHAM. St. Mary

G5 Sheet. 144. Map Ref. T.M. 084 778
Tower UNCERTAIN Church probably Decorated

Height of Tower approx:	55ft.
Internal Diameter Grd:	20ft. 2"
Tower Wall Thickness	4ft.
Bells 1	
Chancel Width	21ft. 8"
Nave Width	23ft.
Nave & Aisles Width	46ft. 5"
Chancel Length	47ft. 2"
Nave Length	44ft.
Thickness of Arcade Walls	2ft. 9"
Thickness of Aisle Walls	2ft. 7"

The church stands by a farm, well away from the five hamlets that make up the parish. It is three miles west of Diss, and consists of a round west tower, (ruinous), nave, chancel, north and south aisles, south porch and north vestry.

The ruined round tower is the largest of the group, being 20ft. in diameter internally and having walls 4ft. thick. The present height cannot be much less than when it was roofed, for three of the four belfry windows are still clear to see. The west window has lost its frame. There was a very large west window on the ground floor, and most of the frame is still here, and below this in the tower wall is a stone coffin lid. The enlarged tower arch is pointed, and above this is a round-headed upper doorway. The frame has been strengthened with bricks, so we cannot determine its original size. There are no fillets to the tower but outside there are two off-sets that reduce the wall thickness by about three inches each time. No such ledges are to be seen inside, and the east side is curved, showing that the original church at least, was built with the tower. The construction is of whole flints of average size and well coursed, that would place it anywhere from 1,000 to 1200. I would think, from the wall thickness alone, that it would be much nearer the earlier date. There is no stair turret, but a wooden bell cote on the nave roof holds the single bell. The bell, recorded by Raven is inscribed:- "T. Osborn Downham Norfolk, Fecit. 1785. Cum Voso Venite."

This large church with two aisles has nothing to show of Saxon or even Norman features. But while the whole is predominantly Perpendicular, see all the windows that are mainly original, there are still traces of the earlier Decorated period. The aisles were erected, so presumably there was a church already standing, and the chancel has features of this period. The piscina with its ogee arches and floriated cusps and the south priest's doorway are all of the 14th. century. The font is also from this period. The clerestory was added towards the middle of the 15th. century when the church was fitted with all new windows.

VISIBLE RUINS

S43. ASHFIELD THORPE. St Peter.
I7 Sheet. 156. Map Ref. T.M. 201 623

The interesting remains of this round tower and one corner of the church stand in the private garden of a farmer. The two sections of the tower are held by heavy chains, and the tasteful gardens around the ruins should make Christians ashamed of the way some ruins are left to be covered by undergrowth.

S44. BUXLOW.
Sheet. 169. Map Ref. T.M. 435 610

The remains of the round tower can be seen in the garden of a cottage. Ref; "Suffolk Institute of Archaeology and Natural History". Vol 18. pp 147-155 by Claude Morley Esq .They can still be seen today.

S45. LITTLE WHELNETHAM.
Sheet. 155. Map Ref. T.L. 889 600

In the churchyard of St. Mary Magdalen, 9ft. 2" from the east wall, are the foundations of a circular building. The external diameter is 25ft. 7" and the walls are 3ft. thick. The circle is complete although it was broken for four internments from 1783 to 1852, so if as appears probable these are the foundations of a round tower, the tower arch has been closed in to complete the circle when restoring it after the internments. Although rare, this would not be unique for two churches to stand in one churchyard.

RECORDED EVIDENCE OF ROUND TOWERS
NOTHING VISIBLE

S46. ALDEBURGH-ON-SEA.

Messent tells us there was a flint round tower built in 1926, on to the Roman Catholic Church at Aldeburgh-on-Sea. It became unsafe and was demolished in 1955. There are no signs of this tower now at the church which is still in use.

S47. BECCLES ENDGATE.St. Mary.

Two sites in Beccles have been claimed for this church, with the dedication of St. Mary. The most widely held view, is that it stood to the south of Beccles, near the railway bridge at the end of Kemps Lane. The evidence to support this claim is that human bones were found when the railway cutting was made, and they have also been found in nearby gardens, which points to a graveyard on the site. The other site, which is thought to be the Sandy Lane-Rigbourne Hill-Banham Road area, is now a residential estate, but it is surprising that no evidence has come to light of human remains, either from the builders, or the householders tending their gardens. Both these sites will no doubt have their champions for years to come, and it is not my aim here to say which is correct. Whether St. Mary's Endgate had a round tower is what I would most like to know, but even this is very much in doubt, as no records to my knowledge have given the shape of the tower.

Queen Elizabeth I we are told, gave orders to demolish the church because it was no longer required, but this was not carried out, for by 1750 we hear that the church is in a state of ruins, with portions of the tower "four feet thick still standing." This is the only indication that it may have been circular in shape. It also appears that parts at least of the ruins were visible until early in the 19th. century, so it is strange that so little is known of the shape of its tower, or its site.

S48. HALESWORTH. St. Mary.

Pevsner tells us that the present square tower completed in 1430 replaced a round tower the foundations of which were found inside the present church near the font. Something that must have happened to many of these towers when a much larger church was built.

S49. HASLEWOOD. Nr. Aldeburgh.

Dr. Hele's book on Aldeburgh 1870 tells us "The base of a round tower was found at the west end of the ruins of Haslewood." Ref. Messent.

S50. IPSWICH. St. George.

There are records that this church once had a round tower. Roy Tricker records that it fell into disuse after the Reformation and was finally destroyed by fire in 1764.

S51. WORLINGHAM PARVA. St. Peter

Sheet. 156. Map Ref. T.M. 459 893
Tower and Church Middle SAXON

Tower External Diameter	15ft. 3"
Tower Internal Diameter	7ft. 9"
Tower Wall Thickness	3ft. 9"
Length Internally	39ft.
Nave Width Internally	12ft.
Nave Wall Thickness	3ft.
Apse Wall Thickness	2ft. 9"

The lost village of Worlingham Parva, of only 117 acres, had a church in Saxon times, the foundations of which were found during the building of the Beccles-by-Pass road in 1980.

The first signs were bones unearthed during the digging for a gas main. Work on that section of the road ceased while the Suffolk Archaeological Unit carried out a rescue dig. I witnessed the foundation walls of the church exposed, and saw a narrow apsidal church with a round western tower, and quarter-round fillets between tower and church. The walls were complete, with no opening for a north or south doorway, or opening into the tower. Thus we must assume that flints were used as the doorsteps into this building. Most of the apse lay under a farm track and so was not excavated, but the curved eastern wall left no doubt that this was the shape of the east end.

While the Suffolk Archaeology Unit would not date the church any nearer than the 10th to 12th century, my experience of the other round tower churches, satisfies me that the width of the nave fixed it firmly in the middle period of 900 to 1,000. The wall thickness and fillets gave good Saxon indications, and the fact that the two western corners of the foundations were still there and of flints proved their pre-Conquest date, for if they had been of dressed stone, and therefore later, they would have been missing for use in other buildings when the church was demolished. I disagree with the Suffolk Unit's possible shape of the church, for they suggest that it had short side walls for a chancel arch at the end of the nave. I have yet to see a Saxon chancel arch in any round tower church, in fact, a large number do not have one to this very day.

At the end of the excavations and research, the site was covered and now the road passes over the site of the church.

UNRELIABLE EVIDENCE OF ROUND TOWERS

The churches listed here have been called round towers in error by a number of writers.

BROOME

This was a miss-print for BROME, as Broome is a village just north of the Suffolk border

DARSHAM

This was included in the text of *"Peeps from the Past"* 1892, but it has a square tower.

NOWTON

This is an early church, and is mentioned in Domesday, but it has a square tower.

RUSHMERE. St. Andrew.

This church near Ipswich has a square tower.

RUSHMERE. All Saints.

There is no village of Rushmere with a church dedicated to All Saints, but Rushmere near Lowestoft, has a round tower church of St. Michael.

THORNHAM PAVA. St. Mary.

This small Saxon church is thatched, as is its small Saxon square tower. It looks just as the round towers might have looked in their early days. But that does not make it a round tower.

WESTLETON. St. Peter.

This large and wide church has a 14th, century square tower, and no signs of its ever having been different.

BURGH. St Peter.

This is not exactly a deletion. It should be understood that the village of Burgh St. Peter is just, and only just in Norfolk. The tower of this church is square. The Suffolk village is BURGH CASTLE. This village has a church of St. Peter with a round tower.

DUNWICH. St. James.

While there are several records of this round tower, they all stem from one source, the words of the rector who wanted to change the shape. It is however, and always has been a square tower. It is built of red brick internally, but cased in flints outside to give it an ancient look. The intention to alter the shape was probably found impossible. Refs. "Round Tower Churches Society Magazine" Vol. 11 p.5.

In 1986 I studied the two articles by Claude Morley F.R.S. F.Z.S., in *Preceedings of the Suffolk Institute of Archaeology & Natural History"* Vol.18. Part 1. 1922. page 8, states, Shipmeadow has a round tower. There is no evidence of this. Page 25. refers to Debenham and Walpole as having had round towers. There is no corresponding evidence, and I doubt if there ever was. Debenham has a large square tower that is SAXON, so it is hardly likely to have had any tower before this.

CHURCH NOTES - ESSEX

E1. BARDFIELD SALING. Sts. Peter & Paul

Sheet. 167. Map Ref. T.L. 686 265
Tower and Church 1380

Tower Height	53ft. 6"
Internal Diameter Grd:	11ft. 6"
Tower Wall Thickness	3ft. 2"
Nave Ridge Height	36ft.
Bells 1	
Chancel Width	15ft. 1"
Nave Width	20ft. 10"
Nave & Aisle Width	31ft. 8"
Chancel Length	12ft. 10"
Nave Length	58ft. 6"

This church stands on level ground about four miles west of Braintree. There are few houses near by. It consists of a round west tower, nave, chancel (part), south aisle and south porch.

This is one of the very few R/T churches that can trace its origins back to its beginning by documents. It is also the last R/T church to be built (as far as we know), until the building of Higham Church near Newmarket in 1861.

The tower is circular for its full height with no battlements; but a stair turret, built with the tower on the south side, reaches to the bell chamber. Here we can see clearly that this stair turret was built with the tower as one unit, and not as an added structure, or built into the thickness of the walls. None of the earlier towers have a turret such as this, and the nearest is possibly the one at Rockland St. Peter. The four double-light belfry windows are still of the Decorated period, and the tower has not suffered any alteration. There are no fillets, which we would not expect to see at this date, but the tower is sectionised by stone string courses. The one bell is dated 1768. There is a Sanctus Bell window where the upper doorway usually is, showing the change of use of this doorway now a stair turret gave access to the upper floors.

There is a fine panelled ceiling to the ground floor of the tower, and I have not seen another like it, but it seems to be Victorian. The bell frame is obviously a local effort, probably from 1768 when the bell was hung. Two triangular frames are used to support the bell which is rung by the wheel. On the wall of the floor below is further proof of local workmanship, for there is a rough wooden capstan, secured to the wall as though to make sure it would be there when it might be wanted again to lower the bell..

The church is constructed of small flints with no coursing, as was the case after Norman times. Some Roman tiles and medieval brick in small quantities are scattered among the flints. Although of a much later period than the main group of these churches, there have still been changes over the 600 years of its life. The church held the 600th anniversary of its founding with a number of events in 1980. The first thing we notice is the short chancel and no east window. The chancel was shortened in Victorian times, and then, the east wall had a Rose window. During the last war, a bomb damaged the east wall, and on rebuilding, the window was not replaced. Note the blocked up arch over the south porch, where the south aisle was shortened by blocking up one bay. The south porch is Victorian, thus telling us when this happened. The north door is blocked up with flints and cemented, and besides this, outside are the remains of a Holy Water Stoup, showing this was the main entrance in early days. There are some Roman tiles and early bricks round these remains.

Inside, the remaining three bays of the south aisle have piers of four clustered columns with spurs between. The arches have two hollow chamfers. The nave roof has four tie-beams with wallplates and a plastered ceiling. Preserved behind glass are early examples of Essex 'Straw Platting' that used to fill the tracery of the chancel screen.

E2 BROOMFIELD.St Mary

Sheet. 167. Map Ref. T.L. 705 105
Tower SAXON. Church Uncertain

Tower Height	32ft.	Chancel Width	15ft. 9"
Spire Height approx:	35ft..	Nave Width	21ft. 9"
Total Height approx:	67ft.	Nave & Aisle Width	39ft. 7"
Internal Diameter Grd:	15ft.	Chancel length	35ft. 4"
Tower Wall Thickness	3ft. 8"	Nave Length	42ft. 8"
Bells 6			

This church and village is now virtually a suburb of Chelmsford, and serves more as a parish church of a town than as a village church. There is still a small green to the south of the church to remind us of its earlier role. The plan is of a round west tower with spire, nave, chancel, north aisle, north vestry and south porch.

The tower is circular for its full height with no battlements. It is surmounted by an octagonal spire in the Essex style with a shingled roof. A cast iron staircase leads to the top floor of the tower. There are four dormer windows in the spire, and three round-headed belfry windows at the top of the tower. These windows appear to have been restored, and the whole frames are in red brick which is thinner than modern brick. They are closed with louvres. On the ground floor are three more round-headed windows with heads in Roman tiles and their jambs are in tiles and flints. There is no sign of an upper doorway and the tower arch is wide and round-headed. The tower is curved on its eastern side that implies the tower and church were built together, but with a very thick wall on the east at 5ft.10", this could mean that the church was added to the tower, or more likely, rebuilt. I have noted a few similar east sides in Norfolk. The six bells were cast by John Warner & Sons London, in 1874/5, and presented to the church by Mr. H.C. Wells, a churchwarden. They were rehung in an iron frame in 1912. Two old bells inscribed "John Dier Made Me 1580", and "Miles Graye Made Me 1613" were recast by Warners to form part of the peal. A third was smashed when it fell to the floor early in the 19th. century. Between the tower and church are splays, not in our accepted style of Saxon fillets. They seem more like a straight extension on to the church which may have been rebuilt, or just as easily another way of joining the two when built together. I base my Saxon dating on the wall thickness, the round-headed windows, and the flints used in the jambs as well as Roman tiles. Neither Normans, nor later builders would have used flints when other materials were available.

The church and tower walls we must note are quite differerent. The tower is of whole flints of all sizes with just occasional pieces of Roman bricks or tiles, while the church walls, at the south and west are of whole flints, mainly of a different colour to the tower, and masses of Roman tiles. The S/W nave corner is entirely of Roman tiles, (plate 35), and also the N/W, and N/E nave corners, as well as the S/E corner of the chancel. This indicates a very large source of Roman materials, and might mean that these could have been used after the Conquest in place of dressed stone. The chancel has been extended by about 10ft., as we can clearly see the original S/E corner, in Roman tiles. A similar pattern of walling has been used for the extension, and the Roman tiles probably came from the old east wall. The north aisle has six bays with octagonal piers and pointed arches with double chamfers of the 15th. century, which also dates the chancel arch. The south porch is a fine timbered structure on a base of flints and stone facings. All the church windows appear to be Victorian copies of Decorated and Perpendicular windows, except three south chancel windows that appear to be original outside, although they have been restored within. These three windows, and the east window, contain the stained glass of Rosemary Rutherford, the daughter of the rector who had the living during the last war years. In the base of the tower is a true 'Fresco' painted by Miss Rutherford before the stained glass work for which she became famous.

E3. LAMARSH. The Holy Innocents

Sheet.155. Map Ref. T.L. 890 361
UNCERTAIN

Tower Wall Height	41ft.
Spire Height approx:	20ft.
Total Height approx:	61ft.
Internal Diameter Grd:	10ft. 8"
Tower Wall Thickness	2ft.10"
Nave Ridge Height approx:	35ft.
Bells 1	
Chancel Width	21ft. 9"
Nave Width near Chancel Arch	21ft.
Nave Width at West Wnd	20ft. 4"
Chancel Length	18ft. 9"
Nave Length	41ft. 3"

This church stands on a level site one and a half miles north of Bures on the Suffolk/Essex border. It has a round west tower, with spire, nave, chancel, south porch and north vestry.

The tower is circular for its full height with an overhanging octagonal spire, roofed with red-brown tiles. There is one belfry window facing south, the east window is blocked, and the north and west side of the tower is missing its natural wall and now has an inner and outer skin of lath and plaster and so has no windows in this section. About a quarter of the tower has been restored in this way. The section is about a ten foot segment from S/W to N/W and a brick pier at either end prevents further falls. The fallen section has been bridged with poles spaced about fourteen inches apart and covered with laths and plaster. The wall thickness thus empty, has been used to provide a stairway to the first floor. A doorway in the north internal wall about eight feet up is reached by a short ladder fastened to the wall, and inside this doorway is a wooden stairway leading within the inner and outer skin of this fabricated wall to the first floor. The one belfry window is near the top of the wall section of this tower, The first floor south window, looks very much like a Saxon round-headed slit window. The round head was supported by boards while the mortar set, and the whole window including the jambs is of selected flints, although the head is not set back on the jambs. However, I have seen many windows with their heads not set back that I am certain are Saxon, so the possibility is still there of this being a Saxon window. There is one large bell, and the bell, and the bell frame seems to be locally made, and is in the style of the one at Bardfield Saling. The bell bears the date 1695 and replaced a set of bells which had been sold some years previously. The spire is dated 1865, and may at this date have replaced an earlier spire.

The church walls are cement rendered and the corners are buttressed, so the original quoins cannot be seen. The south doorway has a four-centred head of Tudor brick, and the south porch is 15th. century. The windows, although very much restored in Victorian times, still have parts of their original frames, and range from Early English to Perpendicular days. We cannot learn much from this church, for while the nave and chancel are wide, and do not appear to be pre-Conquest, the layout of the walls it will be seen is very irregular, and points to early work. But the tower has positive Saxon signs, if only with one window, and it has walls only 2ft. 10" thick. Apart from this one tower window, the earliest dateable features are the Early English east windows, although these have been altered, yet they still seem to be of the 13th century. There is one more Early English window in the south of the chancel.

E4. GREAT LEIGHS St. Mary the Virgin

Sheet. 167. Map Ref.T.L. 739 156
Tower SAXON, Nave & Chancel NORMAN

Tower Height	39ft. 3"
Spire Height approx:	35ft.
Total Height approx:	74ft. 3"
Internal Diameter Grd:	16ft. 1"
Tower Wall Thickness	3ft. 8"
Bells 5	
Chancel Width	19ft. 6"
Nave Width	24ft. 6"
Chancel Length	35ft.
Nave Length	47ft. 4"
Nave Wall Thickness N & S	3ft. 6"

The village stands astride the A131 road S/W of Braintree, but the church is over a mile away in a quiet side road called Church End. Just north of the church is the river Ter, which gives its name to the neighbouring village of Terling. Only a block of cottages and Lyons Hall stand near the church, and the presence of the Hall, may explain why the church should have been built here, if indeed the site of the Hall is as ancient as the church itself.

The plan of the church is a round west tower with an octagonal spire, nave, chancel, south porch and north vestry. The tower is the earliest part of this church, and we must call it Saxon on the evidence of the Norman west doorway that cuts through the earlier pilaster buttress, and upon the wall thickness.

The tower is constructed of largely uncoursed flints and rubble with some mixture of Roman brick. It was repointed in 1979. There are five narrow buttresses or pilasters to a height of about 10ft. at N, W, S N/W and S/W. The Norman workmen cut through the west pilaster to insert the west doorway, and this is further proved by Miss Couchman's remarks after her inspection of the tower. "The Norman west door is an insert, it cuts the western pilaster buttress; also packing stones, can be seen between the sides of the doorway and the main build of the wall". The tower is circular to the top of the walls and there are no battlements, but an octagonal spire of the Essex style surmounts the tower and overhangs the walls. It is almost identical to the one at Broomfield, and is covered with Canadian cedar shingles, renewed in 1978. Four dormers in the spire serve as belfry windows, for the five bells are right at the top of the tower walls. The five bells are inscribed "Miles Graye Made Me. 1634". They were rehung by H. Bowell & Son in March 1888.

If the weather vane is correct, then this church is not on an east/ west alignment, but roughly N/W to S/E. The bell openings have sharply pointed triangular heads with louvered openings and are divided into two lights. Below the bells are six other windows, the upper three are at north, west and south, with the heads at belfry level, i.e. 34ft. 6" from the ground, while the other three, placed below the others are at first floor level or 17ft. 6" from the ground. Between the two west windows is a clock, not seen so often these days. It is a Tucker clock, installed in 1869, and there is another at Cranwich in Norfolk. There is no upper doorway to be seen and no fillets between tower and church. On its eastern side, internally, the tower is completely flat, and quite a lot of this has been repaired with brick that seems to be Victorian. So although at first sight, it appears to have been built on to an earlier church, the extent of the repairs make this just a little doubtful.

We shall now turn our attention to the church. Although my studies have shown that quite probably the naves of Essex Saxon churches were wider, or that they were late Saxon, from 1,000. onwards, as we have only six examples the evidence we have must be carefully examined. Everything in this church points to a Norman building, especially the thickness of the nave walls. Therefore, it was probably when the Norman doorway was inserted into the tower that the nave was widened to this Norman church. The nave walls are built of flints and rubble with pieces of Roman brick. At the west end of the north wall are two Norman round-headed windows, while further east is a square-headed Perpendicular with three lights. In the north chancel are two Decorated windows although these appear to be almost completely Victorian. Three Decorated style Victorian windows are in the south wall of the chancel. Quite near to the simple priest's door is a large block of conglomerate, and other pieces can be seen in the south chancel wall. There is a blocked Low-side window to the west of the priest's door at 2ft. 6" from the ground. A three-light Perpendicular window is in the south of the nave, but the tracery has been renewed. Next to the porch is the third Norman round-headed window, and again it appears to have the original stone in the outer frame. The porch seems to have been rebuilt in Victorian times, as it is all modern brick, but there are some whole flints, a little masonry and a few early tiles in the base. To the west of the porch is a Decorated window that appears to be almost entirely original although rather worn. The south doorway inside the porch is a simple Early English pointed doorway, but over this, can be seen the outer arch of an earlier Norman doorway, with chevrons and leaf mouldings. The Norman features, together with the wall thickness must therefore place the nave and chancel in the Norman period, while the tower, must be before the Conquest, to a church that has disappeared.

Two special features to note are, the Dog Rapper's seat, just inside the south door, and the finest board listing the Rectors that I have seen. It is the work of the Rev. John Bryant. As well as the list of rectors, is a list of their accomplishments, together with heraldic shields of their families or colleges; 13 in all.

E5. SOUTH OCKENDON. St. Nicholas

Sheet. 177. Map Ref. T.G. 596 829
Mainly NORMAN

Tower Height	56ft.
Height of String Course	38ft.
Diameter at Grd:	14ft.
Nave Ridge Height	38ft.
Bells 1	
Chancel Width	16ft.
Nave Width	22ft.
Nave & Aisle Width	49ft. 11"
Chancel Length	24ft. 4"
Nave Length	37ft. 10"

The church stands on level ground to the south of the village green. But this village is now a residential part of the Greater London belt. It has a round west tower, nave, chancel, north and south aisles, north chapel and south vestry.

In this very Victorianised church and tower, we have only the north nave doorway, a fine example of Norman work on which to base our judgement of its age. This doorway is certainly Norman, and the nave and tower measurements and wall thickness seem to fit this period, but this is as far as we can go.

In 1856, George Buckler published his book *"Twenty-Two Churches of Essex"*. He published a detailed plan and a N/W view of the church which are far different from what we see today. From today's plans and photos however, we can see the alterations made in Victorian times after 1856. His whole book is so thorough that we can rely on the descriptions and measurements.

The tower was 37ft. high and capped with a flattish lead cone. It was in three storeys with an early Perpendicular west doorway. The Victorian restoration has raised the tower from the string course (top table) with a new belfry stage and battlements to 56ft. The four new belfry windows, resting on the string course are pseudo Norman. The old belfry windows are now blocked, and a stair turret has been built outside the tower, with an outside door and two windows to light the stairs. The west door has been altered to a pseudo Norman, and the whole has been refaced with knapped black flints and a large amount of blocks of masonry, including many wall ties about 14 inch by 4 inches, (see chapter 12). A new south aisle and vestry were added at the same time.

Looking at the plan it is more easy to see that the general layout of the early church, (almost certainly Norman), has remained. But just how much of the old walls are here we do not know because of the overlay of knapped flints. If as I believe, the tower, nave and chancel were here first, although Buckler thinks that the north aisle was built at the same time, because there was a small slit window to the west of the north porch, but it is not here now. If the north Norman doorway has not been reset, this aisle, with the other parts must be Norman. The north porch and north chapel are 15th. and 16th. centuries respectively. Restorations and improvements were carried out from time to time, including most of the windows being changed to the Perpendicular style, but almost all these features have now disappeared with the Victorian alterations.

E6 PENTLOW. Sts. GREGORY & GEORGE

Sheet. 155. Map Ref. T.L. 812 461
Tower NORMAN, Church SAXON

Tower Height	51ft.
Internal Diameter Grd:	13ft
Tower Wall Thickness	4ft. 3"
Nave Ridge Height	34ft.
Bells 5	
Chancel Width	16ft. 5"
Nave Width	20ft. 8"
Chancel Length	26ft. 5"
Nave Length	38ft11"
Nave Wall Thickness N.	2ft. 8"
Nave Wall Thickness S.	2ft.10"

The church is on a slight rise in a valley, close to the river Stour and Cavendish, and just south of the Suffolk border. It lies hidden behind a clump of trees, down a short lane. It has a round west tower, nave, apsidal chancel north chapel and south porch.

This church and tower, are firmly based in the periods above, and are confirmed by the research of the Taylors. The church walls are constructed of whole flints, the four nave corners are all built of selected flints (plate 40) and the apsidal chancel, requiring no corners is clearly of the same build as the nave. This is a clear indication that all the walls are of the same pre-Conquest period, and the uncoursed construction with large mortar gaps would seem to place it in the middle Saxon period. The selection of the flints for the quoins, is not for shape, but rather for size, and all shapes of large sized flints have been used, cut to give a sharp corner, some flat ones used to give depth, and here and there some smaller ones, either to fill in, or they may be repairs. The walling does not show the selection for size and coursing as the late Saxon period in Norfolk, but then the Norman tower is not of the same finish as its Norfolk counterparts, which may of course be due to the availability of sufficient evenly sized flints. The church walls, however, show the large mortar gaps so common in the middle Saxon period.

There are no fillets, and the confirmation of a Norman dating for the tower is simply that the Saxon church was towerless and almost certainly entered by a west doorway. Inside the tower to the east we can see the flat east side of the tower, which is the nave west wall, showing that the tower was added to the church and therefore later. Also the tower arch, or actually the west doorway, for it is more elaborately carved inside the tower, is Norman, and the tower wall covers part of this stonework. We can see therefore, that the Normans replaced the original west doorway with a fine example of their carved stonework, and when later a tower was added, this covered part of their earlier work, thus proving that the tower was later than the Norman doorway. The tower wall thickness 4ft. 3" measured at the west window confirms my statement of Norman measurements, while at the east, (nave west wall), it measures 3ft. 3". The upper doorway is 1ft. 11" wide by 4ft. 7" tall but nothing original has been left. Over the Norman doorway is the carving of a muzzled bear; Gissing also has one, but what is the significance? The tower is completely circular and battlemented, and above the nave roof it retains its flattened side towards the east, giving it an oval appearance. There are three belfry windows, one Perpendicular and two Y-tracery Early English. As the Perpendicular window is on the south, the main entrance side, and the earlier windows on the west and north, I would think that these are original, and the south window was changed later, more for appearance than because it required renewing. The first floor is the ringing chamber, and has three rectangular windows, with the west one still retaining its wooden lintel inside, but the north and south are now cemented. They are splayed for only half the wall thickness, and then a rectangular opening has been formed, framed with dressed stone with no splay. This is a much later alteration. The ground floor also has three windows, rather unusual in these towers. A west Perpendicular window of two lights, and north and south have very narrow slit windows, still with their wooden lintels going right through the wall thickness. The Norman tower doorway has one circular engaged column and two of squared stones with simple bases. Voluted and Decorated capitals are below a Decorated abacus. Chamfered imposts and plain stones for the inner arch. There are no imposts or decoration towards the nave.

The church windows are mainly Y-tracery of Early English date, though some have been restored in Victorian times, and the Kemps' chapel on the north has a Perpendicular window which helps to date this part. This is a very simple but interesting church.

E7. BARKING. St. Patrick

I spent little time at this church in 1975 noting only the main facts, as it was not in our East Anglian style. David Vinnels devoted an article to it in the *"Round Tower Churches Society Magazine"* vol.17.*

The church was designed by Arthur Eric Wiseman and was consecrated in 1940. It was designed to seat 300 and cost about £10,500. It consists of a nave with narrow passage aisles, north and south transepts, both ending with apses and a chancel sited within the eastern round tower. Joined to and forming part of the church are the church hall and church rooms.

It was constructed with a reinforced concrete frame, and faced with yellow-brown Dutch bricks. The font bowl is of polished bronze and the church possesses a stone from St. Patrick's Armagh Northern Ireland presented by the dean of Armagh Cathedral. It was placed in the chancel wall.

RECORDED EVIDENCE OF ROUND TOWERS NOTHING VISIBLE

E8. ARKESDEN. St. Mary. Sheet. 154. Map Ref. 483 346

Near Audley End; Messent records,and also Essex Record Office, that the foundtions of a Norman round tower were found when the present west tower was built. At this time the church was heavily restored. The south arcade has circular piers and the north arcade octagonal piers.

E9. BIRCHANGER. St. Mary. Sheet. 154. Map Ref. T.L. 507 228.

Near Bishop's Stortford, Pevsner records the north aisle is 1899 and there are two Norman doorways, one at least has been reset. The round tower seems to have been destroyed in the 18th. century. Pevsner records the nave as Norman and the chancel as Early English.

E10. WICKEN BONHUNT. St. Margaret. Sheet 154..Map Ref. T.L. 499 333

The church was restored and enlarged in 1858/9. It is an early church with a chancel 30ft. long by 12ft. wide and the nave is 40ft. long. When excavating for a new west tower in June 1958 a very perfect foundation of a round tower about 10ft. across internally was found with a small tower arch (presumably narrow). Very detailed records of the restorations are in the Essex Record Office and we have photo copies in our Records.

WEST THURROCK. St. Clement.

This was not a round towered church as is sometimes suggested. Excavations have established that underneath the present square tower, lie the remains of a round church. The round nave is under the tower, and the chancel lies under the present nave.

CHURCH NOTES - CAMBRIDGESHIRE

C1. BARTLOW. St. Mary.

Sheet. 154. Map Ref. T.L. 586 452
Tower & Church SAXON

Tower not measured	
Chancel Width	17ft. 5"
Nave Width	21ft. 9"
Chancel Length	31ft. 4"
Nave Length	41ft. 5"
Nave Wall Thickness	2ft. 7"

Five miles N/E of Saffron Walden, Bartlow St. Mary, one of only two round tower churches left in Cambridgeshire has been so much restored that little can be learned regarding its age. The fact that only once, on a preliminary visit was I able to ascend the tower to the first floor, means that there may still be something to discover at some later date. The plan is of a round west tower, nave, chancel, north porch and south vestry.

The tower is battlemented and circular for its full height. The embattled parapet has recently been renewed with modern brick and is entirely out of keeping with the character of these churches. All the cement rendering has now flaked off the tower, and there is a stone string course at about eaves height. At the string course, the wall steps in about four inches, and there seems to be a slight taper from here to the top. The four belfry windows appear to be Early English lancets, except the east, which is wider and shorter (cut off by the roof) probably when the roof level was altered. There is a large fillet to the south of the tower, almost like a buttress, and a large triangular one on the north. Whether or not there were any fillets here originally I cannot say, but certainly these do not fit into any pattern of these early towers. There are two circular windows on the first floor of the tower, one at the north and the other at S/W They have dressed stone frames however, so from the outside at least, they have no claim to be pre-Conquest. But there are faint signs of three more, although these do not show at all inside the tower. The two that are open, show as square openings within the tower, and at the same level on the east, is an upper doorway with a flat lintel of boards. My research has shown that a number of these Saxon circular windows were altered in later years with dressed stone, so they may have been altered.

All the windows of the church are decorated except the east, which is Victorian in the Perpendicular style. Although the windows have all had some restoration, they nevertheless retain enough original stone to be called Decorated. The north porch 15th. century and the entrance has a squared head label with quatrefoils in the spandrels and diagonal buttresses. The church has two 15th. century wall paintings.

C2. SNAILWELL. St. Peter

B6. Sheet. 154. Map Ref. T.L. 642 676
Tower & West wall of church SAXON

Tower Height	49ft. 9"	Chancel Width	19ft. 2"
Internal Diameter Grd:	10ft. 10"	Nave Width	23ft. 9"
Tower at West Window	3ft. 8"	Nave with Aisles	48ft. 2"
Nave West Wall Thickness	2ft. 11"	Chancel Length	29ft. 4"
Nave Ridge Height	43ft. 9"	Nave Length	36ft. 11"
Bells 3			

The church stands in the village, two miles north of Newmarket and not far from the small green. It is on a small knoll with a ditch or moat round part of the churchyard. The land rises towards the south. The church consists of a round west tower, nave, chancel, north and south aisles, north vestry and south porch.

It is quite easy to see that the tower was built against an earlier towerless church, for on the first floor, the flat face of the nave west wall can be plainly seen, and long gaps show where there is no bond, even of the plaster between the two buildings. There is evidence here also of rough blocking with flints, but no definite shape either of a nave window or an upper doorway.

The tower is constructed of fairly well coursed flints, most of an average size, while there is a band of large flints about 20ft. up, and also some odd large ones near the base. Although the tower was added to the church there are no fillets at the joins to north or south. The four double-light belfry windows with round heads, divided by a central shaft, are built of dressed stone and are at the wall

face with no carving or recessing as is usual with Norman work. They are Norman is style, and we must call them Norman, for there are a fair number of Norman belfries. that have no recessing. Below these, at first floor level, are a north, south and west round-headed slit window with dressed stone frames and the round heads are cut from a single stone. This, according to Baldwin Brown and the Taylors, is a Saxon feature, but there are so many like this found in East Anglia and the apparent non existence of dressed stone, leads me to date them as Early Norman. The ground floor west window is not much larger, but it has a large internal splay and is faced internally with dressed stone. The tower is finished with a plain parapet and a bell cote on the east side, now empty but occupied by a small bell until 1978. The tower roof is lead and almost flat, but in the form of a shallow cone. The weather vane is in the form of St. Peter's key.

The Rev. Kightley informed me that there were originally three bells in the tower rung by the wheel and one small bell in the bell cote. In the 1700s one bell disappeared or was disposed of. In 1978 the remaining three bells were overhauled at the Whitechapel Foundry and all rehung inside the tower to be chimed only.

While everyone so far has dated this tower as early Norman about 1090, which was also my judgement at first, but a visit in 1979 showed that in eight or nine places, just below the parapet string course, and evenly spaced, a number of flints had fallen out. These appeared to be roughly like the openings of Saxon circular windows. Their position also equated with those at Forncett St. Peter, St. Paul's Norwich (now destroyed), and the blocked up windows in Burnham Norton and Bungay Holy Trinity. Hoping to obtain confirmation of this, I ascended the tower, but although at this point there was a great deal of patching up and repairs with flints and chalk clunch, they were so widespread that no relation to the outside patches could be gained. These must therefore remain a question mark, for although I feel certain that these were Saxon circular widows . I have no positive proof. May I hope that one day a trial opening will be made.

The inside of the belfry windows were interesting because the dressed stone frames are only one block thick at the outer face of the tower wall. Each window is a large round-headed opening constructed entirely of flints and other stones, with the facing of dressed stone that appears to be a dressing only of this flint opening and in no way a support for the walls above, the arrangement of the flints at the heads are in a non-radial mode, or as Baldwin Brown terms them *"Tredington fashion"*. These openings are in purely the Saxon style, as is also the wall thickness. The facing stones including those of the lower tower windows it now seems certain have been added in the early Norman period.

Turning now to the church, while doubtless from the foregoing, a Saxon church must have been here, only the lower part of the nave west wall remains and the Victorian restoration has destroyed almost all the early work. the octagonal piers of the arcades are too slender for the weight they carry, and with the walls, they are taking a lean outwards. The nave has a single hammer-beam roof containing many early timbers, and carved figures look down from alternate hammer-beams, and the wall plates are also carved. The chancel has a double piscina from the time of Edward 1 (1272 to 1307) with very deep basins, but the heads are new this being probably the oldest feature.

There are three interesting pictures in the vestry; the earlier painting shows the tower with a fairly tall slender spire, and no clerestory windows, but we think that these were just left out by the artist. A later print before the Victorian restoration shows the spire gone and the south aisle battlemented, while an interior water colour of about the same time, shows the plaster scored as of blocks of stone.

C3. WESTLEY WATERLESS. St. Mary the Less

Sheet. 154.Map Ref. T.L. 618 562
Tower fell 1855. Church Early English

This towerless church lies five miles SS/W of Newmarket and two and a half miles east of Six mile Bottom. The tower fell in 1855 and an excavation in 1951 determined that the tower was round with an internal diameter of nine feet. Tradition says it was a Saxon tower, and also several sources including *"Magna Britania"* by Lysons, says the Saxon tower had a later top stage with pointed belfry windows.

The church with north and south aisles is built of flint rubble with a mixture of Tudor bricks. The eight windows of the nave are Decorated but one Early English lancet is in the south wall of the chancel. There are some interesting brasses to be seen.

CHURCH NOTES - SUSSEX

SX1. LEWES. St. Michael

Sheet. 198. Map Ref. T.Q. 409 100
Tower most probably SAXON

Not Measured
Bells 1

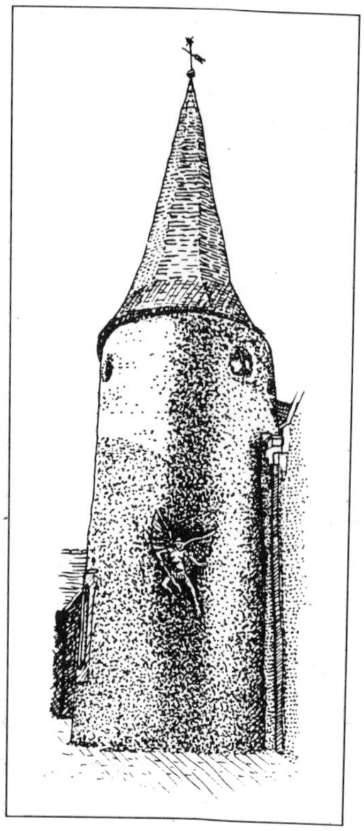

St. Michael's is in the main street of Lewes and is right under the castle and close to the river Ouse. It consists of a round west tower with spire, nave, chancel, north and south aisles and north transept.

The round tower, circular to the top is the only ancient part of the church. *"Cassells Gazetter"* of 1895 says, "St. Michael's was rebuilt in 1775 and restored and enlarged in 1885." This must refer to the church as distinct from the tower, and the 1775 rebuilding need not mean from the foundations upwards. V.C.H. vol. 8 page 745, considers it to be 12th century. This no doubt refers to the tower only.
"Saxon Churches of Sussex" says:- "13th century. The tower east wall, lower part, is flattened to fit the nave. This flat part narrows upwards above the tower arch so that the nave roof is shaped to fit the tower round wall." While Arthur Mee says:- "The 18th, century St. Michael's has kept its Norman tower."

So most writers think that the church is 18th. century, and there is nothing showing to prove otherwise, but the tower is called Norman, 12th. and 13th. century.

I have been able to do little research on this tower and have not seen any of the interior above the ground floor. The writer of *"Saxon Churches of Sussex"* has certainly been on the first floor, and the flat east side would indicate the tower being built against an earlier church. That church must certainly have completely disappeared. My notes of 1975 says there is no ladder to reach the first floor, and one of at least 20ft. would be required. The interior of the ground floor has been heavily restored and rendered. The round tower is about 40ft. high, and surmounted by a spire rising about another 30ft. and covered in shingles. The tower is now cement rendered and pebble-dashed. The four belfry windows near the top of the stone tower are circular with quatrefoil stone inserts. The unusual shape for belfry windows, and their position would seem to indicate they are Saxon circular double-splayed windows, especially as the 12th. and 13th centuries did not appear to make this type of window.

As I have not been able to study closely, either these windows or the interior of the tower, we must wait the opportunity to do this at some later date. There was no sign of an upper doorway from the nave, and where this would probably have been, was covered by a modern wall painting. The north aisle has wooden piers to the arcades and the north transept is used to house the organ.

SX2. PIDDINGHOE. St. John

Sheet. 198. Map Ref. T.Q. 435 031
Tower & Church Probably SAXON

Not measured
bells 3

This ancient church stands beside the river Ouse like the other R/T churches in Sussex. It still stands in its small village. There is a round west tower with spire, nave, chancel, north and south aisles and south porch.

The round tower is about 35ft. high with an octagonal spire roofed in shingles that rises another 20 to 30ft. There are five slit belfry windows irregularly spaced, and two other slit windows in the tower, one on the first floor and the other on the ground floor. Two of the three bells have no inscription and the other is dated 1713. Although I have not had the opportunity to ascend the tower or to measure the tower and church the local church guide dates the tower as 12th century. This is the same as nearly all other round towers have been dated, with no features of the 12th century being present. The suggested dating at the head is based on my assessment of a large number of these towers, and the fact of Norman work being present in the church, but the tower wall being too thin for the Norman period. There are no fillets or stair turret and an 18ft. ladder would be needed to reach the first floor. The unusual weather vane of a fish is that of a salmon trout, but it has been mounted upside down. A further indication of the antiquity of this site, is the record that before the churchyard was enlarged in 1882, it was circular. The east window is of three lancets of the 13th century, and the aisles unlike those of East Anglia, are under one roof from the peak of the nave. There is much more to be learned at this church, for I have been unable to give it the attention it requires.

SX3. SOUTHEASE. No Dedication

Sheet. 198. Map Ref. T.Q. 423 053
Tower & Church SAXON

Tower Height approx:.	35ft.
Spire approx.	15ft.
Total Height approx.	50ft.
Internal Diameter Grd:	8ft. 4"
Tower Wall Thickness	2ft.10"
Chancel Width	16ft. 8"
Nave Width	16ft. 4"
Chancel Length	9ft. 8"
Nave Length	35ft. 11"
Nave Wall Thickness N & S.	2ft. 7"

The church is on a slope to the west of the small village green, and with the cottages clustered round the green still in the style of our English village. Like the other Sussex round towers this church is also near the river Ouse. It consists of a round west tower with spire, nave, chancel and south porch.

This delightful church, still in its village setting has lost most of its original chancel, yet still has its ancient charm. It still has every sign of being a Saxon church, and the flat east side of the tower internally, shows that it was added to an earlier church as was St. Michael's in Lewes, still in Saxon days. The tower is round for its full height and tapers slightly all the way up, and is crowned by a circular spire, covered with shingles and surmounted by a cross. As well as the flat east side of the tower, the measurements also show that the east side is thinner, the nave west wall at this point being only 2ft. 2". The wall measurements alone declare this building to be pre-Conquest, for no Norman walls were ever so thin. There are no fillets, and here again a ladder will be needed before one can reach the upper floors.

Some of the older quoins of the church appear to be sandstone rather than the limestone used in the later repairs. V.C.H. calls the church Saxon, although calling the tower Norman before 1150. The wall thickness however rules this out,. There is only one belfry window slightly east of north, and this is glazed. The only other window in the tower is the small round-headed window in the west face that is about three feet from the ground. This window is framed with red and yellow bricks. Above this window is part of the frame and sill of another window that has been blocked up long since. The south porch is of flints with red brick quoins, and roofed in red-brown pantiles. There is no sign of an upper doorway from ground level.

The church once had a south transept, and I was told that it once extended much further east, which would account for its very short chancel. The archway to the old transept can still be seen, and inside this is double-light ogee-arched window of the 14th. century. The tower arch is now closed in and has a modern door.

CHURCH NOTES - BERKSHIRE

B1. GREAT SHEFFORD. St. Mary

Sheet. 174. Map Ref. S.U. 380 754
Tower & Church SAXON

Tower Height Not measured.		Nave Width	18ft. 10"
Internal Diameter Grd:	14ft. 5"	Chancel Length	25ft. 5"
Tower Wall Thickness	3ft.	Nave Length	53ft. 8"
Bells 6		Nave Wall Thickness N & S	3ft.
Chancel Width	19ft. 2"		

St Mary's stands in a narrow part of the Lambourn valley, four miles downstream from Lambourn on the B4000 road, a fine avenue of limes leads us to Great Shefford Church. It consists of a round west tower with an octagonal top, nave, chancel and south porch.

The *"Hungerford Rural District Official Guide"*, calls the tower Transitional Norman with a 15th century octagonal belfry stage. The church is mainly 12th. century it states. While the *"Victoria History of Berkshire"* dates it all except the octagonal belfry as Transitional Norman.

But an extract from *"West Shefford Parish Register"* 1693-1778 says:- "The church is classed by Lysons (Magna Britannia) among Saxon Edifices; how justly may be judged from the shape of the tower." The font it says is "Pure Saxon."

These writers show the wide divergence of opinion, and the truth is, I believe, somewhere between them. The wall thickness of both church and tower, and the width of the nave, not only have good indications of a Saxon date, but my research has proved, time and time again, how these measurements are a great aid to dating these churches. Especially when there are Norman features present, then thinner walls than those used by the Normans, give a positive dating to the earlier date. There are a number of Norman features, by which we can say that tower and church are at least Norman, and the wall thicknesses prove they were here before the Conquest.

The tower is curved on the east internally, showing it was built with the church, and the south nave doorway has definite Norman columns at the jambs. The pointed arch however, that has prompted the early writers to call it Transitional Norman, seems to be the doorway has been altered. The original doorway is from the Norman period, or before 1175. The east chancel window is Perpendicular, but outside, can be seen parts of two Norman windows, destroyed when the larger window was installed. The wide Gothic tower arch, must therefore also be an alteration from the time the south doorway was altered.

The tower which has an upper doorway with a pointed head, and faced with dressed stone, has its circular stage divided by a stone string course, and windows that appear to be Norman rather than later.

B2. WELFORD. St. Gregory

Sheet. 174. Map Ref. SU. 409 731
Probably a 19th century Rebuilding

Internal Diameter Grd:	12ft. 1"
Tower Wall Thickness	5ft. 2"
Nave Width	18ft. 8"
Nave & Aisle Width	48ft. 4"
Chancel Length	31ft. 9"
Nave Length	53ft.

The village of Welford is built on both banks of the river Lambourn and linked by two bridges. The church consists of a round west tower with spire, nave, chancel, north and south aisles and south porch.

There is a wide divergence of opinion on just how much of this church was rebuilt in the last century, some writers even contradicting their own statements. The *"Official Guide of Newbury Rural District"* states:- "The church of Welford was rebuilt in the 19th century, with the same tower and spire re-erected. The lower part of the tower is Norman and circular, and the Early English spire rises from a dainty crown of gabled lancets. Much of the original masonry has also been reused in the nave and chancel."

"Cassell's Gazetteer 1895" states:- "The church of St. Gregory dating from Saxon times, was partially rebuilt in 1885 and retains a curious tower. The chancel is Early English, and contains sedilia, the north aisle is Early English, and the south aisle is Decorated work. The tower is Norman." Where, therefore, is the Saxon part?

Murray's Berkshire tells us:- "The church has a round flint tower from which rises a graceful octagonal late 12th. century spire. The body of the church, consisting of nave, aisles and chancel was rebuilt 1852-5 from designs by T. Talbot Bury."

This I believe to be nearest the truth, for it is hard to see a tower that is sound being pulled down to be rebuilt it the same style. It may well have been recased, for at 5ft. 2" the walls are either Norman, or Saxon with a very thick casing which is hardly likely. My notes state the tower is constructed of cut flints and rough masonry. There is a stair turret on the north, but no fillets between tower and church. No upper doorway was to be seen. The tower is flat on its eastern side, but whether this was from the original building, or resulted from the rebuilding I have not been able to discover.

Norman, Early English, and Decorated styles are to be seen inside the church, all looks new, although we are told that the sedilia is the original, but re-cut. What then can we trust? With the limited time I could spare at this location, I must leave the church and tower with a big question mark.

CHURCH NOTES

OTHER ROUND TOWERS IN THE BRITISH ISLES

Besides the foregoing R/T Churches, the British Isles has quite a number more, which however, do not belong to our East Anglian style of flint churches. The list I have at present is as follows:-

ABERNETHY. Perthshire. Scotland. A freestanding tower in the style of those in Ireland, but capless. It does not appear to taper as much as these. It is however, otherwise much the same as the Irish.

BRECHIN. Angus. Scotland. A tower very much the same as the Irish round towers with a later cap.

COCKSBURNSPATH. Near Duns. Berwickshire. No one is certain whether the church or the tower was built first, and various dates are given. Some say 14th century for the gable and 16th. to 17th. century for the tower. One thing is certain, the top 12ft. or so of the tower was added in 1827. A photo I have depicts a round tower, built of rough masonry, about the same height as our East Anglian round towers, but narrower. The parapet is plain, suggesting a flat roof, and the tower is clasped over half way by the nave west wall in the same manner that some Irish round towers have been incorporated into churches.

CROSSMICHAEL. Kirkcudbrightshire. Scotland. This is the parish church which is standing and in full use. The tower is thought to be of 1611, which is the date on the bell in the tower. The church is later and replaces an earlier church on the same site. They are both built of local stones and not flints.

DEERNESS. Orkney. A church with two round towers at the east end stood here, but Dr. Hibbert of York who visited the site in 1832 reported that the whole building had recently been demolished. Their internal diameters is said to have been about 6ft.

DERVAIG. Isle of Mull. This is another round tower in the Irish style attached to a church.

EGILSAY. St. Magnus. Orkney. A round tower still stands at the west end of the ruined church. This is another in the Irish style. A recent photo I have is of the tower being restored, possibly as an Historic Monument.

LARGS. Ayrshire. Reported to me but not confirmed.

STRATHPEFFER. St. Agness. Invernesshire. Dedicated in 1892 with the chancel unfinished. Completed in 1899. It also has an upper doorway to give access to the aisle roof.

PEEL .Isle of Man. This round tower with its ruined church stands within the ruined castle. It is similar to the Irish, but much shorter.

LLANDYSILLIA. St. Tysilio. Montgomeryshire. This church is recorded by Pevsner.

PENPONT. BRECKONSHIRE. Built in the Romanesque style by Gilbert Scott.

TORTEVAL. St. Phillippe. Guernsey. A 19th century church and tower. This tower has also appeared on a Guernsey stamp.

SANDOWN. St. Patrick. Isle of Wight. This is a Roman Catholic church and was built in 1929 of dressed stone in the Irish style.

HEATON. St. Francis. Near Newcastle-upon-Tyne. Ref. by Messent says, "This is a brick round tower in modern style and does not resemble our East Anglian Towers in any way."

BRIXWORTH. All Saints. Northamptonshire. This is really a Saxon stair turret against a square tower.

HIGH WYCH. St. James. Hertfordshire. This is a modern tower and church, and built of dressed stone.

NORTHOLT. St. Joseph the Worker. Middlesex. In spite of the dedication this church is Anglican. This is a modern church and tower built in concrete in 1967.

POXWELL. St. John the Evangelist. Near Weymouth. This tower, it is said, was built on the foundations of a Saxon round tower at the beginning of this century in Weymouth stone. It was demolished in 1969.

LONDON. all Souls. Langham Place. This church, used by the B.B.C. has a round tower that is unusual for it stands on circular columns.

HALE. St. John. Near Farnham Surrey. This is a modern round tower that replaced an earlier tower of the same shape. It is similar to those in East Anglia.

GUILFORD. St. Nicholas. Surrey. The present church is 1870/75. Tradition says, a Saxon church with a round tower stood here. This is the 3rd. or 4th. church on this site.

TOOTING. St. Nicholas. Surrey. *"Little Guides"* Surrey; records "St. Nicholas had a 12th cent. round tower. It was rebuilt in brick in 1833".

FAVERSHAM ABBEY. Kent. In 1965 the foundations of a circular tower were found to the south of the church. It is believed to have been a circular stair turret.

GODMERSHAM. Kent. This church once had a round tower, but I have no further information.

OSPRINGE. Sts. Peter & Paul. Near Faversham Kent. Extract from *"Ospringe Parish Magazine."* The steeple was built of flints and round, and over the steeple was a tall spire of 50ft. or more in height. It seems the whole fabric was decayed, for on Friday 11th. Oct. 1695, while the bells were being rung, the whole tower collapsed but no one was hurt.

IRISH ROUND TOWERS

The Irish Round Towers are all built of the local stone, so do not compare with our East Anglian counterparts, They are about 90ft. tall, and have as many as seven floors on which valuables and people could take refuge. Their construction renders them fire-proof for even their roofs are of stone. There are 125 examples known. 23 have disappeared, 12 are doubtful as being of the original style. But 67 surviving examples are regarded as being of the original style and 23 are said to be later copies of these ancient towers. Lennox Barrow's book *"The Round Towers of Ireland"* is the finest text book on these other interesting Round Towers.

ROUND TOWER CHURCHES ABROAD.

East Anglia appears to have the largest group of round towers anywhere in the world. While there are a number in other countries, nowhere are they in such numbers. After East Anglia, Germany has more than any other country, twenty that are known to me, mainly through the assistance of H. de Olde of the Netherlands. Most are believed to date from the 12th. century, so although some writers believe that ours were copied from the continent, the relative quantities in each locality seems to indicate that they followed the East Anglian examples. The following list contains all those known to me:-

GERMANY.	
NIEDERSACHSEN	Beckendorf.
	Heesligen.
	Luderburg.
	Selsingen. Still partly round on the north, the remainder is polygonal.
KLOSTERKIRKE	Lorch Ehm.
SCHLESWIG-HOLSTEIN	Barmstedt.
	Bosau.
	Friedrichstadt.
	Kaltenkirken.
	Kosel.
	Neukirken.
	Oeversee.
	Pronsdorf.
	Ratekau.
	Rellingen.
	Süderstapel.
	Süsel.
	Warder.
	Weddingstedt.
	Wesselburen.

Barmstedt, Kaltenkirken and Wesselburen, originally round, have been surrounded with brick, but they still show their round form. Bosau, Süsel and Warder are not round any more, although at Bosau, small amounts of the original round tower are still visible.

ANDORRE	Capella-Santa Colonna
CZECHOSLAVAKIA	Rip
FRANCE	Uzes. (Gard) St. Theodorat.
	Echingham. (Pas-de-Calis)
ITALY.	S. Apollinare-in-Classe.
	S.Apollinare-in-Nuovo.
	S. Claudio-al-Chienti.
	Pisa. Leaning tower.
	S. Vitale.
NORWAY.	Altmark.
POLAND	Inowoods.
	Strzelno.
	Zarnow.
SOUTH AFRICA.	Johannesburg
SWEDEN	Blantarp.
	Bollerup
	Hammarlov.
	Hammarlunda
	Ska.

BIBLIOGRAPHY

Barrow George Lennox.	Round Towers of Ireland Academy Press.		1979
Batcock Neil.	Church in Transition 950 - 1200. Oxford University Committee for Archaeology No. 17. "Parish Churches of Norfolk in 11th. and 12th. Centuries."		1988
Batcock Neil.	East Anglian Archaeology No. 51. "Ruined and Disused Churches of Norfolk"		1991.
Blomefield Francis	History of Norfolk.		1736.
Braun Hugh.	Parish Churches. Architecture and Development. Faber and Faber 1970.		
Brown G. Baldwin.	Arts of Early England Vol. 2. Anglo-Saxon Architecture	London.	1925
Bryant Hugh.	County Churches Suffolk 2 vols.	London.	1912.
Buckler George.	Twenty-Two Churches of Essex.	London.	1856.
Cassell's Gazetter.			
Cautley H. Munro.	Suffolk Churches and their Treasures.	Adlard.	1937.
Cautley H. Munro.	Norfolk Churches.	Adlard.	1949.
Clapham A.W.	English Romanesque Architecture Before the Conquest. Oxford.		1930.
Clapham A.W.	English Romanesque Architecture After the Conquest. Oxford.		1934.
Cox Charles .	County Churches Norfolk. 2. vols.	London.	1910.
Cox Charles.	Little Guides Series. Essex. Methuen.		1909.
Ditchfield P.H.	Editor Memorials of Old Norfolk.	London.	1908.
Dixon Box. K.	Twenty-four Essex Churches. Essex Countryside.		
Editor. Carter Alan.	East Anglian Archaeology No. 15.		1982.
Fernie Eric.	Architecture of the Anglo-Saxons. Batsford.		1983.
Fisher E.A.	Greater Anglo-Saxon Churches.	Faber & Faber.	1962.
Fisher E.A.	Anglo-Saxon Towers.	David & Charles.	1969.
Gage John.	Society of Antiquities. Archaeologia Vol. XXIII		1829.
Gem Richard.	"How should we Periodise Anglo-Saxon Architecture" 'Anglo-Saxon Church Papers'. Council for British Archaeology. Research Report. No. 60		1986.
Gem Richard.	The English Parish Church in the 11th. and Early 12th. century. A Great Rebuilding. Monograph. No. 17.		1988.
Gunn John.	Ancient Architectural Remains in the Church of Beeston St. Lawrence Norfolk. Proceedings of the Archaeological Institute.		1847.
Gunn John.	Saxon Remains in the Cloisters of Norwich Cathedral. Norfolk & Norwich Archaeological Society Vol. 8.		
Harrod Wilhelmine & Linnell C. L. S.	Shell Guide to Norfolk.	Faber & Faber.	1957.
Heywood Stephen.	Round Towers of East Anglia. Minsters & Parish Churches. The Local Church in Transition. 950 - 1200. Monograph No. 17.	Oxford.	1988.
Heywood Stephen.	Norfolk Round Towers. Historical Atlas of Norfolk.		1993.
Hodgkin R.H.	History of the Anglo-Saxons.	Oxford.	1952.
Knights Mark.	Peeps at the Past. Editor.	London.	1892.
L'Estrange John.	Church Bells of Norfolk.	Norwich.	1874.

Linnell C.L.S.	Guide to Letheringsett Church.		1952.
Lysons.	Magna Britania.		
Mee Arthur.	King's England Norfolk.	Hodder & Stoughton.	1940.
Mee Arthur.	King's England. Suffolk.	Hodder & Stoughton.	1941.
Messent Claude.	Ruined Churches of Norfolk.	H.W. Hunt. Norwich.	1931.
Messent Claude.	City Churches of Norwich.		1932.
Messent Claude.	Round Towers to English Parish Churches. Norwich.		1958.
Mortlock D.P. & Roberts C.V.	Popular Guide to Norfolk Churches. 3 volumes.		
Mortlock D.P.	Popular Guide to Suffolk Churches. 3 volumes.		1988.
Morley Claude.	Proceedings of the Suffolk Institute of Archaeology & Natural History. Vol. 18 Part I.		1922.
Murray's.	Berkshire Architectural Guide. John Betjeman & John Piper.	London.	1949.
Orange A.J.	Story of Feltwell.	Norwich.	1970.
Parker J.H.	Architectural Notes of the Churches & other Buildings in the City & Neighbourhood of Norwich. Proceedings of the Archaeological Institute.		1847.
Pevsner Nicholas.	Buildings of England. Suffolk. Penguin.		1961.
Pevsner Nicholas.	Buildings of England. Norfolk. 2 volumes. Penguin.		1962.
Raven. J.J.	Church Bells of Suffolk.	Jarrold.	1890.
Raven J.J.	Proceedings of the Suffolk Institute of Archaeology. Vol. IV.		
Rigold. S.E.	Review of Messent's Round Towers to English Parish Churches. Arch. Journal CXV.		1958.
Rodwell Warwick.	Anglo-Saxon Church Building. Aspects of Design & Construction. Research Report No. 60.		1986.
Stenton Frank.	Anglo-Saxon England, 2nd. Edition.	Oxford.	1947.
Thornhill E.	Historical Rambles in East Anglia.	Exeter.	
Taylor & Taylor	Anglo-Saxon Architecture. 3 vols. Cambridge.		1965
Whitelock Dorothy.	Anglo-Saxon Chronicle		
Woodward Samuel.	Society of Antiquaries. Archaeologia vol. XXIII.		1829

Friends of the Round Tower Churches Society Magazine. 1973 to 1988.

Round Tower Churches Society Magazine. 1988 onwards.

Hungerford Rural District Official Guide.

Little Guides. "Surrey".

Newbury Rural District Official Guide.

Saxon Churches Sussex.

Victoria History of Berkshire.

West Shefford Parish Register. 1693 - 1778.